Music for Inclusion and Healing in Schools and Beyond

T0355345

Music for Inclusion and Healing in Schools and Beyond

Hip Hop, Techno, Grime, and More

Edited by

PETE DALE, PAMELA BURNARD, AND
RAPHAEL TRAVIS JR.

OXFORD
UNIVERSITY PRESS

Oxford University Press is a department of the University of Oxford. It furthers
the University's objective of excellence in research, scholarship, and education
by publishing worldwide. Oxford is a registered trade mark of Oxford University
Press in the UK and certain other countries.

Published in the United States of America by Oxford University Press
198 Madison Avenue, New York, NY 10016, United States of America.

Library of Congress Cataloging-in-Publication Data
Names: Dale, Pete, editor. | Burnard, Pamela, editor. | Travis Jr., Raphael, editor.
Title: Music for inclusion and healing in schools and beyond : hip hop,
techno, grime, and more / edited by Pete Dale, Pamela Burnard, and Raphael Travis Jr.
Description: New York : Oxford University Press, 2023. |
Includes bibliographical references and index.
Identifiers: LCCN 2023032485 (print) | LCCN 2023032486 (ebook) |
ISBN 9780197692684 (paperback) | ISBN 9780197692677 (hardback) |
ISBN 9780197692707 (epub)
Subjects: LCSH: Popular music—Social aspects. | Popular music—Instruction
and study—Social aspects. | Culturally sustaining pedagogy. |
Rap (Music)—Moral and ethical aspects. | Music therapy for teenagers. | Hip-hop.
Classification: LCC ML3918 .P67 M825 2023 (print) | LCC ML3918 .P67 (ebook) |
DDC 306.4/8424—dc23/eng/20230712
LC record available at https://lccn.loc.gov/2023032485
LC ebook record available at https://lccn.loc.gov/2023032486

DOI: 10.1093/oso/9780197692677.001.0001

Paperback printed by Marquis Book Printing, Canada
Hardback printed by Bridgeport National Bindery, Inc., United States of America

Contents

Foreword

Enter the phrase 'Music saved my life' into a search engine and see what happens. When I did it, 0.68 seconds later 560,000 results appeared. The phrase comes up in confessional blog posts about the power of music and articles on mental health; it is the title of dozens of songs, a Mary J. Blige world tour, self-help books, and memoirs; it adorns hoodies, t-shirts, and coffee mugs and a variety of other merchandise. Taking the experiment a step further, I narrowed the search. 'House music saved my life': 107,000 hits. 'Hip Hop saved my life': 43,300. On a whim I checked a few other phrases. 'Calculus saved my life': 6 hits. 'Organic chemistry saved my life': 0. 'World history changed my life': 0.

Music, calculus, organic chemistry, and world history are all subjects taught to teenagers and young adults around the globe. Among these, music is taught far less often than the others. And yet, music in general, and especially genres such as Hip Hop, house, techno, and grime, are embraced as a life-saving force by young people struggling to make their way through adolescence and into adulthood. Fortunately, popular music is being taken more seriously by educators and administrators, and even genres whose presence would once have been unwelcome in schools, if not forbidden, have now found a place in institutionally sanctioned activities and spaces. Popular music programs, ensembles, and curricula are appearing more frequently, and practitioners—including DJs, rappers, and producers—have been hired as full-time faculty.

Convening an interdisciplinary mix of educators, scholars, and practitioners, *Music for Inclusion and Healing in Schools and Beyond* is part of a movement that argues that effective pedagogies can be built around the cultural values and imperatives of musics and their communities of origin that have traditionally been excluded from or marginalised in educational institutions. In this foreword I would like to amplify this work with a broad appeal: that it is vital for any scholarship and pedagogy on these genres to centre the artists and communities who create these musics. Before continuing, I should contextualise this appeal by making clear who I am and who I am not. I am a scholar, educator, and advocate who has taught a variety of popular music genres, particularly Hip Hop, at the university level since 1999. I am a musician and have spent time learning the art of the Hip Hop DJ and have spent countless hours engaging with and observing Hip Hop artists. I am not, however, primarily a practitioner of the genres that I study and teach. I am also a privileged white man with tenure and research funds, which explains as much of my success in promoting Hip Hop in academia as my research, teaching, and advocacy. But even given this power and privilege, this success has only come because I have been able to work in partnership with exceptional practitioners outside of academia, and most of them people of colour. With this in mind, I offer three exhortations that draw both on my own experience and perspective and on the perspectives and experiences of the remarkable artists with whom I have collaborated over the years.

Open the gates. Kuttin Kandi is a pioneering DJ, a legendary name in the world of turntablism who has been active in the community for decades. She is also an educator, a mentor, a writer, and an activist. She is, in short, as qualified as anyone to teach the art, culture, and history of the Hip Hop DJ, and Hip Hop in general. However, like many practitioners with similar qualifications, she has found herself subject to academic gatekeeping. She was once asked by a faculty member at a local university to recommend someone to teach a Hip Hop course. They were dealing with an awkward situation—a faculty member (an academic and non-practitioner) had taught the course in the past, but students complained that it felt disconnected to the genre they knew and loved. 'We need someone to teach this class', the professor said, and then asked, 'Do you know anybody who [can teach it] who has at least a master's [degree]?' 'I took a little bit of offense to it', Kandi recalls, 'because you're asking me for a resource, knowing that I could probably teach this class myself but don't even have a BA [bachelor of arts degree]'.[1] This is just one example of the academic gatekeeping she has experienced; she has observed exclusionary practices in the organisation of conferences, panel discussions, and other public events where Hip Hop is centred but the most authentic voices of Hip Hop are left out. I have heard similar stories from other artists. What is insidious about this gatekeeping is that artists are often simultaneously exploited and excluded; they are consulted for their expertise, almost always without compensation, and then shut out from the initiatives they assist.

This gatekeeping also hurts students. This is a point well made by David Spellmon, a North Carolina–based educator and author of *Just Like Music: Social Emotional Learning Inspired by Hip Hop* (Spellmon, 2020). 'Hip

Hop can add immense value from an academic perspective', he explains. 'The whole notion of inviting the culture of the students (Hip Hop) into the classroom is a form of Culturally Responsive Instruction, but the challenge is maintaining the rigor, which can be done with a gifted educator'. However, when we shut educators from the culture out of the classroom and, as in the situation Kuttin Kandi described, assign less qualified instructors, 'there will be an inauthentic feel if the educator does not fully understand the importance of Hip Hop to their students [and it] will create a disconnect between students and educators'.[2] This is not to say that only Hip Hop artists can teach Hip Hop, but we risk alienating students if our pedagogy does not resonate with their lived experience of the music they hold so dear.

We—those of us on the inside of educational institutions or networks—must open the gates to practitioners. (Our ultimate goal should be to remove any barriers altogether, but opening the gates is a necessary first step.) This can take many forms: we should invite them to perform, lead workshops, and teach courses; we should make space and facilities accessible to them; we should consult with them for their expertise and compensate them for their time. And as Junious Brickhouse, a dancer and educator and the executive director of the non-profit Urban Artistry, told me, we should always aim to develop ongoing, sustainable relationships. 'Give me a chance to show you what I have studied my whole life', he asks when he is invited into academic spaces. But he cannot do that if he is treated as a 'spectacle', brought in to add some colour to a public event or demonstrate diversity in a superficial, tokenistic way—only to be ignored thereafter.[3]

As the chapters in this volume attest, the benefits of moving from a practice of gatekeeping to gate-opening are immense. I will offer an example of my own. A few years ago, I was invited to give a talk at the University of Michigan. I asked if, as part of my visit, I could bring some artists I knew who worked in nearby Detroit to meet with students. One of the artists, Deidre Smith, an MC who performs as D.S.Sense, made such a good impression that a faculty member, Mark Clague, successfully lobbied to have her hired to teach a rap songwriting class. At the end of the semester—her first time teaching at a university—Smith wrote in a Facebook post that she was 'crying tears of gratitude' upon seeing student evaluations. Students testified that the course was 'amazing', 'inspiring', and 'the coolest', that it boosted their self-confidence and self-expression and offered them a 'safe haven'. After attending a performance that showcased the students' work, Clague wrote this to Smith: 'Seeing the students perform was revelatory for me and I can only begin BEGIN to imagine the positive and transformative impact you have had on these students' lives'.[4] Less than a week later, Clague wrote to Smith that she was approved to teach two additional classes that would build on her first offering, and thus provide students the means to progress to more advanced levels of rap songwriting. All I did was crack open the gates a tiny bit; Mark Clague opened them further. D.S.Sense did the rest, compellingly demonstrating the unique value of her art and pedagogy to the university.

Move the music from periphery to centre. Consider the history of popular music in educational institutions. Typically, and perhaps always, the music enters at the periphery. Whether jazz, rock, or Hip Hop, the music first has an extracurricular existence, taking root in student clubs or after-school programs. And this is often where the music stays. If it progresses any further, it may enter the curriculum as an elective, but never part of a sequence of advancing levels and never to fulfil a degree or graduation requirement. Opening the gates, therefore, only accomplishes so much if the music remains on the margins, if students can easily finish their schooling without ever encountering it in a class or other required activity.

As an example of the trajectory from periphery to centre, consider the place of Hip Hop at the University of North Carolina at Chapel Hill, where I have taught since 2006. In the 1990s there was a student Hip Hop organisation, and Michael Eric Dyson, then a professor in the Department of Communication, often addressed Hip Hop in his courses. But Hip Hop was not widely embraced at UNC. For example, Dyson was heavily criticised by parents and alumni in 1996 when he cited rap lyrics at a commencement speech; the university administration did nothing to defend him.[5] (Dyson left UNC in 1997.) As far as I know, Hip Hop had little or no presence in my department, Music. When I introduced Hip Hop into my teaching in 2007, I was met with no real resistance, though a colleague made sure to tell me how much he hated the music. Nor did I find any roadblocks when I proposed hiring Hip Hop artists to co-teach with me or when I created the Beat Lab, a space that houses turntables, drum machines, synthesisers, and production stations. However, I secured external funding to hire the artists and purchase the equipment through grants and donations; I cannot be sure what the response would have been had these initiatives required existing departmental funds. The only time I felt thwarted in my efforts was when I proposed hiring a well-known Hip Hop producer who had expressed interest in teaching a beat-making course at UNC. The resistance came at the dean's level when

I was told that there was no way the university could hire the producer since he did not have an advanced degree.

Although Hip Hop's presence grew steadily at UNC, it still existed at the margins of the department. We brought a few Hip Hop artists in to teach the occasional class but could only hire those who had graduate degrees, and they were only ever part-time instructors. Courses focused on Hip Hop could only be taken as electives and fulfilled no requirements for music majors. It was only in the past few years that a more fundamental shift in the role of Hip Hop began. In fact, the two most important achievements in moving Hip Hop from periphery to centre came only in 2022: the revamping of our curriculum to allow music majors to focus their studies on Hip Hop (and other popular genres) and the hiring of our first full-time faculty member in Hip Hop composition and performance—the producer, composer, songwriter, and entrepreneur Suzi Analogue (Zachary, 2022).

I will cite three lessons to draw from the trajectory of Hip Hop at UNC. First, moving any music from periphery to centre requires the full (or majority) participation of the unit or institution. No single advocate is sufficient to chart this course. Second, it requires systemic change. One of my mantras has been that it should be possible for beat makers and banjo players to be music majors at UNC. (This mantra reflects the popularity and cultural importance of both Hip Hop and bluegrass to the state of North Carolina, as well as my penchant for alliteration.) But this could never be possible within the system that had existed for decades. My mantra could only become reality with the adoption of a new curriculum, one that reimagined the music history and theory sequences, that challenged the definition of musical literacy as the ability to read Western printed notation, and added new courses in popular musics.[6] Even this was not sufficient: we also had to prioritise the hiring of new faculty proficient in popular musics and eliminate the requirement that graduate-level degrees were required of all faculty. A third lesson is that moving Hip Hop from periphery to centre requires sustained commitment. This move is ongoing at UNC, and it is too early to gauge its success; but there will be no success without the continued funding of Hip Hop activities and a commitment to a cultural shift in which students studying Hip Hop (and bluegrass, for that matter) are taken as a seriously and are given as much chance to succeed as any other student.

Evaluate. If Hip Hop, house, grime, and other contemporary popular genres are to have a robust, authentic, and sustained existence within our educational systems, their value needs to be communicated to all stakeholders: students, teachers, administrators, funders, and the public. This goal is well served by developing robust and rigorous evaluation mechanisms. Unfortunately, the outcomes we most desire from our engagement with students are often the hardest to measure, whether because of the difficultly of assessing causality or because the most desired impacts manifest themselves months or years after students have left the classroom. I will offer a few suggestions for addressing these challenges, with the understanding that there is so much more to say. (Fortunately, there is a wealth of excellent ideas on the subject offered throughout this volume.) For one, evaluation should be part of curriculum design and not relegated to brief peer reviews or a fifteen-minute window accorded to students on the last day of class. Feedback and input should be collected regularly and be integral to the structure of the course or activity. Second, in addition to assessing knowledge acquisition and skill development, we should seek to measure broader areas of growth, both among students and in our curricula. Here are a few questions I would ask: Do students, especially those whose communities have traditionally been marginalised or oppressed, feel more included? Do curricula represent the diversity of students' identities and experiences through course materials and staffing? Do the educational materials and activities encourage students to develop empathy for others? Do students feel empowered to express themselves in ways that feel authentic to them? Do curricula offer pathways to further artistic development and potentially employment? Third and finally, students (current students and alumni) as well as practitioners should be involved in the development of evaluation practices and materials. Yes, we educators are the experts in our fields, but what is so clear from the following essays is that those who are truly dedicated to music-related activities that promote inclusion and healing in schools and beyond must centre the agency of the communities that nourish these musics and the agency of our students who find these musics so life-giving. We do well to look to them for guidance and wisdom.

To close I want to continue to centre the work of practitioners by giving the final word to the Ugandan b-boy, educator, and promoter, Kaweesi Mark. Mark found purpose and community as a homeless, orphaned teen on the streets of Kampala when he started learning Hip Hop dance through the non-profit organisation Breakdance Project Uganda. Years later, he continues to work with BPU but has since founded Break-Fast Jam, 'an initiative that nurtures and promotes dance, art, hip-hop and urban culture'.[7] When I recently asked Mark what he sees as the benefits that can arise from students interacting with Hip Hop, he provided the following list: 'Being inspired by how people with nothing/less created a powerful global movement; Building connections with people around the world; Being inspired by the positive ground breaking contributions of Hip Hop worldwide; Learning about the power of creativity & innovation; Reflecting on their lives.'[8] I think most of us who do this kind of work do it for exactly the reasons Mark describes. We want to foster connection, creativity, innovation, and reflection. We want to inspire and be inspired. From my perspective, this is not only a powerful final message but also an apt way to describe the goals of *Music for Inclusion and Healing in Schools and Beyond*.

Mark Katz

References

Jared, S. (2023). *Music curriculum spans genres, includes applied learning.* https://college. unc.edu/2023/01/music-curriculum-applied-learning/.

Spellmon, D. (2020). *Just like music: Social emotional learning inspired by Hip Hop.* Positive Archer Publications.

Zachary, C. (2022). *Renowned artist Suzi Analogue appointed to music faculty.* https:// music.unc.edu/2022/06/27/suzi-analogue-appointment/.

Contributors

Martin Ainscough studied Music at Salford University and has been working with Musical Futures since 2008. Martin is an Assistant Headteacher at a secondary school where he has responsibility for developing authentic, real-world learning across the curriculum. As a music teacher, Martin has gained experience of delivering a wide range of courses at key stage four, including GCSE, BTEC, NCFE, and RSL Music Performance. He is currently a Director at Musical Futures and is also an SLE (Specialist Leader of Education) in Music, offering support and leadership training for teachers in other schools.

BREIS (breeze) is the founder of Student of Life, a Hip Hop–inspired arts organisation that uses motivational talks, live rap performances, interactive workshops, and learning strategies to inspire creativity and engage students more. BREIS is a critically acclaimed rap artist. His music and wordplay explore the human condition with an Afro surrealist perspective. His latest project, Arise & Shine, is full of hard-hitting, clever lyrics over a musical backdrop of Hip Hop, reggae, and funk. BREIS is also the author of *Diary of a Creative Mind* and *Brilliant Rappers Educate Intelligent Students*.

Pamela Burnard is Professor of Arts, Creativities, and Educations at the Faculty of Education, University of Cambridge. She has published widely with twenty-five books (most recent being *The Routledge Companion to Creativities in Music Education*, 2023). Along with over one hundred articles, her work advances the theory and practice of multiple creativities across education sectors including early years, primary, secondary, further, and higher education, through to creative and cultural industries. She is coeditor-in-chief of the international journal *Thinking Skills and Creativity*. Current funded projects include 'Choices, Chances and Transitions around Creative Further and Higher Education' (Nuffield) and 'Creative Learning for Boosting Bio-Economy within HEI Curricula (CL4Bio)' (ERASMUS). She is an Elected Fellow of the Royal Society of Arts (RSA), Fellow of the Chartered College of Teaching UK, and Fellow of the International Society for the Study of Creativity and Innovation (ISSCI). She is an Adjunct Professor at the Universities of Lisbon and Western Sydney. She sits on the advisory board of the *Global Institute of Creative Thinking* (GIoCT) and is a trustee for *Da Vinci Life-Skills Biophilic Education* and Co-I (Co-Investigator) of the AHRC-funded Contemporary Urban Music for Inclusion Network (CUMIN).

Alex H. D. Crooke has a transdisciplinary background in adolescent mental health, sociology, and music therapy. His work explores intersections between music, well-being, culture, and social justice. Combining these theoretical strands with practice as a beat maker, DJ, and designer, Dr Crooke's work involves research, teaching, consulting, and instrument development.

Pete Dale has worked as a musician, music promoter, school music teacher, and latterly as an academic specialising in music education. His interest in using tech-based contemporary popular musics to enhance inclusion stems from his work in schools, where he found that encouraging DJing and MC rapping in the classroom allowed much greater engagement with otherwise hard-to-reach learners, especially disaffected boys. He is passionate about encouraging social and cultural recognition of the value of Hip Hop, post-Hip Hop, and the full range of electronic dance musics. Pete is Lecturer in Music Education within the School of Arts and Creative Technologies at University of York and is Principal Investigator of the AHRC-funded Contemporary Urban Music for Inclusion Network (CUMIN).

Jabari M. Evans is an Assistant Professor of Race and Media at the University of South Carolina and the Institute of Rebooting Social Media at Harvard University. He is also Executive Director of The Brainiac Project Inc., a non-profit focused on creating opportunities and pathways for creative youth in low-income urban communities of colour. Jabari's research focuses on subcultures that Black creative youth develop and inhabit to communicate with digital media tools and technologies.

Lambros Fatsis is a Senior Lecturer in Criminology at City University, London. His research focuses on police racism and the criminalisation of Black music (sub) culture(s), fusing Cultural Criminology with Black radical thought. Lambros is also a member of the Prosecuting Rap Expert Network and an advisor at the Brighton-based youth music charity, AudioActive.

Elliot Gann is a licensed child and adolescent clinical psychologist by training. Dr Gann is a long-time beat maker and Executive Director of Today's Future Sound (TFS) who has been working with TFS in Bay Area schools and community settings, and across the globe using Hip Hop beat making and culture as a mental health, educational, social-justice, and cross-cultural intervention.

Nathan Geering is the Director of Rationale Method Accessibility Innovation Company and Director of Rationale Arts Registered Charity. Nathan specialises in accessibility innovation and strives to make work that heightens accessibility for both disabled and non-disabled artists and audiences. He also runs a registered charity called Rationale Arts that innovates Hip Hop elements to enhance healthcare in both medical and educational settings.

Simon Glenister's background is a mixture of twenty years of experience working in local government settings with young people in challenging circumstances alongside a career as a professional musician, touring internationally and specialising in music technology. Founding Noise Solution in 2009, the organisation uses an innovative evidenced-based combination of one-on-one music mentoring, focussed on beat making, and a bespoke digital platform designed to share participant's success stories with family and professionals whilst capturing nationally benchmark-able well-being data. Noise Solution has proven its highly statistical significance in impacting on well-being of populations that other statutory organisations often struggle to engage with. On a mission to take the 'wooly' out of arts impacts, Simon is an advocate of the importance of impact capture, impact management, and the use of theory to inform practice. Simon's work in this area is underpinned by a research master's degree, undertaken at Cambridge University's Faculty of Education in 2016–2018, researching digital youth work and well-being.

Fran Hannan is currently Managing Director of Musical Futures and has been with the organisation since 2005, initially as a project manager and in various leading roles since then. During most of that time she also worked for ArtForms, the lead organisation of the music hub for Leeds. Fran had previously studied music at Chetham's School of Music and then Nottingham and Bretton Hall (University of Leeds) before beginning her career as an instrumental teacher (cello) and school teacher. She remains passionate about music and music education in all its forms and is currently co-principal cellist for Harrogate Symphony Orchestra.

Simon Hayhoe is a Reader in Education at the University of Bath, a Centre Associate in the Centre for the Philosophy of Natural and Social Science at London School of Economics, and an Associate of the Scottish Sensory Centre at University of Edinburgh. His current work focuses on visual impairment and the arts, accessible and inclusive technologies, impairment and ageing, and social-science research methodology. Hayhoe's most significant project investigated the use of mobile technologies and their use by older adults with disabilities, which was sponsored by a Horizon 2020 grant from the European Union (2016–2020). He is currently coeditor of the Routledge book series Qualitative and Visual Methodologies in Educational Research. He has won several awards and fellowships, including a Fulbright All Disciplines Scholar's Award and fellowships of the British Computer Society and the Metropolitan Museum of Art (New York), and was a Temporary Advisor to the World Health Organisation (2019–2021).

Mark Katz is John P. Barker Distinguished Professor of Music at the University of North Carolina at Chapel Hill and Founding Director of the U.S. State Department hip hop cultural diplomacy program, Next Level. His five books include Capturing Sound: How Technology has Changed Music (2004, rev. 2010), Build: The Power of Hip Hop Diplomacy in a Divided World (2019), and Music and Technology: A Very Short Introduction (2022). He is co-editor of Music, Sound, and Technology in America: A Documentary History (2012) and former editor of the Journal of the Society for American Music (2012–15). In 2015 Katz was recognized by the Hip-Hop Education Center in its inaugural awards ceremony, and in 2016 he was awarded the Dent Medal by the Royal Musical Association for his contributions to musicology. He is currently at work on Rap and Redemption on Death Row, a co-authored book with incarcerated musician Alim Braxton, and a third edition of Capturing Sound.

Ian Levy is an Associate Professor and Graduate Director of School Counseling at Manhattan College in New York. He is a New York City native, and former High School counselor in Manhattan, Brooklyn, and the Bronx. Dr. Levy's research examines Hip Hop based practices in schools as a culturally responsive approach to counseling wherein students process difficult thoughts and feelings through the writing, recording, and performing of emotionally themed music.

Douglas Lonie has over fifteen years' experience researching the impacts of music and arts participation on individuals and communities. His mixed-methods PhD (University of Glasgow, 2008) explored the impact of music on adolescent mental health. As Research and Evaluation Manager at the National Foundation for Youth Music (2008–2014) and Senior Consultant at BOP Consulting (2014–2020), he has worked with hundreds of cultural organisations across the United Kingdom and internationally exploring the personal and social impact of art and culture. Dougie has designed and led research and evaluation for UNESCO, Bloomberg Philanthropies, Arts Council England, Creative Scotland, and British Council Arts. In 2018 he was a Global Cultural Fellow at the University of Edinburgh, leading conversations on the role of culture in developing empathy within and between communities. In 2020 he co-founded the research organisation *tialt—there is an alternative*, seeking to develop impact evaluation practice that is more theory-led, creative, inclusive, and fun.

Kiran Manley lost her older sister, Promila, in a car accident in 2000, subsequently suffering a delayed traumatised grief reaction and a creative block that lasted ten years. During this time, she trained as a secondary English teacher, and enjoyed a fruitful career in museum and gallery education. After her father died in 2010, she discovered therapeutic writing and her writer's block came undone. Already holding a BA and MA in Literature, Manley decided to do an MSc in Creative Writing for Therapeutic Purposes to share what she had learnt about self-healing through creativity. She then set up Hip Hop HEALS, a mental health project that uses Hip Hop to tackle health inequalities in marginalised groups, particularly for Global Majority people, young people, and men. In 2020 she was selected for Lloyd's Bank's School for Social Entrepreneurs to develop Hip Hop HEALS into a social enterprise business, with a grant of £1000. Manley also hosts and produces 'Glowitheflow' podcast on therapeutic Hip Hop.

Beate Peter is a cultural sociologist at the University of Groningen and interested in the role that music plays for the formation of communities. As an interdisciplinary scholar with a PhD in popular music, she works with a range of methodologies to uncover hidden voices and stories of marginalised communities. Currently, Beate works with Unity Radio, engaging young people from challenging backgrounds in the elements of Hip Hop through workshops and VR.

Inka Rantakallio is a postdoctoral researcher in Musicology at the University of Helsinki with an interdisciplinary background in Study of Religions (MA) and Musicology (PhD). She is also known for her work as a music journalist, public speaker, and DJ. Her current project (Academy of Finland, 2021–2024) focuses on feminist women rappers, gender, race, and whiteness in Finnish Hip Hop. Her PhD dissertation (2019) focused on discourses of authenticity, spirituality, and atheism in Finnish underground rap. She has co-edited three books (in Finnish) on music and/ or Hip Hop studies. Her research interests include Hip Hop, popular music, gender, race, worldviews, religion, identity, and discourse.

Rawz is an MC and Poet. Growing up in one of the United Kingdom's most deprived areas, Northfieldbrook (Greater Leys) in Oxford, he first discovered lyric writing in his early teens. It was an essential way to channel his emotions and organise his thoughts. A self-guided therapy. Since then, Rawz has performed his craft all over Europe both as a solo artist, and with the Inner Peace Records collective, which he helped to form alongside other artists from Oxford and London's Hip Hop scenes in 2015. He has collaborated with musicians from all over the world and shared stages with some of his childhood heroes. Rawz's music and lyrics share his exploration of our interconnected worlds, and his responses to them, promoting outer change and advancement through inner reflection and positive action. Rawz does this while covering an unlimited range of topics including love, capitalism, nature, community, crime, science, religion, and more.

Jim Reiss began his career as a DJ in the 1990s before starting to share DJ skills with young offenders in 2000 then later as a workshop facilitator for North Yorkshire County Council. He is the Managing Director of DJ School UK, industry consultant for the foundation degree in DJ skills at Leeds Conservatoire, and a panel member for MUSIC: Leeds launchpad funding applications. Jim was one of the consultants to AQA exam board during the development of the specification for using DJing at GCSE level. He has developed a range of Unit Award Scheme accreditations in DJ skills with the AQA board.

Austen and Scott Smart previously known as Brodanse and Austen/Scott, were regular fixtures at fabric, the UK's leading nightclub. The co-founders of Danse Club Records collaborated with music powerhouses like Groove Armada and Armin Van Buuren. In 2016, they established FutureDJs, launching an innovative study programme for DJ-ing and music production taught by sixty tutors across the UK. This led to the world's first graded DJ exams with the London College of Music and the publication of *FutureDJs: How to DJ* (Faber Music, 2020). In 2019, they pivoted to Virtuoso, working with major name artists to transform global music education. Leveraging their eight-year experience with leading education providers, they now help develop artists into educators and create inspiring, scalable curriculums.

Johan Söderman holds a position as professor in Child and Youth Studies at the Department of Education, Communication, and Learning, University of Gothenburg. Söderman is also a Reader in Music Education at the Faculty of Fine and Performing Arts, Lund University. For almost twenty years, Söderman has published articles and books regarding Hip Hop in relation to learning and education. Currently, Söderman is involved in the project In the gangster rap era—Educational and Youth Cultural Implications, which is financed by the Swedish Research Council.

Raphael Travis Jr. is a Professor at Texas State University in the School of Social Work. His research, practice, and consultancy work emphasise healthy development over the life course, resilience, and civic engagement. He also investigates creative arts, especially Hip Hop culture, as a source of health and well-being for individuals and communities. He is author of the book *The Healing Power of Hip Hop*. His latest research, linking arts engagement and well-being, appears in a variety of academic journals and book chapters.

The Collaborative Research for Education, Art, and Therapeutic Engagement (CREATE) Lab led by Dr Travis partners with researchers, educators, artists, and community-based organizations focused on better understanding the educational, health, and therapeutic benefits of music and art engagement. Dr Travis is also the founder and Director of FlowStory, PLLC. FlowStory promotes the empowering aspects of Hip Hop culture as a critical tool for learning, growth, and well-being across all ages, but especially with youth in family, education, therapy, afterschool, and summer program settings.

Introduction

Pete Dale, Pamela Burnard, and Raphael Travis Jr.

Music for Inclusion and Healing in Schools and Beyond emerges from the AHRC-funded two-year network project Contemporary Urban Music for Inclusion Network (CUMIN) which began its funding period at the outset of 2022. The background of both the network and this book (which is primarily made up of chapters from those who have presented in our CUMIN workshops and 2023 conference) is a concern that contemporary popular musics (Hip Hop, grime, drill, EDM, house, techno, reggae, and more) do not receive the educational, cultural, and social recognition which they ought to command. This situation needs to be redressed because, as we show in this book, the potential individual and community benefits arising from such recognition are huge.

What is the educational, cultural, and social recognition that contemporary popular musics ought to command? UK newspaper *The Independent* reported in 2015 that 'Hip-hop is the most listened to genre in the world, according to Spotify analysis of 20 billion tracks' (Hooton, 2015). Meanwhile, there is an estimated global audience of 1.5 billion for dance/electronic music according to the 2019 International Music Summit report (Watson, 2019). Hip Hop, house, EDM, grime, and so on: these musics are what most people in the world today are listening to. Nonetheless, Hip Hop is 'frequently excluded' from even popular music education according to the *Journal of Popular Music Education*, let alone the mainstream music curriculum (Smith and Powell, 2018: 3). In the United Kingdom, the current National Curriculum for Music emphasises the need for school children to be exposed to 'music from great composers and musicians'. Some rock and pop repertoires have found a place in schools over recent decades, but electronically generated contemporary popular music (a far more ethnically/racially diverse music, typically) remains marginalised. This (educational) issue is explored in Part One of the book in particular. However, the broad problem pertains not only to schools but also to mainstream culture.

Pete Dale, Pamela Burnard, and Raphael Travis Jr., *Introduction* In: *Music for Inclusion and Healing in Schools and Beyond*. Edited by: Pete Dale, Pamela Burnard, and Raphael Travis Jr., Oxford University Press.
© Oxford University Press 2023. DOI: 10.1093/oso/9780197692677.003.0001

Think DJ decks: is the DJ just someone who spins platters and presses buttons but lacks real musical/creative skills? Some will say 'yes', of course, but Part One of this book strongly suggests otherwise. Is a rapper really a musician? *The Guardian* suggested in late 2022 that some today still regard rap as 'tuneless, artless or without merit' (Nicholson, 2022), and yet rap-based music is some of the most popular in the world today. In short, much of the field(s) of contemporary popular musics is today kept at the educational and cultural margins despite a towering popularity in the inner cities and beyond. A core purpose of *Music for Inclusion and Healing* is to argue that huge benefits could arise if this situation were to be redressed.

Among these benefits is an impact on wellness that seems to arise from opportunities for music-making or music-related activities that engage with these (educationally/culturally marginalised) contemporary popular musics. Part Two of the book drills into those therapeutic gains, evidencing the benefits that would appear to have arisen and querying/exploring/ enhancing the potential for detailed and robust evaluation of such impacts. In Part Three, meanwhile, the book examines the question of evaluation of this impact, carefully examining issues as to *what* changes and *why*, as well as asking *how* the change can best be measured.

These concerns—educational, therapeutic, and the evaluation of impact(s)—can in fact be taken as related pieces, to some extent. That is, the question of wellness is far from being extra-scholastic in character: if you do not feel well, you will not learn well. The therapeutic potential of Hip Hop and other contemporary popular forms is highly pertinent to broader questions about what schools do, what they do well, what they could do better, and so forth. Learning new skills, learning to DJ or MC, learning about music, meanwhile, are doubtless good for almost anyone's mental health. The book does not separate its three sections on the grounds of some mutually exclusive distinction among educational, therapeutic, and evaluative concerns, then: these areas overlap and support one another, or at least they can do. Those toiling in the field of education will find much to consider from Part Two: questions of well-being, of healing and of recovery from trauma that, sadly, are much needed by many learners within a wide range of (not just urban) schools. Those with a special interest in 'The Healing Power of Hip Hop' (to quote the title of Raphael Travis' landmark book on this topic), meanwhile, will be enlivened by the considerations of what schools sometimes do *to* people (which is not always positive) and what they could potentially do *for* and *with* people (if, for example, they offered a curriculum that is more engaged with contemporary and electronically driven popular forms, as the chapters in Part One tend to propose they should). Both Part One and Part Two are about the pleasures, benefits, and potentials of making or working with/around contemporary popular musics, in other words, but they focus separately upon education and therapy as an organisational principle within the book's structure.

Part Three, meanwhile, provides vital insights for readers interested in both the therapeutic-orientated and education-orientated aspects of the book. The focus here is 'Impact and (Evidence-Building) Evaluation'. Part Three asks how therapeutic and/or educational impacts are best identified, measured, and put to work for evidence-based evaluation. Why is it important to evaluate impact? For one thing, the kinds of extra-scholastic organisations that are often discussed in this book require robust evidence of measurable impact in order to unlock the funding that is so often essential for the survival of such organisations. Funders, that is, want to know *what will change* as a result of an intervention based in some way around contemporary popular musics, such as rapping or beat-making workshops: What will the impact be and how do you know that this impact will arise? How will evidence of the impact be measured? What factors can make it more or less robust? How can the risks of either decreased agency or increased alienation be addressed through ethical evaluation practices? How can the evaluation of quality (and impact) of practices and programmes be measured in ways that organisations, institutions, artists, practitioners, educators, researchers, and therapist workforces can achieve 'quality' based on evidence? We argue and provide evidence that different figurations of 'quality' can be both political and ethical. While quality remains a quantifiable, recognizable, and measurable thing that can be objectively assessed and ultimately attained, there is an urgent need for professional standards to 'go beyond quality' and thus to recognize 'quality' as *processes of becoming*. Developing critical understandings and new applications of diverse forms of evaluations for diverse programmes, practices, and projects, utilizing integrated and interdisciplinary approaches that combine artistic, scientific, and robust methods, listening conventions and socio-musical relations, are long-awaited.

The three sections that make up the main body of the book, then, are intended to weave together to present a broad argument that the kinds of contemporary popular musics cited in the subtitle of this book have educational and extra-scholastic as well as therapeutic benefits. Heretofore, these benefits have been growing in practical application, and yet they remain under-used and under-theorised relative to their potential for beneficial impacts. These impacts are clear to see, up to a point, but a more robust and secure evidence base in terms of measurable impact would be wise, the book proposes. The potential 'beneficiaries', here, could be 'people in general' (if we can put it like this), but also, more specifically, there are good reasons to think that those who dwell and strive to survive in our inner cities are particularly likely to benefit from an enhanced openness to contemporary popular musics (Hip Hop, grime, house, and more) in schools, beyond schools, in therapeutic applications, and so forth.

We make no apology for a strong interest in inner-city lived experience: there, we find a greater need for wellness, a greater need for schools to feel welcoming rather than alien, a greater need for creative opportunities in an urban world that can feel devoid of creativity for so many. We will also tend to find in the inner city (particularly in the United States) a higher level of ethnic diversity. This not only is reflected in the field of Hip Hop (which, incidentally, we capitalise throughout the book on grounds that it is a full-blown cultural arena and not just a genre of music) but runs across the forms of contemporary popular music at the heart of this book. Detroit-born DJ Ash Lauryn, for example, recently stated on a BBC Radio 4 documentary that 'some people hear the word "techno" and they think "all-male, all-white line-ups, hoards of fist-pumping zombie bros"—but that ain't the whole story'. In Lauryn's view, 'the radical politics of techno live on, you just need to know where to look . . . To me, techno has always been political and it has always been black' (Lauryn, 2022). Whatever the colour of one's skin, we all need creativity in our lives: unfortunately, however, formal and structured opportunities for creative expression can be limited in inner cities all over the world.

The editors of the book and the contributors are working to turn this situation around: we would contend that creativity is good for your health, good for learning, and good for citizenship. Consequently, this music-related 'bull' needs to be grabbed by its proverbial 'horns'. We need to understand where these goods (good health, good learning, good citizenship, and more) come from, certainly, and what exactly they are: but moreover, as a (global) society, we need to seize the opportunity that can arise when marginalised (and yet immensely popular) contemporary forms are offered up for creative agency among too often marginalised people.

This book is not focused upon one specific genre of music. Rather, we see a set of genres that form the cultural centre of much contemporary life in our inner cities and beyond. They are typically based around electronic music production: 'beat making', programming, digitally cutting and splicing and generating sounds with (typically) a heavy, synthetically created beat and strident electro-bassline beneath them. They often have their stylistic origins in the inner cities of the United States (although not always: grime is widely understood as uniquely British, and drill has had its own genesis in the United Kingdom, for example, whilst Hip Hop music has differing characters and flavours around the world in its innumerable iterations and reiterations). They often feature rapping, although some relevant and contemporary forms are more likely to include melodic vocals whilst much EDM has no voice on it. They come with a whole panoply of extra-musical signs and symbols: trainers, insignia on clothing, special terminology, inventive creation of dialect, perhaps even preferences for particular kinds of food or films or computer games and so forth. (Musics that fall outside of those upon which we are focussed—Western art musics and the broad field of 'rock and pop', for example—also contain such signs and symbols, of course: the signs and symbols differ, but the 'habitus' (in Bourdieu's sense) is an *expression* of class rather than being its fundament, and, therefore, the fact that signs and symbols differ does not constitute a structural difference; but it is notable that some signs and symbols are kept at the margins in many 'official culture' contexts whilst being at the cultural centre of the (other) mainstream in other contexts).

In truth, some of the most popular contemporary musics have been swept beneath the carpet (Burnard *et al.*, 2023). It may not have been a deliberate decision on the part of individuals, but such has happened. Take the school syllabus: it would be an injustice to say that the UK exam boards have been entirely ignoring rapping, beat making, and so forth (although not every country can say the same, probably). On the contrary, some UK exam boards have shown an impressive openness to, say, DJing, rapping, performance on laptops and even 'beatboxing' (imitating percussion using the human voice, that is) (Dale, 2017: 119–123). Nonetheless, we know that many school music departments eschew such (contemporary) modes of musicking, presumably in fear that a technology-based performance will not be treated respectfully no matter what it says in the exam syllabus. Consider, in this regard, some comments from a teacher who was formally interviewed as part of the 2019–2020 'Tech Champions' project led by Musical Futures in association with Ableton (Dale, 2020). The teacher, a classically trained musician whose practical application of music technology for teaching and learning purposes was regarded as 'outstanding' according to the project's evaluation report, stated that they had never used technology for an assessed GCSE or A-level performance and they 'couldn't imagine doing that', as they are

> nervy of the assessment process, moderation process, things like that. I'd love to do it but I'm nervous . . . I have a genuine fear that people [who do moderation] don't understand the use of technology. Even in composition I get nervy with it, '[At] what point is it the student's work' and so on and so on.

Such is a serious obstacle to the full integration of Hip Hop, grime, house, EDM, and suchlike (and associated modes of composing and music-making) in school-level education: if the teachers are nervy, they are likely to be apprehensive and 'play it safe'; and the net result for many learners is that they become less likely to achieve well in Music as a school subject, or to select it from the studying 'options' they are given around the age of fourteen. Meanwhile, the 2015 announcement of Kanye West's appearance on the UK's annual Glastonbury festival bill was met with a petition against it and vocal disapproval from several quarters. Emily Eavis, lead figure in the Glastonbury festival in recent years, has claimed that she 'actually had death threats in 2015' as a direct result of the decision to place West on the bill. Similar disapproval occurred when Jay-Z and Stormzy were added as headline acts within the Glastonbury line-up (2008 and 2019, respectively) (Eavis, 2019). Why should these artists, all of them wildly popular around the world, be unwelcome at or deemed unsuitable for Glastonbury? It may be naked racism at play here, of course: each of these performers has Afro-diasporic heritage (they are 'Black', that is). However, it may be that something a bit more subtle (and perhaps more pernicious) is at play: a feeling that the electronic sounds, the rapped vocals, the whole assemblage of signs and symbols and so forth, mean that this kind of music just is not right for Glastonbury. If people enjoy that kind of thing, fine; but it does not belong in 'our' musical world: this, it seems likely, is what many objectors to the inclusion of Kanye West, Stormzy, and Jay-Z had at the forefront of their minds.

Such objectors are often 'just' fans: rogues, perhaps, who lack the objectivity and fairness that we can expect from journalists and other influencers of the cultural establishment(s) in the field(s) of music(s). Are these fans, who would start a petition against a rapper performing at Glastonbury, really at odds with the mainstream view of contemporary popular musics, though? Consider, in that regard, the expressed views of US politician Ben Shapiro: 'In my view, and in the view of my music theorist father who went to music school, there are three elements to music . . . There is harmony, there is melody and there is rhythm'. Shapiro adds that

> Rap only fulfils one of these, the rhythm section. There's not a lot of melody and there's not a lot of harmony. And thus, effectively, it is basically spoken rhythm. It's not actually a form of music. It's a form of rhythmic speaking. Thus, beyond the objectivity of me just not enjoying rap all that much, what I've said before is that rap is not music. (Roberts, 2019)

In the age of social media, no one ought to be surprised to hear that these comments were widely met with vitriolic rebuttals. Why Shapiro and his father would feel comfortable in assuming that melody, harmony, and rhythm are more important than, say, timbre, structure, or texture is a mystery; no serious musicologist ought to accept such a tidy assumption about what is most important in music or their assumptions about the compositional layers of rap music. Shapiro's view that 'rap is not music' is extraordinary for its bluntness, unpleasantness, and ignorance, of course, but is it really so far from the dominant view in the mainstream, official culture with regard to contemporary popular musics? Ordinarily, we can expect a bit more subtlety in terms of public attitudes to these musics, but in the end I would suggest that Shapiro is saying what a lot of people, from politicians and policy-makers to the fabled 'man in the street', think about the contemporary field.

To steal away the very ontological basis of these musics *qua* musics— to deny them even the category of being music, as Shapiro so clearly has attempted to do—has significance. Millions of Jay-Z, Kanye West, or Stormzy fans are not going to suddenly turn away from what they love on the basis of a politician's categorical denial that these musics are worthy of the name, of course. Nonetheless, the refusal to accept rap as musical has its effects: it helps to structure a negative public attitude to rap as an artform, it helps to reinforce the idea that some kinds of creativity have higher standards and qualities than some other kinds of creativity, it helps to despoil the sense that rap is an accomplishment or attached to the broader Hip Hop culture, and it helps to put these musics down. On one level, that does not matter too much: the aforementioned acts are wildly popular all over the world, as we have said, and far more famous than Ben Shapiro will ever be. However, the likes of Shapiro have helped to maintain a situation where this *de facto* contemporary popularity is not adequately reflected in, say, what gets focussed upon in a school classroom, what soundtracks dominant culture, what gets public subsidy. The custodians of the official culture have kept contemporary popular musics at the margins: our argument, in this book, is that rethinking this situation is an urgent necessity.

Book Structure: Summary of Chapters featured in Parts One, Two, and Three

As stated, the book is divided into three main sections. **PART ONE** is on 'Curriculum and Music Education'. **CHAPTER 1** sets the tone for the whole book: Lambros Fatsis informs us, in a chapter titled 'Beat(s) for Blame: UK Drill Music, "Race" and Criminal Injustice', that drill music has been effectively criminalised in the United Kingdom. Reaching back to calypso as a contextual example, Fatsis shows that the story is an old one: music made by Black people pushed to the margins, marginalised, and even criminalised/banned. What happens, though, if this music is taken out of the socio-cultural margins and given the mainstream recognition that its actual popularity would seem to demand? In **CHAPTER 2**, Jim Reiss tells us about 'DJ School UK and Beyond: My Journey as a DJ and DJ Educator' (to quote the chapter title) and his efforts to do just that. Jim works in schools, beyond schools, supporting teachers, supporting learners, even supporting the UK exam boards at times with his expert knowledge of DJ skills. His chapter charts his journey from school days to the present in a manner that demonstrates how some of the problems Chapter 1 had identified might be redressed through practical activity in and beyond schools.

Following this, **CHAPTER 3** by Johan Söderman examines ' "Bildung Life": Holistic Ideals of Hip Hop Education' from a Swedish perspective. The chapter identifies an 'educationalization' of Swedish hip-hop that started in the early 2000s, resulting in what has been referred to by some scholars as 'Folkhemsrap' (referring to the Swedish word 'Folkhem', which has been used as a synonym to 'the welfare state' by politicians). Again, the problems identified by Lambros Fatsis are given a tonic by this Swedish example: electronically generated contemporary popular musics such as Hip Hop can be embraced and, if and when they are (as would seem to have occurred in this Nordic example), a highly valuable 'sense of citizenship' can arise. **CHAPTER 4** by Pete Dale follows this, entitled 'Technology and the Music

Curriculum: Maximising Inclusion, Diversifying Options'. Dale's argument, in short, is that music education in UK state schools is in peril today, despite some benefits that initially arose from the replacement of the 1987 'O-level' (which did not recognise the guitar-based popular music that had become dominant in the decades since World War II as being worthy of curriculum coverage) with the GCSE (which jumped that hurdle at least to the extent that guitars, drums, and 'pop and rock' became part of the curriculum). Focussing on the example of the Musical Futures/Ableton project 'Tech Champions', Dale argues that the decline of music in schools might be reversible if, but perhaps only if, music technology is more fully recognised for its value in music education. Technological music-making equipment (DJ decks, DAWs, launchpads, etc.) need to be more widely used, and tech-orientated contemporary genres (grime, house, Hip Hop, EDM, and so forth) need to be more fully included.

Fran Hannan and Martin Ainscough, the leading figures in the United Kingdom's influential Musical Futures organisation, are the authors of **CHAPTER 5** on 'Musical Futures and Music Technology in Mainstream Music Education'. As Jim Reiss does in Chapter 2, Hannan and Ainscough use their personal histories as the starting point for the discussion, showing that whether one has taken the traditional route of classical music-orientated music education (as Hannan has done) or come from a more 'informal learning' background (as is the case with Ainscough) one can and should take an open-minded and learner-centric approach to music teaching. The chapter goes on to discuss the Tech Champions project (as examined by the previous chapter) and the thinking behind it, concluding with some strident observations about the state of music education in the United Kingdom today. Part One concludes with **CHAPTER 6**, 'Rethinking Learning with Future DJs, Virtuoso, and Beyond' by Austen and Scott Smart, two brothers who have made a significant contribution to DJ education in the United Kingdom with their Future DJs organisation and, more recently, their new company Virtuoso (which extends beyond the DJ orientation with content based around beat making, music production, and so forth). Starting, as do Chapters 2 and 5, from the life experiences of the chapter authors (including their experiences of music in school), the chapter describes the Smart brothers' journey from professional work to educational work before exploring the concept of the DAO (Decentralised Autonomous Organisation). The DAO, the chapter argues, could provide a path toward community governance and enhanced inclusion of learner interests.

Within **PART TWO** we have personal narratives alongside professional expertise and practice insights about Hip Hop culture as a path to healing and well-being. We have individual testimonials of transformation through Hip Hop culture in **CHAPTERS 7 and 9.** Across the chapters we find strategic opportunities and points of leverage to move the needle on health and well-being through the lens of Hip Hop culture. These chapters offer a deep dive into the minds of artists seeking to embody change, to be walking, breathing, relational vehicles of change for individuals and communities. **CHAPTER 7** takes us on a journey of discovery, healing, collective-well-being, perseverance, and artistic brilliance through Hip Hop. In **CHAPTER 9,** we also experience a journey of discovery, healing, resilience, and art-driven transformation through Hip Hop, drum and bass, EDM, and other music and art experiences. In both, the results were the desire to share the power of art with others to help them on their journeys. These are honest accounts of successes, challenges, triumphs, and missteps, but ultimately healing, wellness, and generosity along the way to embracing roles as agents of change.

Across chapters is a focused attention to the culturally specific realities of students' lives and what will likely resonate with them within the context of often inequitable and traumatic environments and experiences. Alongside qualitative examples, we also have quantitative data to help us add to existing evidence about how musical experiences contribute to healing and wellness.

In **CHAPTER 8,** we see data to further support how music can help people to feel better, do better, be better, have a better sense of belonging, and be invested in better conditions for the communities they care about. In this instance the evidence supports how music can be empowering through the ways we naturally experience music in our daily lives, but also how there is often intentionality and purpose in how people are listening. While there are opportunities for our helping professionals—social workers, counsellors, educators, and others—to create meaningful music-driven strategies to help students learn and grow, students are also doing this on their own with a clear rationale. At the same time by knowing how and when music is useful and empowering for students, the chapter helps us to see how we can better leverage student musical preferences, such as how those that prefer Hip Hop might uniquely benefit from professionally mediated music-driven approaches that employ Hip Hop music. At the same time while we see what contributes to empowering engagement, we see factors that contribute to risky engagement, offering similar opportunities to think about ways to potentially inhibit risky engagement.

An additional layer of cultural consistency and alignment is explored through the Therapeutic Beat Making model used by the work of Today's Future Sound in **CHAPTER 10**. These are in-depth case examples of working directly with the social reality and lived experiences of youth—but around the globe. Youth voices, community needs, and culture are not only solicited, but celebrated and amplified. The idea of Therapeutic Beat Making is explored from its emphasis on (a) relationships/being relational, (b) being expressive, and (c) the self-concept. Its significance alone as an incredibly engaging tool is important, as is beat making's ability to be a precursor to other more analytical-cognitive-processing-oriented activities, a regulating type of 'cognitive preparation' like mindfulness activities (Chris Jeter, personal communication, January 28, 2023). But the attention to building community, cultural sensitivity, and investing in developmental well-being is what comes to life in this chapter.

Health and well-being are explored through lyrics, through emcees/rappers, through everyday people, but also, in **CHAPTER 11**, through breakers and choreographers. All of this provides a further glimpse into the expansiveness of Hip Hop culture. The Sound Pad project centres dancers/breakers-as-teachers and inclusive education as pathways of well-being. Breaking culture, attention to gaps in opportunities for inclusivity, and being proactive about meeting cultural needs—in this case those with visual impairments—are shown to be incredibly meaningful.

We also hear directly from educational settings in **CHAPTER 12**. Within a case example among Chicago youth, the idea of Connected Learning within a Hip Hop–based education program is explored as a pathway to positive mental health, where students positively develop in these safe, supportive face-to-face and digital spaces. Identity once again emerges here as meaningful, as we validate these innovative ways to positively affirm identity and the short- and long-term value of doing so.

Chapters in **PART THREE** focus on evaluation. In **CHAPTER 13**, London rapper BREIS writes about 'The Hip-Hopification of Education and Its Evaluation'. The aim of this chapter is to highlight the need to challenge and disrupt teaching practices that no longer serve us in an ever-changing complex contemporary life. It explores how the Hip-Hopification of Education sees a meeting of works where Hip Hop 'signs in' and enters education. Where storytelling is featured strongly and sits at the centre of my Hip Hop Literacy program, which aims to make learning more fun and provide an understanding of Hip Hop, whilst simultaneously improving literacy skills.

It also helps us further understand and equip our young people for the future. This chapter shares outstanding students' verses that expose their vulnerability, their writing skill and knowledge of self, and BREIS take on the practice of evaluation. In **CHAPTER 14**, entitled 'Translating Evaluation and Research into Practice: What Matters for Socially Engaged Arts Programmes In and Beyond Schools', author Pamela Burnard addresses socially engaged practice that is distinctively collaborative, often participatory, and involves collaboration and participation with people as the medium or material of the work. Practices are designed to forge direct intersections with the community and social issues and can involve partnerships among artist practitioners, educators, evaluators, and researchers in and across educational sectors and engaging communities. These programmes are generative, communal sites that support and innovate practice. The role of *evaluation*, a reflexive process involving judgments about the quality and effectiveness of practice matters to how we draw together, understand, review, and report on socially engaged arts programmes. On the other hand, the role of *research* and reporting on the impact of socially engaged arts programmes (such as the arts-mental health relationship and health effects of diverse/urban musics engagement and dance participation) is often unclear or oversimplified. When teachers and arts practitioners want to evaluate their own practice and/or research their practice, they often, though not always, try to do this in partnership with researchers. Recognising the importance of translating practices into evaluation or research matters. This chapter invites us to ask *what matters* when we pay attention to situations when practitioners change their ways of enacting practices because they are acting as/with evaluators or as/with researchers or simply adapting/adopting 'evidence' from other evaluations or research, to improve what they are doing.

This is followed in **CHAPTER 15** by 'Untangling Earphones—Power, Voice, and Agency in Participatory Music Impact Evaluation', where Douglas Lonie explores different positions in the 'evaluation structures' that can affect much participatory music practice. The 'tangled earphones' of the title refers separately to funders of music interventions, the organisations and practitioners that deliver music programmes, and the participants themselves. Reflecting on research cases from over fifteen years of work in this field, this chapter aims to 'untangle' some of the points of contradiction that can lead to uncritical and substandard evaluation practices. Themes of control, agency, and power in impact evaluation design and practices are addressed. The discussion proposes that, if applied uncritically, these practices may have the opposite effect of the intended positive impacts of participatory music projects (i.e., 'unvoicing', diminished agency, and increased alienation). The chapter concludes with a set of considerations to enable researchers and practitioners to develop approaches to evaluation that are more critical and reflective. Through this process of collective 'untangling', we aim to listen more clearly to the various voices represented in participatory music and understand where these voices may need greater or lesser amplification when exploring and presenting the impact of such interventions.

In **CHAPTER 16**, author Beate Peter is concerned with young people's voices in spoken word popular music projects. In this chapter, entitled 'Evaluating Young People's Voices in Spoken Word Popular Music Projects', it is argued that for projects that engage young people with and through music, it is important to consider their voice in all its iterations, which includes young people's artistic voice. Using the concept of voice, this chapter shows how projects need to be designed in a way that captures young people's voices throughout the project and includes the non-verbal (i.e., musical) dimensions of their voices as forms of communication. Such inclusion necessitates the creation of intersubjective meaning through the negotiation of hierarchies, knowledges, expertise, and agency. As a result of the negotiation process, the role of the researcher can be redefined. By acknowledging the different epistemologies of the project participants, impact beyond the anticipated outcomes can be uncovered. Focusing on participation as an inclusive method, young people should be included in the planning, delivery, and evaluation of projects. Given a certain flexibility and space within projects, unintended outcomes can be identified through and responded to by the young people themselves. This way, impact becomes a phenomenological variable and allows for various forms of data and types of analysis to be used for the evaluation of projects.

Then what follows is **CHAPTER 17** where author Simon Glenister writes 'Evaluating Well-being Outcomes of the Social Enterprise "Noise Solution": Digital Approaches to Outcome Capture'. This chapter aims to demonstrate how technology can be applied to solve commonly held problems faced by arts organisations in demonstrating outcomes of their work, while also potentially improving them. *Noise Solution* delivers one-on-one music technology mentoring with youth, often referred by external agencies because they are at a point of crisis. The intention being to improve well-being. Self Determination Theory (Ryan and Deci, 2000) or SDT is used as a lens with which to inform the design of both mentoring and a bespoke social media 'like' platform facilitating the sharing of highlights and video reflections of each young person's mentoring experiences, weekly, and securely with their identified stakeholders. Each young person's feed also facilitates the capture and analysis of quantitative well-being data. The combination of mentoring, capturing, and sharing of highlights with stakeholders may contribute to fulfilling basic psychological needs identified in SDT.

The book ends with **CHAPTER 18**, written by Inka Rantakallio and entitled 'Who Is Heard and Who Gets to Belong in Hip Hop? The Counterspaces of Women and Gender Minority Rappers in Finland'. This chapter analyses the impact and evaluation of four initiatives that have sought to enhance the inclusion of women and non-binary practitioners in the Finnish Hip Hop music scene: (1) the D.R.E.A.M.G.I.R.L.S. group, (2) Matriarkaatti (Matriarchy) multimedia platform, (3) Hip Hop feminist anthology *Kuka kuuluu?*, and (4) Monsp bootcamps and mixtapes. The four examples provided women and non-binary people identifiable access opportunities to practice live performance and/or studio work and to create counterstory to the hegemonic White male narrative in Finnish Hip Hop. The chapter argues that these projects functioned as 'counterspaces' that challenge stereotypes and norms and help develop alternative communities, narratives, and a sense of belonging through validating the participants' experiences as minorities. Theoretically, the chapter builds on critical whiteness studies and intersectional Hip Hop feminist theory in analysing gender and race as intersecting identities and whiteness and patriarchy as systems of power. The chapter's evaluation of impact is based first and foremost on the perspectives of those participants in these projects, and secondly, on the response of other music industry stakeholders. More generally, the chapter calls attention to factors which contribute to inclusion and exclusion of women and marginalised people in Hip Hop and Popular Music scenes.

* * *

Hip Hop, grime, EDM, house, techno, and suchlike represent the mainstream of contemporary popular music, in fact. This needs to be better reflected in educational, cultural, and social terms. Such contemporary popular musics can and have supported wellness and healing, can and have had huge benefits for musical learning and enjoyment, can and have impacted on people's lives around the world in extremely positive ways. This unique book seeks to account for those positive impacts, theorise them, and help to extend and advance their impact. Contributing authors invite readers to rethink the possibilities and potentials for contemporary popular musics to gain the prestige that their actual popularity would suggest they should already command.

References

Burnard, P., Dale, P., Glenister, S., Reiss, J., Travis, R., Gann, E. and Greasley, A. (2023). Pursuing diversity and inclusivity through Hip Hop music genres: Insights for mainstream music curricula. In C. Randles and P. Burnard (eds.), *The Routledge Companion to Creativities in Music Education*. London: Routledge.

Dale, P. (2017). *Engaging students with music education: DJ decks, urban music and child-centred learning*. Routledge.

Dale, P. (2020). *A reflective report on Musical Futures' Tech Champions project*. https://www.musicalfutures.org/wp-content/uploads/2020/07/MF-TC-PROJECT-report.pdf?x89258.

Eavis, E. (2019). *I had death threats for booking Kanye for Glastonbury*. https://www.theguardian.com/music/2019/oct/30/emily-eavis-glastonbury-50-festival-anniversary-trapeze-books-extract.

Hooton, C. (2015). *Hip-hop is the most listened to genre in the world, according to Spotify analysis of 20 billion tracks*. https://www.independent.co.uk/arts-entertainment/music/news/hiphop-is-the-most-listened-to-genre-in-the-world-according-to-spotify-analysis-of-20-billion-tracks-10388091.html.

Lauryn, A. (2022, September 26). *Techno: A social history, Episode 1* [Radio broadcast]. BBC. https://www.bbc.co.uk/programmes/m00199y6.

Nicholson, R. (2022). *Everyone Can Rap review: An incredibly heartwarming Hip-Hop contest*. https://www.theguardian.com/tv-and-radio/2022/oct/02/everyone-can-rap-review-an-incredibly-heartwarming-hip-hop-contest.

Roberts, M. S. (2019). *US political commentator Ben Shapiro says rap isn't real music*. https://www.classicfm.com/music-news/ben-shapiro-thinks-rap-isnt-music/.

Smith, G. D. and Powell, B. (2018) Introduction to the special issue on Hip Hop, or how not to other the other. *Journal of Popular Music Education*, 2(1/2). https://doi.org/10.1386/jpme.2.1-2.3_2.

Watson, K. (2019). *IMS business report 2019: An annual study of the electronic music industry* https://thegroovecartel.com/news/international-music-summit-ims-ibiza-2019-business-report/.

PART I
CURRICULUM AND MUSIC EDUCATION

1

Beat(s) for Blame

UK Drill Music, 'Race', and Criminal Justice

Lambros Fatsis

Introduction

UK drill music, a British offshoot of Chicago drill, broke into the mainstream in 2018 as breaking news that blamed this new rap subgenre for rising levels of violence and 'criminality' (Fatsis, 2019b, 2021b, 2021c). Echoing dominant prosecutorial rhetoric, logic, and tactics that make crimes out of drill rappers' rhymes, such panic-stricken discourse continues to scream its hyper-punitive message with ear-piercing frequency—despite the near-total lack of tangible evidence that could link drill music to violence (Fatsis, 2019b; Ilan, 2020; Lynes *et al.*, 2020; Fatsis, 2021b; Fatsis *et al.*, 2021). Alas, the affective resonance of legal penal[1] reasoning sounds louder than the protestations of law reform and human rights organisations, leading legal professionals and experts in criminology, youth justice, and rap music (Garden Court Chambers, 2020; Fried, 1999, 2003; Dennis, 2007; Kubrin and Nielson, 2014; Nielson and Dennis, 2019; Fatsis, 2019b: esp. 1303; Lutes, *et al.*, 2019; Ilan, 2020; Lerner and Kubrin, 2021; Owusu-Bempah, 2022a, 2022b). Reflecting on such jarring dissonance between judicial reason and factual evidence, this chapter critically discusses how and why Black music genres[2] like UK drill become targets of state-sanctioned, racialised criminalisation—in a socio-cultural and political context that regards Black music(s) as noise to be eliminated, rather than as music to be appreciated (Fatsis, 2021b: 37–40). Starting with a brief overview of what UK drill music is and how it is prosecuted and policed, the reasons why drill is criminalised the way it is are explored in turn. This is followed by a discussion of what such discriminatory suppression reveals about a legal penal culture that does violence to principles of truth, fairness, and justice that it otherwise pretends to uphold.

Lambros Fatsis, *Beat(s) for Blame* In: *Music for Inclusion and Healing in Schools and Beyond.* Edited by: Pete Dale, Pamela Burnard, and Raphael Travis Jr., Oxford University Press. © Oxford University Press 2023.
DOI: 10.1093/oso/9780197692677.003.0002

What Is UK Drill and How Is it Policed?

UK drill music is the latest subgenre or stylistic branch in the rap family tree. It originated in Chicago in the mid-noughties, but travelled across the Atlantic and took root in the UK rap music scene soon after. Unlike other rap music, UK drill is moodier and darker in sound and more graphic in its violent imagery. As such, rap lyrics are often (mis)taken for real-life descriptions of crimes committed, rather than as first-person narratives that may be partly or purely performative, fictional, hyperbolic, or fabricated even, as is the case with many other music lyrics or literary works. Crucially, drill rappers consciously exploit stereotypes of violence, 'gangsterism', and 'ghetto life' as a sought-after commodity to be consumed online by followers whose clicks, views, likes, and shares can and do yield material rewards (Evans, 2020; Stuart, 2020; Schwarze and Fatsis, 2022). Rather than offering a simple 'authentic', voice rappers are highly attuned to the commercial relations of their work. They deploy themes of violence and crime that they know to be very marketable (Quinn, 2005). A central impetus and theme of the music is the desire to become a successful drill rapper to escape poverty. The violence in drill is part of the genre's conventions and part of its commercial appeal too—as evidenced by the huge popular following that UK drill enjoys—boasting chart-topping hits, sold-out gigs, headlining festival line-ups, and endless playlists on YouTube and Spotify (Mohdin, 2021).

Approached as anything other than the music genre that it actually is, however, drill has become indelibly marked by the stigma of the accusations levelled against it. Imagined, depicted, and targeted as a cause of violent crime and a source of moral decay, UK drill finds itself at the sharp end of punitive law and order ideology, politics, and policy—through a panoply of repressive legal tactics whose authoritarian shirttails are showing, despite elaborate disguises offered by the sheen of procedural fairness that technical, legal jargon thrives at camouflaging. A brief, but hopefully instructive, overview of such legalistic contrivances is offered in turn—as an inventory of policing and prosecutorial techniques that are deployed against an artform that is seldom recognised as such—scarred, as drill is, by criminalising practices that have become so institutionalised that a growing body of rigorous interdisciplinary scholarship has emerged to scrutinise them.[3]

Blamed by the Home Office and the Met Police for London's rising knife crime, without any concrete evidence to suggest such a link (Fatsis, 2019b; Ilan, 2020; Lynes *et al.*, 2020; Fatsis, 2021b; Fatsis *et al.*, 2021; Fatsis, 2022),

UK drill gained notoriety as a suspected front for gang membership and collective offending by the Crown Prosecution Service (henceforth CPS) and the Government's Serious Violence Strategy (Fatsis et al., 2021; Fatsis, 2021b). Stubbornly maintaining that gangs use drill music and social media to celebrate violent crime, the CPS has even produced specific legal guidance on 'Gangs, drill music and social media' to facilitate decision making in 'gang' related offences (CPS, 2021). What started its life as a music genre, therefore, soon became seen through the prism of law enforcement—mentioned *by name* in *specific* legislative guidance drafted for it. By contrast, it might be worth mentioning that across the Atlantic, in 2022, the Restoring Artistic Protection Act was introduced in the US House of Representatives (Halperin and Shanfeld, 2022), seeking to protect artists from the use of their music as legal evidence in criminal and civil cases, following similar legislative moves at the state level in New York and California. In fact, on the same day that that a New York Senate State bill became law[4]—promising to get rap lyrics out of courtrooms—in the hallowed turf of British jurisprudence, ten young Black boys appeared in Manchester Crown Court, facing charges that relied heavily on rap lyrics and videos (Quinn et al., 2022: 419–20). This case rightly became a *cause célèbre* that generated mainstream publicity and well-attended protests against the 'rap on trial' phenomenon (Kubrin and Nielson, 2014; Nielson and Dennis, 2019; Lerner and Kubrin, 2021).

Such practices continue unabated in Britain's courtrooms—unruffled by the scholarly, legal, or public outcry against them (Kingsley, 2021; Fatsis et al., 2021; Fatsis, 2021c).[5] The CPS, for example, had no qualms about publicly stating that 'it was not aware of any cases where drill music had been wrongly used as evidence in the past' (Ball and Lowbridge, 2022), on the *same day* that they heard ample evidence to the contrary, in a 'listening exercise' that was aimed at helping the CPS review its guidance on the use of drill as 'evidence'.[6] These evidence-gathering techniques include the use of lyrics, music videos, and still images obtained from music videos: as direct evidence of wrongdoing, as confessions to an offence, or as expressions of intent to commit an offence. The use of such material, however, is also used indirectly through the imposition of Criminal Behaviour Orders (CBOs) that require drill artists to inform the police twenty-four hours in advance of their intention to publish any videos online, while also demanding that they give a forty-eight-hour warning of the date and locations of any planned live performance. Such 'ancillary orders',[7] as they are known, also prevent suspects from associating with certain people, entering designated areas, wearing hoods, or using social media and unregistered mobile phones.

The police also request the removal of drill music videos from YouTube and monitor the playing of UK drill music on air by requesting radio stations to pluck drill tracks out of their playlists—as Met Deputy Commissioner Sir Stephen House disclosed at a Police and Crime Committee meeting of the London Assembly (London Assembly, 2021, from 02:15:18 to 02:19:40). The London Metropolitan Police has even formed a Drill Music Translation Cadre, consisting of police officers who act as rap expert witnesses, decoding lyrics and translating them into evidence for the prosecution (Quinn, 2018). In fact, the Met boasts an entire operation known as Project Alpha, which involves more than thirty staff (Crisp and Dodd, 2022a). Launched in 2019, Project Alpha was set up by the National Police Chiefs' Council (NPCC), the Home Office, and the Metropolitan Police Service (MPS) to scour so-cial media sites in search of 'gang-related music linked to serious violence' (Railton, 2022), prompting serious concerns about racial profiling and po-tential privacy violations on a large scale by youth violence experts (Crisp and Dodd, 2022b).[8]

Defined as 'gang-related music' by none other than a Project Alpha op-erative (Railton, 2022), drill is analysed, policed, and prosecuted as such—without placing the very term 'gang-related music' under critical scrutiny and without questioning the qualifications and credentials of cops who pose as 'experts' on music genres they have little or no demonstrable specialised knowledge of, or rigorously trained professional expertise in (Ward and Fouladvand, 2021; Fatsis, 2022).[9] This is important to note, relying as the prosecution of drill does on narratives, intelligence, and testimony that are produced by law enforcement professionals who are insufficiently knowl-edgeable to accurately analyse, interpret, or reliably opine on rap music culture—without being insensitive to, or inadequately aware of, the ar-tistic conventions of the genre (Dennis, 2007, Nielson, and Dennis, 2019; Ilan, 2020). (Re)presenting drill music as 'gang-affiliated' is a case in point, suggesting as such terminology does that drill is a criminal outfit (which it is *not*), rather than an artform (which it actually *is*).

What makes such 'dangerous associations' (Williams and Clarke, 2016) be-tween gangs and drill credible, however, are the emotive connotations that the term stirs up: 'a lazy shorthand to refer to street-crime involving young, marginalised people of colour' (Fatsis *et al.*, 2021). Attributing so-called gang membership and involvement in collective offending is one of the ways in which racially minoritised groups become disproportionately criminalised. Not only is there is no accurate or reliable definition of a 'gang' (see, e.g., Hallsworth and Young, 2008; Smithson *et al.*, 2013), but the ones that are officially used are too broad and selectively applied to particular communities and groups of people that are (racially) criminalised (see, e.g., Alexander, 2008; Gunter, 2017; Owusu-Bempah, 2017, Williams and Clarke, 2018; Nijjar, 2018; Fatsis, 2019a; 2019b; Phillips *et al.*, 2020; Clarke and Williams, 2020; Paul, 2021; Monteith *et al.*, 2022). A fleeting glimpse into the relevant legislation that is weaponised in the state's war against drill tells us as much, so 'the law' takes centre stage in turn—as a racialising and criminalising tool that creates the suspects it seeks to police, prosecute, sentence, and incarcerate.

'Gang-Related Music'

Having already looked at the dubious logic and spurious use of the term 'gang-related music' to describe and criminalise drill music and having alluded to the alluring mythology of irresponsible 'gang talk' (Hallsworth and Young, 2008), introducing the official definition of gangs that is used when drill takes the defendant's seat in court seems appropriate. I do this to justify and substantiate the scepticism that critical scholars reserve for this official definition. Section 34(5) of the Policing and Crime Act 2009 defines acts as 'gang-related' if the targeted group: (a) 'consists of at least 3 people', (b) 'uses a name, emblem or colour or has any other characteristic that enables its members to be identified by others as a group', and (c) 'is associated with a particular area'. Evidently, such a definition is hopelessly vague to carry any weight. It could be applied to gown-wearing graduands, lanyard-holding conferees, or high-vis vested marathon runners. That does not happen, of course. In the context of drill music, however, things are different: anyone who raps on camera with at least two other people, wearing T-shirts with the drill collective's name or logo in their neighbourhood, can be identified as a gang member and prosecuted as such. The recent discrediting of the Met's Gang Matrix, following a landmark legal challenge led by Liberty on behalf of UK rapper Awate and UNJUST UK, stands out as an indicative case study on unlawful and discriminatory policing based on the very gang-mongering that continues to proliferate in court, with drill as a prime suspect. Yet, what the Gangs Matrix scandal amounts to is more forcing the Met to concede

(a) that the Gangs Matrix database was unlawful, (b) that it breached the right to a private and family life, and (c) that it disproportionately targeted young Black people (Liberty, 2022). It also reminds us that the music one makes or listens to suffices as a criterion for inclusion in the Matrix. In 2018, before drill became popular, it was UK grime music that was targeted—as a 2018 Amnesty International report duly noted (Amnesty, 2018). Now, the suspect genre is, of course, drill (Rosa, 2022).[10]

Evidence of Bad Character and Joint Enterprise

Beyond the largely unfounded accusations of 'gang-banging' culture explored above (see also: Fatsis, 2021c; Fatsis et al., 2021; Fatsis, 2022), drill also finds itself (mis)treated, and certainly (mis)interpreted, as evidence of bad character—or as a justification for securing joint enterprise convictions (Owusu-Bempah, 2022a, 2022b). Section 98 of the Criminal Justice Act, 2003, defines bad character evidence as 'evidence of, or of a *disposition towards*, misconduct' rather than evidence that 'has to do with the alleged *facts* of the offence with which the defendant is charged' (emphasis added). Based on such a definition, drill music material is therefore relied on as evidence of the defendants' 'bad character', due to stereotypical associations between rap and 'criminality' rather than based on incontrovertible evidence of wrongdoing (Kelley, 1996; Krims, 2000; Keyes, 2004; Kitwana, 2005; Kubrin, 2005; Deveraux, 2007; Ilan, 2020: 47; Kubrin and Nielson, 2014; Bramwell, 2015a, 2015b; Bramwell, 2018; Fatsis, 2019a, 2019b; Ilan, 2020; Lynes et al., 2020; Fatsis, 2021b; Owusu-Bempah, 2022a, 2022b).

Similar in logic, but somewhat different in inflection and style, joint enterprise is a legal doctrine that allows the court to show guilt by association between defendants. Given the broad scope of such legislation, it is possible to convict individuals of crimes *without* committing the criminal act they are charged with, or even being at the scene of the crime. To introduce such 'evidence' in court, prosecutors present such material in conjunction with witness statements that are produced by relevant 'experts' (usually police officers, 'gangs experts', and forensic linguists), who may also be instructed to give evidence in court. Such cases are usually based on arguments that involve a matter-of-factly presentation of drill-related material, made without adequately interrogating the artistic, literary, or fictional nature of the 'evidence' that is brought before judges and jurors (Fried, 1999; Dunbar et al.,

2016; Dunbar and Kubrin, 2018; Stoia *et al.*, 2018; Nielson and Dennis, 2019).
Not unlike the garrulous gang discourse peddled by cops and prosecutors,
joint enterprise has also sustained considerable critical attack for its dispro-
portionate use to convict young Black people (Clarke and Williams, 2020;
Hulley and Young, 2021). This has continued even after a 2016 Supreme
Court ruling found that joint enterprise resulted in over-charging and over-
convicting secondary suspects (Mills *et al.*, 2022; Waller, 2022). As such, it
is hardly surprising to hear that '[r]ap videos and lyrics are typically being
admitted to build group prosecutions against Black children and young
men, often tried under 'joint enterprise' laws that enable 'secondaries' (not
suspected of having committed the substantive offence) to be tried for the
same crime as the 'principal' (the person suspected of the substantive offence)' (Quinn et al., 2022: 2). No case exemplifies such politics of 'penal excess' (Brown, 2002) better than the (ab)use of drill in court that occurred in
the well-publicised conviction of the 'Manchester Ten' (Legane, 2022). This
case involved ten teenagers in Manchester, who were charged not for *making*,
but for merely *downloading*, drill music tracks or *watching* drill music videos;
this was accepted as incriminating evidence of gang conspiracy (Pidd,
2022a). While this case is hardly coincidental, given the 'vastly expanding'
number of cases involving drill as evidence (Quinn et al., 2022: 2; Swann,
2021), it nevertheless demonstrates how the law conspires in manufacturing
suspects to be criminalised—prompting a Manchester MP and shadow culture secretary (Lucy Powell) to rail against such a verdict (Pidd, 2022b).[11]

The preceding snapshot of legalised racial injustice—exemplified by the
clampdown on a Black music genre—undoubtedly makes for shocking
reading, but it should hardly occasion surprise. The racialised criminalisation
of Black music and the policing against Black Britons are nothing new
(Fatsis, 2021a; 2021b: esp. pp. 35–37; Fatsis, 2023a). Both remain disturbingly alive and well today, urgently reminding us of the enduring presence
of racism—as an ideology of political (mis)rule and legalised injustice that
normalises, institutionalises, and legitimises 'dehumanizing social policies
of structured inequality' (Gordon, 2022: 10–11). Extreme though this assertion may sound, it is difficult to deny or ignore—unless the legacy of a long
and ignoble history of racism as an 'atmosphere [that] impregnates every element of social life' (Fanon, 1956: 129) is spirited away, occluded, or elided,
as it very often is (Fatsis, 2019c). The remainder of this chapter, therefore,
takes this issue up, devoting its attention to the very socio-cultural, political, and institutional mentality, worldview, and ideology (=racism) that

turn Black cultural expression into a criminal and cultural offence (Fatsis, 2021b: 38–41). The chapter then ends with some concluding afterthoughts, on why attuning ourselves to the racialised criminalisation of drill sharpens our scholarly and political consciousness, by shattering deeply ingrained mythologies about the legal penal system: as a constellation of fair, impartial institutions that are imbued with democratic, egalitarian, and ethical principles of justice (Williams, 1993; Quigley, 2007; Owusu-Bempah, 2017; Fatsis, 2021a; Fatsis and Lamb, 2022).

Why Is Drill Music Policed and Why It Matters

The punitive arsenal that has been mobilised against UK drill music raises the question of why a(ny) music genre would be singled out as a threat to public safety. The answer is actually quite straightforward and is contained in just one word: racism. Understanding how racism operates as a mental furniture that upholsters our socio-cultural and political imagination, however, is much trickier that letting a single word do so much of the interpretive weight-lifting that is necessary. Indeed, what is required of us is to accept the role of racism as a default setting rather than a system error of the very socio-cultural and political context we are educated and socialised into. Instead of approaching racism as a 'disposition of the mind [or] a psychological flaw' (Fanon, 1956: 127) that is *episodic, accidental,* or the unfortunate outcome of a few isolated incidents that suddenly erupt out of nowhere, it is understood here as *systemic, structural,* and institutional(ised). Racism is the residue of historical processes that are rooted in the era of imperial-colonial rule, but continue to assign negative value to biological or cultural differences; these are historical processes that are perceived as 'alien', incomprehensible, and inadmissible to a (majority) 'white' (supremacist) society and its socio-cultural, political, and judicial institutions.[12]

Such an understanding of racism as 'the ordinary means through which [. . .] the practice of dehumanizing people produces racial categories' (Gilmore, 2007: 24) is vital to identifying and contextualising how and why forms of Black creativity and public expression are denied *as artforms*; so they can be policed instead as noisy violations of 'normative, respectable, cultural codes' (McKittrick, 2021: 162) that are regulated and outlawed by 'the law'. To think about racism as the ideological script that justifies (and literally produces!) the state-sanctioned, racialised criminalisation of Black

music genres like drill, therefore, is to treat racism as an active ideological ingredient, within an economic and political system that creates social
infrastructures (=institutions) that: allocate resources, value social lives, and
arrange people in a hierarchy (=scale) that orders (=ranks) us according to
our status on that scale, be it racial, economic, or heteronormatively gendered along binaries of inclusion/exclusion and belonging/non-belonging,
which foster social divisions that fester as forms of social inequality and
injustice.

Simply put, 'the feeling of threat' that drill represents in the penal and public
imagination 'depends on *the acceptance of [racist] cultural stereotype[s]*'
(Sibley, 1998: 123; emphasis added) that cast drill rap(pers) as a threat
in the first place. Such racist stereotypes about blackness and 'criminality'
(Gilroy, 1987a) function as a readily available 'depository of anxieties about
mixing [. . .], merging' and the sharing of public space (Sibley, 1998: 127)
that quickly translate into calculations of 'risk', surveillance technologies, and
legislation that keep those who are deemed as 'Other(s)' in their place: as
outcasts and misfits, who ought to be consigned to the margins of civic life
(Fatsis, 2021a). Targeted as aesthetically out of tune [=noise], culturally out
of place [=*un*belonging], and politically out of order [=disorderly] (Fatsis,
2021b: 38–40), drill—like so many of its Afrodiasporic music traditions before it (Fatsis, 2021b; Fatsis, 2023a)—becomes (policed as) *unwelcome noise*,
produced by *cultural 'aliens'* who do not belong *here* and are *politically threatening* to a social order that is racialised (by default) as 'white'.

Lest we are lost in high theory, illustrating much of the above through
some examples seems eminently sensible, if not entirely necessary, as
a way of demonstrating patterns of continuity in the policing of Black
music(s) across time (history) and space (geography). Countering popular
misconceptions about the unique and unprecedented ills that drill ostensibly
brings in its wake, it is important to remind ourselves of the longer history
of policing against Black, or Afrodiasporic, music(s) from the era of colonial
slavery. While it is not possible to offer a detailed account of such centuries-
old practices, a detailed discussion of which can be found elsewhere (Fatsis,
2021b; Fatsis, 2023a, 2023b), a few snippets of such history are nevertheless
considered in turn, by way of illustration. Difficult though it may be for us
today to imagine that so upbeat and playful a genre like calypso would come
into the orbit of law enforcement, our historical memory would be better
served by reminding ourselves of an anonymous eighteenth-century calypso
that describes the plight of the colonised as follows:

Can't beat me drum, in my own, my native land.
Can't have we Carnival. In my own, my native land.
Can't have we Bacchanal in my own, native land. (Robinson, 2020: 246)

A few centuries later, another calypsonian, Atilla [*sic*, 1938] the Hun, would express a similar sentiment about the banning of calypso by British colonial governors, in the lyrics of his 1938 hit 'Banning of Records' (which was itself banned).[13]

Imagine our records being banned from entering in our native land.
That they are obscene I must deny, but all things look yellow to the jaundiced eye.
I think they're ungenerous to attempt to take our music from us.

Skipping a few decades, we find ourselves in twenty-first-century Britain, where rappers Krept & Konandescribe in their single 'Ban Drill' (2019) how:

They took my videos down, said it's too violent
I can't do a show, it's getting stopped by Trident
It's slowing down my income, they're tryna ban drill.

Facile though it may seem to compare the criminalisation of drill with (much) earlier Black or Afro-diasporic music genres, it is impossible to overlook striking similarities that speak of how the logic of surveillance, regulation, containment, and control informs the policing of Black artistic expression by colonial and post-colonial authorities alike. Atilla the Hun (*né* Raymond Quevedo) has documented such practices beyond his music, in his magisterial book on calypso/*kaiso* (Quevedo, 1983: esp. 27, 55–58, 60–63),[14] where he lambasted such measures as 'wicked', 'nefarious', 'perverse', 'pernicious', and 'dictatorial' (Quevedo, 1983: 60, 63). Would not the same words ring true, however, if they were applied to the suppression of drill? Thinking and saying so does not equate or pretend that the policing against Black music(s) is the same all the time, or that its history amounts to a linear and unbroken sequence of events. Rather, it is to stress that situating the policing and prosecution of drill in the context of the longer (colonial) history of policing against Black music(s) points to the legacy of racist logics and tactics that remain virtually unchanged.

Inviting historical parallels, therefore, does more than simply remind us of the banning of drumming, dancing, and musical performance under British colonial role; of police regulations against Carnival celebrations (in the Caribbean and in Britain); or of the clamping down on reggae soundsystems, bashment, and grime raves (Fatsis, 2021b; Fatsis, 2023a, 2023b). It also forces us to acknowledge that not *all* music is penalised the way Black music genres are, if at all (Binder, 1993; Fried, 1999, 2003; Dunbar, *et al.*, 2016; Dunbar and Kubrin, 2018; Nielson and Dennis, 2019: 114). Were this not true, the list of genres sketched above would look rather different. To deny this is to deny and ignore the specific and unique history of policing that Black music genres have endured (and resisted!) from the era of colonial slavery to the present day (Fatsis, 2021b; Fatsis, 2023a); as sonic embodiments of threatening 'difference' and 'otherness' that do not just depart from Western-European 'soundscape norms' (Charles, 2018: 7) but act as receptacles of Black cultural pathology that breeds lawlessness. This familiar and deeply ingrained racist mythology can be recognised from seminal texts like Hall et al's. (1978) *Policing the Crisis* and Gilroy's (1987b) *There Ain't No Black in the Union Jack*, which have masterfully decoded and exposed the (ongoing) reality (Fatsis, 2021a). To further deny this is to deny that drill, like so many of its stylistic predecessors, is *selectively* singled out and *racially* criminalised. There are other music genres (Binder, 1993; Fried, 1999, 2003; Dunbar, *et al.*, 2016; Dunbar and Kubrin, 2018) and artforms (hooks, 2006: 134–44; Fatsis, 2023c) that never find themselves translated and transformed into 'evidence' in criminal proceedings. To avoid misunderstandings, this is not to advocate for the criminalisation of other music genres too, but to stress that the *racial(ised)* criminalisation of drill and so many other Black music genres before it tells us more about 'white' supremacist ideology than Black pathology.

With this realisation in mind, the take-home message of this chapter should be that understanding how and why drill is policed and prosecuted the way it is *matters* because it helps us understand the logic, function, and consequences of racism: as a form of administered, state-sanctioned inequality that is *enabled*, rather than *opposed*, by 'the law'. This in turn compels us to question the legitimacy of legal penal functionaries (police, prosecutors, and judges), when they are found to make decisions with little or no evidence that can withstand critical scrutiny. And this should ultimately encourage us to confront the ugly realities of racism—not just in the legal penal system, but in the cultural sphere too, inviting us to listen to and think with Black music genres, as sources of knowledge about the social world around us (Fatsis, 2021b; Fatsis, 2023a, 2023b). This involves *re*-cognising (literally, rethinking) Black music(s) as instruments of intellectual, cultural, and political life (Fatsis, 2019a, 2021b; Fatsis, 2023a, 2023b) that blast out 'sonic critiques of colonialism, racism, structural inequalities, and other forms of violence' (McKittrick, 2021: 50–51). Thinking politically with rap as our guide, therefore, involves hearing rather than silencing rappers' voices—even when what they 'spit'[15] does not sound pretty, prim, or proper. It is therefore appropriate and only fair to give the final word to legendary rapper KRS-One (1988), whose beats and rhymes (in *Necessary*) have been tugging at my sleeve and tapping on my shoulder as this chapter was written. I hope it proves as useful (to you) as it is necessary (to me):

> When some get together and think of rap, they tend to think of violence
> But when they are challenged on some rock groups, the result is always silence
> Even before the Rock and Roll era, violence played a big part in music
> It's all according to your meaning of violence and how or in which way you use it
> Oh no, it's not violent to show in movies the destruction of the human body
> But yes indeed it's very violent to protect yourself in a party
> And, oh no, it's not violent when under the Christmas tree there's a look-alike gun
> But, yes, of course it's violent to have an album like KRS-One
> By all means necessary, it's time to end the hypocrisy.

References

Åberg, E. and Tyvelä, H. (forthcoming). 'Writing about this reality is a way to get away from this reality'—Re-reading the misrepresentations of Nordic 'gangsta rap' in two contemporary Nordic welfare states' [Draft article, sent as personal communication with the authors on March 26, 2022.

Alexander, C. (2008). *(Re)thinking gangs*. London: Runnymede Trust.

Amnesty International. (2018). *Trapped in the matrix: Secrecy, stigma, and bias in the Met's gangs database*. Amnesty International. https://www.amnesty.org.uk/files/reports/Inside%20the%20%20matrix.pdf.

Andrews, K. (2016). The problem of political blackness: Lessons from the Black Supplementary School Movement. *Ethnic and Racial Studies*, 39(11): 2060–2078.

Ball, J. and Lowbridge, C. (2022). *CPS to review guidance on using drill music as evidence.* https://www.bbc.co.uk/news/uk-england-nottinghamshire-60070345.

Basu, D. and Lemell, S. J. (eds.). (2006). *The vinyl ain't final: Hip Hop and the globalisation of Black Popular Culture.* London: Pluto.

Bernard, J. (2021). *Joint.* London Literature Festival. https://www.youtube.com/watch?v=Qp8lYH0hGzg.

Binder, A. (1993). Constructing racial rhetoric: Media depictions of harm in heavy metal and rap music. *American Sociological Review*, 58(6): 753–767.

Bramwell, R. (2015a). *UK Hip-Hop, grime and the city: The aesthetics and ethics of London's rap scene.* London: Routledge.

Bramwell, R. (2015b). Council estate of mind: The British rap tradition and London's hip-hop scene. In: J. A. Williams (ed.), *The Cambridge Companion to Hip-Hop.* Cambridge: Cambridge University Press, pp. 256–262.

Bramwell, R. (2018). Freedom within bars: Maximum security prisoners' negotiations of identity through rap. *Identities*, 25(4): 475–492.

Brown, M. (2002). The politics of penal excess and the echo of colonial penalty. *Punishment and Society*, 4(4): 403–423.

Carinos, E. (2020). 'Fuck le 17!'. Rap français et forces de l'ordre'. *Droit(s) et hip-hop.* https://halshs.archives-ouvertes.fr/CRESPPA/hal-03383746v1.

Charles, M. (2018). MDA as a research method of generic musical analysis for the social sciences: sifting through grime (music) as an SFT case study. *International Journal of Qualitative Methods*, 17: 1–11.

Clarke, B. and Williams, P. (2020). (Re)producing guilt in suspect communities: The centrality of racialisation in joint enterprise prosecutions. *International Journal for Crime, Justice and Social Democracy*, 9: 116–129.

Cowley, J. (1996). *Carnival, canboulay and calypso: Traditions in the making.* Cambridge University Press.

CPS (2019). *Sentencing—Ancillary orders.* https://www.cps.gov.uk/legal-guidance/sentencing-ancillary-orders.

CPS (2021). Gang related offences—Decision making in. https://www.cps.gov.uk/legal-guidance/gang-related-offences-decision-making.

CPS (2022). *Pioneering 'gangs' unit set up to tackle those who 'live by crime'.* https://www.cps.gov.uk/west-midlands/news/pioneering-gangs-unit-set-tackle-those-who-live-crime.

Crisp, W. and Dodd, V. (2022a). *Met police profiling children 'on a large scale', documents show.* https://www.theguardian.com/uk-news/2022./jun/03/met-police-project-alpha-profiling-children-documents-show

Crisp, W. and Dodd, V. (2022b). *Met police did not consult us on children's data project, say youth violence experts.* https://www.theguardian.com/uk-news/2022/jun/05/met-police-children-data-project-alpha-youth-violence.

Dennis, A. L. (2007). Poetic (in)justice? Rap music lyrics as art, life, and criminal evidence. *The Columbia Journal of Law & the Arts*, 31: 1–41.

Deveraux, A. (2007). 'What chew know about down the hill?': Baltimore club music, subgenre crossover, and the new subcultural capital of race and space. *Journal of Popular Music Studies*, 19: 311–341.

Dillon, N. (2021). *New York lawmakers introducing bill to limit rap lyrics as evidence in criminal trials.* https://www.rollingstone.com/music/music-news/ny-state-senators-bill-legislation-rap-lyrics-evidence-criminal-trials-1258767/.

Dunbar, A. and Kubrin, C. E. (2018). Imagining violent criminals: An experimental investigation of music stereotypes and character judgments. *Journal of Experimental Criminology*, 14(4): 507–528.

Dunbar, A., Kubrin, C. E., and Scurich, N. (2016). The threatening nature of 'rap' music. *Psychology, Public Policy and Law*, 22: 280–292.

Evans, J. (2020). 'We [mostly] carry guns for the internet': Visibility, labour, social hacking and chasing digital clout by Black male youth in Chicago's drill rap scene. *Global Hip Hop Studies*, 1(2): 227–247.

Fanon, F. (1956). Racism and culture. *Présence africaine (Paris)*, VIII-IX-X (June–November): 122–131.

Fatsis, L. (2019a). Grime: Criminal subculture or public counterculture? A critical investigation into the criminalization of Black musical subcultures in the UK. *Crime Media Culture*, 15(3): 447–461.

Fatsis, L. (2019b). Policing the beats: The criminalisation of UK drill and grime music by the London Metropolitan Police. *The Sociological Review*, 67(6): 1300–1316.

Fatsis, L. (2019c). When police racism is denied, does it go away?. *British Society of Criminology Blog*. https://thebscblog.wordpress.com/2019/08/28/denying-institutional-racism/.

Fatsis, L. (2021a). Policing the union's Black: The racial politics of law and order in contemporary Britain. In F. Gordon and D. Newman (eds.), *Leading Works in Law and Social Justice*. London: Routledge, pp. 137–150.

Fatsis, L. (2021b). Sounds dangerous: Black music subcultures as victims of state regulation and social control. In N. Peršak and A. Di Ronco (eds.), *Harm and Disorder in the Urban Space: Social Control, Sense and Sensibility*. London: Routledge, pp. 30–51.

Fatsis, L. (2021c). Stop blaming drill for making people kill. *The British Society of Criminology Blog*. https://thebscblog.wordpress.com/2021/10/18/stop-blaming-drill-for-making-people-kill/.

Fatsis, L. (2023a). From overseer to officer: A brief history of British policing through Afro-diasporic music culture. In R. P. Cavalcanti, P. Squires, and Z. Waseem (eds.), *Southern Perspectives on Policing, Security and Social Order*. Bristol: Bristol University Press, Chapter 3.

Fatsis, L. (2023b). Arresting sounds what UK soundsystem culture teaches us about police racism and public life. In M. Charles and M. W Gani (eds.), *Black Music in Britain in the 21st Century*. Liverpool: Liverpool University Press, pp. 181–197.

Fatsis, L. (2023c). Decriminalising rap beat by beat: Two questions in search of answers. In E. Peters (ed.), *Music in Crime, Resistance and Identity*. London: Routledge, pp. 63–77.

Fatsis, L. (2022). When cops analyse drill, but get it wrong still. *StopWatch*. https://www.stop-watch.org/news-opinion/when-cops-analyse-drill-but-get-it-wrong-still/.

Fatsis, L., Ilan, J., Kadiri, H., Owusu-Bempah, A., Quinn, E., Shiner, M. and Squires, P. (2021). Missing the point: How Policy Exchange Misunderstands Knife Crime in the Capital. *Identities Blog*. https://www.identitiesjournal.com/blog-collection/missing-the-point-how-policy-exchange-misunderstands-knife-crime-in-the-capital [Accessed: January 9, 2023].

Fatsis, L. and Lamb, M. (2022). *Policing the pandemic: How public health becomes public order*. Bristol: Policy Press.

Fried, C. B. (1999). Who's afraid of rap: Differential reactions to music lyrics. *Journal of Applied Social Psychology*, 29(4): 705–721.

Fried, C. B. (2003). Stereotypes of music fans: Are rap and heavy metal fans a danger to themselves or others? *Journal of Media Psychology*, 8: 2–27.

Garden Court Chambers (2020). *Drill music, gangs and prosecutions—Challenging racist stereotypes in the criminal justice system.* https://www.gardencourtchambers.co.uk/events/drill-music-gangs-and-prosecutions-challenging-racist-stereotypes-in-the-criminal-justice-system.

Gilmore, R. W. (2007). *The golden gulag: Prisons, surplus, crisis, and opposition in globalizing California.* Oakland, CA: University of California Press.

Gilroy, P. (1987a). The myth of black criminality. In P. Scraton (ed.), *Law, Order and the Authoritarian State: Readings in Critical Criminology.* Maidenhead: Open University Press, pp. 47–56.

Gilroy, P. (1987b). *There ain't no black in the Union Jack.* Abingdon: Routledge.

Gordon, L. R. (2022). *Fear of Black consciousness.* London: Penguin.

Gunter, A. (2017). *Race, gangs and youth violence: Policy, prevention and policing.* Bristol: Policy Press.

Gunter, A. and Watt, P. (2009). Grafting, going to college and working on road: Youth transitions and cultures in an East London neighbourhood. *Journal of Youth Studies*, 12(5): 515–529.

Hall, S. (1993) What is this 'Black' in Black popular culture? *Social Justice*, 20(1–2): 104–114.

Hall, S. (1975). *Africa is alive and well and living in the diaspora.* Paris: UNESCO.

Hall, S., Critcher, C., Jefferson, T. *et al.* (1978). *Policing the crisis: Mugging, the state and law and order.* London: Macmillan.

Hallsworth, S. and Young, T. (2008). Gang talk and gang talkers: A critique. *Crime Media Culture*, 4(2): 175–195.

Halperin, S., and Shanfeld, E. (2022) *RAP Act introduced in Congress would bar the use of lyrics as evidence in court proceedings.* https://variety.com/2022/music/news/rap-lyrics-crimimal-evidence-congress-bill-legislation-1235327683/.

Hill, E. (1997). *The trinidad carnival.* London: New Beacon Books.

hooks, b. (2006). *Outlaw culture: Resisting representations.* Abingdon: Routledge.

Hulley, S. and Young, T. (2021). Silence, joint enterprise and the legal trap. *Criminology & Criminal Justice*, 22(5): 714–732. https://doi.org/10.1177/1748895821991622.

Ilan, J. (2012). "The industry's the new road": Crime, commodification and street cultural tropes in UK urban music. *Crime, Media, Culture*, 8(1): 39–55.

Joshi, T. (2022). *Spitting innocence: The use and abuse of drill lyrics in court.* https://www.rollingstone.co.uk/politics/features/prosecuting-uk-drill-rap-lyrics-court-20131/.

Kelley, R. D. G. K. (1996). 'Kickin' reality, kickin' ballistics: 'Gansgsta rap' and post-industrial Los Angeles'. In W. Perkins (ed.), *Droppin' Science: Critical Essays on Rap Music and Hip Hop Culture.* Philadelphia, PA: Temple University Press, pp. 183–300.

Kelley, R. D. G. (2008). *Yo' mama's disfunktional: Fighting the culture wars in urban America.* Boston, MA: Beacon Press.

Keyes, C. (2004). *Rap music and street consciousness.* Champaign, IL: University of Illinois Press.

Kingsley, T. (2021). *Criminologists slam 'misleading' Policy Exchange report linking drill music to youth violence.* https://www.independent.co.uk/news/uk/home-news/policy-exchange-report-youth-violence-b1955691.html.

Kitwana, B. (2005). *Why white kids love Hip-Hop: Wankstas, wiggers, wannabes and the new reality of race in America.* New York, NY: Basic Civitas Books.

Krims, A. (2000). *Rap music and the poetics of identity*. Cambridge: Cambridge University Press.

Kubrin, C. E. (2005). Gangstas, thugs and hustlas: Identity and the code of the street in rap music. *Social Problems*, 52: 360–378.

Kubrin, C. E. and Nielson, E. (2014). Rap on trial. *Race and Justice*, 4(3): 185–211.

Legane, R. (2022). The Manchester ten. *Red Pepper*. https://www.redpepper.org.uk/the-manchester-ten/ [Accessed January 9, 2023].

Lerner, J. I. and Kubrin, C. E. (2021). *Rap on trial: A legal guide for attorneys*. UC Irvine School of Law Research Paper, University College Irvine. https://cpb-us-e2.wpmucdn.com/sites.uci.edu/dist/d/2220/files/2022/08/Rap-on-Trial-Legal-Guide-v1.1.pdf.

Liberty (2022). *Met to overhaul racist gangs matrix after landmark legal challenge*. https://www.libertyhumanrights.org.uk/issue/met-to-overhaul-racist-gangs-matrix-after-landmark-legal-challenge/.

Lippman, A. (2019). 'Law for whom?': Responding to sonic illegality in Brazil's funkcarioca. *Sound Studies*, (5)1: 22–36.

London Assembly (2021). *Police and crime committee meeting*. https://webcasts.london.gov.uk/Assembly/Event/Index/f546d1a1-66c0-452a-961e-d0d1b00ddebe.

Lynes, A., Kelly, C. and Kelly, E. (2020). Thug life: Drill music as periscope into urban violence in the consumer age. *British Journal of Criminology*, 60: 1201–1219.

Lutes, E., Purdon, J. and Fradella, H. F. (2019). When music takes the stand: A content analysis of how courts use and misuse rap lyrics in criminal cases. *American Journal of Criminal Law*, 46(1): 77–132.

Maylor, U. (2009). What is the meaning of 'Black'? Researching 'Black' respondents. *Ethnic and Racial Studies*, 32(2): 369–387.

McKittrick, K. (2021). *Dear science and other stories*. Durham, NC: Duke University Press.

Mills, H., Ford, M., and Grimshaw, R. (2022). The usual suspects: Joint enterprise prosecutions before and after the Supreme Court ruling. *Centre for Crime and Justice Studies*. https://www.crimeandjustice.org.uk/publications/usual-suspects.

Mohdin, A. (2021). *Tion Wayne and Russ Millions' body is first drill song to go to UK No 1*. https://www.theguardian.com/music/2021/may/07/tion-wayne-and-russ-millions-body-is-first-drill-song-to-go-to-uk-no-1.

Monteith, K., Quinn, E., Dennis, A., Joseph-Salisbury, R., Kane, E., Addo, F. and McGourlay, C. (2022). Racial bias and the bench: A response to the Judicial Diversity & Inclusion Strategy (2020–25). Simon Fellowship Report, University of Manchester. https://documents.manchester.ac.uk/display.aspx?DocID=64125.

Nielson, E. and Dennis, A. L. (2019). *Rap on trial: Race, lyrics, and guilt in America*. New York, NY: New Press.

Nijjar, J. S. (2018). Echoes of empire: Excavating the colonial roots of Britain's 'War on Gangs'. *Social Justice*, 45(2/3): 147–162.

Olsen, J. (2004). *The abolition of white democracy*. Minneapolis, MN: University of Minnesota Press.

Owusu-Bempah, A. (2022a). The irrelevance of rap. *Criminal Law Review*, 2: 130–151.

Owusu-Bempah, A. (2022b). Prosecuting rap: What does the case law tell us? *Popular Music*. 41(4): 427–445. https://doi.org/10.1017/S0261143022000575.

Owusu-Bempah, A. (2017). Race and policing in historical context: Dehumanization and the policing of Black people in the 21st century. *Theoretical Criminology*, 21(1): 23–34.

Paul, S. (2021). *Tackling racial injustice: Children and the youth justice system: A report by JUSTICE*. Justice.

Perry, I. (2004). *Prophets of the hood: Politics and poetics in Hip Hop*. Durham, NC: Duke University Press.

Pidd, H (2022a). *Fury in Manchester as black teenagers jailed as result of Telegram chat*. https://www.theguardian.com/uk-news/2022/jul/01/fury-in-manchester-as-black-teenagers-jailed-as-result-of-telegram-chat.

Pidd, H. (2022b). *Manchester MP to write to minister over 'guilty by association' verdicts*. https://www.theguardian.com/law/2022/jul/04/manchester-mp-to-write-to-minister-over-guilty-by-association-verdicts.

Phillips, C., Earle, R., Parmar, A. *et al.* (2020). Dear British criminology: Where has all the race and racism gone? *Theoretical Criminology*, 24(3): 427–446.

Pritchard, W. (2022). *'I wanted to show their innocence': Teenage drill rappers take centre stage in bold new play*. https://www.theguardian.com/music/2022/nov/04/uk-drill-project-barbican-interview.

Quevedo, R. (1983). *Atilla's Kaiso: A short history of Trinidad calypso*. Mona, Jamaica: University of West Indies Press.

Quigley, B. (2007). Letter to a law student interested in social justice. *Depaul Journal for Social Sciences*, (1)1: 7–28.

Quinn, E. (2005). *Nuthin' But a G thang: The culture and commerce of gangsta rap*. New York, NY: Columbia University Press.

Quinn, E. (2018). Lost in translation? Rap music and racial bias in the courtroom. Policy@ Manchester Blogs. http://blog.policy.manchester.ac.uk/posts/2018/10/lost-in-translation-rap-music-and-racial-bias-in-the-courtroom/.

Quinn, E., White, J. and Street, J. (2022). Introduction to special issue: Prosecuting and Policing Rap. *Popular Music*, 41(4): 419–426. https://doi.org/10.1017/S026114302 2000642.

Railton, M. (2022). Analysing gang-related music linked to serious violence. College of Policing. https://www.college.police.uk/article/analysing-gang-related-music-linked-serious-violence.

Robinson, C. J. (2020). *Black Marxism: The making of the Black radical tradition*. Chapel Hill, NC: University of North Carolina Press.

Roks, R. A. and Van Den Broek, J. B. A. (2020). *Cappen Vor Clout?* hdl.handle.net/1765/132478.

Rosa, S. K. (2022). *The Met could be sued over its racist gang database*. https://novaramedia.com/2022/03/15/the-met-could-be-getting-sued-over-its-racist-gang-database/.

Schwarze, T. and Fatsis, L. (2022) Copping the blame: the role of YouTube videos in the criminalisation of UK drill music. *Popular Music*, 41(4): 463–480. https://doi.org/10.1017/S0261143022000563.

Sibley, D. (1998). The racialisation of space in British cities. *Soundings*, 1(10): 119–127.

Sivanandan, A. (2008). *Catching history on its wing: Race, culture and globalisation*. Pluto Press.

Smithson, H., Ralphs, R. and Williams, P. (2013). Used and abused: The problematic usage of gang terminology in the United Kingdom and its implications for ethnic minority youth. *The British Journal of Criminology*, 53(1): 113–128.

Stoia, N., Adams, K. and Drakulich, K. (2018). Rap lyrics as evidence: What can music theory tell us? *Race and Justice*, 8(4): 330–365.

Stuart, F. (2020). *Ballad of the bullet: Gangs, drill music and the power of online infamy*. Princeton, NJ: Princeton University Press.

Swann, S. (2021). *Drill and rap music on trial.* https://www.bbc.co.uk/news/uk-55617706.

Waller, N. (2022). *Gang narratives and broken law: Why Joint Enterprise still needs fixing.* https://www.crimeandjustice.org.uk/resources/gang-narratives-and-brokenlaw-why-joint-enterprise-still-needs-fixing.

Ward, T., and Fouladvand, S. (2021). Bodies of knowledge and robes of expertise: expert evidence about drugs, gangs and human trafficking. *Criminal Law Review,* 6: 442–460.

Williams, P. and Clarke, B. (2016). Dangerous associations: Joint enterprise, gangs and racism: An analysis of the processes of criminalisation of Black, Asian and minority ethnic individuals. *Centre for Crime and Justice Studies.* https://www.crimeandjustice.org.uk/publications/dangerous-associations-joint-enterprise-gangs-and-racism.

Williams, P. and Clarke, B. (2018). The Black criminal other as an object of social control. *Social Sciences,* 7(234): 1–14.

Williams, P. J. (1993). *The alchemy of race and rights.* London: Virago.

Discography

Atilla the Hun (1938). The banning of records. Decca.

KRS-One (1988). Necessary. *By all means necessary.* Boogie Down Productions.

Krept and Konan (2019). Ban drill. EMI.

2

DJ School UK and Beyond

My Journey as a DJ and DJ Educator

Jim Reiss

Introduction

This chapter is as an autobiographical synopsis of my journey as a tutor of DJ skills in the United Kingdom. It focuses on the learning I gained, the challenges I faced, and the successes I achieved. I am an advocate of the power of DJ equipment and contemporary popular musics (from Hip Hop to house and far beyond) for inclusion, and I strongly believe that DJ abilities require a level of skill and musicianship at least equivalent to traditional instruments. I am not a professional writer or an academic. The easiest way for me to address the themes in this book is in the first person, focusing on my personal experiences.

Formative Years

I grew up in Bradford and, around my teenage years, in Leeds (both in North Yorkshire) without a musician in the house but with plenty of music. The genres represented by my family included progressive rock, dub reggae, punk, synth pop, ska, soul/blues, heavy metal, and world music, to name a few. In school, by contrast, my music lessons focused on the Western classical tradition. I had no interest in learning about the composers, or how to play any traditional instrument, but I could appreciate the depth of Beethoven's Ninth Symphony and the melodies of Saint-Saëns' *Carnival of the Animals*. I loved music, and I made mix tapes (programming songs in the order I wanted them), but I never imagined, and was never given reason to believe, I could have a career in the music industry.

Jim Reiss, *DJ School UK and Beyond* In: *Music for Inclusion and Healing in Schools and Beyond*. Edited by: Pete Dale, Pamela Burnard, and Raphael Travis Jr., Oxford University Press. © Oxford University Press 2023.
DOI: 10.1093/oso/9780197692677.003.0003

Then Hip Hop became popular. I noticed the musician in Hip Hop acts was manipulating turntables, using them as the instruments. I started experimenting. Next, house music came along and I realized they were using turntables to program songs live, while also adding instrumentation in the way they blended parts of songs to play simultaneously. I bought turntables, learned the craft, and found my place in the industry.

I enjoyed seeing people happy with the music I shared when DJing much more than I enjoyed any ego boost I gained as a performer. I loved being able to draw on all my musical experiences in my DJing by sampling Beethoven and Led Zeppelin, Bob Marley, and Hugh Masekala. I recognized that no one was teaching others how to do this, and that successive generations were still feeling that secondary-school music education was not relevant to them, however much they enjoyed listening to music.

First Steps Sharing Skills

While I was working with a band in 2001, I reduced my DJ residencies and starting demonstrating DJ equipment in retail shops. The hours suited my band responsibilities. It was during this time that a retail customer asked me to demonstrate what I was doing to a group of young offenders. I had been warned that the session would be challenging, that behaviour of these 'hard to reach' young people might be offensive, or even dangerous. In fact I got as much of a buzz from the session as I had from any gig up to then. The engagement, respect, and attentiveness were amazing, but there was one thing above all that made me want to do more of this work with young people: the fact that they recognized that they were the musician, that they were culturally represented and that they were being creative. I realized I could provide that pathway for learners that I was never offered.

I made myself available to youth centres, the youth justice system, community organizations, and sometimes schools in and around West and North Yorkshire: anywhere young people loved music but weren't offered it in culturally relevant formats. I did the work as a sole trader, alongside my DJ gigs and band work. Like most demonstrators and mentors, I had to unlearn my own practice and break it down so I could build up a scheme of work to help me teach. Although the scheme of work gave me a framework on which to work flexibly, it didn't really directly benefit the young people at that time. It did help me persuade headteachers and organization leaders that I was worth taking seriously, though. The teaching itself was totally informal. By the nature of the settings, it had to be flexible and adaptive to whatever age/music taste/youth sub-culture I was faced with at any given session. I always got excellent feedback, nearly always got 100 percent engagement, and started to make real progress. Centres began asking for repeat visits and longer-lasting projects. This enabled me to get the young DJ learners deeper into the art form.

Formalizing Reasons for the Work

I'm not good at marketing, but it was impossible not to notice which elements of my sessions were of most interest to young learners, so I used to list these to prospective youth organizations:

Cultural relevance: When I first started, I used to take my vinyl turntables, but this meant I was constrained to using my own vinyl collection. If the kids didn't like my songs, I was effectively as useless to them as Bach had been to me. So I started to take CD players and CDs I had burned MP3s onto, which allowed me to include up-to-date tracks of the most current music, in all genres, meaning that my young learners really could always find something that represented them culturally. The feeling of empowerment and the amount of focus a music educator can get when a young person feels culturally represented should never be underestimated. In my opinion, it is the foundation of the success in all my sessions. If, on a rare occasion, I did not have a specific song, I could have it by the next week (assuming I was going to have a repeat visit). To really achieve success, though, I had to stay up-to-date with all the varied techniques of mixing constantly evolving music. As a music lover, this part of my work was a pleasure.

Instant accessibility: CD players removed the tactile requirement to place a needle on vinyl. Although I love teaching how to use vinyl, I also recognize that to be truly inclusive I must respect that some young people in the twenty-first century have had no interaction with anything other than touchscreens or buttons. To play a song on CD DJ players, you simply hit the big shiny button that flashed green. Because of this, young learners in most settings intuitively knew how to get things started. The accessibility of these newer technologies for DJing helped me include children and young people with a variety of Special Educational Needs who may not have had the motor skills to operate vinyl players.

I couldn't help but notice what the organization staff, youth workers, and teachers saw value in, so I started to list these benefits too:

Level of demand of skills taught: Many youth organizations planned short courses of four to six weeks allowing young people to learn enough to produce a short but reasonably competent mix of music. Often the resultant work would then be shared at some kind of celebration or 'gig'. Even in these cases, organization management may still have been so certain that DJing was 'just pressing buttons/not a real instrument' that they would fail to recognize the level of skill achieved by the learners. Many youth organizations who bought into DJing as a one-off activity, like it was a cake to be consumed, didn't seem to understand that by not allowing repeat sessions for those young people who wanted them, they may have added to that young person's disrespect of authority and the feeling of being a misunderstood youth.

Increased life skills: Self-esteem, self-confidence, and well-being data has been produced time and time again to show increases in engagement over short-run music projects, and DJing has the same outcomes. I collected qualitative evidence for team-working, reflective practice, and mentoring skills from the comments overheard by learners.

Facing Barriers

Around 2007, while marketing my services to schools in particular, I started to recognize the antipathy mainstream education had toward the use of DJ skills in music classes. Many organizations welcomed me as useful for 'nurture' projects, recognizing the engagement levels in hard-to-reach students, but very few saw any value in using DJing as a musical instrument in mainstream curriculum delivery. As I had history as both a DJ in the contemporary sense (playing records to audiences as an entertainer) and in my work as a recording and gigging musician with bands (using the techniques of turntablism to add samples and 'scratching' to original compositions), I fundamentally knew that the turntable was an instrument that required at least an equivalent level of skill to the more traditional instruments. However, I felt and feel that this is rarely recognized by the music establishment.

At the same time, I started to meet antipathy from much of the established DJ community for my work teaching DJ skills. Automation in modern DJ equipment allows some DJs to achieve results without skill or creativity.

A mindset that 'it's just pushing buttons' began to be voiced across the DJ community, especially from the older generation of vinyl players toward the newer users of digital technology. Meanwhile, I was embracing the new technologies due to their accessibility but also because they allowed the development of completely new techniques that had never been possible on vinyl turntables (e.g., cue drumming, live re-editing with loops). These new technologies included DJ controllers that by this time were becoming more and more reliable, while still being low cost, and so were especially accessible to the beginner 'bedroom dj' market who could not have considered vinyl turntables anyway. I quickly understood that 'tarring all with the same brush' devalues the level of skill being achieved in those students learning this still-evolving art form.

Concurrently to the above, the UK government introduced its policies of 'austerity' in response to the banking crisis of 2008. This very quickly led to less and less youth clubs being able to employ me, even though many of the young people still requested DJ workshops.

In 2010, the UK government introduced the English Baccalaureate (EBacc) as a 'performance measure' with which to compare schools. In short, the practical result of the introduction of the EBacc was that mainstream educators had to prioritize a curriculum based on English, math, and the sciences over and above the arts, including music in all its forms. Consequently, the work I was delivering, developing, and learning so much about was being devalued by mainstream government policy, by older generations who didn't understand it, and by educators who still didn't see its value as a musical instrument. My work was becoming harder to deliver as less funds were available for youth work nationwide. At the same time, I had reached a point where I had created a reliable and flexible method of informal teaching, a curriculum that tied into the mainstream music curriculum in the United Kingdom, a transferable list of the benefits of a DJ education, data showing the benefits of DJing as an engagement tool, and a hunger to discover more about the ever-evolving art form I loved.

An idea started to formulate in my mind that the young people I was working with should be able to have their efforts recognized at levels equivalent to the existing music grades for traditional instruments. I also realized that I would not be able to continue working as a sole trader in an economic climate where my clients (mainly youth centres and schools) had no funds. I decided to incorporate a non-profit company that could apply for and use grant funding to continue to deliver my work.

It Didn't Exist, So We Had To Invent It

I set up DJ School UK in 2013 in Leeds with the following simple aims:

1. Supply accessible, engaging, and educational DJ and music production tuition, projects, and workshops.
2. Use our activities to raise self-esteem and teach life skills, especially to the hard to reach, disadvantaged, or otherwise vulnerable.
3. Generate income from corporate and private customers to subsidize our services to young people who will benefit the most.
4. Raise the profile of our art form by formalizing accreditation for DJs as musicians to levels equivalent to traditional instrumentalists.

From the outset, one of our policies at DJ School UK was to be as inclusive as possible. I had noticed vast differences in general behaviour and attention between open-to-all youth provision such as youth groups, on the one hand, and targeted sessions for particular parts of the youth population (e.g., 'Youth Justice', 'Autistic Spectrum', 'Economically Disadvantaged'), on the other hand. At first, funding was mainly only available for the latter context, the targeted groups. However, DJ School UK was set up with a desire to be inclusive of all youth groups, welcoming attendees from all backgrounds. In something of a compromise, we allowed those who could not afford our participation fees to attend to access (made possible thanks to our grant funding) and charged those who could afford to pay. This policy meant that music and DJing were the unifying factors in our sessions, which was exactly what we wanted: there was no 'race to the bottom', and any differences between the young people, in terms of their socio-economic background, were far from obvious. Everyone got on with learning, sharing skills, and making music. An unexpected benefit of this was that we created peer networks that were hugely beneficial to young people who otherwise generally felt excluded for one reason or another.

A core principle for DJ School UK is to refuse to accept hierarchies for any reason. We believe that, for example, a newcomer aged twelve should have as much chance of discovering a new technique or song as an eighteen-year-old who has been learning DJing skills for a long time: our priority is: *everyone learning together*; we aim to avoid the competitive and exclusive value systems that are common to many educational contexts. In the main, we managed to successfully create such a learning culture: typically, the newcomer aged twelve would share their knowledge with the skilled eighteen-year-old without the older student questioning it. We encouraged all learners to accept that, in this relatively new and still-evolving art form, *any of us at any level could have something to show someone else.* This extended to the tutor team, myself included: I would happily lead as a role model by declaring that I hoped my students would end up teaching me things. Often, they did just that.

In terms of cultural relevance, we at DJ School UK enjoy sharing our understanding of music history. We use current music and trace the samples it uses to search back through time, discovering new artists, genres, and styles with our students. We reinforce this method of expanding genre-knowledge by stressing that both house and Hip Hop music were created due to a *lack* of funds for traditional instruments, or a lack of training, among groups of people who typically felt a prejudice against them due to their race, sexuality, or some other characteristic. We advise our students that they have as much chance of creating a new scene as the pioneers of DJ culture had.

For students who are especially interested in music history, we trace the roots of this music backward to jazz, blues, ragtime, and the meeting of African rhythms with Western instruments. By suggesting that the roots of current music can be linked to escaped slaves and deserting navy conscripts maintaining folk traditions and joining together in music-making, we aim to stress the importance of inclusivity through music even in the face of huge barriers such as colonialism. This again empowers our young people and gives them something that is much easier for them to relate to than the Western classical tradition alone.

DJ School UK was very fortunate that the local 'Music Hub' Leeds Music Education partnership (LMEP), which was set up in response to the UK government's National Plan for Music Education, was extremely supportive of our aims and methods. They gave us a funding boost and additional network development right from the outset. The system of Music Hubs in the United Kingdom was established in 2012 and has been reported as quite hit-and-miss: a survey by Ofsted (2013) found that 'music hubs, working at their very best, can challenge and support school leaders to bring the numerous benefits of a good music education to all pupils . . . However, Her Majesty's Inspectors found few examples of such good practice.' We would suggest that LMEP, who have been with us throughout our development, must be of the 'very best' type that Ofsted mention. The first partnership we had in 2014/15 involved us being funded to reach out to 10 local schools in the LMEP network and offer DJ activities as 'first access' to music. We once again came up against the prioritization of the EBacc subjects in UK schools and found that in certain cases, in fact especially in those schools with catchment areas of mainly high economic disadvantage, we could not give our sessions away for free. The schools in these areas found it hard to achieve the targets set by education policy for their students, and the school administration seem to have believed they could not allow the students any 'off curriculum' time beyond the EBacc subjects. We tried to argue that a little music might generate more respect for the schools, but very few were prepared to try it at that stage. Other schools, often with existing music provision, jumped at the chance, and we were able to run the project with excellent responses in terms of recruitment to our own extra-curricular DJ clubs.

As DJ School UK continued to deliver to schools and other community organizations, plus under funding from a variety of grant-giving organizations, I noticed there was a lack of standardization in evaluation methods among groups. The data we were requested to collect was always different, and this made comparing overall outcomes from our activities difficult.

We developed DJ Clubs in 2016 with funding from the UK's Youth Music organization (a national charity funded through Arts Council England). These DJ Clubs followed our fully inclusive model, applying standardized evaluation across all attendees. This has been our flagship activity and still runs today. We have collected seven years of standardized data, which we can now use to explain to funders and schools what we achieve, and what data they will get from us, rather than asking them what they want us to collect.

As a non-profit organization, we re-invested every penny we could into additional equipment for our learners. We consulted the young people and, aside from a few expensive examples of industry standard kit, we focused on standardizing accessible equipment so more learners could play at once. The availability of digital controllers and DJ software assisted us here as they were even more accessible than CDJ decks, and more affordable. We quickly had a space where up to thirty learners could gain first access, or eight learners could focus on entry-level equipment knowing that, as their skills progressed, they could move onto more challenging industry-standard equipment, preparing them for real-life scenarios if the opportunity arose.

Raising the Profile of the Art Form in Education Settings

In 2016 I was invited to work with the AQA exam board on the GCSE specification for students wanting to use DJ skills in the performance element of
their qualification (published in 2018). As this tied in so well with our fourth
aim (raising the profile of DJing, in brief), I was happy to do this. I am still
hoping for more time and attention to be paid to this in future revisions: there
is room for improvement in the AQA specification for DJs.

As part of our efforts to develop qualifications and assessment strategies
for DJing, I approached all the organizations who managed the music grades
system in the United Kingdom. Their focus was only just turning to music
technology, and none were interested in the performance aspect of DJing.
I felt they were too busy trying to encompass everything that was not a traditional instrument into one pigeonhole. I instead registered and trained with
the AQA (a leading UK exam board) Unit Award Scheme (henceforth UAS),
where I realized I could draw up my own curriculum for DJ skills applicable
to multiple levels of ability and on varied formats of equipment. This resulted
in a far more DJ-friendly set of accreditations available to DJs. The AQA UAS
does not count as a qualification in itself but can be used to show progress
through three levels of skill and prove to parents, teachers, and others what
a young person has achieved. This AQA UAS is based on my original flexible
scheme of work and so also gives my tutor team a recognized framework on
which to base their teaching.[1]

Recognizing the impact we were having in and around the city of Leeds
and the application of DJing at all levels of music education, but specifically
in engaging young people not interested in traditional instruments, LMEP
supported us to deliver continuing professional development (CPD) and
teacher resource packs to aid delivery of our AQA UAS curriculum. This
meant we soon had a cohort of schools where music departments felt confident to buy their own DJ equipment and incorporate DJ skills in their own
scheme of work.

As mentioned earlier we have over the years developed our own methods of
data collection and evaluation, mainly to satisfy the reporting requirements
of the Youth Music charity and other funding providers but also as we have
seen opportunities to expand the data set we collect and the methods of
analysis. We have created a 'culture of form-filling' in our DJ club sessions
where we have managed to explain the value of completing our forms to our
young people. All learners quickly know that feedback forms are read and

that comments, requests, or concerns are picked up, meaning these are a method for us to hear youth voice and for the young people to air worries privately without needing to be outspoken in sessions themselves. After each session, each attendee completes a paper feedback form giving themselves a self-assessed score. These are based on how they feel about their abilities in DJing, music production, and music in general; how confident they feel; how easy it is to understand the tutors; and whether they feel confident that they are properly explaining their thoughts and queries to us (or, alternatively, if they worry that they are having difficulties communicating with us). They also write a little sentence regarding what they have done, if they have had any feedback from anyone else, how that feedback made them feel, and what they want to do next week. We also have tick boxes that relate to whether they composed anything, shared a skill, worked in a team, shared any musicianship, or did a recording. We use the self-assessed scores to analyze how they feel as they progress. Over the years, we have come to recognize a strong correlation with the Dunning Kruger theory whereby new learners who find everything accessible score themselves highly at first, then reduce their self-assessment as they realize how much more they can learn. We also see the same pattern in learners who are moving on to new challenges, formats of equipment, or genres of music. Advanced learners generally settle into a mid-range self-assessed score as they are more humble about their abilities. We use the other notes to pinpoint how engaged someone is (plans made/ plans achieved) and how confident they feel in the space (feedback/sharings/ recordings done). All this is backed up as our tutor team also note any events they notice and we see strong correlation over time of learners recognizing their abilities and understanding their achievements after they have been with us for longer periods.

We especially listen out for reflective comments and keep a record of how the depth of understanding of DJ skills can be demonstrated in how a learner reflects on their work. For example, a new DJ may say 'that was rubbish I wish I was better' whereas a more experienced learner may say 'I dropped one mix where I was trying to achieve too much at once, I need to practice or maybe rethink how I do that mix'. A second, more musical example would be 'this mix sounds bad' from a beginner whereas a more experienced DJ could say 'I was experimenting with two songs and hadn't realized when the vocalists came in, they ended up clashing, plus the two songs are out of key, but I think if I try and mix over the drum breaks the blend should work and I may achieve a nice key change'. Finally, we triangulate all the data on an individual basis with qualitative comments from parents, carers, support staff, or school teachers to pinpoint where young people's self-assessment is reinforced by others or where pastoral issues may be responsible for a dip in self-assessment and where that learner may benefit from additional support.

Has Anything Changed?

Throughout our evolution as DJ School UK, we have been advocating for the inclusion of DJ skills in mainstream education. Since 2021 (the end of the COVID-pandemic 'lockdowns' in the United Kingdom) we have seen an increase in interest from this sector. I am unsure whether this is because schools are recognizing the value of engagement in music and more specifically the power of offering DJing to those who love music but who aren't interested in traditional instruments, or if we are only just meeting a new cohort of music teachers who have grown up with dance-music culture and who inherently understand that this culturally relevant art form is valuable. Despite this increased interest that we have been receiving lately, we still find many schools will not make time for the activities we offer. We waste a lot of time preparing tenders and plans for work with music teachers only to find the plans are halted by school management/executives. This is still especially prevalent in those schools who are struggling to achieve the EBacc at the levels expected of them, and thus those often in lower-achieving, economically disadvantaged areas with parents who cannot offer as much home support. As the new National Plan for Music (June 2022) is non-statutory, it seems schools can do this. The data for a wider curriculum, with culturally relevant music included, evidences benefits to well-being and to overall GCSE/BTEC scores in those schools who do include it (Gill, 2020), suggesting that improved EBacc outcomes could be a knock on effect of this change. However, I suspect the schools sometimes feel they have no choice but to prioritize the EBacc as an immediate priority at the expense of the curriculum-enhancement offer we make.

Over the last few years, we have also faced an increase in competition from the private sector. As a non-profit organization dedicated to helping children with our art form who rely on raising our own funds, it is a new hurdle for us to compete with private interests who can spend more on marketing. It is especially heart-breaking when private educators let young people down due to their own management or business plans being flawed. This risks reinforcing a sense among vulnerable children that nothing is worth doing and 'everything is rubbish'. We appreciate that some work done in the private sector aids our cause: Future DJs (now Virtuoso), for example, have actually developed music grades 1, 3, and 5 in the United Kingdom, in conjunction with the London College of Music Examinations (LCME) (see Chapter 6 in this book for more information about that). I would hope that other exam boards will develop grade exams for DJs, just as LCME/Future DJs have done: I do not see the LCME grades as the last word in DJ grade exams, although they are certainly a step in the right direction. Just as a guitar, violin, or flute teacher can select a grade syllabus to suit the needs of the learner, a range of DJ grades from a range of exam boards should be the goal.

Another problem we find with our competition in the teaching of DJ skills is DJ tutors who do not cover the full range of genres available in DJ culture. If a young person wants to learn Hip Hop DJing but their tutor can only teach house, for example, then the tutor is effectively repeating the same exclusive methods that kept popular music out of the picture in music education for so long: just as the best guitar tutors can teach classical, folk, jazz, rock, and other styles, DJ tutors ought to develop the widest possible range of teaching skills. Otherwise, if the tutor fails to develop such flexibility, in many cases a DJ tutor's teaching will not be culturally relevant and therefore not actually engaging to the young person.

Finally, there are some DJ tutors who teach only how to *use* the equipment and are not skilled at imparting the *creative process*. In the worst cases, such tutors even rely on automation functions on the decks, whereby little musicianship is actually taught. These tutors devalue the serious work done by dedicated DJ tutors in the eyes of mainstream educators, perpetuating the myth that DJing is 'just pressing buttons'.

Looking Back: Looking Forward

DJ School UK turned ten years old on May 3, 2023. We have one of the biggest DJ education studios in the United Kingdom (probably the biggest) with the widest range of equipment available for young people facing challenging life circumstances. We have a team of tutors who can teach all techniques in all genres across all formats of equipment. We have a strong system of data collection and evaluation. Excluding the lockdown years 2020–2021, we average 1,377 individual students taking part in our activities per year. At least

50 percent of these are facing some kind of challenging life-circumstance. At any given time in the average year, we have seventy to one hundred core students working on some kind of long-term project. Approximately 75 percent of these projects results in at least one accreditation for the student. All those who spend more than six weeks with us are offered the opportunity to gain these accreditations. Our students can complete Arts Award, the AQA Unit Award Scheme, receive our support through GCSE and up to foundation degree level, and through our network our students can be signposted onto a variety of local work-experience, further-education, or career options. We have a handful of ex-attendees who are enjoying successful careers in the music industry and a further fifteen to twenty in higher education studying music or a music-related subject.

Some may say we have achieved our aims, but we do not believe so. The culture of DJing was built on continuously experimenting with combinations of music. Through this, new genres, techniques, and styles were developed. The equipment-manufacturing industry is constantly developing new hardware and software, which opens up new options to DJs. As we are youth-led, we fundamentally believe we need to keep our ear to the ground, making sure we are up to date with both the music and the equipment as the culture continues to develop. We rely on our young people to help us with this and we never assume, as tutors, that we know it all. The continuous evolution of this art form is one of the reasons it is culturally relevant to successive year groups and youth movements. We want to do our best to continue to deliver it accessibly and offer it to all.

References

Gill, T. (2020). *The relationship between taking a formal music qualification and overall attainment at key stage 4: Cambridge assessment research report.* Cambridge, UK: Cambridge Assessment.

Ofsted. (2013). *Music in schools: What hubs must do.* https://assets.publishing.service.gov.uk/government/uploads/system/uploads/attachment_data/file/413107/Music_in_schools_what_hubs_must_do.pdf.

3

'Bildung Life'

Holistic Ideals of Hip Hop Education

Johan Söderman

Introduction

Over the past fifteen years, Hip Hop–based education has gained ground in academic literature (Lamont Hill, 2009; Petchauer, 2012; Love, 2015), and research has to a large extent focused mainly on formal schools and how Hip Hop can be used in classrooms as part of educational tools or methods. In music-education research there has consequently been a greater interest in how Hip Hop has moved into in the classroom (Kruse, 2016, 2020), and the Scandinavian contribution to this scholarly discussion consists of analytically tying Hip Hop education to particular perspectives on learning and pedagogy that traditionally has been based in after-school activities and civil society (Sernhede, 2002; Söderman, 2007; Dankiç, 2019; Ringsager, 2018; Ringsager and Madsen, 2022). Through the lens of these educational activities, the aim of this chapter is to discuss how Hip Hop education parallels the essence of the Nordic Bildung practice and philosophy that permeates them. The chapter also discusses the ways in which Hip Hop invigorates the contemporary understanding of Bildung.

The field of Swedish Hip Hop studies has mainly been situated in the understanding of the emergence of Hip Hop culture as sequential to the transformation of Sweden from a previously (mainly) homogeneous nation into a multicultural society (Sernhede, 2002; Söderman, 2007; Sernhede and Söderman, 2011). This change was particularly noticeable during the 1990s, and Hip Hop music has been regarded a soundtrack to that change, primarily because Hip Hop music and culture came to enable Swedish youths with immigrant backgrounds to identify with Black American experiences as portrayed in Hip Hop lyrics and MTV music videos (Sernhede, 2002; Söderman, 2007; Sernhede and Söderman, 2011; Snell and Söderman, 2014).

Johan Söderman, *'Bildung Life'* In: *Music for Inclusion and Healing in Schools and Beyond.* Edited by: Pete Dale, Pamela Burnard, and Raphael Travis Jr., Oxford University Press. © Oxford University Press 2023.
DOI: 10.1093/oso/9780197692677.003.0004

When young people outside the United States began to make their own Hip Hop music, they did not simply imitate American Hip Hop, but rather created new variants of Hip Hop with a distinctive local touch (Bennett, 1999). In addition, this can be seen as an example of Hip Hop as extremely local (Forman, 2004). When the first generation of Swedish rappers started to rap in Swedish language in the 90s, the music genre grew in popularity in Sweden, and Swedish became the main language of the genre (other popular music genres at the time were often sung in English). At the same time, young people with foreign backgrounds started to identify with the narratives and experiences of Black America as it was portrayed in American Hip Hop. In addition, Hip Hop was part of the popular mainstream culture, but young people with foreign backgrounds were more able to mirror their own living conditions in relation to Hip Hop music than the majority of youths were able to—especially how the life in multicultural suburban public housing areas in Sweden's major cities paralleled American residential areas that were also separated from the white majority population. In Sernhede (2002), these multicultural suburbs were even described as 'reservations' by their young citizens. As a metaphor for social exclusion this links to and contributes to understanding also the rise of a particular language change that was expressed in and through songs of Swedish Hip Hop group the Latin Kings who contributed to establishing new words in the Swedish vocabulary. These words were sprung from the Swedish multicultural suburban cultural slang and contained both Arabic, Spanish, and other language influences, and a new sociolect arose as a kind of dialect within the specific socio-economic group. This also linked to the African American identification with its distinct similarities with Ebonics (or African American Vernacular English). In Swedish multicultural suburbs it came to be referred to as 'Immigrant Swedish' and 'Kebab Swedish' or even 'Hip Hop Swedish' (Kotsinas, 1998).

In retrospect, it is also possible to see how an educational discussion about Hip Hop and learning took off in the early 2000s through academic literature such as Sernhede (2002) and Söderman (2007). However, Swedish underground Hip Hop in amateur settings was highly influenced by the Each One Teach One philosophy that has spread throughout the global gospel of Hip Hop although originating from the time of slavery in which Black Americans were denied education (Chang, 2005). Mainly so it was the messages in Each One Teach One philosophy of how the older, more experienced in Hip Hop taught their younger peers that fitted well with, for instance, Swedish welfare-state ideals of social justice and emancipation—a topic that has been scholarly discussed internationally by for instance historian Lars Trädgårdh (2010, 2018). Indeed, Hip Hop from the late 90s and early 2000s has even been referred to by scholars as *Folkhemsrap*, referring to the Swedish word *Folkhem* (in English: 'home of the people'), which has been used as a synonym to 'the welfare state' by politicians during the 1900s since it is an effective metaphor for the welfare state's homelike and embracing ambition to be a welcoming home for all (Bredström and Dahlstedt, 2002). By linking to this metaphor it is implied how well messages from Hip Hop connected with that particular welfare-state ideology of equality and social rights, in turn linking Hip Hop also to the emancipatory educational tradition called *Folkbildning* in Swedish (popular education), which has internationally been referred to as Nordic Bildung (Brooks, 2020; Andersen and Björkman, 2017). In his definition of Nordic Bildung to an Anglo-Saxon readership, Brooks (2020) describes it as 'the power of educating the whole person'. This educational tradition contains a form of pedagogy that has been developed within Swedish civil society and study associations for over a century, and that is now part of the Swedish public-funded *Folkbildning* sector (Nordic Bildung and 'Folkbildning' will further be used synonymously in this chapter).

All over Sweden, after-school activities in study associations that are based on Hip Hop have occurred since the early 2000s. Swedish study associations are state funded but are at the same time connected to NGO's and popular movements within civil society, such as the labour, temperance, and evangelical movements. Even political parties and churches are involved as membership organizations in these study associations; the Social Democratic party are, for instance, involved in the study association *ABF* (*Workers' Educational Organization*); the former state national church, Church of Sweden, runs the study association *Sensus*; and Muslim organizations are behind the study association *Ibn Rushd*.

Nordic Bildung from an international outlook

The educational movement that still offers alternatives to traditional school was founded over a century ago. The concept of Nordic Bildung includes certain perspectives on the very process of learning, which has become institutionalized as a particular state-funded educational sector in which the study associations are included. But this tradition is not only Swedish, rather it is established as part of the Nordica and its self-image and is as such closely related to the democratic process in Scandinavia. Although the institutions of Nordic Bildung vary from country to country, the idea and philosophy remain a common feature. The aim or meaning of this educational tradition lies close to the English concept of *empowerment* through education. From a global and historical perspective, African American intellectual W. E. B. Du Bois expressed similar thoughts about self-education. During his stay in Berlin between 1892 to 1894, Du Bois was highly inspired by German Bildung theories, and he experienced how European high culture played a significant role in how Du Bois, as a Black man, was welcomed in Germany. In contrast to the race segregation in the United States, Du Bois, with his aristocratic appearance, was not judged by color in the same way in imperial Germany as he was in the States (Barkin, 2005). This experience made him believe that Bildung would help Black Americans to gain more influence and respect in society. Accordingly, Du Bois was also convinced that people would be able to attain empowerment and emancipation by means of holistic educational ideals rather than instrumental and narrow ideals of, for instance, vocational education. Instead, Du Bois' views on education can be seen as the direct opposite to those of political leaders who advocated practical training for minoritized people during the late nineteenth and early twentieth centuries. Du Bois' prioritised what, in Bourdieusian terms, we can refer to as cultural capital: this, Du Bois believed, offered the path to influence and extensive class mobility that he experienced in late nineteenth-century Germany. During this time, European class society almost seemed to conceal racism to the young Du Bois, who did not experience discrimination and racism during his two-year visit in imperial Germany (Barkin, 2005). His embracing of Bildung and it line of thinking thus also share common ground with the ideas about education and democracy expressed by contemporary peer John Dewey. Decades later, Paolo Freire raised similar critiques against cramming and teaching-for-tests culture in schools, which he described as 'banking'. Interestingly, Du Bois, Dewey, and Freire were also contemporary with Nordic Bildung proponents who, on the other side of the Atlantic, argued for the importance of holistic perspectives on education in contrast to narrow and instrumental views.

Although both historical and contemporary Bildung advocates rarely do agree on the use of a common definition of the concept, they do usually tend to stand united in what Bildung is not—instrumental tendencies within education politics being the common denominator for Bildung proponents (Burman and Sundgren, 2010). From a Swedish perspective, the importance of educational ideals from the German philosopher Wilhelm Von Humboldt cannot be stressed enough. The rhetoric beyond Bildung and academic freedom is often referred to as the Humboldtian heritage (Östling, 2018). Burman (2017) states that within Swedish education discourse both 'Humboldt' and 'Bildung' tend to be used as ideological markers, opposite towards certain instrumental tendencies in society and formal education system. Two clear such tendencies are the short-term utilitarian thinking, which is reflected in the fact that education is nowadays often perceived in terms of economic prosperity and that knowledge is reduced to competitiveness in the international market (Burman, 2017).

The Complexity of Nordic Bildung in Theory and Practice

While traditional formal education has a clear beginning and a predestined ending, Bildung is a timeless process, truly lifelong. It has an intrinsic value and is critical of the 'useful knowledge' represented in traditional education settings. 'There is nothing as useful as useless knowledge'; this phrase is commonly articulated by Bildung advocates of the Swedish popular adult education tradition (i.e., *folkbildning* in Swedish), which is related to the fact that no one can really tell what knowledge will be needed in the future. For instance, who was able to foresee the pandemic and what kind of knowledge that were needed to handle the lockdown? Given the lack of a common definition, using the concept of Bildung inevitably means dealing with some contradictions that are embedded in different definitions of the very concept. These can be illustrated by how, for example, Bohlin (2011) on the one hand emphasizes Bildung as based on a focus on the individual in terms of personal development, upbringing, and the cultivation of 'good taste', while also stressing Bildung by distinguishing what it is not—that is, all those thing that can be perceived as representing the uncultured. Although he does not define what that means, it does however imply such things as perhaps unmotivated opinions, poor manners, and un-reflected ignorance.

The term Bildung semantically indicates both the verb 'to form' and the noun 'picture'. That is, Bildung has to do with forming and shaping, but also picturing and foreshadowing (Gustavsson, 1996). Bildung involves aspects of free human development, as well as of human formation. Within this lies a double feature: a bottom-up approach, in which the human forms herself (collectively and individually), and a top-down approach, in which someone (often from the bourgeois environment) educates (the verb 'bildar' in Swedish) citizens of a lower societal class. This dual role of Bildung is shared with the Greek concept of paideia, which indicates the all-around development of humans' intellectual, artistic, and physical capacity. In this process there will be individuals who through the Bildung process transmit knowledge from an agreed cultural canon. Focusing on both content and process then becomes of importance, or the concept of Bildung will lose its significance (Varkøy and Söderman, 2014). The classical concept of Bildung is historical and therefore may not always relate directly to the social perceptions, changes, and cultural conditions of our time. Bildung can be seen both as a constantly relevant educational concept and yet, simultaneously, as representing historical educational ideals that are out of date in our time.

An individual described as being 'bildad' is usually regarded as cultured or cultivated, like the young Du Bois with his aristocratic performance in imperial Germany (Barkin, 2005). Bildung in this sense directly parallels the thoughts of Dewey in his classical work *How We Think* (1910), in which a clear difference is marked between the state of having access to information and the state of being intellectually educated. The intellectually educated man is formed through what Dewey calls the training of Mind, which is a process that leads to cultivation. The Bildung process takes time, rarely generates any swift economic dividends, and therefore does not always harmonize with the educational principles of our time, which promote 'efficiency' in the 'knowledge society' leading to a state of constant 'employability'. However, a closer look at the Bildung philosophy portrays beliefs about knowledge and learning as being a relationship between the colloquial and the new, unknown, and unfamiliar. The individual is perceived as breaking away from the mundane, to venture out into the unknown and thereby gain new experiences. The journey is therefore a central metaphor in the concept of Bildung. As manifested in Johann Wolfgang von Goethe's classic 'Bildungsroman' (educational novel) *Wilhelm Meister's Journeyman Years*, the hero leaves home to go out into the world, only to come back rich in experience and knowledge. In this context Bildung can be considered a steady process, without a preset purpose and without formal ending. In addition, for the young Du Bois his Bildung journey to Germany was life changing, and he repeatedly referred to it as 'the happiest time of his life (Barkin, 2005).

In Humboldtian terms (von Humboldt, 2000) the process of Bildung is associated with the interplay between internal processes of thinking (insight, reflection, and knowledge), on the one side, and processes of doing (that is external activities, materials, and objects), on the other. This means that while Bildung may not have any goal in itself, it still is connected with a certain movement towards deeper knowledge both in the mind, and as manifested in how humans organize different aspects of their life, nature, and the world. Only in the meeting with the world can Bildung become manifested or distinct. Humboldt also stressed the importance of meetings with inspirational others as crucial for the necessary Bildung strive. In order for an inter-personal meeting to be inspirational in Bildung terms, however, the distance between the parties must be enough for admiration to be turned into inspiration. You have to want to intertwine parts of the other persons traits to your own personality, meanwhile still keeping your own confidence because, as Humboldt puts it, Bildung is never about oppression.

Bildung contains many philosophical dimensions and has no goal beyond itself, like Humboldt claimed. Put in Dewey's words, this means simply that the purpose of education is education. Undoubtedly Bildung contributes both to the democratic development of society and to personal growth toward global citizenship (Gustavsson, 1991). Knowledge that constitutes the concept of Bildung contributes to creating greater tolerance and openness, and an expanded framework of understanding in society and therefore plays an important role in the development of democracy in global citizenship.

All in all, Nordic Bildung can be described as a pedagogy for developing new ways of thinking—from the state of only being able to express opinions, to the higher state characterized by insights of the complexity of existence. Despite the clearly emancipatory knowledge ideals, Nordic Bildung has also served as a means to cultivate or even discipline the people, by immersing them in enough knowledge in order for them to replace old habits with more cultivated ones. This educational tradition has for instance evolved from and through temperance and labour movements (Ambjörnsson, 1988; Elias, 1989). Due to this duality, Nordic Bildung can be discussed as holding dual functions: although the 'right' culture, taste, or behaviour should be conveyed to the people, education should at the same time serve as an emancipatory power. This duality is to some extent also found in the African American philosophy of Each One Teach One, which permeates Hip Hop culture. The Each One Teach One of Hip Hop can in a Swedish context be seen as interacting with the lens of Nordic Bildung philosophy. Both these traditions hold visions of education as emancipation and are based on principles of apprenticeship—principles that those who have gained knowledge and skills by dedicating themselves to the various crafts that exist within Hip Hop culture are expected to communicate and pass on these skills to novices. As a result of the Nordic bildung educational tradition, there are young people without formal training who, being masters of valued and respected forms of musical knowledge, have become respectable teachers-agents of Hip Hop culture. These masters can be seen as enthusiasts. The role of the enthusiast has been celebrated in historical popular movements, and today 'the enthusiast' almost constitutes the cornerstone of the self-image of Swedish civil society, for instance in the sports movements (Söderman, 2023).

Music in Nordic Bildung Practices

In contemporary Sweden, many young people with foreign backgrounds (first- and second-generations immigrants) use Hip Hop music in emancipatorical ways that can be connected to historical functions of music within the folkbildning tradition (Snell and Söderman, 2014). Göransson (2010) writes that people have flocked to social movements, such as the revivalist movement, simply because of their musical elements. Brändström, Söderman, and Thorgersen (2012) write about Musical Folkbildning. For over a hundred years, people in Sweden have learned music through study associations, in folk high schools (non-formal institutions for adult education that generally do not grant academic degrees), and in social movements. Today there is an extensive musical infrastructure within 'Folkbildning' in Sweden. It consists of local/community music halls run by various study associations, as well as high-level music education programs, such as the jazz music education program at the folk high school of Skurup (i.e., Nylander, 2014). The musical branch of 'Folkbildning' has clearly contributed to what is usually described by international media as the 'Swedish music miracle', and it has contributed to Sweden becoming a leading international music nation, competing with the United States and the United Kingdom (among others) in exporting popular music.

In the beginning of the 2000s, organized leisure activities connected to Hip Hop occurred in Swedish study associations. Today, in the 2020s, there are many opportunities for young people interested in Hip Hop to be creative and develop their skills in different kinds of pedagogical activities that are state funded and free of charge. The Hip Hop activities of the study associations that take place in young people's leisure time are organized forms, which means that they can be considered as non-formal learning (Eshach, 2007). Although Hip Hop–related activities have a definite frame-work, there are no definite objectives such as a curriculum or policy. The study association is also a prerequisite for many young people to be involved in the artistic activities that are available (most often with an emphasis on the artistic elements of Hip Hop culture). In these Hip Hop–related activities young people can develop their interests in dancing, writing Hip Hop lyrics, or engaging in music production.

Accordingly, the emergence of Hip Hop activities in Sweden can be regarded as a consequence of the societal and demographical changes that occurred mainly during the 1990s. More recently, Hip Hop culture has also energised music activities in study associations that had a previous domi-nance of rock groups, and Hip Hop also gradually became a means for reaching out to youths who are living in the segregated suburbs. In the next section I will report on the main characteristics of these by drawing on my own previously conducted studies.

Hip hop Activities Outside School—Personal Cultivation, Organic Education, and Entrepreneurship

Through study associations and other Nordic Bildung–oriented Hip Hop ac-tivities in Sweden, my previous studies have shown how Hip Hop connects with Nordic Bildung in a sort of (1) *organic education*. Also, the activities themselves, together with the encompassing settings, generate (2) *personal cultivation*, but also give rise to (3) *entrepreneurship* mainly in relation to the realm of the Swedish welfare state. In the following I will further demonstrate my main findings related to the three categories in italics above, in order to carry out a summarizing final discussion, regarding how Hip Hop activities can be seen as a path to a Bildung life.

1. Organic Education

The Hip Hop activities that take shape can be seen as non-formal learning. Eshach (2007) distinguishes non-formal learning from the informal since the former has a structure in its activities in contrast to the informal, which can take place in all kinds of settings. Non-formal learning has a frame within the activities but lacks certain curriculum in opposition to formal learning (Eshach, 2007). The concept of organic education is inspired by Gramsci's notion of the *organic intellectual* (Gramsci, 1971), by which he meant individuals without formal education but who are nonetheless deeply involved in society. As a result of the Nordic Bildung tradition, the enthusiast is highly valued, as mentioned earlier in this chapter. Said (2012) celebrates the amateur, which can be seen as synonymous to the enthusiast, as someone who in opposition to a more professional work posture does not follow fixed working hours. Instead, amateurs are guided by their passion and creative enterprises. In Hip Hop activities, there are young people without formal training who, being masters of valued and respected forms of musical knowledge, have become respectable teachers-agents of Swedish Hip Hop culture. They can be regarded as enthusiasts who connect to historical equals from the Nordic Bildung tradition.

In addition to the connection to Nordic Bildung, there is a philanthropic approach that appears through expression of the will to help and support others, which are in line with the global Hip Hop philosophy of Each One Teach One. According to this approach, it is important to support the participating young people to be able, in time, to shoulder leadership on their own terms. One Hip Hopper in Söderman (2018) underlines how older participants gradually are given more responsibilities and trust:

> We have tried to tell the older ones, 'you're in charge'. Some of the younger are also put in charge, but only for a few days to try it out. They can come in here and try to run the studio. But most importantly is that the older kids are responsible and in charge, because they were here longer. Those who are active, run the place. They basically have the mandate to rule and it affects people. Like one guy he was like 'shit, I'm important, I can't just go about doing anything'. Then others think that they want to be important too.

By trusting youths to gradually manage the studio, they inevitably become invited to get organically acquainted with the role of the educator or teacher in a way that not only is beneficial in terms of Bildung but also contributes to recognizing the role of the teacher. It is also an example of how the spirit of Each One Teach One works in practice. One participant in Söderman (2018: 212) talked about the importance of mentors:

To be honest, I've been quite lucky to have mentors around me. Lifestyle has always been in focus and you've always been told what Hip Hop is really about.

The notion of 'what Hip Hop is really about', in this context, signals that it is more encompassing than the culture and music. Hip Hoppers in Söderman (2018), for instance, talk about their negative experiences from school and express that they never felt at home there. One of the participants claimed Hip Hop as an arena leading to learning, with a reference to one of his peers:

> School isn't very good for him, school isn't going so well. But the thing with having Hip Hop, it's really like—they've got the studio, they can go there and write and that's some fun. We joke a little with him, saying that a rhyme is sixteen lines and you can write a lot of them, but you can't write one little essay at school under one page. So, you've got to capture their interest. A rapper can be very fast, writing in the studio and that kind of thing for only, like, 30 minutes. (p. 213)

To summarize the philosophy behind the *organic education*, it is creating an alternative to formal education, and this non-formal education can be regarded as a whole way of life, which means that human beings cannot avoid teaching others. In the Nordic Bildung practice, the message of Each One Teach One becomes extra strong in a pedagogical setting—it produces organic Hip Hop education, generating implications both for the individual and on more collective level.

2. Personal Cultivation

As previously stated, the study associations that have incorporated Hip Hop as part of their activities bear a long tradition of connections with popular movements and civil society. However, Hip Hop activities not only involve the format of organization, but also include certain values that are transmitted from, for instance, the labour movement (i.e., Ambjörnsson, 1988) to contemporary pedagogy. This is particularly so regarding the fostering and personal cultivation of study association activities, as evidenced in previous studies (Lundin and Söderman, 2014; Söderman, 2018, 2019, 2021). Often, personal cultivation appears to accompany the music-making parts of pedagogy, by the emphasis on keeping the habitats of activities neat and tidy, but also including the transferring of certain ideals, such as issues of equity and equality, through study-circle-style discussions on rap lyrics, for instance. Ringsager and Madsen (2022) discern similar disciplinary regimes or fostering tendencies within Danish after-school Hip Hop activities, which they see as an expression of social technology.

Personal cultivation can, for instance, be shaped through the use of contracts for behaving well. In a study by Lundin and Söderman (2014), the leaders of the study association's Hip Hop activities claimed to use such contracts with the youths in order to get them to develop 'common sense':

> You need to learn to be considerate of others, avoid damage. It's important so that the activities can continue. If the studios and premises are damaged, or used for selling drugs, we won't be able to continue. That's why there has to be rules. (Lundin and Söderman, 2014: 252)

Similar contracts are also used in several other Hip Hop–related education settings and may also include compliance with directives of 'doing well in school' or at work. A requirement to follow rules, such as taking care of recycling, tidying up after yourself, or being in charge of the keys, for instance, could be part of the contract. One Hip Hopper in Söderman (2018) talks about how it is possible to learn from and take responsibility for the study association's Hip Hop activities: 'We're new to it. There's a lot you don't understand right away, so you have to learn it'. The quote may act as an example of an individual learning process, as well as showing how a fostering pedagogy will work. One of the participants in Lundin and Söderman (2014) talked about controversy between breakdancers referring to themselves as part of the 'old school' scene, and others whom they claim to be 'new school'. He said that younger Hip Hop participants show inadequate respect for their older peers, even directly disrespecting them, noting that the controversy might depend on the fact that newer forms of breakdance tend to be more technically advanced. Breakdance, however, has a fairly long history, which another participant emphasizes as important: 'The young people who come here with shitty attitudes; we try to talk to them and to respond in a respectful way', indicating that the participants take it as their responsibility to foster their younger peers.

The leaders of Hip Hop activities talk about the way 'a good structure' functions in a disciplinary way, particularly for less advantaged participants.

There is a belief that Hip Hop is an effective tool for reaching this partic-ular group of young people, and that the activities within the study asso-ciation are helping them to start self-education processes. However, the culture of promoting good character and personal cultivation does not stand un-contradicted. Some participants in Lundin and Söderman (2014) gave voice to the position where rules are said to be too many and limit the creative processes. In accordance with Brändström *et al.* (2012) it might also be the case that all forms of education contain a certain degree of 'sym-bolic violence' (i.e., Bourdieu, 2000), in this case in the form of regulations regarding participation. Popular movements have historically been de-pendent on people with middle-class backgrounds, taking on the role of preaching the value of sobriety or of leading a life as a Godfearing citizen. A 'good character' training occurs also in Söderman (2021) in the form of leaders fostering responsibility through providing help with simple things like doing homework, but also through fostering the cultivation of socially just behavior and good moral values through participating in varied peda-gogical activities.

3. Entrepreneurship

A sort of entrepreneurship occurs within the Hip Hop activities. It can be expressed in how different networks become available for the participants. These various valuable networks enable them to fund activities, like public shows and events. There are examples in Söderman (2021) of how leaders of the Hip Hop activities develop contacts with politicians and promi-nent representatives of NGOs within civil society. There are also motives on the part of the decision makers to cooperate with the Hip Hoppers. In Söderman and Söderman (2020) it is demonstrated that the connections with the municipality include, for instance, the imperative that civil society associations should become something to put on display in order to pro-mote values of a 'creative city' (Florida, 2006). Study associations, under the umbrella of civil society, are still in part state- or municipality-funded. This engages youths in Hip Hop activities within a particular association structure: the youths take responsibility for funding and accounting, both financially but also regarding certain activities and certain commitments, such as promoting and organizing events and festivals (Söderman and Söderman, 2020). For some leaders, this structure provides a platform to enable a certain type of welfare state–based entrepreneurial career based on Hip Hop. In Söderman (2021), for example, entrepreneurial skills are found to have occurred in relation to a particular Hip Hop association based in Malmö, where one of the founders has used it as type of springboard for his future career. Years after his career had evolved, it was possible to establish himself as a rapper and also as a socially committed activist. Through this double position he could establish important networks outside of his Hip Hop organization, meanwhile still bonding with new members. The founder later became the artistic director of a cultural institution in Stockholm and took part in the Swedish branch of the Eurovision song contest, and also worked on developing a political party's arts policy. Furthermore, he educated students in artistic colleges on postcolonial theories and conducted work on diversity issues at the national Swedish Television company (SVT) as well as for one of the national study associations. (Söderman, 2021: 471). In addition, it is important to point out that the tight relationship between the Swedish welfare state and civil society (i.e., Trädgårdh, 2010) perhaps made the rapper's Bildung journey possible.

This type of entrepreneurship also leads to practical experiences that in turn create educational synergistic effects. In Söderman (2018) it is reported how participants, in order to organize an event, are seemingly fostered into these types of networks and connections through booking a municipal recreation centra, contacting a local fire department to arrange for security, and putting up emergency exit signs to contacting local commercial sponsors, including a food store chain for catering, and a local housing company and an energy company to contribute to finances.

Social media has become a central arena for everyday life. Gillberg (2007) paints a picture of what she calls the Renaissance man of our time—a key player in the so-called attention society in which digital visibility, for example, is highly valued. Gillberg describes the Renaissance man of our time as an activist with many occupations, a social entrepreneur who is visible on social media and whose main asset is their personal brand. This perspective makes it possible to understand the entrepreneurship of Hip Hop. It is also in this particular social climate that the role of multitasking Hip Hopper emerges with a protean career. In the Swedish context networking and building personal brands lead to access to funding and incorporation of the activities in study associations, which in turn can be regarded as a form of developing entrepreneurship that suits the Swedish welfare state and civil society well.

Discussion

The Hip Hop activities described and analyzed in this chapter are still clearly intertwined with Nordic Bildung ideals in ways that make them appear as potential alternative routes to education compared to contemporary traditional school. Specifically so, the disciple pedagogy that emerges in the analysis can be traced back to the Each One Teach One philosophy that likewise is characterized by senior youths teaching their younger peers (Söderman, 2007). A similar pedagogy permeates also the popular and Bildung-oriented sports movement in Sweden, in which senior youths are recruited from within the sports club or association to train rookies (Söderman, 2023). This way of organizing educational settings thus appears to be built on how people tend to naturally teach each other; parents teach their children, older siblings teach their younger siblings, and those who, for instance, have played football a little while longer teach it to the following novices. This in turn indicates not only that humans have the capacity to learn, but also that people cannot avoid employing the role of educator and also that this is highly supported through activities and organizations collected under the overarching umbrella of Nordic Bildung. These are signified by their distinction from traditional school by not being determined by the existence of a teacher—rather they are based on a high degree of trust. Contrary to formal education, however, organic education and processes of Bildung consequently seem to invoke youths with aspirations to take on leading roles in relation to new and even younger participants. This pedagogy of trust not only generates and resonates the level of trust in society at large (i.e., Putnam, 2000) but also serves as an illustrative opposite example of how control and test-based formal education rests partly on the distrust of youths and learners. The organic education that arises within the Hip Hop activities, of which the trust-driven disciple pedagogy is an example, can thus be seen mainly as a nursery garden for future professional work life. By enabling youths to gain the opportunity to learn how to work through trusting them to lead Hip Hop activities, they additionally become active in gaining skills also beyond the aesthetic Hip Hop elements. The particular merging of Each One Teach One with Nordic Bildung ideals create a unique educational atmosphere for this.

Although Hip Hop is a highly contemporary and modern aesthetic expression, it is interesting to note how it has developed into such a natural part of this historical tradition. The personal cultivation that occurs through Hip Hop activities links to the emancipatory ideals surrounding the early labour movement and seemingly contributes to teaching a new generation, in a completely different kind of cultural setting, the same valuing of cultivation as a key worth. The structure of the Hip Hop activities itself teaches these values, and the engaged Hip Hoppers act in accordance and contribute to teaching new generations those same values by setting up rules and reflecting on the importance of minding for instance the premises and equipment. Consequently, spaces arise for young people to engage in a pedagogic way as a consequence of the rendezvous between the Each One Teach One philosophy and the Nordic Bildung tradition, where the remix of popular culture and historical tradition creates an educational context built on holistic ideals. That allows young people to learn from two educational settings—the enthusiast tradition and the disciple model where youth teach their younger peers. Rather than maintaining dichotomous roles of educator versus the educated, these roles are intertwined by the fact that the more experienced teach the novices and thereby organically learn how to be educator. A part of the setting in which these processes occur is the realm of Swedish civil society, which is often linked to governmental and municipal funding. Since most Swedish cultural expressions and organizations are funded in similar ways, Hip Hop becomes an arena in which to teach and be taught how this system works, and how to best benefit from it—since the educational tradition and the public organization of Bildung activities in Sweden are so intertwined, and to a large extent disconnected from commercial markets.

Hip Hop culture, with its aesthetic expressions, emerged in socially disadvantaged areas like the Bronx and Harlem in New York. Accordingly, it is not surprising that holistic pedagogic methods occur in opposition to more formal education, with regard to Hip Hop culture's history in which a marginalized individual's conquest of knowledge has been central. Contemporary Nordic Bildung cannot look the same as it did hundred years ago, as Lorentz and Bergstedt (2006) have pointed out. Perhaps Hip Hop is the global pedagogical movement of today and can be considered the clearest example of contemporary Nordic Bildung. Training takes place through Hip Hop and produce self-confidence and knowledge, which contribute to the empowerment of all humans involved in Hip Hop pedagogy, especially marginalized young people with immigrant backgrounds who can strongly identify with Hip Hop and Black Americans experiences.

For almost two decades, the promotion of a personal cultivation has been supported within the ideology of the Swedish Hip Hop activities. These have been regarded as ways of helping young people to get on or stay on the right track but also as a method to foster good values among young people, including the aforementioned personal cultivation. In short, Hip Hop's values often parallel the ideology of the Nordic welfare-state model (i.e., Trädgårdh, 2010, 2018). That said, Ringsager and Madsen (2022) take a strongly critical stance toward 'rap programs' from a Danish context (p. 276). In their view, this welfare fostering within after-school Hip Hop activities forms part of a (potentially pernicious) social technology 'that involves the risk of reproducing societal marginalization, particularly of racialized youth' (p. 259). Nonetheless, it can be countered that Hip Hop institutionalization can contribute to the development of a highly valuable interest in teaching and pedagogy for its participants. This is expressed through a wish to contribute to supporting and helping others, which in turn relates to a philanthropist approach evolving from a mixture of the Nordic Bildung tradition and Hip Hop's Each One Teach One philosophy. On the one hand, enabling participants to take on responsibilities and trusting them to perform are central to the Hip Hop activities and make out what might be seen as a pedagogy of trust in contrast to the societal distrust that often unfortunately occurs in traditional schooling environments. On the other hand, promoting personal cultivation will contribute to a musical transformation by the risk of disarming a counterculture of resistance, while making it more available for youth to engage in. In addition, it thus becomes central, with a dual approach that highlights the complexity of Bildung life within Hip Hop practices.

The Each One Teach One philosophy intertwined with Nordic Bildung in all takes on the form of a seeming 'success story'. It is reminiscent of the connotations in the expression 'the American dream' while to a large extent also reminiscing the idea of a classical Nordic and European 'Bildung journey' that has been described already in literature from the nineteenth century. On a personal level, Each One Teach One is about emancipation and rising above one's own conditions—sometimes against all odds. Hip Hop in Swedish civil society constitutes a possible encounter for Bildung in Humboldtian terms. According to Humboldt, the process of Bildung must have both a physical expression connected to worldly matters, through which the individual can reflect knowledge in both internal and external processes, for instance by adapting practice in accordance with gained insights. Based on the finding I have presented, Hip Hop may very well be said constitute one such worldly, contemporary expression. The idea that Hip Hop could make Bildung possible today rests on the educational value of Each One Teach One, a value that offers possibilities for reflecting one's own experiences in relation to others. Through this (popular) cultural uniqueness, Hip Hop consequently not only has the potential to invigorate the concept of Bildung through music in civil society in Sweden—it has achieved this already, and continues to extend such invigoration.

References

Ambjörnsson, R. (1988). *Den skötsamme arbetaren. Idéer och ideal i ett norrländskt sågverkssamhälle 1880–1930.* Stockholm: Carlsson.
Andersen, L. R. and Björkman, T. (2017). *The Nordic secret: A European story of beauty and freedom.* Lidingö: Fri tanke.
Barkin, K. (2005). W. E. B. Du Bois' love affair with imperial Germany. *German Studies Review,* 28(2T: 285–302.
Bennett, A, (1999). Hip hop am Main: the localization of rap music and hip hop culture. *Media, Culture and Society,* 21(1): 77–91.
Bohlin, H. (2011). *Vad är medborgerlig bildning?* https://www.diva-portal.org/smash/get/diva2:450475/FULLTEXT01.pdf.
Bourdieu, P. (2000). *Konstens regler. Det litterära fältets uppkomst och struktur.* Norra Rörum: Brutus Östling Förlag.
Bredström, A. and Dahlstedt, M. (2002). *Folkhemsrap? Motstånd och anständighet i svensk hiphop.* Linköping: Linköping University Press.
Brooks, D. (2020). *This is how Scandinavia got great: The power of educating the whole person.* https://www.nytimes.com/2020/02/13/opinion/scandinavia-education.html.
Burman, A. (2017). I akademiska kristider åberopas Humboldt. I *Respons.* http://tidskriftenrespons.se/recension/i-akademiska-kristider-aberopas-humboldt/.
Burman, A. and Sundgren, P. (2010). *Bildning: texter från Esaias Tegnér till Sven-Eric Liedman.* Daidalos.
Brändström, S., Söderman, J. and Thorgersen, K. (2012). The double feature of musical 'folkbildning': Three Swedish examples. *British Journal of Music Education,* 29(1): 65–74.
Chang, J. (2005). *Can't stop, won't stop: A history of the Hip Hop generation.* New York, NY: St Martin's Press.
Dankić, A. (2019). *Att göra hiphop: en studie av musikpraktiker och sociala positioner* Lund: Universus Academic Press.
Dewey, J. (1910/1997). *How we think.* Chelmsford, MA: Courier Corporation.
Elias, N. (1989). *Sedernas historia.* Stockholm: Atlantis.
Eshach, H. (2007). Bridging in-school and out-of-school learning: Formal, non-formal, and informal education. *Journal of Science Education and Technology,* 16(2): 171–190.
Florida, R. (2006). *Den kreativa klassen framväxt.* Göteborg: Bokförlaget Daidalos AB.
Forman, M. (2004). Ain't no love in the heart of the city. In M. Forman and M. A. Neal (eds.), *That's the Joint!: The Hip Hop Studies Reader.* Abingdon: Routledge, pp. 155–157.
Göransson, B. (2010). *Tankar om politik.* Falun: Ersatz.
Gramsci, A. (1971). *Selections from the prison notebooks.* London: Lawrence & Wishart.
Gustavsson, B. (1991). *Bildningens väg: tre bildningsideal i svensk arbetarrörelse 1880–1930.* Göteborgs universitet.

Gustavsson, B. (1996). *Bildning i vår tid: om bildningens möjligheter och villkor i det moderna samhället.* Stockholm: Wahlström och Widstrand.

Hill, M. L. (2009). *Beats, rhymes, and classroom life: Hip Hop pedagogy and the politics of identity.* New York, NY: Teachers College Press.

Kotsinas, U-B. (1998). *Ungdomsspråk.* Uppsala: Hallgren & Fallgren.

Kruse, A. J. (2016). Toward Hip Hop pedagogies for music education. *International Journal of Music Education,* 34(2): 247–260.

Kruse, A. J. (2020). 'Take a back seat': White music teachers engaging Hip Hop in the classroom. *Research Studies in Music Education,* 42(2): 143–159.

Love, B. L. (2015). What is Hip Hop -based education doing in nice fields such as early childhood and elementary education? *Urban Education,* 50(1): 106–131.

Lorentz, H. and Bergstedt, B. (2006). *Mångkulturell folkbildning: pedagogiska utmaningar I ett postmodernt samhälle.* Lunds universitet.

Lundin, J. and Söderman, J. (2014). Unity—Hiphop, socialt kapital och lärande i Studieförbundet Vuxenskolan. In M. Askander, J. Lundin, and J. Söderman (eds.), *Coda. Andra antologin om musik och samhälle.* Malmö: Kira förlag.

Nylander, E. (2014). *Skolning i jazz. Värde, selektion och studiekarriär vid folkhögskolornas musiklinjer.* Linköping: Linköping Studies in Behavioral Science, Linköping University.

Östling, J. (2018). *Humboldt and the modern German university: An intellectual history.* Lund: Lund University Press.

Petchauer, E. (2012). *Hip Hop culture in college students' lives: Elements, embodiment, and higher edutainment.* Abingdon: Routledge.

Putnam, R. D. (2000). *Bowling alone: The collapse and revival of American community.* New York, NY: Simon and Schuster.

Ringsager, K. (2018). Solution or a 'fake sense of integration'? Contradictions of rap as a resource within the Danish welfare state's Integration Project. *Journal of World Popular Music,* 5(2): 250–268.

Ringsager, K. and Madsen, L. M. (2022). Critical Hip Hop pedagogy, moral ambiguity, and social technologies. *Anthropology & Education Quarterly,* 53(3): 258–279.

Said, E. (2012). *Representations of the intellectual.* Vintage

Sernhede, O. (2002). *Alienation is my nation: Hiphop unga mäns utanförskap I det nya Sverige.* Stockholm: Ordfront.

Sernhede, O. and Söderman, J. (2011). *Planet hiphop. Om hiphop som 'folkbildning' och social mobilisering.* Malmö: Liber.

Snell, K. and Söderman, J. (2014). *Hip Hop within and without the academy.* Lanham, MD: Lexington Books.

Söderman, A. and Söderman J. (2020). Swedish Hip Hop youth association 'The Movement' goes online. *The Oxford Handbook of Social Media and Music Learning.* Oxford: Oxford University Press, pp. 177–195.

Söderman, J. (2007). Rap(p) i käften. Hiphopmusikers konstnärliga och pedagogiska strategier Musikhögskolan i Malmö. Lunds universitet.

Söderman, J. (2018). Folkbildande raptivister och pedagogens renässans. In I. E. Sorbring and T. Johansson (eds.), *Barn- och ungdomsvetenskap: En grundbok.* Dover, DE: Liber, pp. 205–217.

Söderman, J. (2019). Folkbildning and creativity in leisure time Hip Hop: Towards a pedagogy of trust. In A. Sparrman (ed.), *Children's and Young People's Leisure Culture.* Kulturanalys Norden, pp. 84–96.

Söderman, J. (2021). Double features of organic music education in a post-industrial city. *The Routledge Handbook to Sociology of Music Education.* Abingdon: Routledge, pp. 467–478.

Söderman, J. (2023). Om folkbildningsmässig särart I idrottsrörelsens studieförbund SISU Idrottsutbildarna. *Utbildning och lärande*, 17(1): 25–43.

Trädgårdh (2010). Rethinking the Nordic welfare state through a neo-Hegelian theory of state and civil society. *Journal of Political Ideology*, 15(3): 227–239.

Trädgårdh (2018). Scaling up solidarity from the national to the global: Sweden as welfare state and moral superpower. In N. Witoszek and A. Midttun (eds.), *Sustainable Modernity.* Abingdon: Routledge, pp. 79–101.

Varkøy, Ø. and Söderman, J. (2014). *Musik för alla. Filosofiska och didaktiska perspektiv kring musik, bildning och skola.* Studentlitteratur.

Von Humboldt, W. (2000). Theory of bildung: Teaching as a reflective practice. *The German Didaktik tradition*, 57–61.

4

Technology and the Music Curriculum

Maximising Inclusion, Diversifying Options

Pete Dale

Introduction

Did you enjoy music classes much when you were at school? Responses to this question will certainly elicit strong affirmation from some individuals: 'yes, I loved it!', that constituency might say. However, there is much evidence to suggest that most will not respond in this way. One broad indicator of this, in the United Kingdom, would be the numbers who select Music at Key Stage 4 (the last stage of compulsory school education that runs from thirteen or fourteen years of age to sixteen years of age). In 2020, the *Cambridge Assessment Research Report* found that uptake of GCSE Music was 7 percent (Gill, 2020: 6). Whilst this is only a modest fall from the from 7.4 percent found by Cambridge Assessment in 2009/10, it is a small number compared with the 20 percent uptake for PE and 36 percent opting for Art at Key Stage 4 reported by QCA in 2002 (quoted in Lamont and Maton, 2008). Alexandra Lamont and Karl Maton (2008) have suggested (again, based on QCA findings from 2002) that GCSE Music uptake in 'the early 2000s' was 8–9 percent. Whilst this would appear to be an improvement on the percentages for the UK's pre-GCSE qualification known as the O-level (Lamont and Maton suggest that this was around 5–6%), it would seem that Music has been on (at best) a steady downward trajectory, in terms of its popularity as a Key Stage 4 option in the United Kingdom, for around twenty years.

Music, then, looks to have been at its moment of least popularity in the pre-1987 days of the O-level, as a UK pre-A-level subject option. The replacement of O-level with GCSE in 1987 (whereby rock and pop began to appear in the curriculum[1]) may have given the subject a bit of a boost, in terms of numbers, but it has always been a minority option. This may be partly due to an assumption, and not always an unspoken one, that 'musicians' are

Pete Dale, *Technology and the Music Curriculum* In: *Music for Inclusion and Healing in Schools and Beyond.*
Edited by: Pete Dale, Pamela Burnard, and Raphael Travis Jr., Oxford University Press. © Oxford University Press 2023.
DOI: 10.1093/oso/9780197692677.003.0005

inevitably a rarity within any given set of people. (I say that this assumption is not always unspoken based on ten years spent as the music specialist in UK schools: I recall, for example, having to patiently explain to a PGCE Music trainee whom I was mentoring that it is unhelpful to ask a class 'Are there any musicians here?' because we ought to be assuming that 100% of the learners in each class are musicians, unless we are going to abandon practical music-making work with all but that special minority of supposedly-genuine 'musicians'.) For a long time, schools expected Music to run as (typically) the smallest class among the subjects students could opt into: it was taken as read that there would be fewer 'bums on seats' here than in any other discipline among the subject options. Most schools, along with the Department for Education and its school inspectors, regarded this as an inevitability that had to be accepted despite the relatively expensive staffing cost. To quote the 1977 Department of Education and Science report *Gifted Children in Middle and Comprehensive Schools*, there are 'very small numbers of exceptional children whose musical needs probably require individual assessment and provision'; otherwise, there is a risk that 'apparently reasonable decisions taken to meet the needs of the majority of pupils can adversely affect' that special constituency of (musically) 'exceptional' children (DES, 1977: 84).

Those days, in which music was viewed as an educational expense that was indispensable for children from less-advantaged backgrounds, look to be fading—at least in the United Kingdom's state education sector (the 'public schools', as they say in the United States). *Music Education: State of the Nation*, a 2019 report by the All-Party Parliamentary Group for Music Education, the Incorporated Society of Musicians, and the University of Sussex, found 'a fall of over 20% in GCSE music entries' and a fall of 1,000 in numbers of secondary school music teachers in the United Kingdom across the five years leading up to the report (Daubney *et al.*, 2019: 3). Many schools today are not offering Music as an option at all, post–Key Stage 3 (KS3 being the eleven-to-13-or-14-years-of-age bracket in which all children have an entitlement to one hour of Music per week): Daubney and Mackrill (2018) have reported 'no option for GCSE music in 18% of the responding schools' within their study, with 464 UK schools having participated in the research. The evidence looks robust and tallies with my findings in the Tech Champions project, which I discuss below. The idea that the (capital M) discipline of Music ought to be included in the curriculum of all schools has gone: at Key Stage 5 (the sixteen–nineteen age bracket of post-compulsory education in the United

Kingdom), many students are having to travel long distances if they want to do an A-level in Music or Music Technology.

'Music as a subject could be facing extinction', the BBC has reported, attributing this fear to Ally Daubney (lead author of the aforementioned *Music Education: State of the Nation* report, Daubney *et al.*, 2019) (Burns, 2017). This feels like it is probably something of an exaggeration: it is hard to imagine Britain's private schools allowing Music to disappear from the curriculum entirely. Doubtless the conservatoires have a fair chance of surviving even if the state schools abandon Music altogether, although the ecology of music education would look very different if state school instrumental and vocal teaching was no longer an option for conservatoire graduates: the 'employability' statistics that Higher Education institutions are measured by might look very different in that case. Most readers will presumably hope that Daubney's claim does not come to fruition: it would surely be a pity if the twenty-first-century British education system gave up entirely on one of the oldest academic disciplines. The signs are not promising, however: the very fact that a *National Plan for Music Education* (HM Government, 2022) was deemed necessary in 2011, with an updated plan published in 2022, is indicative of the vulnerability of the discipline; other school subjects have not been repeatedly singled out in this way. (The 2021 House of Lords' report *A National Plan for Sport, Health and Wellbeing* [House of Lords, 2021] is a stand-alone document that looks at fitness and physical activity rates across the nation, not just in schools; I have found no other 'National Plan' governmental reports besides this one and the two *National Plan*[s] *for Music*.)

Music's new *National Plan* is careful in its language: the government would 'like' every school to plan for improvements in its Music offer, and the report suggests certain things 'should' happen (2021: 5), but the Musicians Union have stated a concern that the guidance 'is non-statutory, suggesting that accountability could be a challenge where schools do not engage with the plan' (Musicians Union, 2022). Those who are concerned about the plight of Music Education should surely be pleased that the UK government are at least trying to intervene in some measure. Nonetheless, the governmental direction of travel needs to be eyed critically.

The new *Model Music Curriculum: Key Stage 3*, published in March 2021, is a key document for such purposes. Its first prescription for the curriculum content that learners should have been exposed to by the age of fourteen is 'an aural knowledge of some of the great musical output of human civilisation' (2021: 6). This precedes (literally, but a wider priority seems to be implied) the requirement for children to experience 'creative processes', musical understanding, and musical knowledge, with the latter receiving a heavy focus on 'notation' (2021: 6). It is not entirely clear what HM Government means by 'great', here, but there is good reason to suspect that they are not taking the word in its size-related traditional sense (by which we might assume they mean large-scale works such as the symphony or the 'concept album') and that, rather, they essentially mean 'really good' when they say 'great' (as is common in vernacular speech today). Many teachers will doubtless take 'great musical output' to mean the baroque and classical music of, roughly, the early eighteenth century to the mid-nineteenth century: my daughter, for example, only heard Schoenberg at school in her Key Stage 4 GCSE studies, never at Key Stage 3. That said, and in fairness to the 2021 *Model Music Curriculum: Key Stage 3*, we should note that some Romantic and twentieth-century compositions are cited in the guidance for suitable listening, followed by some film music, a section of popular music (covering blues, rock, pop, and a piece of hip-hop but no electronically driven dance music of any kind) and some (arguably rather tokenistic) examples of music from around the world.

If it is indeed the case that the literal prioritisation of 'The Western Classical Tradition up to the 1940s' in the UK government's *Model Music Curriculum: Key Stage 3* (2022: 10) signals a desire to ensure that all children in the United Kingdom are exposed to this music, the question remains as to whether such prioritisation is wise. Is this the best way to revitalise the popularity of Music as a curricular option among today's school children? Is prioritising the great tradition (with 'great' here intended to denote both quality and scale of influence/importance over the centuries) of Western art music the best way to try to enable this music to regain some of the cultural status that we all know it has lost over the last fifty years or so? Alternatively, might other strategies be viable and perhaps more effective as both revivers of the popularity of Music as a curriculum choice and revivers of the popularity of Western art music (or, as most will put it, 'classical music')?

The purpose of the present chapter is to propose something of an alternative strategy on both counts (an alternative strategy to make Music more popular as a KS4 option in Britain's schools *and* a strategy to make classical music seem, to put it frankly, less alien). Across 2019–2020, I worked on the 'Tech Champions' project with the United Kingdom's Musical Futures organisation (a very well-established not-for-profit organisation that has done much to widen the curriculum and develop practical methods in music education in the last two decades) alongside the Ableton company (leading manufacturers of music tech hardware and software that is popular with many DJs and 'beat makers' around the world) and ten secondary state-school music departments. Interested readers can learn more about Musical Futures at www.musicalfutures.org. Data collected from the Tech Champions project suggests that it is possible to inspire large numbers of children to opt for Music as a GCSE or BTEC subject (a KS4 option, that is) despite the downwards trends discussed above. The project also showed that a Music department can retain all the traditions of the discipline—a school choir, school band or orchestra, traditional ensembles such as string bands, and so forth—alongside the most up-to-date curriculum content including all forms of electronically generated contemporary popular musics (Hip Hop, grime, EDM, and so forth). These findings suggest that treating classical music as 'just another music' (worthy of study, of course, but music like any other music in the end) and engaging with contemporary popular musics (and the attendant modes of music-making) may in fact be the best way to maintain Music as a school subject that is popular, exciting, and genuinely relevant to not only contemporary tastes but also more traditional musics.

The Project

'Tech Champion Teacher' was announced in February 2019 by Musical Futures, in partnership with Ableton, as a new music-education-facing project for teachers interested in 'exploring and developing innovative approaches within their classrooms using music technology' (quoted in Dale, 2020: 6). Free copies of Ableton Live software and their Push 2 hardware were offered to participating schools. With one month provided for interested schools to apply for participation in the project, Musical Futures was inundated with over fifty applications. Once selections from these applications had been made, ten schools took part in the project, each receiving enough copies of Live and Push 2 to allow teaching with whole classes (up to thirty learners in a class being common in British schools thus fifteen pieces of hardware allowed pairs of children to engage in practical work simultaneously). I visited all ten of the schools, undertaking lengthy interviews with music teachers in each school (with ethical clearance provided by Manchester Metropolitan University, the institution at which I was tenured at the time). During my visits, I saw the music technology deployed in a range of ways, from pairs of children working in tandem in a single room with headphones and splitters (as can often be found with keyboard work in schools) to Push 2 being integrated into small group work in practice rooms where traditional instruments (from violin, piano, and voice to guitars and drums) were used in conjunction with the music tech.

Musical Futures was set up around 2005 in collaboration with Professor Lucy Green of the UCL Institute for Education (Green 2008). It has placed a special emphasis on informal learning throughout its existence. The Tech Champions project can be summarised as an attempt at continuing to support this mission (including the informal learning principle) whilst expanding the established Musical Futures methods with more technology and with music technology such as Push 2 treated as a performance instrument. Performance with music technology was an area about which the teachers were particularly enthusiastic (Dale, 2020: 19–21) and which Musical Futures and Ableton's Simon Lyon (who jointly delivered in-service training teachers from the participating schools, with some input from this author) were very keen to encourage.

The ten participating schools stretched from the central lowlands of Scotland to Cornwall, from Essex to Lancaster, from South Wales to West Yorkshire and beyond: a wide spread of British schools in geographical terms. Most were situated in rural areas or were on the edge of, or near to, small or medium-sized towns. One school had no data available on ethnicity within their Ofsted inspection reports, the others were all 'mostly white' (or 'minority ethnic below average' and so forth) other than one school which was listed as having a 'large number of . . . other ethnic origins'. Two of the schools were 'vast majority white British'. Two of the schools were all-boys, the others were all mixed gender. Six schools were listed as 'below average' for measures of disadvantage (proportions of 'pupil premium' learners, for example) and one of these was described by Ofsted as 'well below' the national averages. Three of the schools were reported by Ofsted to be 'higher than average', one of which was 'well above'. Three of the schools were rated as 'Outstanding' or 'Excellent' in their most-recent inspections, four schools were rated 'Good', and one school had been told it 'Requires improvement'. The current inspection rating of the other two schools was unclear from the documentation in the public domain.

For non-British readers, it is worth clarifying that 'mostly white' learners in a school is not unusual in this country: the UK government recently reported a white population of 87 percent (HM Government, 2021), although the phrase 'minority ethnic below average' indicates that some of these schools were, as it were, more white than the (current) norm. Taking the data from the last paragraph as a piece, we can reasonably conclude that, in the main, these were (primarily) not inner-city schools even though economic disadvantage was nonetheless in play to varying extents. This tallies with the impression I gained during my visits: these seemed to me to be fairly typical British schools that were mostly in pleasant-enough areas but would no doubt have had pupils facing significant socio-economic disadvantages. The 'vibe' in the schools was typically welcoming and calm (I tended not to see disruptive behaviour in classrooms and corridors), and the music teachers often spoke of their headteachers or their management teams as being highly 'supportive' of music as a curriculum area.

Findings that Emerged during the Research Period

The first finding of significance was that all of these schools appeared to have exceeded the 7 percent average take up of Music as a Key Stage 4 option. All the schools reported around 10 percent (at the minimum) of their learners opting for music. Several evidenced well over 10 percent, and one was able to show me evidence of around 25 percent of the children opting for Music whilst another evidenced over 40 percent opting into Music. Another school spoke anecdotally of over 40 percent opting into Music, although I was not able to see any evidence of this, though it seemed credible: I certainly saw large GCSE classes in that school. What was crystal clear was that Music was popular enough in most of these schools to allow more than one Key Stage 4 Music class to run concurrently within a single year group: at a time when numbers are reported to have been falling for decades (from a starting point as a minority-choice in the first place, as indicated above), Music was a clearly popular option in the schools that participated in the Tech Champions project. I saw well-populated classes full of eager learners and could see that multiple Key Stage 4 classes were timetabled (Dale, 2020: 46). To put that in context, the school that I worked in from 2003 to 2012 did not attract enough learners to run even one KS4 class most years. The idea of more than one class running within a single KS4 year group was unthinkable; there just was not enough demand.

How was such popularity with students achieved within the Tech Champions schools? I found that the schools offered a curriculum of the greatest possible breadth. Not only were contemporary popular musics of the (broadly speaking) electronically generated kinds taken seriously (for example, posters advertising the school's 'Rave Cave' in which DJing with Serato and music-making with launchpads were welcome) but also all forms of contemporary popular musics more broadly (from Dua Lipa to Arctic Monkeys). Breadth of coverage was highly evident on wall displays, which would typically include information about classical composers, traditional instruments, or the rudiments of music (pitch, rhythm, timbre, and all that). The point is, these schools had music departments that evidently allowed higher-than-average proportions of learners to feel confident in ticking the box marked 'Music' on their options forms. Nearly all of the schools were offering a wide range of traditional music-making opportunities alongside the music technology offer: orchestras, string ensembles, brass and wind bands, jazz bands, big bands, boys' choirs (one of which had won a county-level competition), even campanology at the local church and Japanese Taiko drumming at one school. Beat-heavy contemporary popular musics had not displaced more traditional musics, then: moreover, the contemporary was complementing the more traditional curriculum.

It is notable that, although nearly all of the teachers had been 'classically trained', they were all markedly willing to develop knowledge, skills, and understanding with technology such as that which Ableton supplied to them. Several of the teachers were acting in advisory/training roles for PGCE courses, moderation roles for exam boards, and even advisory roles for national education bodies. These were excellent practitioners, then, but they were also—and crucially—noticeably open to the full range of musics and music-making modes that exist in the world today. By making the effort (and it was clear that it had been an effort for many of the teachers, with time in evenings and weekends having been given up so that they could 'get their head around' Push 2 and the Live software), their departments were blossoming.

Regarding the use of music technology as an instrument for performance assessments (a key impetus behind Tech Champions, as noted above), some nervousness about the credibility of such music-making for GCSE and BTEC assessments was notable among certain teachers. One teacher, for example, revealed that 'I have a genuine fear that people [who do moderation for the exam boards] don't understand the use of technology' (Dale, 2020: 20). Another teacher, who was undertaking moderation of GCSE Music performance assessments for a leading exam board at the time, argued that such fears are unfounded in her experience. A third teacher spoke of hiring a DJ educator to help them assess a DJing performance they wished to submit for a student's GCSE assessment. Such was necessary because they were certain

> about how incredible [the learner's] performance was, but we were anxious because we didn't necessarily know all the skills that [the student] was doing . . One music teacher that I spoke to said 'well, the examiner's probably not going to understand so just put whatever!' I thought, 'how can they listen to it and not understand?' . . . We marked it as best we could, justified it on the form and we'll just have to see [what the moderators say] in the Summer. (Dale, 2020: 20)

The findings of the study, then, do suggest that school music teachers are anxious, at times, about the attitudes of 'the music establishment' (if I can put it like that) toward electronically generated and beat-heavy contemporary popular musics and their modes of music-making. Bias, prejudice, and even outright ignorance are commonly heard, as was indicated by the aforementioned experiences reported by the informants in this study. That said, several exam boards (in the United Kingdom, at least) are adapting more and more to DJing, MCing, beatboxing, and suchlike in their recent specifications: there is certainly room for improvement but, nonetheless, there is a growing openness from the likes of OCR and AQA that is worthy of applause (Dale, 2017: 120–123).

Dumbing Down?

The data above strongly suggests that openness to contemporary popular musics (and the attendant modes of music-making) can do much to encourage greater uptake of Music as a Key Stage 4 option in British schools (and, thereby, the survival in education of a discipline that is said to be under threat of extinction). What, then, are the causatives for the delay in greater embracement of these musics and the equipment with which these musics can easily be made? One factor, as hinted at above, even in the case of the teachers participating in the Tech Champions project, is a form of internalization of prejudice: teachers seem to fear disapproval from colleagues, exam boards, and, most likely, school inspectors, and, as a result, many keep music technology and the contemporary popular musics that rely on that technology somewhat at arm's length. Doubtless this accounts for at least part of the problem, but it is not the whole story: teachers are not just imagining bias against, say, the idea of DJ decks as a musical instrument or the idea that music-making can be worthwhile even if it is done without the use of notation; the bias is out there (Dale, 2017: 89, 114–115).

One causative factor for the bias in question (or, more likely, multiple biases) is a fear of 'dumbing down', no doubt. Sometimes equating DJing with 'painting by numbers', commentators will often object that a DJ 'just' pushes buttons. One can object, of course, that a piano player is also 'just' pressing levers that trigger hammers, a flautist is 'just' pressing buttons (of a sort) that adjust the length of a column of air, and so forth. One can invite a non-DJ to have a go at, say, beatmatching (without the sync function) or to attempt to perform the transformer scratch (a notoriously challenging DJing trick) and see whether they still consider DJs to be lacking in skill. One can deploy these and other strategies (inviting them to read a text such as Mark Katz's *Groove Music* monograph on *The Art and Culture of the Hip Hop DJ*, 2012, for example) to persuade the sceptic that DJs really are musicians and that the DJ decks are a real musical instrument. In the end, however, it might not be easy to persuade some of the more committed sceptics: they, it seems, 'just know' that the technology is doing the work for the DJ, for the beat maker, for the performer of contemporary popular musics.

Some comments from teachers involved in the Tech Champions project form a pleasing tonic to such dismissive attitudes. Consider, on this score, the following remark from the oldest of the Tech Champions teachers, a classically trained practitioner (and, we can note, flautist) with decades of experience in the classroom:

> Someone is pressing something at a [particular moment in musical] time, pressing different things, doing it well, doing it in time and making decisions—it's not a flute, but you're still pressing things on a flute and doing things at the right time. So I'm just saying, 'GCSE Music, you can do it, this is your instrument now, you can do it'. (Dale, 2020: 19)

The optimistic positivity of the teacher's general attitude is striking, as is the willingness to recognize that pressing buttons (or levers or whatever) is musical if and when it involves real-time musical decision-making, involves musical precision ('doing it well'), involves musical *skill*. Such optimism about the potential of music tech to kindle musicality in children, as well as a willingness to see the technology as a musical instrument on which students could do assessed performances, was the norm among the Tech Champions teachers. Several of them spoke about the way that technology allowed their learners to work practically in the first instance but with 'music theory' being slipped in afterwards in a manner that, due to the practical work having come before the theoretical work, was highly effective: 'In terms of achievement, they are experimenting with things in a more complex way without even thinking about it', as one teacher put it (Dale, 2020: 26).

There is no question that technology commonly allows easier access to music-making: very often it causes frustration to be replaced with elation. One of the Tech Champions teachers reported that 'a student who's never looked at a keyboard before, and we get quite a few coming up from primary school who've never tried to play a keyboard before, I think that can be a little bit nerve-wracking: trying to work out what the notes are' (those who have spent years teaching music in schools, such as this author, will recognize the veracity of this statement). For this teacher, however, it is possible to 'develop a good piece of music using music technology': in her words, 'keyboard skills are, like, a different set of skills that could come after' (Dale, 2020: 25). However, if music becomes so easy to make, will the students actually be learning anything of any significance? The Tech Champions teachers seemed to feel that indeed they would:

> If it makes music accessible for all, and if that Push controller is allowing people to have success that they wouldn't have had before, because they couldn't play perfectly in time, then I think that's a wonderful thing. Obviously those really talented musicians can create music in whatever way they want, but as a tool for allowing it to be accessible for everyone, I think it's wonderful. (Dale, 2020: 25)

Meanwhile, 'the really high achieving students' were also claimed to be benefitting from the access to up-to-date technology that the Tech Champions project allowed: in reference to a particular student, for example, one teacher stated that 'he's, like, exploring—by himself, because everything's so intuitive—and he's four steps ahead in terms of creating the sonority of the tracks that he wants because he can just go and explore it and it all makes so much sense'. This learner, the teacher insisted, 'can push himself further and further and really play around with the sounds' relative to the middle and lower ability students (Dale, 2020: 27). Many of the teachers said much the same with regard to their higher-ability learners. Middle-ability students also seemed to benefit from exposure to the technology, even if they were adept on traditional instruments: for example, a chord with 'an 11th and a flattened 9th and it's in F# minor—things that will automatically make a kid go "Oh my god, that's too hard!" . . . if we can programme in something like that [i.e., pre-programme the Ableton Push 2 unit such that F#-11(b9) can be played at the touch of a button], it could be a good way of experimenting' with harmony, one teacher suggested. She did not specify whether it was a keyboard player or a guitarist she had in mind, but it is probably one of those two (polyphonic) instruments: either way, F#-11(b9) would be tricky to play for an intermediate player; using technology to allow a learner to explore the sound of this particular chord in some particular harmonic context is valuable, therefore, since they can at least *hear* the harmonic effect even if their playing skills hinder their delivery of the chord as a traditional performer.

To put the last point in context, a brass teacher once remarked to me that she had found composing four-part harmonies in the Bach chorale style a real challenge when (like me) she had done a Music O-level in the 1980s. Bach-style SATB arrangements on staff notation were a core requirement of Music O-level, and such remains in place at A-level as a key requirement. However, it is no longer required for the United Kingdom's post-1987 KS4 curriculum: instead, the GCSE features a mixture of notation-based and non-notation-based skills but no direct requirement for SATB harmonisation in the strict style that is associated with Bach. The brass teacher in question worked peripatetically for many years in the school music department that I led: she was an excellent musician with outstanding teaching skills as well as all the performance skills and musical knowledge she needed for the job. She was, however, not a pianist. She expanded on her point about the challenge of notating four-part harmonies by saying that 'you never knew what it would actually *sound* like'. Although I had some piano skills, I recalled suffering from the same problem: I did not have the keyboard fluency to execute what I had written onto the stave. I therefore had to approach the task as a primarily theoretical challenge: I knew that I should avoid 'parallel fifths' (Bach hated them, although the Ramones and Black Sabbath have shown that it is in fact possible for mass audiences to enjoy them) and suchlike, thus I could put something down on paper that corresponded to the established aesthetic preferences in question. Nonetheless, I did not really know what the harmony I had written down would sound like, in all honesty. If music technology can help learners with proven musical ability in some areas, despite deficiencies in other regards, to get a practical feel for aesthetic rules that we previously understood only in theory, it is hard to see (to use a contemporary phrase) what is not to like. The brass teacher and I were just such learners, but I would contend that, had such technology existed in the 1980s, the learning outcome would have been (to use more contemporary phrases) more a matter of levelling up than dumbing down.

Music technology, in other words, can help advanced learners, intermediate learners, and entry-level musicians: it can help with learning, and for some learners it makes the world of difference; for them, it makes music viable as a practical subject at school where previously it was off the map. For the learner with skills on a traditional instrument and/or knowledge and understanding of 'music theory' in its traditional sense, technology might be an aid rather than the 'be-all-and-end-all'. In any case, though, it is hard to understand why 'Music Technology' gets hived off as a distinct subject from Music. Are these two really a world apart?

Concluding Problematics

Harold Rosen once suggested 'that the linguistic capital of the dominant culture is persistently over-valued and that of the dominated culture persistently undervalued' (1972: 7). What happens if we replace the word 'linguistic' with 'musical'? I would suggest that such a situation largely pertains in the United Kingdom and elsewhere: the musical capital of the dominant culture generally gets overvalued, and that of the dominated culture either gets undervalued or, perhaps worse, ignored. This situation needs to be redressed: music education urgently needs updating.

The Musical Futures/Ableton-instigated Tech Champions project was a significant success for this (ongoing) struggle to update music education. Music, in the United Kingdom's KS4 in particular, has struggled for many years to speak to contemporary music tastes and contemporary modes of music-making. Tech Champions showed that there is space for a reversal of music educations (mis-)fortunes. It also showed that classically trained teachers can widen (if, but only if, they are *open* to widening) their range of teaching skills even if they have little or no previous experience of music technology (as was the case with most of the Tech Champions teachers, at least at the point they entered the teaching profession).

In nearly all of the schools that participated in the Tech Champions project, traditional musical endeavours (choir, school band, and so forth) existed quite happily alongside music tech-based activity. So I can conclude here that: having a 'Rave Cave' turns out not to prevent a school Music department from engaging with the great tradition of classical music and a host of other musics. That said, the 2020 onwards global pandemic arising from the COVID-19 outbreak did hinder the concluding period of the project. As a culmination of the Tech Champions project, 'Musical Futures TV' offered an online 'festival of learning' in 2020 and 2021. This was the best that could be done, in the context of the 'lockdown' restrictions that demanded 'social distancing', as a sharing of the project (with presentations from several of the teachers who had participated in the project). The learning materials that Musical Futures and Ableton made available to teachers through Musical Futures TV (still locatable through 'hashtag' searches of #mufutv2020 and #mufutv2021) are well worth examining: Ableton Push and the Live software it works with are very effective tools for teaching and learning, or so the Tech Champions teachers thought, at least. The curious teacher might well open up a host of possibilities in their school with music technology such as this, and Musical Futures TV 2020 and 2021 is a great place for the uninitiated to start exploring the potential.

Although Tech Champions might have had more impact had it not been for COVID-19, the project was an exciting one for those of us who would like to see music education more effectively integrate Hip Hop, grime, techno, and so forth in the educational mainstream. There is still a long way to go, however. The United Kingdom's 2021 *Model Music Curriculum: Key Stage 3* shows that classical music or, more accurately, Western art music is prioritised by policy-makers (as discussed in the Introduction above). In this chapter, I have attempted to query the wisdom of this prioritisation: it seems to me that listening to Debussy then Drake then the Doors then Dizzy Gillespie then David Guetta then a host of other musics is the best way to keep the great tradition of Western art music alive. By placing this music alongside other musics, and critically analysing them *all* with children in mainstream British classroom, the Western art tradition (Beethoven, Brahms, and the rest of the gang) is more like to feel relevant, interesting, and worthy of attention. Classifying classical music as a class apart does not appear to have helped this music to seem vital. On the contrary, many seem to view Western art music as 'posh music' today; on that basis, classical music seems to often get dismissed.

At the same time, music technology needs to be celebrated for its own sake. With a Push 2 unit or the Ableton Live software, or with DJ decks, or with any of the contemporary array of launchpads, or with GarageBand (and one could go on and on with this list of course), music-making becomes more accessible than it has even been before. Some of the technology is less appropriate for differentiation, of course: GarageBand, for example, has significant limits to the variation of outcome if (as I did in my own practice) one uses the software's set of loops to teach whole classes some basic principles of mixing, re-mixing, and sampling. As I have discussed elsewhere, the most able learners do not always come up with something that sounds all that much different from the music made by those who had previously shown more basic musical understanding and/or skills (Dale, 2017: 153). Some music tech, however, can allow the most able, the less able, and the middle-ability learners to *all* be stretched, to all develop new skills and to make music with a great deal of variety and individual character. With the best of the contemporary music tech on the market, learners in classrooms can make Hip Hop or bhangra, string arrangements or fat beats, hard rock or hardcore techno, and much more besides. Not only enhanced inclusion but also greater attainment are frequent outcomes for the full range of learners.

There remains scepticism about such claims, certainly in the United Kingdom but also around the world. I would argue that the United Kingdom's exam boards are world-leading in their openness to music tech in some ways. Nonetheless, many further improvements to the curriculum specifications need to be made, and there is an urgent need for teachers to receive better training with music tech. Beyond the United Kingdom, meanwhile, it is relevant to mention that I featured many of the themes discussed in this chapter at an Urban Music Studies conference in Germany in 2018 and was advised by the panel chair that my proposals were 'dynamite' to the music-education establishment. There certainly are many, in the United Kingdom and beyond, who think that music needs to remain a minority option that only the gifted should be allowed to do.

Consider, in that regard, a comment from a 'pre-service' teacher that I quoted in my 2017 monograph *Engaging Students with Music Education* (Dale, 2017: 154):

You can't just create music. Calling [computer-aided musical creation] music is like picking up a fork and banging on the table and creating a beat and then saying 'Yeah, that is music'—but it's not, you know? (Vratulis and Morton, 2011: 407)

In fact, percussion ('banging' one thing with another thing) is fundamental to the history of music, from the caveman to the Timpani player to the producer 'punching' beats into a launchpad. In fact, music tech has great potential for complex music-making and is a world away from banging a fork on a table. In fact, anyone *can* 'just create music'; it is our birthright, indeed. It is very worrying that a trainee teacher would make the comments just-quoted, which so clearly suggest that this thing 'music' can be restricted not only as an activity but also as a thing in itself. Hip Hop is music. Grime is music. EDM is music. The best teachers recognise this. The best teachers place those musics alongside a host of other musics and encourage all the learners to make music together, individually, with technology, with traditional instruments, or in any way they please.

References

Burns, J. (2017). *Music 'could face extinction' in secondary schools*. https://www.bbc.co.uk/news/education-39154242.

Dale, P. (2017). *Engaging students with music education: DJ decks, urban Music and child-centred learning*. Abingdon: Routledge.

Dale, P. (2020). *A reflective report on Musical Futures' Tech Champions Project*. https://www.musicalfutures.org/wp-content/uploads/2022/11/MF-TC-PROJECT-report.pdf.

Daubney, A. and Mackrill, D. (2018). *Changes in secondary music curriculum provision over time 2016–18: Summary of the research*. https://www.ism.org/images/images/SUMMARY-Changes-in-Secondary-Music-Curriculum-Provision-2016-18.pdf.

Daubney, A., Spruce, G. and Annetts, D. (2019). *Music education: State of the nation. Report by the All-Party Parliamentary Group for Music Education, the Incorporated Society of Musicians and the University of Sussex* .https://www.ism.org/images/images/State-of-the-Nation-Music-Education-WEB.pdf.

DES. (1977). *Gifted children in middle and comprehensive schools*. HMSO.

Gill, T. (2020). *The relationship between taking a formal music qualification and overall attainment at Key Stage 4*. https://www.cambridgeassessment.org.uk/Images/603850-the-relationship-between-taking-a-formal-music-qualification-and-overall-attainment-at-key-stage-4.pdf.

Green, L. (2008). *Music, informal learning and the school: A new classroom pedagogy*. Aldershot: Ashgate.

HM Government (2022). *The power of music to change lives: A national plan for music education*. https://assets.publishing.service.gov.uk/government/uploads/system/uploads/attachment_data/file/1086619/The_Power_of_Music_to_Change_Lives.pdf.

House of Lords (2021). *A national plan for sport, health and wellbeing.* https://publicati ons.parliament.uk/pa/ld5802/ldselect/ldsportrec/113/113.pdf.

Katz, M. (2012). *Groove music: The art and culture of the Hip Hop DJ.* Oxford University Press.

Lamont, A. and Maton, K. (2008). Choosing music: Exploratory studies into the low up-take of music GCSE. *British Journal of Music Education,* 25(3): 267–282. https://doi. org/10.1017/S0265051708008103.

Musicians Union (2022). *Government publishes new national plan for music education.* https://musiciansunion.org.uk/news/government-publishes-new-national-plan-for-music-education.

Rosen, H. (1972). *Language and class: A critical look at the theories of Basil Bernstein.* Bristol: Falling Wall Press.

HM Government (2021). *Ethnicity facts and figures.* https://www.ethnicity-facts-figures. service.gov.uk/.

Vratulis, V. and Morton, C. (2011). A case study exploring the use of Garageband™ and an electronic bulletin board in preservice music education. *Contemporary Issues in Technology and Teacher Education,* 11(4): 398–419.

5

Musical Futures and Music Technology in Mainstream Music Education

Fran Hannan and Martin Ainscough

Introduction

This chapter is written by Fran Hannan and Martin Ainscough, the two current directors of Musical Futures, which is a not-for-profit organisation providing resources, training, and a community of practice with the aim of making music in schools relevant, engaging, imaginative, and authentic. The ethos of Musical Futures is based upon the work of Lucy Green and her work around informal learning. Fran and Martin begin by reflecting upon their own experiences of music education as learners in order to unpick their own motivations and aspirations for the approaches advocated by Musical Futures and their use within schools. The core focus of the organisation remains centred around the exploration of a pedagogy that places young people at the heart of learning—focused on their music-making and their participatory learning. Musical Futures is student-centred and is about encouraging teachers to think about how their students learn and what they want to learn but most importantly how they learn, as individuals.

Experiences as Learners

For Martin, learning informally (the core principle behind Musical Futures) was how he developed his interest in music. Although he did not have any real music lessons in childhood, his grandad had a piano, which he played 'by ear'. This had a significant influence upon Martin, who taught himself to play the piano by copying ragtime pieces from old audio tapes. Upon

Fran Hannan and Martin Ainscough, *Musical Futures and Music Technology in Mainstream Music Education*
In: *Music for Inclusion and Healing in Schools and Beyond*. Edited by: Pete Dale, Pamela Burnard, and Raphael Travis Jr.,
Oxford University Press. © Oxford University Press 2023. DOI: 10.1093/oso/9780197692677.003.0006

learning about Musical Futures in 2007 during his PGCE year, Martin immediately felt a real connection to the approach, largely because of his own experiences of music at school. Whilst he had a great music teacher who was very inspiring and an excellent musician, he does not really remember learning much from classroom lessons. Much more inspiring was the extra-curricular provision through his involvement in ensembles, such as the jazz band and the informal aspects of being around the music department at lunchtime, in the music studio, and being given the freedom to experiment with computer software such as Cubase. He only began having regular piano lessons at the age of seventeen, completing his grade 5 then grade 8 piano exam before going on to a performance diploma and music degree.

Fran had more of a 'classical' training. Although she attended her local comprehensive school, at the age of sixteen she began attending Manchester's specialist music school, Chetham's School of Music. Having initially considered work as a peripatetic instrumental teacher of cello, she had a change of heart during her first teaching practice of her PGCE as she was able to see how the experiences and opportunities the school offered their students had a powerful effect on their engagement with school. Having learned to play drums as part of her PGCE training at college, the school asked her to help out with the school production, *Some Like It Hot*, and asked her to learn the drum part to play in the band from an audio tape of the music. Fran learnt the drum parts by listening to the tape and working out the drum patterns for each of the show's songs aurally. Following on from this, Fran went on to play with a group of ex-students and staff in Working Men's Clubs, which provided her with an insight into pop-based musical genres and aurally based learning through immersion in informal learning experiences. That experience, after a very privileged musical upbringing, drives Fran's determination to ensure that music learning is inclusive and accessible for all young people—for most people, the opportunity to learn music happens in school, and if learners are not able to grasp opportunities then many of them will never go on to learn to make music. Music should be a lifelong learning experience, not just something for those who are fortunate to have parents who are able to provide instrumental lessons: it needs to be really inclusive. Both Martin and Fran are passionate about inclusivity, and this ethos remains at the heart of the Musical Futures approach to learning.

Early Involvement in Musical Futures

Having spent a short time teaching cello as an instrumental teacher, Fran went on to become a classroom teacher with the majority of her teaching career in primary and secondary schools until 2005. At that point, she joined ArtForms in Leeds, a music and arts service working with children, young people, families, and schools across the city. Soon after, she became involved with Musical Futures working as part of the Leeds pathfinder team. This experience has enabled Fran to develop a deep understanding of teachers' experience in the music classroom in both primary-, secondary-, and community-based settings.

Fran's journey with Musical Futures began in the research phase of the project, which began life as a Paul Hamlyn special initiative. At that particular time, the Paul Hamlyn–funded pathfinder project was divided into three strands, with each strand undertaken by different pathfinders. The Hertfordshire team were focused on Lucy Green's work exploring how popular musicians learn and how that could be translated into the classroom. The Nottinghamshire team were exploring ways to engage students with music and exploring the most effective ways that music services could support the work of schools. In Leeds, the pathfinder team were working with students who were not particularly engaged with the kind of music-making experiences offered within the traditional secondary-school context. Many students can be quite self-contained about their music-making, and rather than engage with anything that was happening more formally in the classroom, these often self-taught musicians, or 'bedroom musicians', were offered support through the Leeds pathfinder projects to develop their skills further or to help to them connect with other like-minded musicians within their peer group—to enable them to participate in the experience of making music with other young people informally. Fran's initial role as assistant project manager of the Leeds pathfinder was to devise projects for learners that were outside of the usual, formal music context within schools. These initially took place in community venues and were designed to support musicians with songwriting, making use of music technology, and developing as performers and composers.

Eventually, Fran began to work with people from the other pathfinder teams and when Musical Futures officially came to the end of the research phase, she joined the national team led by Abigail D'Amore. In 2017 she became managing director and now leads the not-for-profit organisation.

Martin's involvement in Musical Futures began whilst studying for his PGCE. He attended a Musical Futures training course and found it to be a 'lightbulb moment' that helped to make sense of his own experiences at school along with the motivation to use this knowledge to make a change within education to ensure that it had a greater relevance for young people. Martin began his teaching career in a great school that had a specialisation in Performing Arts and a strong belief in the power of the arts to change the lives of young people. The school was fortunate to have four music classrooms, but each one was filled with keyboards, and nearly all schemes of learning centred around learners playing them. Traditional extra-curricular ensembles were thriving in the school, but they had very little influence upon the classroom music experiences of the learners—the two were completely separate.

Reflecting again on his own experiences, Martin began to question how much students were really learning from their classroom music lessons each week. Those learners who could already play were not really being challenged (or engaged) by the work on keyboards, and many other students simply had no interest in learning the 'Harry Potter theme' on the keyboard (or whatever piece was directed in the scheme of work). The head of department supported a trial of the 'In at the deep end' approach from Musical Futures, which needed some investment in instruments, such as electric guitars, amps, and drum kits. The initiative saw a huge impact across the department, particularly for some of the most challenging learners who had previously disengaged from music lessons. Significant numbers of students who had been considered to be 'no good at music' suddenly started to become engaged and would share that they had a guitar or drum kit at home. This interest had always been there for the students, we just had not been providing learners with a place to explore it, or looking for abilities beyond playing the keyboard. Soon, music lessons became a really thriving space. No longer were there 'mono-instrumental' rooms of thirty keyboards—there were a few keyboards, a few guitars, a few drum kits alongside learners who brought in whatever instruments they were learning into lessons. This really opened up the space for authentic learning. The music department launched a hugely popular 'Rock School' with over sixty learners turning up each Wednesday evening, putting on gigs and 'Battle of the Bands' competitions: there was a huge buzz and energy all created and fostered by classroom music lessons. These weekly lessons were now key in challenging, engaging, and encouraging learners in their own musical journeys. One of Martin's students who was involved in the original trial, Reece, is now a key part of the core Musical Futures team as Head of Resource Development. Having gone on to study at the Liverpool Institute of Performing Arts, he brings a unique perspective to our work through his experience as a student and, latterly, professional musician.

Martin's work with Musical Futures continued to grow, leading to him becoming a Director in 2015. His main occupation is as an Assistant Headteacher in a Secondary School where he is able to take the ethos and principles that underpin Musical Futures and apply these across the school, as has been attempted more widely in 2007–2012 with the 'Learning Futures' project (also funded by the Paul Hamlyn Foundation). In Martin's opinion, most learning that happens in schools is 'just in case': we have to teach it to our students in case they need to know it for their examination. However, the Musical Futures approach is more about learning *just in time*. 'There's this task that I've been set, *how do I do this*?' In his opinion, that's the kind of learning we remember and that young people need in order to be successful: real-world learning, working together as a team, problem-solving, authentic learning—that is what Musical Futures has been about from its inception to the present day.

Put it this way: if you were teaching skiing in school through a 'traditional' approach, you might start by ensuring that students had a good knowledge of the sport—maybe exploring the history of skiing in lesson one. In lesson two, we might talk about skiing techniques and research famous skiers. Lesson three, we might put on some protective equipment and make sure we have got it on correctly by completing some peer assessment. By the time students get to lesson four and we finally give them a chance to put skis on, they actually do not really want to ski anymore because 'skiing's boring'. The Musical Futures approach flips this on its head—in lesson one we say 'We're going to put some skis on, but don't worry, I'm going to support you, guide you through, but we're going to learn through the enjoyment of what we're doing'. In Martin's view, it is a more effective, natural way of learning and is how we learn to do things outside of the formal education setting, such as our hobbies, interests, or sports.

Musical Futures prompted similar experiences to those Martin describes in schools across the country. Susan Hallam, Andrea Creech, and Hilary

Figure 5.1 James Tuck – A Musical Futures Tech Champion Teacher at work using Ableton Live alongside an Ableton Push Device

McQueen's evaluation of Musical Futures (Hallam *et al.*, 2017) showed that positive outcomes have included greater engagement with and take-up of music, developing a range of skills for learning, developing performance skills, supporting the school ethos, and a sense of pride with regard to student achievements in music. Hallam *et al.* (2017) also found that results at Key Stage 4 music were above the national average. We would summarise that this happened because schools focused on trying to engage *all* learners, particularly those they were not previously connecting and engaging with. We want every child that comes through the classroom door to think they are a musician through being treated as one.

The Changing World of Music and the Tech Champions Project

The use of a Digital Audio Workstation (DAW) for mainstream, whole-class teaching and learning is, we believe, reasonably standard across schools in the United Kingdom, with many schools making use of this equipment. There is a great deal of variance, however, in how *effectively* the technology is used and how *accurately* the technology, or the approaches to using it, provide a way to authentically create music that young people are listening to outside of the classroom.

The Musical Futures Tech Champions program was developed upon the principles that Lucy Green originally set out in her work (Green 2008) around informal learning back in the early 2000s. One of the central aspects was reflecting the music and instruments that children enjoy, like, and identify with. At the time this was music created by bands with guitars, synths and vocalists, and so on. However, the music children are largely identifying with twenty years later is generally created using DAW software on a computer utilising sampling, software instruments, and effects. If we return to Green's principles, it is clear that in order to engage those young people *we must reflect their interests.* They need the opportunity to explore music using the tools and processes that have been used to generate the music they are listening to, that they see as authentic.

Launched by Musical Futures in conjunction with Ableton in 2019, the aim of the Tech Champions program was to engage ten schools in exploring and developing innovative approaches within their classrooms using authentic tools. The aims for this project have been bold—we have sought to change the culture of music education within schools to reflect the musical interests of our young people. For that purpose, we worked with Ableton to provide the ten schools with Push hardware, Live software, and technical and pedagogical support in using it with classes. Ableton's Live software is very innovative in the way it works, offering the opportunity for a more exploratory, less linear way of creating music. The Push hardware that works with Live is also very tactile, it lights up, and learners can press and play.

Among the Tech Champions teachers, there were some who were already experienced with using music technology in their classrooms, whilst others knew very little about music technology but were keen to develop their confidence and knowledge. Putting those teachers together as a group to share ideas and create a community of practice provided a support network for

Figure 5.2   Musical Futures logo

those who were less confident. The role of Musical Futures and Ableton within the project was to provide experience, resources, approaches, and a pedagogy to develop their confidence to make effective use of this equipment within their own classrooms.

The Tech Champions teachers helped Musical Futures to trial and develop resources within their own classrooms. The mantra of 'take this, use it, innovate and share' was central to the project. It provided a starting point, which said 'take the Push pad and Ableton Live, use this resource we have developed and explore how we can improve it, or develop your own resource and share it with everyone'. This provided a rich set of resources that had been tested and refined in the classroom. The project included a celebration of music tech at Spirit Studios in Manchester, which included performances from the students in participating schools, workshops, and an opportunity for young people to interact with people in the music industry. Sadly, the pandemic curtailed aspects of the Tech Champions project. Instead, we were able to organise an online festival of learning event, #MUFUTV, in 2020, which was so successful we repeated it in 2021. The Tech Champion project demonstrated what can be achieved when barriers are removed. The legacy of the project is a large bank of resources and a strong commitment from

Ableton in supporting music learning in schools. They offer a Push scheme for schools in addition to providing Ableton Live to schools free of charge.

The world of music continues to grow and change, and our role is to ensure we continue to support teachers in moving with it, whether that is a new genre, a different approach to songwriting, or writing music for the screen. Each of these provides opportunities for teachers to integrate technology within their classroom work in different ways. Our role is to connect the teachers with the music in an authentic way and create a resource to support them that we know will work in the classroom so that they can connect authentically with their learners. By de-mystifying the approach, we hope that music teachers will not find it too daunting and will instead see it as a developmental, interesting journey.

The Challenges of Authentic Technology Use in the Music Classroom

If classroom music lessons are to reflect the musical interests of young people, then the use of technology in an authentic & relevant way *should* be ubiquitous in the music classroom. In our experience, it isn't and we believe there are four main obstacles to that happening:

1. Teacher Education

Many music teachers have experienced a classical route through their education—often having instrumental lessons at school, followed by studying music at A-level and university before completing a PGCE and commencing their teaching practice. This can often lead to teachers replicating their own experiences of education within their classrooms. Entry requirements for PGCE courses and teaching roles are often written with the traditional music educator in mind, although there are some exceptions. Candidates for music teaching roles are sometimes asked to sight read or perform a piece of music on a traditional instrument. The problem is, that is looking for a certain kind of person: a certain skill set, which may not pick up those who are highly skilled DJs or users of music technology.

There is also an issue around the support offered to Early Career Teachers (ECTs): the training for them is increasingly being directed at a national level and tends to be quite broad and focused on classroom practice across all subjects. This can hinder ECTs in exploring subject-specific approaches, or stifle the freedom to experiment in their teaching.

2. Skills, Experience, and Authenticity

The second obstacle to the more effective use of music technology in mainstream music education is the need for *authenticity*. There is particular software and hardware required, specific skills, understanding of the genre: these are all imperative if the students are going to find the music authentic in relation to the music they usually listen to.

There are also issues around what is acceptable in the classroom in terms of lyrical content and imagery. For example, many young people today are interested in the subgenre known as *trap*, which has strong associations with illegality. Many songs contain prolific swearing, references to drug and weapon use, misogyny, and racism, which can be really difficult for a teacher to navigate. How can we authentically honour that genre and that students' interests in a classroom where we are also expected to teach values? There is a genuine conflict there, we think.

Although many teachers realise that they need to diversify their own skillset, they can be a bit unsure about where to start. When music is ever-changing, and many teachers just do not know where to start, which is what led us to start up the Tech Champions project and what drives the resources and training that we offer.

3. Classroom Curriculum and Equipment

The third issue is around the curriculum diet offered to learners and the equipment available to them. Within the music curriculum, there can be a tendency to focus solely on looking back historically at music. We are not suggesting that the music of the past should be ignored, as it can provide a rich experience for young people. However, we feel strongly that we need to first start with the interests of the young people to 'get them hooked', then from there we can expand their interests and listening, once they are interested and invested in the world of music.

The other issue around structure is equipment/software and ensuring it is compatible with school networks or systems. This can be complex—when we have previously explored developing resources for DJing, for example, there are not only many different kinds of DJ controllers and software (with different versions of the same software confusing things further), but the software is not always compatible with a school network (mainly because the software has not been designed for networked computers) and so on. The equipment can also be expensive and thus prohibitive for schools to invest in especially considering the current issues around funding in schools. Overall, the structure at both individual school level and at national level is not conducive to music technology being better integrated into school education.

4. School Leadership

Musical Futures has always constituted a somewhat radical challenge to music education norms and, in some senses, wider educational norms. In our experience of working with teachers, they often cite this challenge to the norm as a barrier to implementing changes within their schools. Sometimes these barriers can be nothing more than the perception of individual teachers (in terms of concerns around Ofsted and presumptions about their attitudes toward this way of learning etc.), but sometimes there are very real barriers in terms of restrictions implemented by senior leadership teams who do not fully understand the needs of a creative, practical subject. For example, in our training courses, we hear regularly from teachers that they *have* to make use of written work for students to record their learning, or that they *must have* a particular structure to their lesson, or they *must* assess in a particular way. Many of these approaches simply hinder a teacher's ability to get on with practical music learning. However, Christopher Stevens (the new lead HMI for music education in the United Kingdom) has recently emphasised the importance of 'developing their progression in technical ability, their constructive knowledge, and their expressive knowledge. The key point is that it's about getting better' (Clifford, 2022). These three elements (the technical, the constructive, and the expressive) formed the three pillars at the heart of Ofsted's 2022 'Research review' of music (Ofsted, 2022). Indeed, Christopher Stevens has recently done work with Music Mark, one of the United Kingdom's leading music education organisations, running sessions for teachers that have outlined expectations from a music lesson: our understanding is that this outline, in keeping with Ofsted's 2022 review document, emphasised making music as a technical, constructive, and expressive activity.

Many of our Musical Futures Champion Teachers have successfully navigated Ofsted, through having a clear vision for their subject and being able to demonstrate high levels of learning and engagement from learners. This suggests that the fear of Ofsted disapproval is very much misplaced: Ofsted are open to music being treated as a practical subject with practical outcomes, and we have evidence (from our Champion Teachers' experiences) to show that inspectors respond positively to music lessons that do not result in pieces of writing, do not prioritise abstract knowledge over practical activity, and are open to contemporary popular music of all kinds.

Conclusion

We would agree with Robert H. Woody (2022) that music is not just a nice-to-have thing, it is actually a basic human right. By saying music is just-a-nice-thing it allows it to get sidelined in places like schools, because it is not something for *all*. Then, when times get hard in the financial sense, it becomes easy to reduce it. Music, for us, is a human right that we feel it is our duty as educators to provide for students the opportunity to be involved in.

In order to make that happen, all of us in the world of music education need to be open to music-making that reflects contemporary popular music—that which our young people are listening to. Our role at Musical Futures is to support teachers in this challenge. We encourage variety in music education and see no reason why encompassing beatboxing, DJing, rapping, and music tech should not be achievable. We always ask ourselves, what can we do to facilitate teachers to provide those experiences for their learners? How can we provide training to give teachers the confidence they need? Which artists and professionals can we engage with to ensure what we are doing is authentic? We encourage the teachers to realise that they *can* use music technology to meet the obligations in terms of their curriculum delivery but, additionally, to realise that using music tech can allow them to respond to their students' interests.

It is clear to us that there is a challenge from young people for music teachers to continue to widen the curriculum—Musical Futures seeks to support them in making that happen. We recognise that this represents a major challenge for many music teachers and that there are accountability structures that can often make the approaches we have suggested in this chapter more difficult. However, the arts never remain static, and neither should we. There is a need for teachers to be prepared to learn something new. Take trap, the aforementioned subgenre of music that Martin has recently been working on with his learners—at the start, Martin had no idea how to make a trap drumbeat: it just seemed very complicated. However, after multiple efforts (many of which were simply not good enough, Martin felt), the last one was kind of alright. (The key is in the hi-hat patterns!) If teachers are willing to make the effort, then it can make a big difference to the experience of the students they are working with and encourage them to continue to pursue their interests in music.

A lot of courage is needed for some teachers in those schools who place particular requirements upon teachers that are not appropriate for a practical subject. It is not easy to say to a senior leader 'look, I really don't think this is the best way of achieving this in my subject—what about trying it like this which will ultimately achieve the same aim'. This is where our Champion Teachers provide advocacy and support—they are happy to share their experiences and explain how they work with their senior leadership teams.

Bravery among teachers and trust in teachers are what is needed. The Ofsted inspection framework *does* leave more space for more potential freedom for teachers: the teaching force should take that as an opportunity to innovate and embrace the exciting challenges and opportunities that the world of music holds for us and our young people.

In the end, our core message is that *every child that walks into your classroom is a musician and every music lesson should be focused on helping to develop this musicality in an engaging, practical, and authentic way.* If we all keep that in mind, music education will be a vibrant, life-changing experience for many more young people.

References

Clifford, H. (2022) *Christopher Stevens interview: Living up to high standards.* https://www.musicteachermagazine.co.uk/features/article/christopher-stevens-interview-living-up-to-high-standards.

Green, L. (2008). *Music, Informal learning and the school: A new classroom pedagogy.* Abingdon: Routledge.

Hallam, S., A. Creech, and H. McQueen. (2011). 'Teachers' perceptions of the impact on students of the Musical Futures approach. *Music Education Research* 19(3): 263–275. doi: 10.1080/14613808.2015.1108299.

Ofsted. (2022). *Research review: Music.* https://www.gov.uk/government/publications/research-review-series-music/research-review-series-music.

Woody, R. H. (2022). Are musicians special? Should they want to be? Musicality is fundamental to humanity, not a special talent. https://www.psychologytoday.com/gb/blog/live-in-concert/202211/are-musicians-special-should-they-want-be.

6

Rethinking Learning with Future DJs and Virtuoso

Is a Decentralised, Community-Curated Curriculum the Future of Learning?

Austen Smart and Scott Smart

This chapter tells the story of our journey from school to practice and back to the educational world. Having found music at school a joke, we nonetheless became successful DJs running our own label and travelling the world. In 2016 we formed FutureDJs, in the hope of opening up a new future for music in schools. At first, we met the answer 'no' everywhere, but we were hopeful and eventually met some success in our aim of reinvigorating music education in schools. In this chapter, we discuss some of our experiences and present our next move, which we hope will prove to be the most pivotal one we will have made. Our long-term strategy now is to use the overarching DAO concept to truly unlock the gateway to the creator economy, to demystify the music industry, and to complete our mission to transform creative education. This mission is a central pillar to our post-FutureDJs organisation named Virtuoso. We believe creative arts education has the potential to be radically transformed. We believe everything we do and have done supports the aim of inclusive methods in music education.

Introduction

Our journey through music education has not been a conventional one: we were not involved in music during our school years at all, really. Nonetheless, at times (and particularly in the last eight years) we have interacted at a deep level with UK examination boards, schools, and government, not to forget all

Austen Smart and Scott Smart, *Rethinking Learning with FutureDJs and Virtuoso* In: *Music for Inclusion and Healing in Schools and Beyond*. Edited by: Pete Dale, Pamela Burnard, and Raphael Travis Jr., Oxford University Press.
© Oxford University Press 2023. DOI: 10.1093/oso/9780197692677.003.0007

the teachers, students, and parents we have worked with along the way. We have worked at all these different levels with all these different stakeholders and will report some of our conclusions in this chapter.

It is the centralisation of (music) curriculum development that we have now come to believe needs radical transformation with a view to ultimately becoming decentralised (more on that later) and more relevant to and more in tune with the music that young people listen to today.

The requirement to become a professional artist in today's fast-moving creator world reduces pretty much all barriers to entry. This is something we believe is both a blessing and a curse for a modern-day aspiring musician. Surrounded by hopes of fame and fortune, today's young musician does not have the skills and pathways to get ahead regardless of the fact they are constantly invited to participate in platforms such as YouTube, TikTok, Spotify, and Epidemic. This has become our focus with Virtuoso and is the main topic at the heart of the present chapter.

School Days

Let us take a step back and look at how we came to this realization, what it means, and why it even matters. We attended a state school called Knutsford High, and like many young students we were disengaged, bored, lacking direction, and without role models to look to. Our music lessons were a joke. It was seen as the 'mess about' class at school—something we came to learn is a nationwide problem, not just today but also historically. We will never forget sitting in the managing director of Warner Chappell's office and hearing them say, 'music at school was the mess around class'. Here they were, four of the most powerful people in the music industry who have collectively shaped hundreds, if not thousands, of artists' careers—and yet music at school had completely failed to engage them in the subject that would be at the core of their working lives.

Funnily enough, like the managing director of Warner Chappell, we too were really into music—even if our school did not recognise it. We would make mixtapes for the common room and produce beats on entry-level DAWs (digital audio workstations) such as Apple's Garageband. Scott eventually began DJing when he left school to get a job around seventeen years of age. For the next several years we tried to find our way in the club world, from hanging outside backstage areas to get our music heard by well-known DJs, to spending all of our money earned in record shops on vinyls to play at the weekend. For a while I would write about DJs and take photographs of friends' nights, but wherever we went we would always study the DJ, knowing one day we wanted to be on the stage. We just had to work out how.

Career Development and Beginnings of Future DJs

Our career began to take off, we flew around the world, set up our own label, had collaborations with Groove Armada, and hosted masterclasses with Armin Van Burren, eventually culminating in fifty releases on our own label called Danse Club Records, which we eventually licensed to Armada Music. It was an exciting period and one we look back on with great fondness, playing clubs like fabric. Living in London gave us a true appreciation of the power of sound, curation, and music and the responsibility a DJ has to the people on the dancefloor. It ended abruptly in 2016 when we changed our name from Brodanse to Austen/Scott (because we wanted to break into America and because the term 'Bro' had a bad connotation), and we were forced to re-think what we wanted to do. And then we saw an opportunity and ran with it.

The UK examination board, AQA (Assessment and Qualifications Alliance), had introduced DJing onto their GCSE (General Certificate of Secondary Education) music syllabus, perhaps in a hope that more young people would take music as an option at GCSE. We realised very quickly that very few teachers would have the skills, knowledge, or potentially even appetite to teach DJing. That is where we came in: together with our friends Shaun and Joe Marsden, we formed an organisation called FutureDJs in 2016, specifically to provide specialist DJ educators in schools. It all started with Scott teaching the first 1-2-1 peripatetic DJ lessons to students in four schools across the country. We had found our early adopters and were confident to press on.

We were met with the word 'no' almost everywhere. Those few that did said 'yes' invited us in to do an assembly—we would perform in front of hundreds of children and at the end ask 'who wants to learn?' Without fail, 60+ percent of children would raise their hands, and, of those, more than half were female. This response was staggering, but it did not necessarily mean we would start teaching in that school. Often, we would get knocked back at more senior levels due to a blatant disregard for DJ culture or, more often, a lack of funding. Here we were, another roadshow, another three hundred teenagers excited and another week passing without growing numbers for the business. This was despite our partner Pioneer DJ donating all the decks to us for use in the schools. Hundreds if not thousands of teachers never responded to our letters.

Signs of Success with FutureDJs

We were hopeful: in the schools we did get into, we would have some real success, since engagement levels were very high, with children often learning with us for several terms. Many students would step into the music department for the first time and would start to engage more widely at school. Confidence was building all over the country, and after two years our organisation Future DJs was responsible for teaching one thousand lessons a week, with a nationwide delivery team of peripatetic teachers.

Although the eighty schools that had taken our programme was well short of the projected one thousand schools we had hoped for, we had over sixty peripatetic DJs teaching our curriculum across the country; no one had ever attempted to pull this off before. A couple of students were even starting to take GCSE exams using DJ decks as a performance instrument. We wrote a book, *How to DJ*, published by Faber Music in 2020. We also developed graded DJ exams in conjunction with the London College of Music, a world first. Yes, you can take Grade 1, Grade 3, and Grade 5 exams for DJing in the United Kingdom today. But ultimately it was not enough. Still we were dealing with this STEM mentality, in large part because of the United Kingdom's EBacc system that does not reward and recognise the arts in the same way as core subjects. In 2016 the Education Policy Institute (EPI) showed that the number of entries to arts subject GCSE's in 2016 had fallen to the lowest seen in a decade (Johnes, 2016) with EBacc being regarded by participants as placing pressure on arts entries.

So, as more children said yes, and more schools said no, we started to look to new models to reach those students most at need. And then our hand was forced: almost overnight our business FutureDJs had the tap turned off in March 2021, when the COVID-19 pandemic kicked into full force.

Virtuoso

Our plans for digitalisation accelerated at an unprecedented rate, and we moved from teaching one-to-one to one-to-many. We realised we could teach much more than DJing so rebranded to Virtuoso. Just before the 2020 pandemic began, we built the world's first virtual music classroom, using state-of-the-art technology to provide a truly interactive and engaging experience; again, no one had done anything like this before. We began teaching children remotely and offering remote DJ exams, which resulted in a 95 percent pass rate. This was part of a project that was grant funded by Innovate UK in 2020. We also began running 'how to teach DJing and music production' CPD sessions with teachers. We had success with Music Hubs such as Wiltshire, who had high levels of engagement with teachers in the local area. What enabled this success? The leader of the hub Sophie Amstell was deeply engaged and passionate, allocating some funding to the sessions. The work with students ultimately met an end, however, when technology requirements proved to be too high of a barrier for students in the hardest-to-reach areas in society.

Our next move proved to be the most pivotal and has become a central pillar to our beliefs on the future of music education. We began to

Figure 6.1 Recording Carl Cox's Virtuoso masterclass—Learn how to build the mindset of a top DJ

ask really well-known and highly successful artists to become teachers. We assured them we would structure the courses allowing them to show their brilliant skills. We experimented with live remote events—we ran an initiative with Radio 1 DJ Jaguar to engage one thousand female, trans, and non-binary students with electronic music. This video content, which we named 'Future1000', proved to be the most successful we had created up to that point. Our beliefs deepened and in turn so did our methodology. Eventually, fifty plus artists came through our doors, from techno legend Carl Cox to popstar and singer-songwriter Aluna of the electronic music duo AlunaGeorge. We believed these artists were going to be the most inspiring teachers in the world, and more importantly they were the real deal.

We were able to pull out actionable insights from them and produce educational content that could now be subscribed to at low costs, or for free in the case of schools who needed the help. The response was wonderful: in the case of Jaguar and Future1000, we will never forget the power of the connection created directly with students who were normally isolated and without community. Suddenly, students were learning directly from well-known artists and asking the most important questions to help achieve their own learning goals. We had honed a unique craft of turning artists into educators.

However, this only laid the foundations. The next part was what we believe will prove to be the most important step in widescale adoption. We began to ask questions like, how do we build content around the learners like we did with Future1000, how do we individualise the learning journey, and how do learners curate and share their own learning experiences and actionable insights (much like those in the early days of our own journey)? Today we ask members (learners) who they want to learn from, and we are building unique user experiences for different cohorts depending on their preferences or individual goals and ambitions. One of the biggest challenges with Virtuoso has been to curate the content and artists that learners want.

Our mission with Virtuoso now is to truly unlock the gateway to the creator economy, and to demystify the music industry. Our goal is big. We want to enable fifty million creators across the planet to become artists in the next ten years through structured, high-quality educational content with well-known artists/best teachers at the core of teaching. And we want members to be able to vote on the learning that they require in today's fast-moving digital

Figure 6.2 Award-winning DJ and producer MJ Cole outside of the Virtuoso studios with founders Austen and Scott Smart

world. But there is one final step to making this work, and that is handing everything over to the community of learners and the artists.

The Future Is DAO

We have been looking at the long tail of creators and communities. A concept popularized by Chris Anderson in October 2004 is as follows: 'Forget squeezing millions from a few megahits at the top of the charts. The future of entertainment is in the millions of niche markets at the shallow end of

Figure 6.3 BBC Radio One DJ Jaguar and Austen Smart delivering a Future1000 CPD session to teachers around the United Kingdom

the bitstream'. Our lens however is a radical new funding model through which we believe creative arts education can be transformed. It is called a Decentralised Autonomous Organisation (DAO). DAOs are 'blockchain-native, decentralized organizations that are collectively owned and managed by their members via smart contracts' (Bellavitis *et al.*, 2022: 1) Today, DAOs 'are fuelling new business models for decentralized platforms and have revolutionized crowdfunding' (ibid.). The DAO we plan to create dubbed 'WhatClass' will be designed to curate arts/creative/education projects through a social token design system where users earn tokens for curating education content and can split the benefits with both the creators/artists and teachers. We believe creative arts education has the potential to be radically transformed if adoption becomes more widespread and environments be-come more interoperable. We believe that decentralization is a solution that could enable creators to connect directly with learners and communities at scale (and vice versa), and this will eventually reduce the role and power of middlemen and outdated centralised education institutions if adopted by creators.

If we were able to transition creative arts education and the funding of cre-ative arts education to a DAO, then this would enable ownership from day

Figure 6.4 The moment the first *How to DJ* books were published by Faber Music following years of writing and editing with co-author Tom Dent

one for learners and educators. For the first time, learners will be able to par-take in the growth and success of the educational content and communities they are a part of, from the beginning. And we believe this could include teachers, artists, and creators who are looking for ways to fund innovative, rich music education and create additional micro economies in the form of grants from the community, which could include industry giants backing on-chain education projects. This would mean that individuals have new opportunities to earn a living by participating in these communities both online and offline. This approach enables volunteers, teachers, artists, and educators to be rewarded for the value and contributions they bring. a16z aka Andreessen Horowitz, a leading venture capital firm from Silicon Valley, reported 'video games . . . use a "play-to-earn" model' because 'the unique digital artifacts created in web3 games can be owned by players—and bought and sold by them—virtual economies are springing up in which people can generate income for themselves by playing' (a16z, 2021: 28). Imagine that happening in learning and educational content, so that it becomes collectible and valuable: this, we believe, would be a game-changer. We must make learning inspiring, fun, and collectable.

Decentralised Autonomous Organisation (DAO) in Practice

The DAO structure allows members (including teachers and educators) to benefit from it, and this would provide additional funding to education and creative arts in areas most of need and with high levels of digital poverty. This, we think, could address certain issues we have seen over the last several years in UK music education, such as lack of funding and narrowness of options. The implications for music education (and, more particularly, for inclusion of Hip Hop, techno, grime, and so on) are significant: the DAO can make a difference in this regard because, through joint development of content, opportunities for active learning and making choices (making beats or creating in a genre of your own choosing) are enhanced. Opportunities for joint development of content have often been exploited by marginalised and sometimes impoverished communities (think Bronx in the 1970s, for example, where block parties birthed Hip Hop). However, this has tended to happen in particular pockets of the globe: a DAO member, by contrast, is part of a global community. We believe that, with the rising adoption of the internet around the world, geographical constraints will eventually fall further away, giving users opportunities to work and learn online in manners that just were not previously available.

According to Marty Kaplan, a professor at the University of Southern California, 'Throughout the 20th century, cool was mostly a Western thing. From flappers to hip-hop, people looked to cities like London, New York and Paris for fashion, music and entertainment' (The Economist, 2022). However, according to Kaplan, 'After the cold war, as the world grew richer and more connected, many people feared that the West's cultural dominance would keep growing and ultimately produce a global monoculture'. Kaplan has been reported to hold the view that 'The opposite has happened. Today, a teenager sitting in New York is as likely to listen to k-pop and Afrobeats tracks, a sort of west African pop, as American hip-hop'. Pop culture has gone multipolar, to quote the title of the article from which Kaplan's views have been sourced. We believe that the same could and should happen for music

Figure 6.5 After two years of cancelled festivals, FutureDJs student Amelia Warren opens the mainstage of Amsterdam Open Air festival

education, but in order to do that a highly scalable, decentralised platform is required given the huge size of the problem.

A music education DAO could provide a path toward community governance and curation and inclusion: 'disintermediation' and 'decentralization' are keywords in research on the DAO concept (Zhao *et al.*, 2022; Bellavitis *et al.*, 2022); they are, to say the least, words that imply a situation ripe for greater inclusion and choice. The DAO we are working on would be the Web3 version of a cooperative: a community of people (who care about creative arts education) that contribute to the joint development of content, rather than an out-of-date centralised curriculum being engineered and prescribed to individuals who do not engage with it.

A concept defined by Balaji S. Srinivasan, 'Win and help win', is a good model for learners and famous people alike and is something that we believe can apply to smaller creators with much smaller audiences as well. Can an inspiring music teacher from Hackney, London, win like that? We think it is possibly so, yes, and we think that a DAO structure could help such a teacher a great deal.

Figure 6.6 Outside Pacha, Ibiza, with DJs Green Velvet, Heidi, Derrick Carter, Coco Cole, and Scott Smart (left to right) with Austen Smart (behind) in 2014

Web3 Communities

The future could be a teacher raising money from the community to fund a new music-education project such as a student-owned record label. Or an Afrobeat artist raising the funds to teach their production techniques. The teacher might then help to build value for the students, the school, and the local community. The future can be a micro-community of dub-techno fans commissioning a studio-produced course by niche artist, Maurizio. It could also be a community, all voting on producing a course on Japanese Italo-Disco—and owning it together. In the process of all this, an incredible modern Multipolar curriculum would be built and shared with other learners in the community: that is our vision—everybody teaching one another and co-creating/sharing work with each other that covers all modern music.

Web3 is 'convenient shorthand for the project of rewiring how the web works, using blockchain to change how information is stored, shared, and owned' (Stackpole, 2022). A Web3 community membership could eventually become a valuable financial asset, funded by social capital and belief in a collected mission, in this case to transform creative education. Each contributor—no matter how small—can retain royalties tied to the project's ongoing success. The curation of education could replace centralized out-of-touch education, reduce low-value redundant work, and crowd-fund high-value unique work in creative arts and education.

Ryan Selkis, founder and author of the Messari report, states in his 2022 crypto thesis (Selkis, 2022) that Web3 does three things differently; we believe these pillars can help learning become a personalised and inspirational experience:

1. It creates incentives for portable, open user-generated data. Breaking the Web 2.0 companies. In our use case, we assert this could include expensive education models run by universities and PLCs such as Pearson Education. This in theory would open up a universe of possibilities in creative education.
2. It allows people to reflect on what they want to curate at any given time (this may be possible to achieve in a Web2 model).
3. DAOs will allow learners to align with a tribe or a 'signal booster' (we refer to them as icons) and build a curated education content market around that icon or tribe.

With regards to point 3, Selkis states, 'this opens up the possibilities for alternatives to Google Search that looks less like page rank' (Selkis, 2022). In the case of our creative education DAO this could lead to a more custom user experience tailored specifically to the learner. Filters can be toggled on and off based on one's learning needs, and learners can circle around inspiring teachers that they enjoy learning from. Because of our journey, we have long believed learning should be a personalised and individual experience. This is something repeatedly argued by the late, leading academic and international government advisor to the arts Sir Ken Robinson, who at the time of writing holds the record for the most watched Ted talk of all time—he long argued creative education does not need reform, but needs total transformation.

The Creator Dilemma

Once you have seen the creator dilemma, the music-education dilemma, and looked at these emerging technologies, it is hard to imagine a world where this shift does not happen. We went far with graded DJ exams, but we did not transform things radically enough—in fact we only played further into the failing system.

Now we have the opportunity to solve a world problem of funding for the arts and creative education. We would be able to reduce cost of capital for future education projects such as new music curriculums and build a new funding model for music education all whilst scaling learners/members. These for instance could be the building and opening of new artist-led creative departments in schools and local community centres across the world.

These tools offer a direct way for communities and schools to earn income, while also providing mediums to share (and multiply) the value with its members. 'While Web2 is passive, Web3 makes it active, thus turning communities into functioning micro-economies' (Coopahtroopa and Kinjal Shah, 2021). However, our firsthand experience is of an archaic school system that is already decades behind in many respects with technology and the way people learn, and given the barriers to widescale adoption of crypto, we believe schools will be at the tail end of the adoption curve. Therefore, a digital first school for creators, with curated community education, must be built where people of all ages and backgrounds can be reached from a young age and given the world's best creative education before they are sent on the path of out-of-date music/arts lessons at school like so many millions before them.

Summary

In this chapter, we have tried to contextualise what we have been doing with endeavours such as FutureDJs and, more recently, Virtuoso, as well as Brodanse and our activities as DJs. We also acknowledged that music education failed to engage us despite our interest in music, which was strong at the time and has stayed at the heart of our working and creative lives. We are not the only ones: as we have indicated, you can be near the top of the music industry but have learned effectively nothing about music from the school education system.

We think that needs to change, and we think a DAO-based approach is the one that needs to be seriously considered for a root and branch makeover. There is inclusivity at the heart of the DAO concept: and inclusive music education is more practicable if learning and creating/co-creating are mixed up and inter-contextually shared without geographical constraint. (You are the only DnB fan in your class? Teacher does not know anything about it? You need an online learning community to work and share with.) Learning communities can be functioning micro-economies, with the word 'economy' taken to include (although without being limited to) the financial sense.

We have argued for the DAO in this chapter because we believe it is where things will go. We believe it is the future of learning, and we think this will be a positive development. It is our ambition to contribute to thinking about the way things ought to develop but, perhaps most importantly, to contribute to showing (through the shared practice of Virtuoso, for example) that a different learning matrix is possible. We certainly would assert that this matrix would support inclusion within music education. Genres from hip-hop to house, grime to techno, trap to K-Pop could all find their place in a virtual spread of learning that puts the interests of the learning/sharing/co-creating person at the heart of the decision-making processes. More choice means more inclusion. More choice means learning together. Choices have the potential to be limitless.

References

a16z. (2021). *How to win the future: An agenda for the third generation of the internet* https://a16z.com/wp-content/uploads/2021/10/How-to-Win-the-Future-1.pdf.

Bellavitis, C., Fisch, C. and Momtaz, P. (2022). The rise of decentralized autonomous organizations (DAOs): a first empirical glimpse. *Venture Capital,* 25(2): 187–203. https://doi.org/10.1080/13691066.2022.2116797.

Coopahtroopa, Shah K. (2021). *The rise of micro-economies.* https://coopahtroopa.mirror.xyz/gWY6Kfebs9wHdfoZZswfiLTBVzfKiyFaIwNf2q8JpgI.

Johnes, R. (2016). *Entries to arts subjects at key stage 4: Curriculum and qualifications report.* https://epi.org.uk/publications-and-research/entries-arts-subjects-key-stage-4/.

Selkis, R. (2022). *Crypto theses for 2022: Key trends, people, companies, and projects to watch across the crypto landscape, with predictions for 2022.* https://messari.io/crypto-theses-for-2022.

Stackpole, T. (2022). *What is Web3? Your guide to (what could be) the future of the internet* https://hbr.org/2022/05/what-is-web3.

The Economist. (2022). *How pop culture went multipolar: Fears that globalisation would lead to a worldwide monoculture have proven utterly wrong.* https://www.economist.com/international/2022/10/06/how-pop-culture-went-multipolar.

Zhao, X., Ai P., Lai, F., Luo, X. and Benitez, J. (2022). Task management in decentralized autonomous organization. *Journal of Operations Management*, 68(6): 649–674. https://onlinelibrary.wiley.com/doi/10.1002/joom.1179.

PART II
HEALING AND WELLNESS

7

Power and Connection

Rawz

I'm an MC and poet from Oxford. I first discovered lyric writing in my early teens, and I quickly began to find it essential—a way to channel my emotions and organise my thoughts. A self-guided therapy. I've not studied therapy academically, but I developed my own strategies for processing difficult experiences and situations, some of which played out over a number of years. I live with the benefits of this therapy I created for myself every day.

I grew up in Oxford. I don't feel like I am 'from' anywhere else—it is home. When people think about Oxford, I know that they probably get an image of the university and the world-famous dreaming spires, the prestige and elitism. But I grew up very much on the other side of Oxford. The place I grew up in is actually one of the 10 percent most-deprived areas in the United Kingdom, according to the government's index of multiple deprivations. Things like poverty and crime are higher, and life expectancy is lower than the rest of the city/county/country—it is that stereotypical council-estate area. A lot of people in these areas carry trauma, often multiple traumas. It's argued that being in this environment is itself trauma-inducing. That makes sense to me; I've experienced some of that. Growing up, we were always in financial trouble, and I saw the emotional effect that had on my mum, who was really the only adult in my life. There were mental health issues in my family, and violence and the temptations of crime were never far from my close circles. Along with trouble at school, my friends' various dramas, and other miscellaneous stuff, it is safe to say I found some tough times. One thing that would always bring me back to where I wanted to be mentally was music.

Teachers

Music had always been a big part of my home environment; listening to music was something that I always loved doing. It had been at the back of

Rawz, *Power and Connection* In: *Music for Inclusion and Healing in Schools and Beyond.* Edited by: Pete Dale, Pamela Burnard, and Raphael Travis Jr., Oxford University Press. © Oxford University Press 2023.
DOI: 10.1093/oso/9780197692677.003.0008

Figure 7.1 Rawz

Figure 7.2 Rawz Performing on Stage

my mind for as long as I can remember, but it was in my teens, aged about fourteen or fifteen, that I started to consciously think about making music myself. I think I was drawn to Hip Hop lyrics because they talked about a lot of things that I was going through; poverty, dad not being around, violence, police harassment, friends being so close they felt more like family than my blood relatives did, being on the outside with no hope of finding a way in. I didn't really hear any other forum where that was being talked about in a way I could relate to. I wanted to tell my story, to start writing my own lyrics. But I didn't know anyone at all that was even trying to make music; I had no guidance, or any real sense of where to begin.

The way that I figured out how it was done was by learning other rappers' tracks. I think the first was Coolio's 'Gangster's Paradise'—I bought it for my mum for her birthday. She liked the song, but I think my reasons for choosing this present were at least a little bit selfish. I spent the next weeks and months listening to it on repeat for hours at a time, learning every single word and trying to figure out 'How does he do this? Where do the rhymes land? How does it fit with the beat?' I learned by copying. I did not have any access to instrumentals—that is something people have quite easy access to nowadays with YouTube and so on, but I can remember having to rap over people like Tupac and Notorious B.I.G. so I could try out my verses.

I used to truant from school a lot. The first few years at secondary school were tough for me; apart from the obvious, there were a lot of difficult changes happening in my life, and I think it just all got to be too much. Looking back, I see the school really let me down. They had low expectations of what I could achieve, and I got no support at all. It didn't seem like anyone cared if I skipped lessons, or even the whole day. They completely neglected my emotional needs and their duty to make sure I was safe. To me the thing that says it all is the fact that I dropped music as a subject as soon as I could— I knew I loved music, and I was interested in making it, but I hated the way that it was taught in school. It was so uninspiring and geared heavily towards kids who could read music and were having lessons on piano, clarinet, or some other posh instrument outside of school (paid for by their parents of course). People like me were only allowed to play the coconuts or the wood block alongside them, if we did anything at all—it was just a boring 'mess around' lesson. Plus, to me the teacher was crazy!

When it came to General Certificate of Secondary Education grades (GCSEs), my school didn't enter me into some of them, and the ones they did enter me into I did not do too well in. Although I got close to the highest possible marks in some of the tests (the highest possible mark on my spoken

English test, which I made up on the spot), due to the examination structure at the time, I basically left school with no qualifications and went into un-skilled manual work. I was making bits of money wherever I could and not getting very much fulfilment from life at all. I was just trying to exist and con-tribute to my mum's household bills whenever I could.

All through that time, I guess I always had a hope in the back of my mind that music was somehow going to work out for me. I was still always writing lyrics, and visualising a me that was good enough and confident enough to per-form them on stage. Back then I was doing temporary agency work, picking in warehouses, and labouring on building sites. I would write bars in my head and have to memorise those lyrics as I was walking around the warehouse, or doing whatever manual task on site. When I would get home, I had to write them down straightaway before they ran out of my head. I *had* to. It felt like some-thing very important. Back then, not a lot of people knew that I was writing.

Mentors

My first encounter with people on my estate who were into music was actu-ally through drum-and-bass (DnB) DJing. My friend's older sister's boyfriend was well into DnB; he had taught a lot of my mates at the time to mix drum and bass before I met them, so they were all into it too. I guess he was a bit of a mentor. Everyone was getting their own little DJ set-ups, and we would make the rounds of our smoke-filled bedrooms trying out new mixes and listening to the new records in each other's collections. When our mentor got a new pair of decks, I bought his old ones off him for about 20 or 40 quid; it seemed like a lot of money at the time, but looking back, he gave me a great deal. I've got so much to thank that guy for, but I can't even remember his name now. I've still got the decks; they are not set up anymore though. Once, they were the centrepiece of my bedroom, alongside my collection of speakers rescued from skips and various acquaintances' old surround-sound and hifi systems—the number of speakers I had attached to my little hifi was ridic-ulous! I started off mixing a bit of drum and bass, but quite quickly moved into Hip Hop—it was more my rhythm, my speed. I could appreciate DnB, but it was always something I listened to mainly because my mates loved it. The big plus of getting Hip Hop records was that the B-side would often have the instrumentals. I made a few tapes using those beats, messing about with a couple of friends and recording lyrics through headphones. We did share those tapes with a few trusted others; these were the first times I ever heard my words and voice played back to me and saw other people's reactions to them. This was in the very early 2000s, around 2001 or 2002.

Up until that point I hadn't really shown anybody my lyrics, or even told anyone I was doing it apart from maybe two or three of my closest friends. They were complimentary but didn't really get it. It was definitely something I was doing mainly for myself. I look at it in the way that people keep a diary—they hide it, keep it locked away. I used to hide my writing book underneath my bed or in a drawer in my desk that my mum wasn't allowed to look in. It was definitely something I was doing very privately in the beginning, but in my late teens or maybe early twenties, I found other people who were interested in making music and writing.

Sharing

I eventually found connections with other people to make music with more earnestly. A friend (Stanmore—who is unfortunately no longer with us following an episode of police brutality and prolonged multi-layered systemic neglect) introduced me to someone he knew who was making Hip Hop mixtapes—getting acapellas and remixing them on different beats, then burning his own CDs using a PC, putting them out under the name Danger One. His dad was a reggae and dancehall DJ, and Danger was approaching his Hip Hop mixes very much from a dancehall perspective, even blending the two genres together at times. I had never encountered anything like it before. I found out that he was getting loads of instrumentals—he was downloading them from the early file-sharing networks like LimeWire, and this was very interesting to me. It was in his bedroom that I had my first experience of performing lyrics on a real microphone; he had borrowed one from his neighbour Barry (who was a drum-and-bass DJ) to record voiceovers for his mixes, and it just happened to be set up when I went round one day. We were all messing about with it and I decided to drop some of my verses that I had memorised. They went down very well. Almost immediately we formed a group, but had no clue where to begin. We did not know where to buy a microphone from, let alone how to set one up to record! Eventually we figured out, 'There's this shop in town that sells microphones!' We all chipped in and bought our first microphone as a crew. Later, while I was a participant on a six-week course he was running at his studio Soundworks (where I would finish top of the class and gain my first ever formal qualification), a local music legend Dave Norland sold me a much better microphone for cheap and we were away!

We started recording our music and putting out CDs on our estate for free. We used to go into Tesco and buy a stack of 100 CDs and 100 plastic wallets each, burn our music onto the CDs, print out covers (designed by Danger One) on my mum's printer, and then give them out to anyone that wanted one; it was kind of a self-imposed membership fee. The group grew to about twelve members at its peak, and over the next two or three years we must have put thousands of CDs all over the UK and beyond. If I ever went *anywhere* a stack of CDs would be coming with me! I still sometimes get feedback on social media about those CDs, from all over the place. During that time, we made five collective mixtapes, each with around thirty tracks on them (that was the most tracks you could fit on a CD at the time), plus a heavy smattering of solo projects. In that two- or three-year period we must have released over 200 tracks between us, plus a DVD showcasing other local talent, all self-funded while we were performing various other hustles to make money to survive at the same time.

That was Hip Hop being a therapy for me because I was talking about the things I was going through. With my friends, it was a forum for us to share our feelings and opinions with one another, record our experiences, put it out on the estate, and collect feedback. It wasn't really a conscious decision, but that was the effect—I think we all needed it. One thing that always sticks in my mind from that period, something that still gives me motivation to this day, is when a total stranger came up to me in the pub saying, 'you're Rawz aren't you? That album you made helped me through my divorce'. It was the first time I thought 'Wow, what I've been doing has actually helped someone get through a hard time, in the same way that other people's music helped me all those times'. That gave me the motivation to keep going, but also the confidence to think 'I must be alright at this, people are enjoying it'.

Understanding

I started to want to develop and understand my craft a little bit, and went to a poetry course that was being run at a local community arts centre called Fusion Arts. Firstly, that opened my eyes to seeing what I was doing as a form of art: I had never looked at it in that way before. Secondly, it gave me more tools and made me think more about what I was writing: thinking of every word that I am putting on the paper being a choice, thinking about *what* I was saying and *who* I was saying it to.

The leader of the course, a poet named Steve Larkin, was impressed with what I was doing and asked me to help out the next time that he ran it. That led to me travelling all over Oxfordshire with him over the next year or two, working in different spaces, teaching poetry to young people. This helped me grow as an artist, to refine my craft, and to think about *how* I was doing it, and *why* I was doing it. Around the same time, I was asked by a veteran youth worker called Marsha Jackson to take part in a youth project in my local area run by the Leys Community Development Initiative (CDI). Knife crime was really on the rise in the area at the time, so the local youth club was doing anti-knife crime projects. I started working with eleven- and twelve-year-olds at Soundworks (which was attached to the local community centre) exploring the subject of knife crime with them. We ended up making a track that was them expressing how they felt about the stabbings and violent crime that was going on where they lived, helping them to share that with people. I still see a lot of those kids; I think that project really bonded us, and a lot of them are involved with some kind of community work themselves now. We ended up doing a conference at the Oxford United football stadium (which is on my estate) with the Head of Thames Valley Police in attendance—I was able to have a conversation with him and let him know my opinions and how I felt. It was Hip Hop that got me in that chair, through the work that I had been doing.

Employment

Then the funding ran out for both of those projects at the same time: I was told 'Don't come into work next week'—it was literally that abrupt. I was feeling that I really wanted to keep doing this work, and a couple of my friends (Kymel and Daniel) wanted to carry on doing it as well. So, encouraged by my mum, we started the Urban Music Foundation—this was in 2009. I feel it is important to note that, as I write this, both of the community centres I mentioned were scheduled for demolition in 2022, and both of the charities that facilitated this life-changing work for me are under threat through lack of available space and constant battles to find funding. I honestly don't know what I would be doing now had I not had these opportunities, and I worry about a generation that may not have these positive influences in their lives.

When I started the Urban Music Foundation, I wanted to share with people this therapeutic tool that had taken me from leaving school with no qualifications, to starting my own business and becoming a much more well-rounded person, knowing myself well enough to help others get to know themselves. I've been running the Urban Music Foundation ever since, as Daniel and Kymel moved on to doing other things with more secure incomes after a year or two, but they were both happy for me to keep it going on my own—it is thirteen years old now. I've worked with people from age five to ninety-five in all sorts of different settings using mainly lyric writing and poetry (other artforms too) as a tool for connecting people with one another, connecting people with themselves, and helping people to express themselves. I do a lot of work now with young people who are engaged in the criminal-justice system and young people who are struggling in mainstream education.

I've done an annual summer project with the Youth Justice Service here in Oxfordshire for the last ten years or so, the most recent iteration in conjunction with IF Oxford Science & Ideas Festival (which I am a trustee of) called 'What IF?' We work with small groups of, as they call them, their most 'hard-to-reach' young people—people that other services have struggled to 'engage with'. I've never had any trouble working with those sorts of people. We start off with the question 'What If?' and let them expand on that to tell any story they wish. We have had tracks about '*What if the world was ending?*', '*What if I never got arrested?*', '*What if my Mum would have never divorced my Dad?*', '*What if my brother hadn't died in that car crash?*' That is our starting point, and then some of my colleagues and I help them to make a track around this question and record a video for it. Social workers, probation officers, parents, and whoever else are always amazed at the insights they get into these young people's lives and their psyches from just a three-minute track. They say things like 'I've been working with this kid for a year and they haven't let me in as much as they just did in this three-minute track'.

I look at it now as a language; for me music is a language. Someone once said to me that music is what emotions sound like. That makes total sense to me. You can hear a chord on the piano, or a strum of a guitar, or a sample, and that can express feelings more vividly than hours of conversation. It is an amazing tool for engaging with people and helping people to express themselves, and for understanding people. The strap line on my Urban Music Foundation business cards reads 'Connecting people with themselves and each other through music'.

Therapy

That's what is so powerful about this therapy. I call it a self-guided therapy. I still look at it as that in my own practice as well. It's me giving myself a therapy session by asking myself questions and answering them, then sharing the results with other people in the hope that it will help them too.

I developed a project recently called 'Digging Crates' working in collaboration with friends and colleagues from our Hip Hop collective Inner Peace Records (formed in 2015) and the Pitt Rivers Museum in Oxford. The museum was basically set up as a military research facility; they were trying to gather information from all over the world to help them create more effective weapons for expanding the British Empire. In its essence the Digging Crates project is about healing multi-generational trauma—the legacy of colonialism and slavery. We worked with a group of African musicians to explore the museum's collection of African musical instruments and some of the other items that were taken from Africa by British colonisers. We worked with the African musicians to reinterpret the objects from the collection, taking audio samples from some of the instruments in the collections and also from recordings we made of the musicians playing their own music inside the museum. We then used these samples to create new Hip Hop tracks that we also wrote and recorded inside the museum. This is Hip Hop as a tool for healing from trauma in a very deep sense.

This was a hugely spiritual experience for me. I had underestimated the spiritual impact that it would have on me—I thought that it was just going to be fun to make tracks in the museum and sample some old instruments, but actually, the project gave us a way to talk about the weight of the history of slavery and the outrageous abuses of the British Empire and colonialism, and share our views with one another. It gave us a chance to inform academics and researchers in the field about the impact that it has had on us as non-academic people that are living with the legacies of these events. We made a documentary film and an EP (available at diggingcrates.bandcamp.com) from all of our reflections.

Gifts

Now, I'm an experienced youth worker, teacher, mentor, musician, and entrepreneur. I've performed my craft all over Europe, both as a solo artist and with the Inner Peace Records collective. I've collaborated with musicians from all over the world and shared stages with some of my childhood heroes. My music shares my exploration of our interconnected worlds, and my responses to them, promoting outer change and advancement through inner reflection and positive action. I do this while covering an unlimited range of topics, including love, capitalism, nature, community, crime, science, religion, and more. I would not be here if I had not stumbled across this tool in the mud, and been helped to polish and sharpen it by so many caring people along the way.

I think that maybe the most important thing that writing lyrics and making music has given me is that it helped me to realise the power that I have to control my own destiny, and the power and influence that I hold over others through what I choose to do and say. I think the reason that I started writing was partly because I felt voiceless, powerless. I had a vague notion that if I could get good enough at rapping, people would start listening to what I had to say. Now people are starting to listen.

I would like to share a piece of spoken word with you that I was commissioned to write for a three-day fringe event called MARMALADE held by a group of community, arts, and volunteering organisations in Oxford, bringing together funding bodies, charities, community groups, and other organisations to focus on issues linked to community action. I performed this piece to begin a debate on the subject of power and how it could be shared differently.

Power

Powerless

Done to

Not with

Devoid of the ability,

Influence or resources to create meaningful change

'They won't help me so how can I help myself?'

'If they don't care, why should I care about my health?'

'We've been waiting for so long

for somebody to do something

we've given up asking'

We've given up trying

And the power

And the buck just keep on passing

And the power

And the buck

Just keep on passing by

How can we do things differently?

A lack of power means no hope
Hopelessness is my friend's neck
In a rope
Hanging from a tree
Feeling like he had no power
To decide who he was going to be

Power
Is an opportunity
An opportunity rarely
Truly afforded to my community

Is power given?
Or taken?
Is power given?
Or taken away?

How can we do things differently?

Devoid of strength
A powerless victim
Lacking the capacity or authority to act
Seeing someone in need and being powerless to help
Anger
Sadness
Disgust and mistrust
Of power

Who can give me power?

If I ever had power,
Who took it away?

I know
That my power is hidden
Concealed
By those that claim to hold it on my behalf
By those that would give out fish everyday
Before they would issue a permit

To cast my line in waters owned by no one
And only cared for by me
My power is the basis of their authority
Their power is my community
If I refuse to let my power be used
Their sovereignty becomes defused
Illusory
Useless
Ineffective
Powerless

Is power given?

Or taken?

Is power given?

Or taken away?

How can we do things differently?

I have power
The power of speech
The ability to do
The ability to say
Whatever I choose
The ability to act
To help
To nourish
My community

Power is time
Power is resources
Power is truth
And influence
And support

Power is mine to give

Power is mine to receive

Who can give me power?

Who can take my power?

Greed is hoarding power
Holding power
Withholding power
Controlling power
Spending no time
Wasting resources on ticking boxes
Giving out tins of sardines
When there are bigger fish to fry
Wasting time
Bending truth
To keep the illusion of power
At the top of the tower
Out of reach
Behind a screen
A screen to cast shadows on
Shadows of hope

How can we do things differently?

Who can give me power?

Is power given?

Or taken?

Is power given?
Or taken away?

Power is mine to give
Power is mine to receive

Power is knowledge

Knowledge is power
Honesty
Knowledge of self
Knowledge of the power we hold in ourselves
Trust
Not needing a permit to improve
Or to feed each other
When help is needed, who can we turn to
Who can we trust?
If not our brother?
Or our sister?
Our grandmother?
Who knows us better than us?

If we have knowledge
Of ourselves
If we have time
For ourselves
If we have resources
For ourselves
If we have influence
And support
And truth
Then we have power

Now

How can we do things differently?

—RAWZ

To close, I want to share another piece with you: the fourth track from my 2021 collaborative album *ONE TWO*, created with my good friend, the talented singer/songwriter Tiece (also part of Inner Peace Records). The track is called 'One To My Two'. In it I talk about my first experiences encountering music as a form of expression, describing it as if it is a physical entity, my first love. On the album notes I wrote:

This one is an ode to the first love of my life.

The beat has a nostalgia to it that had me thinking about old times even as I was making it, and the subject matter pretty much chose itself. The lyrics are about music, particularly hip hop music and culture. Music really helped me get through some tough times as a kid and is still a huge part of my life today. I imagined it embodied as a person and wrote a song for them.

Hear the full track along with the rest of the album at www.innerpeacereco rds.bandcamp.com

These are my lyrics for the track.

ONE TO MY TWO
You, you're a part of me
It's You that cause my heart to beat
You're my spark in the darkness
In the dance you move my feet
And bring love from my past to me

From the first time we met
I couldn't even talk to you yet
Had to build up my strength
Compose my first sentence
You stayed there in my head
It's like I couldn't tear myself from your presence
You were there when I first played the drums on the table
Showed me a style to relate to
Though I never stayed faithful
And you strayed too I could never hate you
I just played cool
Through the hard times you showed me the truth
We set fire to the roof
You brought bap to my boom
The sun to my moon
You're the 1 to my 2

You, you're a part of me
It's You that cause my heart to beat

You're my spark in the darkness
In the dance you move my feet
And bring love from my past to me

Now look how we grew together
You kept me warm in the coldest weather
Just for that I'm yours forever
You brought gifts no bar can measure
Absorbed my devils
I feel sure when I talk to you
I just call on you
And you're there when I'm feeling blue
This plans never falling through
It's all for you
You set me free

You, you're a part of me
It's You that cause my heart to beat
You're my spark in the darkness
In the dance you move my feet
And bring love from my past to me

—RAWZ

You can find more of my work and connect with me online in the following places. I will be genuinely pleased to hear from you regarding this chapter or any other related thoughts or actions, as it's been a very cathartic experience writing it.

Facebook: www.facebook.com/realrawz
Instagram: www.instagram.com/rawz_official
Twitter: www.twitter.com/realrawz
Bandcamp: www.Rawz.bandcamp.com
Linktree: https://linktr.ee/rawz_official
Thank you for reading my story; I hope it helps.

8

Intentional Uses of Music

Hip Hop, Healing, and Empowerment for Youth Self-Care and Community Well-Being

Raphael Travis Jr., Alex H. D. Crooke, and Ian P. Levy

Introduction

Building on an understanding of how music in general, and Hip Hop more specifically, can positively impact mental health and well-being, this chapter examines how active and intentional uses of music can promote empowering music-related outcomes that link to both personal and community well-being. The chapter's findings can help us more strategically provide opportunities for students to use music, including Hip Hop, for academic, social, and emotional well-being, with or without professional support.

After the onset of the COVID-19 pandemic, mental health challenges exacerbated already disturbing trends in persistent sadness and hopelessness (CDC, 2023), and suicide-related behaviours (CDC, 2023), for many, especially for children and adolescents (Newall and Machi, 2020). An early 2022 poll found that 58 percent of adolescents 'personally know someone who has considered self-harm or suicide' (Zogby, 2022). Moving to the global landscape, it was found that 'clinically elevated child and adolescent depression and anxiety were at 25.2% and 20.5% respectively, which is double pre-pandemic rates and highest among older adolescents and girls' (Racine *et al.*, 2021: E1). A report from the Mental Health America (MHA) screening program found that 2020 had the most people report frequent thoughts of suicide and self-harm (Reinert, Nguyen, and Fritze, 2021).

The COVID-19–era climate of youth mental health was so critical that the American Academy of Pediatrics, the American Academy of Child and Adolescent Psychiatry, and the Children's Hospital Association collectively declared a national emergency in child and adolescent mental health (AAP, 2021). Similarly, the US Surgeon General (2021) issued an Advisory on Youth

Raphael Travis Jr., Alex H. D. Crooke, and Ian P. Levy, *Intentional Uses of Music* In: *Music for Inclusion and Healing in Schools and Beyond*. Edited by: Pete Dale, Pamela Burnard, and Raphael Travis Jr., Oxford University Press.
© Oxford University Press 2023. DOI: 10.1093/oso/9780197692677.003.0009

Mental Health, which focused on actions that can be taken by stakeholders within the youth mental health ecosystem (e.g., families, educators, health-care administrators, media and entertainment). It is essential to identify clear and concrete pathways to healing and wellness for youth. Building on an understanding of how music in general, and Hip Hop more specifically, positively impacts mental health and well-being, this study examined predictors of active and intentional uses of music to promote personal growth and development and community well-being.

Limited Access to Formal Mental Health Services

Many opportunities to address mental health exist with and without professional help. Trends that indicate professionals cannot keep up with demand for youth service needs (Mau, Li, and Hoetmer, 2016; Adjapong and Levy, 2021), and young people's resistance to seeking or following up with initial visits with professional help (Goodwill & Yasui, 2022), suggest that a large portion of young people needing professional mental health support are not getting it and are engaging in some sort of self-care.

Therapeutic uses of creative arts in general, and music more specifically, have been examined in discussions of intentional use of the arts for self-care and self-health (DeNora, 2013; McFerran and Saarikallio, 2014; Levy, Emdin, and Adjapong, 2022; Ortega-Williams, 2021; Schwan, Fallon, and Milne, 2018; Spors, 2022; Stewart Rose, and Countryman, 2021). *Intentional use* is personally initiated use of music that is purposeful toward an objective experience or goal. It is not mediated by a professional. In a recent study of over 3,200 university students, listening to music was by far the most common strategy for dealing with stress, with 68 percent of the group compared to the next category of active leisure activities (e.g., dance, exercise, sports, physical activity) at 43 percent (Reiss *et al.*, 2021). At the same time, there continues to be a gap in research about what is associated with favorable and less favorable outcomes from intentional music use. There is also limited information on the relationship between intentions and the outcomes of intentional uses of music. *Self-care, self-help, self-management,* and *self-musicking* include a variety of functional pathways for perceived 'effectiveness' in achieving the desired outcomes. It may be via distraction, doing something active and productive, writing or journaling, listening to music, or other ways (Town *et al.*, 2022). This may be self-initiated for explicit functional/

productive or therapeutic reasons, or tools to assist people in self-care like recommendations on 'self-help against self-harm' sites and similar public-health initiatives (Fenton and Kingsley, 2022).

These realities suggest we have crossed a threshold and are within a new dynamic era regarding mental health and how people cope. This is important for youth in terms of their social, emotional, and academic well-being. We must better understand how young people utilize their available resources in relation to their mental health, and the opportunities they perceive to exist to enhance their self-care, self-help, and self-management skills. Based on what we know about the significance of social and emotional development in general and the connection with academic engagement and development (Durlak *et al.*, 2011; Taylor *et al.*, 2017), we recognize how better self-care in this regard can help with functioning in all aspects of life, socially, emotion-ally, and academically. We must also be attentive to the unique, cascading, and overlapping factors of oppression, alongside the unique transformative developmental opportunities we have from a life course perspective (Halfon and Forrest, 2018; Russ *et al.*, 2022) for Black youth and other minoritized groups.

Hip Hop culture has historically spoken to these unique social realities, and at once to both individual and community well-being (Travis, 2016: 37–41). We realize that engaging Hip Hop culture is but one of several music-driven pathways to well-being. We must continue to build upon what we know to be even more specific about what might help predict who is likely to benefit from practices and prevention efforts that seek to promote effective self-care, self-help, and self-management.

The following study adds to our understanding of why and how people in-tentionally use music to promote their own well-being, what factors may help predict empowering and risky music engagement, and whether Hip Hop cul-ture is associated with more empowering or risky music engagement.

Background

Recent data continue to suggest a substantial need for mental health care among youth. For example, according to the World Health Organization (WHO), among those aged fifteen to twenty-nine, a leading cause of disability is depression, and the fourth leading cause of death is suicide (WHO, 2023). Developmental timing is also important with approximately 75 percent of mental health disorders developing before twenty-four years of age, and 50 percent by age fourteen (Kessler *et al.*, 2005; McGrath *et al.*, 2016).

However, on the one hand, 40 percent of mental health professionals participating in a recent study say they are not able to keep up with the demand (APA, 2021). On the other hand, children and adolescents often do not seek professional support for mental health problems. Reasons given include a lack of knowledge about available support, perceived stigma and embarrassment, a lack of trust, and fear of non-confidentiality (Radez *et al.*, 2021). Further, among those that do access care, many do not continue, or feel continuing is a challenge (SAMHSA, 2020). Trends suggest that a large portion of young people needing professional mental health support are not receiving it and are engaging in some sort of self-care or intentional music- or music-culture-oriented experiences. Opportunities to support self-care and self-health for mental health have been discussed as important parts of the mental health treatment continuum, alongside health promotion, prevention, and treatment strategies (Travis *et al.*, 2021: 556).

Research suggests that self-help works—both guided and self-guided (Bennett *et al.*, 2019). The specific helpful techniques found in a review were: seeking social contact/help, physical activity, displacement/mimicking techniques (i.e., a similar, less harmful activity such as holding an ice cube), relaxing/comforting techniques, sensory techniques (including self-soothe boxes), fun/diverting techniques, aggressive techniques (such as screaming/ tearing something up), and creative/reflective techniques (Fenton and Kingsley, 2022). CDC and NAS also actively promote tools and resources for youth self-management of mental health (National Academies Press [NAS], 2022).

In addition to self-care and self-health, efforts to improve mental health may be a part of public-health and health-promotion efforts, from universal prevention to targeted prevention initiatives based on their presenting symptoms, and active treatment based on a formal mental health diagnosis. Universal or primary prevention includes strategies targeting the general population with the goal of avoiding negative mental health outcomes (National Academies Press, 2016). Selective prevention includes strategies working with individuals that are at excess risk for potential development of mental health concerns. Indicated prevention efforts on the continuum are akin to secondary prevention for individuals that demonstrate some mental health symptoms but do not have a formal diagnosis (National Academies Press, 2016). It is hoped that symptoms do not progress to a clinical level requiring a formal mental health diagnosis.

Again, music has been a major area of exploration within discussions of intentional use of the arts for self-care and self-health, but also for use in professionally mediated therapeutic strategies (Levy, Emdin, and Adjapong, 2022; McFerran *et al.*, 2020; Rodwin *et al.*, 2022; Travis *et al.*, 2021; Washington, 2018). In a recent systematic review Rodwin *et al.*, (2022) highlighted how most studies report significant effects for mental health outcomes related to social and emotional improvements and reductions of internalizing symptoms for adolescents. Further, a typology of music-based interventions emerged to help show the consistency and contrasts among effective processes to improve well-being. Three distinct, but overlapping, categories for interventions were identified including combinations among the three: (1) somatosensory, (2) social-emotional, and (3) cognitive-reflective. Most effective interventions combined two or all three (i.e., holistically integrated) strategy categories (Rodwin *et al.*, 2022).

School-Based Concerns

Recent research from Choi *et al.* is an excellent example about the importance of school-based environments in preventing or not exacerbating negative mental health outcomes like depression (Choi *et al.*, 2023). Mistreatment, disrespect, inequitable, and non-supportive practices toward Black students in schools inhibit connectedness. It can be helpful to support the implementation of more school-based prevention interventions that consistently promote school connectedness and directly target the needs and experiences of Black students. Social workers are well positioned to offer school-based prevention resources that are free to students and families, which may also be helpful in alleviating disparities regarding both cost and accessibility of culturally adapted mental health resources (Brown and Grumet, 2009). If students appear to enjoy school and value the information taught at school, then it will be worthwhile for practitioners and researchers to continue exploring the role and utility of school-based prevention interventions (Erbacher and Singer, 2018).

Hip Hop Culture and Expressive Arts

The expressive arts align with core elements of Hip Hop culture. They include but are not limited to writing, poetry, dance, visual art, music, play. The expressive arts are often used with attention to the physical body, addressing the negative effects of trauma, and cathartic release (Malchiodi, 2023). These engaging and creative vehicles fit nicely alongside Hip Hop's core elements of MCing and deejaying, breaking, graffiti, and knowledge of self. Hip Hop culture is widely accepted as mainstream in contemporary societies. However, it is also culturally responsive for many individual communities whose unique culturally specific social realities and developmental narratives are reflected within the lyrics (Levy and Wong, 2022; Travis, 2016).

While not absolute, substantial evidence suggests that Hip Hop culture offers individuals a voice, validates their experiences, and provides opportunities to embrace the journey of self and community improvement (Travis, 2016). Hip Hop culture has moved from a regional culture to a global culture specific to realities of the communities and people that embrace and identify with it (Chang, 2005; Colectivo and Alim, 2023; Nafar *et al.*, 2023). Hip Hop integrated strategies have shown to be engaging and empowering, but also to inhibit stress, anxiety, and depression (Alvarez, 2012; DeCarlo and Hockman, 2004; Elligan, 2000; Gann, 2010; Hadley and Yancy, 2012; Levy, Emdin, and Adjapong, 2022; Levy and Travis, 2020; Travis, 2016; Travis, Rodwin, and Allcorn, 2019; Travis and Deepak, 2011; Tyson, 2004; Viega, 2016, 2018; Washington, 2018).

An important aspect of this is that parallel to promoting positive well-being is facilitating agency in one's own developmental well-being—a goodness-of-fit between the evolving person and their environment, a regulation with internal senses, and a sense-making of the external environment (Hambrick *et al.*, 2019; MacKinnon, 2012). Thus, Hip Hop integrated strategies often have micro- and macro-level goals (clinical personal goals [e.g., self-regulation] intertwined with equity and social-justice goals [e.g., better community conditions]). When we discuss equity and justice, it is also aligned with inhibiting trauma-inducing environments (Jasiri X, 2023). It validates a targeting of broader social determinants of health—racial, economic, criminal justice, education—while also targeting specific outcomes that can be measured directly. More specifically, improving conditions that can help inhibit negative well-being outcomes of stress, anxiety, and depression are significant because of the longer-term implications; there are clear links to allostatic load, longitudinal developmental outcomes (De France *et al.*, 2022; Halfon and Forrest, 2018), and academic engagement (Simons and Steele, 2020).

Empowering and/or Risky Engagement as Outcomes *and* Processes

An important aspect of empowering engagement is that it can occur along-side risky engagement. Empowering engagement includes ways of engaging music or other aspects of the culture that have the potential to help a person to *get better* in some way, such as to feel better (esteem), to do better (resilience), to be better (growth), to better belong (community), and for better conditions (change) (Travis and Bowman, 2011). Risky engagement includes ways of engaging music or other aspects of the culture that facilitate attitudes or behaviours that have the potential to decrease mental or physical well-being of the individual *or others*. That these can occur alongside one another suggests that even as people engage music or Hip Hop culture in ways that allow them to feel or do better in some areas of well-being, it can also *simultaneously* contribute to attitudes or behaviours that can decrease mental or physical well-being of oneself or others in some way (Travis, 2016: 69). For example, feelings of empowerment may occur with youth learning to experience positive emotions in general to feel better, or have a better sense of self, but through a dependence on external validation, materialism, or the victimization of others.

New research by Evans (2022) crystallizes this dynamic at the community level when talking about the risk embedded in empowering engagement as an artist/creator. For example, with esteem, resilience, or community-related expressivity (i.e., either aligning with narratives about, or a real-world building of, a strong sense of self; coping with economic, racial, and other marginalizations; and creating a better sense of belonging within perceived priority social communities) it can be a result of risky attitudes and behaviours:

> While global fame and riches were goals, the youth we study also sought clout to gain local reputation. Clout allowed them to compete, collaborate, and connect within the larger hip-hop community of cultural producers. Still, it often did so at a price, as clout often meant exaggerating

street credibility in ways that could become lethal. This, in turn, made participants ambivalent over their tactics for attention and fame. (Evans and Baym, 2022: 2673)

Risks were equally found among those that identified as women:

Female respondents primarily described capping as exaggerating affiliation with high-status men, display of luxury material items, and projecting sexual availability on social media. Though often more sought after than their male counterparts, their visibility also appeared wrought with inner conflict about their celebrity. (Evans and Baym, 2022: 2676)

Intentional Music Use and Positive Development: Which Comes First?

Music and *self-care*, *self-musicking*, *self-management*, or *self-help* has been an especially meaningful part of understanding personal efforts to improve mental health without significant professional support. Researchers have continued to explore these everyday intentional uses. By engaging in self-care, individuals have the ability to regulate emotions, actively learn and grow, and contribute to their own development, building on what is most empowering, and inhibiting what is most risky, akin to healthy and unhealthy uses of music (Levy, Emdin, and Adjapong, 2022; McFerran and Saarikallio, 2014: 2). Self-initiated care and well-being are especially important for youth and young adults of color, who often rely on culturally grounded tools to address disparate levels of psychosocial stressors (Levy, Emdin, and Adjapong, 2022).

An important study from McFerran *et al.* (2018) investigating intentional use of music by young people sought to further differentiate how to best help youth reporting mental health challenges in comparison to flourishing young people. The assumption, based on prior research, was that flourishing youth are more likely to use music 'to promote positive states of being', while those with mental health problems use music to ruminate and intensify anger or sadness (Garrido, Eerola, and McFerran, 2017; McFerran, Garrido, O'Grady, Grocke, and Sawyer, 2015; McFerran and Saarikallio, 2014). Ultimately, they found that a brief music-therapy intervention was helpful in reducing young people's distress. However, the intervention was also appreciated by youth as a way to help them be more conscious of and positively modify their music use (p. 577).

Even if we were not confident that *all* youth were likely to engage music to promote positive states, research by Levy provided evidence that through Hip Hop–integrated strategies it was possible to increase readiness to engage in positive change strategies. Levy (2019) found that after participating in Hip Hop and Spoken Word Therapy (HHSWT) there was a significant increase in high school students' readiness to change around coping with emotional stress or any negative feelings (i.e., moved from preparation to action). The study also found that social and emotional growth was prominent in the lyrics students created, and in their reflections about group experiences. They identified new coping skills, described increased emotional self-awareness, and embraced a stronger self-image (i.e., both in terms of voice and agency) (Levy, 2019: 6–7). Levy, Emdin, and Adjapong (2022) talk about the potential value of adding motivational interviewing (MI) to HHSWT for a more facilitator-led process anchored in a well-established evidence-based model. It is the non-facilitator potential that is also of interest. Similar patterns of empowerment and social and emotional development were found by Travis (2013) when closely examining research about lyrics created within therapeutic settings.

Hip Hop Culture, ICE, and Emotional Pathways

Interacting with the ever-present developmental narratives in any type of music, but especially Hip Hop music, opportunities often exist for emotional experiences that contribute to positive development. Koelsch (2015) outlines key music-evoked emotional experiences that manifest including: evaluation, resonance, memory, musical expectancy and tension, imagination, understanding, and social functions of music. Travis (2016) suggests that these are critical pathways in facilitating positive development. For example, the emotional effects in imagining yourself in the role of someone triumphing over the most adverse life experiences in strong and enduring ways can be so powerful that they engender confidence, self-awareness of personal skills and abilities, empathy toward people in similar situations, or a renewed motivation for better in life and to make healthier decisions (all evidence-based indicators of positive development [EMPYD]). Further discussion of potential developmental opportunities at the neural level from regular music engagement is made by Bruce Perry in an interview with MacKinnon (2012: 214):

> One of the fundamentals of neural change is activity- or use-dependence. Any neural network that is activated in a repetitive way will change. Therefore, if we want to provide reorganising, patterned, repetitive input to reach the dysregulated or poorly organised neural networks involved in the stress response, we can provide patterned repetitive rhythmic somato-sensory activity.

Hip Hop and Empowerment: A System for Therapeutic Change

As a guiding conceptual tool for health promotion, prevention, and intervention efforts, the Hip Hop and Empowerment framework offers significant room for professional autonomy in creating and facilitating motivational therapeutic experiences (Travis, 2013, 2016). The more cognitive-reflective (Rodwin *et al.*, 2022) and expressive (McFerran *et al.*, 2020) activities in this framework use existing Hip Hop–related content as prompts and tools to explore developmental themes, process emotional triggers, and facilitate individual and community improvement through the lenses of esteem, resilience, growth, community, and (social) change (Travis and Deepak, 2011; Travis, 2013; Travis and Bowman, 2015; Travis, Gann, Crooke, and Jenkins, 2019; Travis, Rodwin, and Allcorn, 2019).

The Present Study

There continues to be a gap in research about music engagement and well-being that explores empirically what helps predict favorable (i.e., empowering) and less favorable (i.e., risky) music engagement. Included in this is how differences may exist across subtypes of empowering and risky engagement, between levels of affinity for Hip Hop culture, and by symptoms of depression and anxiety. There is limited evidence about the relationship between reasons for listening to music (i.e., intentional use) and music-engagement outcomes. We need a better understanding as to how empowering music engagement is associated with why and how people engage with music. Such an improved understanding could add to literature seeking to identify opportunities to help young people engage with and through music in positive ways—for social, emotional, and academic well-being.

Intentional Use, and Empowering and Risky Music Engagement

Travis and Deepak (2011) introduced the ideas of the simultaneous presence of empowering and risky music engagement, and the need for clients and practitioners to be able to negotiate the two in service of positive developmental results. Recent research (Travis, Bowman, Levy, and Crooke, 2020) suggests that patterns in empowering and risky engagement may be changing, or at least are worthy of continued exploration in the context of music-integrated self and professionally mediated care. Research has continued to examine patterns of music engagement, but also *the intent* of engagement, asking whether prior predictors of music engagement have continued to be impactful, and whether empowering engagement subscales (i.e., resilience, growth, and community) have provided any added value in understanding intentional music use (Travis, Bowman, Levy, and Crooke, 2020).

First, 45 percent of empowering music engagement was explained, and it aligned with previous research showing that hours listening to music, and time spent exploring one's own race/ethnicity, predicted empowering engagement. Additionally, (a) listening specifically for motivation and for personal and community improvement, (b) having enough friends that care (i.e., connection), and (c) prioritizing lyrical analysis over listening mainly for the beats (i.e., cognitive-reflective processes), each were statistically significant additions to the model predicting empowering engagement (Travis, Bowman, Levy, and Crooke, 2020).

Empowering engagement subscales demonstrated favorable reliability scores (i.e., resilience = .808; growth = .771; community/change = .647). Two risky engagement subscales emerged from a factor analysis with favorable reliability, risk subscale 1 = .784 (n = 5) and risk subscale 2 = .879 (n = 4) (Travis, Bowman, Levy, and Crooke, 2020). Empowering and risky engagement were not associated at the global level; but resilience-empowering engagement and risk subscale 2 were inversely related. Those that tend toward resilience-oriented engagement (i.e., themes of positive coping, a validation of experiences, self-awareness) were significantly *less* likely to have risk subscale 2 types of engagement (i.e., music listening associated with greater comfort with use of Molly [i.e., 'ecstasy'], codeine promethazine, pills, and cocaine). We found that those with more community-oriented empowering engagement (i.e., music listening associated with social awareness, social relatedness, self-expression, social identity) were significantly *more* likely to have risk subscale 1 types of engagement (i.e., music listening associated with greater comfort with or thinking about alcohol use, marijuana use, casual sex, violence, and drug sales to make money).

Among individuals that claimed Hip Hop as a favorite genre and who listed Hip Hop artists as their favorite artists ('Hip Hop Heads'), findings differed in this study from prior findings. In prior research, *rap* music engagement was found to be more empowering and less risky compared to other music engagement (Travis and Bowman, 2012), however this time Hip Hop Heads were significantly more likely than those that did not prefer Hip Hop music as a favorite to have empowering engagement and more likely to have risky engagement.

Again, the purpose of the present study is to continue to add to our understanding of active and intentional use of music to promote empowering music engagement, but also to develop predictors of both empowering and risky engagement. Findings can help provide better assessments for who might be especially amenable to music-based health-promotion and therapeutic strategies, whether it is through self-care or professionally mediated activities. Our evidence suggests that Hip Hop culture and other expressive arts can be used for academic, social, and emotional well-being, with and without professional support.

More specifically, our research questions have asked: (1) Is there an association between empowering and risky music engagement? Are there differences by depressive or anxiety symptoms? (2) What factors contribute to empowering music engagement? Does intentional music use add to prior predictors of empowering music engagement? Does a positive and supportive relationship (i.e., friendship[s] or 'connections') add to predictors of empowering engagement? Does depression or anxiety help predict empowering music engagement? (3) What factors contribute to risky music engagement?

Research Setting and Procedures

The present study occurred at a large university, which is a Hispanic Serving Institution, in the Southwest United States. The research was approved by a University Institutional Review Board, and all proper consents were approved and received. The university regularly holds multiple new student orientations at the start of the academic year to help groups of incoming first-year and transfer students acclimate and gain a greater understanding of their new-higher education environment. The study questionnaire was distributed at the conclusion of several of these new-student orientations.

Participants in the present study came from a convenience sample of 350 incoming freshmen and transfer students. During an orientation for new students, participants were recruited to participate in the study, and upon agreement they completed the thirty-question questionnaire. Ages ranged from seventeen to nineteen, and 61 percent identified as female. When looking at self-reported race and ethnicity, 28 percent identified as Latino/Hispanic, 12 percent identified as Black, 5 percent identified as multi-racial, and 40 percent identified as white.

The present research used single-source cross-sectional self-report data. The cross-sectional design was chosen to explore covariation between an area with more consistent and substantive evidence (i.e., individual and community empowerment framework for empowering and risky music engagement) and an area with novel emerging data (i.e., intentional music use). It is a first step to determine whether there are relationships between intentional music use and types of empowering (or risky) music engagement without introducing excess complexity. Self-report is used because the investigated concepts are very subjective and personal perspectives on music engagement (Spector, 2019: 130). The study and questionnaires were introduced at the start of orientation presentations and completed after the main program of the workshop ended. Participants came from one orientation session per day, over the course of three days. Data collection in each session lasted approximately thirty minutes. Across the three days, there were 350 fully completed questionnaires available to use in analyses.

A single questionnaire, the Individual and Community Empowerment (ICE) Inventory (Travis, Bowman, Levy, and Crooke, 2020), all music version, was used to capture the multiple constructs of interest in this study, as well as single-item proxies for constructs. The larger constructs being measured are empowering music engagement and risky music engagement within the ICE Inventory (with smaller individual empowerment subscales for resilience, growth, community/change empowerment) and reasons for music listening (intentional use of music) along with a series of individual indicators. There are also measurement scales to provide insight into the influences of depressive and anxiety symptoms. Single items and measures act as proxies to capture concepts on listening habits and positive youth development, including spending time trying to find out about race/ethnicity, cognitive-reflective listening with music lyrics, and having enough friends that care. Data were analyzed using IBM SPSS Statistics 25.

Empowering Engagement

Empowering music engagement questions are linked to the original individual and community empowerment scales for rap music that have been adapted to capture the presence of empowering engagement across all preferred music types. At the individual level, music may contribute to individual empowerment through greater esteem, stronger identity, handling adversity, demonstrated resilience, prosocial and health-enhancing attitudes and behaviours, skill-building, and preventing victimization. These are the personal dimensions aligned with feeling, doing, and being better. Community empowerment questions are associated with empowerment related to embracing one's culture, appreciation of cultural resilience, sociopolitical development, and collective action for equity, justice, and collective well-being. Examples of empowerment questions included: 'Hip-Hop music helps me make it through bad times' (individual empowerment) and 'Hip-Hop makes me want to do something positive for my community' (community empowerment). One item was removed from the prior scale because it was not framed in a way that aligned with the other questions and it did not yield the appropriate outcomes. The full scale reliability for the fourteen items is .846.

Risky Engagement

Risky music engagement questions are linked to the original individual and community risk scales for rap music that have been adapted to capture the presence of risky engagement across all preferred music types. The focus has been on individual risk, but a recognition exists for implications beyond the individual. Risky engagement as a full scale of nine items includes the *Risk 1* and *Risk 2* subscales. The older risk subscales were retained because while a new question about Xanax was added to understand perceived interest in Xanax references as a potential health promotive resource, the question format was framed in a more empowering way. Risk subscale 1 items (i.e., Risk 1) included greater comfort with or thinking about alcohol use, marijuana use, casual sex, violence, and drug sales to make money. Reliability continued to be strong for the five items (alpha = .732). Risk subscale 2 (i.e., Risk 2) items included greater comfort with use of Molly (i.e., 'ecstasy'), codeine promethazine, pills, and cocaine (alpha =.874).

Reliability analyses were conducted for scale validation. Mean comparisons (t-tests) were completed for general tests of association. Correlation analyses helped assess alignment, including empowering and risky engagement potential correlation. Multiple linear regression examined predictors of empowering music engagement. Predictors were added based on hypotheses from prior research examining aspects of racial identity development (Travis and Bowman, 2012), intentional music use, having enough friends that care (i.e., connection), prioritizing lyrical analysis over listening mainly for the beats, regular listening to misogynistic lyrics, and depressive symptoms (Travis, Bowman, Levy, and Crooke, 2020). Predictors of risky music engagement were also examined using the same logic from prior research.

RESULTS

That music plays a powerful role in the lives of young people continued to be supported by these data. Each dimension of empowering engagement was supported by large proportion of respondents. A sample of indicator responses helps us see how prevalent these empowering experiences were among people. For example, 90 percent of respondents indicated that music helped them through challenging times. A little less than half (45%) of people felt music made it easier to talk about their problems. Two-thirds (67%) of respondents stated that music was an outlet to express their feelings or ideas about the world. Similarly, almost two-thirds (65.1%) felt that music about making positive decisions motivates them to behave more positively. Seventy percent reported that music has helped them to think critically about the world around them. More than three-quarters (78%) of respondents expressed how they connect better with people that share similar musical interests. While not a part of the empowerment scale, that 55 percent stated how music that talks about the harmful effects of drugs like Xanax makes them think twice about its use is a testament to the potential for promoting empowering music engagement and inhibiting risky engagement.

Correlations

Empowering and Risky Music Engagement

Overall, these results show no correlation between empowering and risky engagement at the global level, which is supported by existing research. Yet (also supported by our prior research) findings did show several important relationships do exist between particular subscales of these global constructs. For example, empowering engagement was significantly associated with a risky engagement subscale (*Risk 1*). Further, a second risky engagement subscale (*Risk 2*) was significantly *negatively* associated with the *community* empowering engagement subscale. This suggests that certain types of risky engagement may align with different aspects of empowering engagement; empowering engagement may be vulnerable to certain risky attitudes or behaviors.

Anxiety and depression were linked to empowering engagement ($r(376) = .218$, $p < .001$. and $r(376) = .232$, $p < .001$. respectively). Prior findings of empowering engagement were linked to less depressive symptoms in personal daily activity (Travis and Bowman, 2012) and then for less depressive and anxiety symptoms within interventions (Travis *et al.*, 2019; Levy and Travis, 2020). These prior research examples were negative associations. In the present sample, it is a 'positive' correlation. Depressive symptoms were positively and significantly linked to all three subscales of empowering engagement, resilience ($r(376) = .234, p < .001$), growth ($r(376) = .115, p = .025$), and community/change ($r(376) = .135, p = .009$).

However, at the same time, the community empowerment subscale was associated with less Risk 2 engagement ($r(376) = -.134$, $p = .009$). Perhaps there are elements of empowerment that are more preventive for higher-risk substance-use engagement. Further, anxiety symptoms were associated with resilience ($r(376) = .287, p < .001$) and community empowering engagement

($r(376) = .220, p < .001$). Significant correlations were also found between youth reporting that they have enough positive and supportive relationships in their lives, on the one hand, and empowering engagement, on the other ($r(376) = .169, p = .001$). These youth were significantly less likely to report depressive symptoms ($r(376) = -.216, p < .001$) and Risk 2 engagement ($r(376) = -.168, p = .001$), but had no association with anxiety symptoms.

Findings suggest that flourishing youth, or youth free of mental health struggles, are not necessarily *better* equipped to or more likely to have empowering music engagement (McFerran and Saarikallio, 2014). Empowering music engagement is found among youth with sufficient positive relationships *and* those struggling with depressive and anxiety symptoms. Neither depressive symptoms nor anxiety symptoms are associated with risky engagement.

Reasons for Use. Respondents that are intentional about music engagement, whether it is for a therapeutic or developmental purpose (i.e., for emotional regulation and for motivation) or practical purpose (i.e., a task) are significantly more likely to have empowering music engagement (regulation, $r(376) = .437, p < .001$; motivation, $r(376) = .385, p < .001$; tasks, $r(376) = .222, p < .001$).

Hip Hop as a Favorite. Those who reported Hip Hop as their favorite genre tended to elicit more empowering *and* more risky messages. A positive trend of empowering engagement exists from least favorite level to highest favorite level. Hip Hop Heads and Non Hip Hop Heads have significantly higher empowering engagement; but those in the middle (i.e., Hip Hop reported as the favorite genre, but no Hip Hop artists listed among their favorite artists) have significantly less empowering engagement. Perhaps these individuals are not as able to quickly and comfortably discern/engage empowering elements or evoke emotions in ways that instigate empowering and developmental pathways or engage more explicitly/proportionately risky content. The difference is not significant between any of the levels, including lowest to highest.

These findings differ from prior research, where those identifying Hip Hop as a preferred genre were more likely to report greater empowering engagement (Travis and Bowman, 2012). Prior research also did not distinguish between those that preferred Hip Hop but did not list a favorite artist as a Hip Hop artist, from those that did. In further contrast, in this study, we found when looking at risky music engagement that the highest level of Hip Hop-as-a-favorite (i.e., also listing a favorite Hip Hop artists) was significantly positively correlated with overall risky engagement, including both the risk subscale 1 and risk subscale 2 $r(376) = .252, p < .001$ and $r(376) = .147$, $p = .004$.

Factors Contributing to Empowering Engagement

Regressions. As shown in Table 8.1, the final model identified how empowering engagement was associated with a range of predictors, including prior research-identified predictors (e.g., identity development), intentional music use (e.g., for emotional regulation and as motivation for getting better), cognitive-reflective processes (i.e., analyze lyrics and not just listen to the beat), and having enough friends that care, $F(11, 336) = 18.086, p < .001$, with an adjusted R^2 at .35.

Replicating Prior Research. As shown in Table 8.1, the model identified how empowering engagement could be predicted by hours spent listening to music and identity development, but Hip Hop being a favorite and listening alone as opposed to socially were not significant within the model, $F(4, 343) = 8.385, p < .001$, with R^2 at .08. Our results indicate that participants who spent more time listening to music and those who spent more time finding out about their race or ethnicity reported a higher level of empowering engagement.

Intentional Use. Addition of indicators for intentional music use resulted in a significant improvement in R^2 to .27. As shown in Table 8.1, the model identified how empowering engagement was associated with using music to regulate emotions, and as motivation for better, but not for completing tasks or activities $F(7, 340) = 19.545, p < .001$. Our results indicate that participants who intentionally use music to increase positive emotions, inhibit negative emotions, do better in life, be a better person, and work toward better conditions for communities and groups they care about reported the highest levels of empowering music engagement outcomes.

Thriving and More. Addition of indicators for thriving/flourishing, cognitive-reflective listening, and potential misogyny resulted in a substantive improvement in R^2 to .35. As shown in Table 8.1, the model identified how empowering engagement was associated with depressive symptoms, analyzing lyrics, and having enough friends that care $F(11, 336) = 18.09, p < .001$. Our results indicate that participants who reported higher levels of depressive symptoms, a tendency to analyze music lyrics, and having enough

Table 8.1 Regression model summary for empowering and risky music engagement

Model	Empowering Music Engagement (n = 347)			Risky Music Engagement (n = 347)		
	β	t	Sig.	β	t	Sig.
Model 1						
Hip Hop as a Favorite	-.070	-1.315	.190	.222	4.174	.000***
Hours Spent Listening	.161	3.072	.002**	.001	.022	.983
Most Often Listen to Music	-.005	-.088	.930	-.015	-.288	.774
Find Out More about Race/Ethnicity	.250	4.817	.000***	.172	3.311	.001**
Adjusted R²	$R^2 = .078$	-1.933	.000***	$R^2 = .075$	4.146	.000***
Model 2						
Hip Hop as a Favorite	-.092	1.911	.054	.218	-.190	.000***
Hours Spent Listening	.091	-1.198	.057	-.010	-.590	.849
Most Often Listen to Music	-.057	3.634	.232	-.031	3.495	.555
Find Out More about Race/Ethnicity	.171	5.066	.000***	.183	-.282	.001**
Intentional Use: Regulation	.270	5.307	.000***	-.017	.835	.778
Intentional Use: Motivation for Better	.272	.535	.000***	.048	-3.519	.404
Intentional Use: Tasks/Activities	.027	-.116	.593	-.195	1.875	.000***
Adjusted R²	$R^2 = .272$	1.106	.000***	$R^2 = .105$	-.318	.003**

(continued)

Table 8.1 Continued

Model	Empowering Music Engagement (n = 347)			Risky Music Engagement (n = 347)		
	β	t	Sig.	β	t	Sig.
Model 3						
Hip Hop as a Favorite	-.006	-.624	.908	.102	-.002	.062
Hours Spent Listening	.050	3.634	.269	-.016	2.565	.750
Most Often Listen to Music	-.028	3.879	.533	.000	.502	.999
Find Out More about Race/Ethnicity	.167	6.228	.000***	.132	-.137	.011*
Intentional Use: Regulation	.200	-.601	.000***	.029	-2.882	.616
Intentional Use: Motivation for Better	.307	4.363	.000***	-.008	1.514	.891
Intentional Use: Tasks/Activities	-.029	4.806	.548	-.155	-1.312	.004**
Depressive Symptoms	.200	2.028	.000***	.077	-2.082	.131
Analyze Lyrics, Not Just Listen	.222	-1.383	.000***	-.068	5.551	.190
Enough Friends That Care	.096		.043*	-.110		.038*
Disrespectful Toward Women/Girls	-.067		.167	.298		.000***
Adjusted R²	$R^2 = .351$		.000***	$R^2 = .193$		.000***

* $p < 0.05$; ** $p < 0.01$; *** $p < 0.001$

friends that care about their feelings and what happens to them reported the highest levels of empowering music engagement outcomes.

Factors Contributing to Risky Engagement

As shown in Table 8.1 the final model identified how risky engagement was associated with a range of predictors, including prior research-identified predictors (e.g., identity development), intentional music use (e.g., for completing tasks and activities), having enough friends that care, and regular listening to misogynistic lyrics $F(11, 336) = 8.54$, $p < .001$, with an adjusted R^2 at .19. Our results indicate that participants who spent more time trying to find out more about their race or ethnicity, and that regularly listen to music that is often disrespectful toward women and girls, are significantly more likely to report risky music engagement. Further, participants that intentionally used music to exercise or help focus on a task, and who have enough friends that care about their feelings and what happens to them, are significantly less likely to report risky engagement.

DISCUSSION

Our society has indeed crossed a threshold and we are now within a new dynamic era regarding how people cope with mental health. Our findings suggest that music engagement is being used intentionally as a concrete resource by youth and young adults to support their mental health. Previous correlations between music engagement and well-being—that is, positive engagement styles were more likely to associated with positive well-being—suggest a unidirectional relationship where the listener's well-being is impacted by their engagement style. The current findings, however, suggest that more nuanced relationships can be observed in this space. For example, we are seeing more people who report anxiety and depression symptoms also reporting that they engage in empowering styles of music engagement. This suggests young people are now consciously employing positive music engagement styles whilst experiencing poor mental health or as an intentional form of coping.

Our findings also highlight the continued impact of distinct, cascading, and overlapping factors of oppression at the individual level, particularly for Black and Brown youth. From a life-course perspective we recognize the significant role of students' environments on their mental health, but also the culturally rich transformative developmental opportunities that exist for Black and Brown youth and other minoritized groups.

After reviewing model coefficients, the most parsimonious (final) model for empowering engagement included a subset of variables from each entered layer: racial/ethnic identity development (layer 1); regulating and motivational intentions for music use (layer 2); depressive symptoms, cognitive-reflective processes (prioritizing lyrical analysis), and having enough friends that care (layer 3). Notably, favoring Hip Hop music was not statistically significant.

For risky engagement, racial/ethnic identity development (layer 1) and depressive symptoms (layer 3) were the statistically significant *positive* predictors. Task-oriented intentions for music use (layer 2) and having enough friends that care (layer 3) were *negative* predictors, meaning they were less likely to have risky engagement. Notably, favoring Hip Hop music was not statistically significant. Results supported a model with 36 percent of variability in empowering music engagement predicted and 19 percent of risky engagement predicted.

Findings support prior research that established that empowering music engagement exists (Travis and Bowman, 2012, 2015) and that these empowering outcomes were not incidental but deliberate and intentional (Travis, Bowman, Levy, and Crooke, 2020). These self-directed experiences, whether it is creating music (Levstek and Banerjee, 2021), listening, analyzing, or otherwise engaging music, can be empowering and have significant positive personal and collective outcomes. Therefore, creating opportunities for empowering intentional music engagement within self-care and self-management of mental health can be especially meaningful. Further, better understanding the specific pathways of empowerment and intentional uses of music can be valuable for traditional therapeutic practices as well.

Results were often consistent with prior research but also helped reinforce newer research on intentional music use. More specifically, findings continue to support the significance of time spent exploring one's own social identity (Levy, 2019; Levy and Wong, 2022; Levy, Emdin, and Adjapong, 2022). That exploring identity was positively associated with empowering engagement *and* risky music engagement may reflect distinctions between positive and negative cultural and/or racial socialization where an absence of strong cultural affirmations and pride can have a deleterious effect on racial or cultural socialization and inhibit a strong racial/ethnic identity (Travis and Leech, 2014). Results also echo the importance of positive and supportive relationships in general (Travis and Leech, 2014) and their value alongside high effort coping, especially among Black youth (Kahsay and Mezuk, 2022). Further, intentional music use (i.e., particularly for self-regulation and for motivation for personal and community improvement) added significantly to the model. This supports prior research suggesting community improvement and equity and justice can be kindled by Hip Hop (Jasiri X, 2023; Levy and Wong, 2022; Travis, 2016; Washington, 2018). Finally, our evidence supports the research of Rodwin et al. (2022) by highlighting the therapeutic value of engaging in cognitive-reflective processes with music, which is prioritizing lyrical analysis and meaning-making over 'just' enjoying the beats in music.

We must use this existing evidence to be explicit about what might help predict who is likely to benefit from specific therapeutic practices. We must also be explicit as to what might contribute to prevention efforts that seek to promote effective self-care, self-help, and self-management strategies. These findings will help us better assess for and support those who might be especially amenable to music-based health promotion and therapeutic mental health strategies (Rodwin et al., 2022) and help us to know whether these strategies support and help students in their self-care or in their engagement and work with professionals in mediated music-based activities (e.g., music-integrated in-school or afterschool educational activities, therapeutic activities, or other youth development activities) (Munson et al., 2021; Munson et al., 2022).

Intentional Music Use: Empowering Outcomes and Empowering Processes

People engage music experiences on their own in ways that align with typologies of most common and effective interventions, (a) somatosensory (active, using equipment, creating, and performing [can be done alone]), (b) social-emotional (interpersonal and interactive, self- and social awareness), and (c) cognitive-reflective (higher-order thinking, meaning-making, and processing). These are captured by the outcomes measured by the ICE inventory (Travis and Bowman, 2015) and the reasons why/intentions for listening (i.e., regulatory, motivational, and task-oriented reasons—first reported by Travis, Bowman, Levy, and Crooke, 2020). Self-driven and intentional use of music has people combine these processes in their own idiosyncratic ways, but then likely in more systematic ways consistent with the overlapping dimensions found in research on effective program strategies (i.e., socio-cognitive [processing and analyzing in groups], socio-somatic, and holistic).

Results also point to potential motivating factors for students that actively use music for the promotion of personal growth and development and community well-being. These individuals actively pursue music experiences for more than just mood regulation (i.e., increase positive emotions and inhibit negative emotions). There is a strong motivational component for more substantive personal and community development. Participants actively used music as a motivational tool for 'better'. This aligns with prior research that discussed the *impacts* of music engagement and found empowering music engagement as pathways to 'better'—feeling better, doing better, being better, better belonging, and better conditions (Travis and Bowman, 2015). This suggests that supportive services can help to leverage the momentum for better and provide tools and resources for individuals to continue their personal self-directed journeys of coping and for betterment (Mushonga and van Breda, 2021). Supportive services can also take a more structured and directive approach by facilitating music-integrated therapeutic experiences. This includes more nuanced approaches that blend the two by helping to eliminate potentially maladaptive self-directed strategies by young people (McFerran and Saarikallio, 2014; McFerran et al., 2015). Results continue to show people engage music content across all genres in ways that are empowering and risky. But more importantly, its impacts on their lives are complex and nuanced. We have ways of measuring this nuance.

Hip Hop, Empowerment and Risky Engagement, and Wellness

First, results of the present study suggest that all genres of music can be empowering and risky. While measures originally derived from an empowering rap-music engagement scale, all current scales and subscales were based on questions asking about 'the music you listen to most ("your music")'. When looking at the relationship between empowering and risky engagement, there was no correlation across the two global constructs. However, when examining the subscales there were significant relationships that became apparent. This supports conclusions from prior research (Travis and Bowman, 2015), which suggested that while reliability subscale scores were not as optimal as the overall scale scores, there was still empirical validity and potential conceptual value in exploring more nuanced analyses based on subscales of empowering music engagement. Further, these empowering outcomes aligned with empowering intentions for use and also aligned with research validating the effective processes within music-based interventions (Rodwin *et al.*, 2022).

While data did not support statistically significant greater levels of empowering engagement, it did support substantial empowering outcomes, and empowering processes for those that have Hip Hop as a favorite, supporting the rationale for tailoring strategies for individuals that embrace Hip Hop culture. Those who reported Hip Hop as their favorite genres tended to elicit more empowering *and* risky messages. A positive trend of empowering engagement exists from least favorite level to most favorite level. However, the difference is not significant *between* any of the levels, including lowest to highest. Alternatively, when looking at risky music engagement, the highest-level group reporting Hip Hop as their favorite was significantly correlated with overall risky engagement, and the Risk 1 subscale.

That Hip Hop is explicitly recognized for both empowering engagement and heightened risk suggests an opportunity to use strengths-based, empowerment-based, and life-course-based frameworks to enhance empowerment and reduce risk in pursuit of academic, social, and emotional competence-building. Further, there was significantly less empowering engagement for the subgroup that reported Hip Hop as their favorite genre but did not list Hip Hop artists among their top three favorite artists (mean = 49.1). This suggests a potential differentiation between those that derive a significant entertainment value from Hip Hop, perhaps in social settings, but do not fully embrace the culture in ways that are empowering.

This suggests that Hip Hop is amenable within interventions for promoting empowerment and inhibiting risk, with application across public health, social work, education, and juvenile justice programming. These are applicable for interventions across the life-course in family/home, educational, therapeutic, and developmental settings—to support self-care and self-management, and traditional interdisciplinary service provision. These include Hip Hop integrated educational (Hicks Harper and Emdin, 2022), therapeutic (Washington, 2018), and violence prevention (Abdul-Adil and Suarez, 2022) strategies.

For Practice, For Self-Care

Findings suggest that we have conceptual and practical tools to more carefully tailor and curate music-based interventions for academic, social, and emotional growth. This is our next challenge. How do we best use baseline assessments such as the ICE Inventory in partnership with our existing intervention typologies (Rodwin *et al.*, 2022; see also McFerran *et al.*, 2020) to help scaffold activities that can be effective for different desired points of emphasis? How do we use our range of effective practice frameworks to be applicable in academic and non-academic settings for groups and for individual students? Finally, based on our evidence of the extensive use of self-care strategies and self-management through music, along with what predicts the most empowering music engagement, how do we also create alternative tools for self-care?

At the same time, results make it clear that we must pay attention to risk alongside empowerment in arts-based strategies. There is not an inverse relationship where empowering engagement means that people are significantly less likely to report risky engagement. How do you also tailor and curate tools to inhibit/prevent risky behaviours, with attention to cultural realities and data demonstrating how risk is not distributed equally? People report both empowering and risky engagement, with some common predictors but also unique predictors. Students that are struggling have the potential for both empowering (e.g., regulating and motivating) and risky engagement (e.g., rumination). Rumination, not explicitly explored in the present study but possible among those with depressive symptoms, would be consistent with prior attention to the negative mental health effects of rumination (McFerran and Saarikallio, 2014) and the responsibility young people can take in being more proactive and discerning in how they engage music to ensure healthier and more desirable outcomes.

Results also suggest some people (e.g., those reporting depressive symptoms) were more likely to engage in risky attitudes and behaviours, but *also* empowering actions. Empowering engagement in these situations may be to combat the risky attitudes and behaviour, or it may be that these individuals are more receptive to empowering engagement. Alternatively, those that reported anxiety symptoms may be seeking support/relief through empowering music engagement, but not taking it to the level of risky attitudes and behaviours. For them, it may be a different type of struggle. They may be anxious, worried, and unsettled . . . but not depressed, and perhaps not as down on their identity, their sense of self, and/or their place in the world. It may be that their world feels less ominous and daunting, a qualitatively different experience.

Using the ICE inventory in assessments, it will be possible to determine who may be more receptive to music-based therapeutic strategies. The findings suggest that more attention is given to both receptive and active engagement of music lyrics by professionals and that youth on a more positive developmental trajectory may not be any more inclined to empowering music engagement. That both youth with depressive symptoms and those reporting more positive and supportive friendships are more likely to report empowering engagement can seem contradictory. However, those that are struggling may have the capacities to be more proactive in engaging their resources if they have some greater developmental assets in place (i.e., the flourishing argument) in comparison to those that feel they do not have the same level of connectedness among their friendships. Perhaps this allows their periods of mental health struggles to be more episodic and less enduring/for shorter durations.

Music as Practical, Music as Play

Intentional exercise and task-oriented uses were associated with less risky engagement. Perhaps these variable relationships are capturing those people that are not as interested in the socio-emotional aspects of music engagement. These individuals use music as a more practical tool as opposed to a therapeutic tool to 'get better' in some way. Even further, those using music for exercise and completing tasks may be engaging in activities more closely aligned with 'musicking', or music as play, with their associated therapeutic and well-being outcomes (Stewart Rose and Countryman, 2021).

While *music-play* is often discussed in the group context, it can also be an individual activity. The study by Stewart Rose and Countryman (2021) provides a rich body of research support for music as play and as a form of self-care within the context of groups *and* as an individual. For example, one young person reflects, 'Sometimes on the bus I'll be fingering, like, playing the notes on my arm and pretending I'm playing my guitar and I can imagine myself performing because the feeling I get is, like, I can almost envision myself there'. Another continues with the dual premises of having freedom and vulnerability, in a self-regulating and grounding way, 'letting go of the pressures of his life and proactively choosing his favourite songs to provide "emotional therapy" . . . it blanks out everything around me and it makes me feel like I'm just here by myself, not in a bad way, more like in a place where I can think to myself' (Stewart Rose and Countryman, 2021: 470–471). Another student shared, 'when I listen to music I feel more myself: you can be who you want to be and how you want to be' (Stewart Rose and Countryman, 2021: 474). These may be about self-regulation, or inspiration for personal and community betterment, but they can also surface in more isolated activities where one values their self-time . . . to focus, to reflect, be in 'flow', and/or to exercise.

Treatment Engagement

Building on important research by Munson *et al.* (2022) and Rodwin *et al.* (2022), our findings can help to understand which music-integrated processes might help with intervention design and efficacy, but also which might simply inspire continued therapeutic engagement, or effective self-care. All three types of Rodwin *et al.*'s (2022) therapeutic processes are identified. For example, it may be that somatosensory dominant responses (i.e., regulating and feeling responses) suggest the value of immediate use of music equipment/technology, like with the "Clip Jamming" technique (Crooke and McFerran, 2019). That is, students can perhaps begin active playing and creating at the start of any session, to help regulate, engage, and build rapport. Meanwhile, for others—for individuals that might score higher on community empowering engagement and intentional use linked to motivation for better community conditions—the more socio-cognitive and holistic approaches might be emphasized proportionally (although not to the absence of other meaningful goals and foci).

Culturally Sustaining Practice and Pedagogy

Finally, when considering the ability to tailor therapeutic, educational, and public-health practices and recommendations to unique individual and cultural preferences, we open the door to tapping into organic culturally sustaining practices like Hip Hop culture. Research highlights the conceptual and empirical value of culturally sustaining practices with teaching and pedagogy (Paris and Alim, 2017) and mental health and counseling practices. Results are also promising in consideration of possible professional-development and skill-building opportunities for greater cultural responsiveness among practitioners.

In Summary: Continuing a Global Movement to Eliminate Inequities and Injustices

Strong evidence of active and intentional uses of music for empowerment and to promote self-regulation, personal growth and development, and community engagement suggests we can more strategically provide opportunities for youth to use the music that they prefer, relate to, and enjoy for academic, social, and emotional well-being, with and without professional support. This is increasingly consistent with existing research and practice (Radez *et al.*, 2021).

The significance of reducing stress, anxiety, and depression because of the impacts across the lifespan and across generations cannot be overemphasized. The value of racial and ethnic identity development for participants within empowering music engagement remains consistent. The ability to improve community conditions to reduce inequities and injustices and mitigate trauma-inducing environments is also essential, along with the recognition of social determinants, including racism, which contribute to these conditions and inequities.

It may be possible to help develop policies and procedures that support intentional and conscious use of music by individuals needing help whether or not they participate in traditional professionally-mediated therapeutic activities. Therapeutic strategies should consider health-enhancing goals as much as goals to inhibit risk and threats to well-being, especially among those that favor Hip Hop music.

Further research is needed on holistically integrated approaches to therapeutic music engagement to help determine the most promising mixes of somatosensory, social-emotional, and cognitive-reflective strategies, and how these can be uniquely tailored to the needs of individuals and communities across settings. Finally, in this new era, research can help us determine how these unique strategies can be used to develop and maintain tools for self-care and self-management.

References

Abdul-Adil, J. and Suárez, L. M. (2022). The urban youth trauma center: A trauma-informed continuum for addressing community violence among youth. *Community Mental Health Journal*, 58(2): 334–342. https://doi.org/10.1007/s10597-021-00827-4.

Adjapong, E. and Levy, I. (2021). Hip-hop can heal: Addressing mental health through hip-hop in the urban classroom. *The New Educator*, 17(3): 242–263.

Alvarez, T. T. (2012). Beats, rhymes, and life: Rap therapy in an urban setting. In S. Hadley and G. Yancy (Eds.), *Therapeutic Uses of Rap and Hip-Hop*. Abingdon: Routledge, pp. 117–128.

American Academy of Pediatrics [AAP] (2021). *Declaration of national emergency on child and adolescent mental health.* https://www.aap.org/en/advocacy/child-and-ado lescent-healthy-mental-development/aap-aacap-cha-declaration-of-a-national-emergency-in-child-and-adolescent-mental-health/.

American Psychological Association [APA] (2021). *Demand for mental health treatment continues to increase, say psychologists* [Press release, October 19]. https://www.apa. org/news/press/releases/2021/10/mental-health-treatment-demand.

Bennett, S. D., Cuijpers, P., Ebert, D. D., McKenzie Smith, M., Coughtrey, A. E., Heyman, I., Manzotti, G. and Shafran, R. (2019). Practitioner review: Unguided and guided self-help interventions for common mental health disorders in children and adolescents: a systematic review and meta-analysis. *Journal of Child Psychology and Psychiatry*, 60(8): 828. https://doi.org/10.1111/jcpp.13010.

Brown, M. M. and Grumet, J. G. (2009). School-based suicide prevention with African American youth in an urban setting. *Professional Psychology: Research and Practice*, 40(2), 111–117. https://doi.org/10.1037/a0012866.

Centers for Disease Control and Prevention. (2023, July 11). *Youth risk behavior survey: Data summary & trends report.* https://www.cdc.gov/healthyyouth/data/yrbs/ pdf/YRBS_Data-Summary-Trends_Report2023_508.pdf.

Chang, J. (2005). *Can't stop, won't stop: a history of the hip-hop generation.* St. Martin's Press.

Choi, M. J., Hong, J. S., Travis Jr, R. and Kim, J. (2023). Effects of school environment on depression among Black and White adolescents. *Journal of Community Psychology*, 51(3): 1181–1200. https://doi.org/10.1002/jcop.22969.

Colectivo, L. L. R. and Alim, H. S. (2023). 5. 'Luchando derechos' in neoliberal Spain: Hip Hop visions beyond racism, xenophobia, islamophobia, and the gentrification of El Raval, Barcelona, Vol. 3. Oakland, CA: University of California Press. https://doi-org/ 10.1525/9780520382817-008.

Crooke, A. H. D. and Mcferran, K. S. (2019). Improvising using beat making technologies in music therapy with young people. *Music Therapy Perspectives*, 37(1): 55–64. https://doi.org/10.1093/mtp/miy025

DeCarlo, A. and Hockman, E. (2004). RAP therapy: A group work intervention method for urban adolescents. *Social Work with Groups*, 26(3): 45–59. https://doi.org/10.1300/J009v26n03_06.

De France, K., Evans, G. W., Brody, G. H. and Doan, S. N. (2022). Cost of resilience: Childhood poverty, mental health, and chronic physiological stress. *Psychoneuroendocrinology*, 144: 1–7. https://doi.org/10.1016/j.psyneuen.2022.105872.

DeNora, T. (2013). *Music asylums: Well-being through music in everyday life*. Ashgate.

Durlak, J. A., Weissberg, R. P., Dymnicki, A. B., Taylor, R. D. and Schellinger, K. B. (2011). The impact of enhancing students' social and emotional learning: A meta-analysis of school-based universal interventions. *Child Development*, 82(1): 405–432. https:// doi.org/ 10. 1111/j. 1467- 8624. 2010. 01564.x.

Elligan, D. (2000). Rap therapy: A culturally sensitive approach to psychotherapy with young African American men. *Journal of African American Men*, 5(3): 27–36. https://doi.org/10.1007/s12111-000-1002-y.

Erbacher, T. A. and Singer, J. B. (2018). Suicide risk monitoring: The missing piece in suicide risk assessment. *Contemporary School Psychology*, 22(2): 186–194. https://doi.org/10.1007/s40688-017-0164-8.

Evans, J. M. (2022). Exploring social media contexts for cultivating connected learning with Black youth in urban communities: The case of dreamer studio. *Qualitative Sociology*, 45: 393–411. https://doi-org/10.1007/s11133-022-09514-6.

Evans, J. M. and Baym, N. K. (2022). The audacity of clout (chasing): Digital strategies of Black youth in Chicago DIY Hip-Hop. *International Journal of Communication (Online)*, 16: 2669.

Fenton, C. and Kingsley, E. (2022). Scoping review: Alternatives to self-harm recommended on mental health self-help websites. *International Journal of Mental Health Nursing*, 32(1): 76–94. https://doi.org/10.1111/inm.13067.

Gann, E. (2010). The effects of therapeutic hip-hop activity groups on perception of self and social supports in at-risk urban adolescents [Unpublished doctoral dissertation]. The Wright Institute.

Garrido, S., Eerola, T. and McFerran, K. (2017). Group rumination: Social interactions around music in people with depression. *Frontiers in Psychology*, 8: 490. https://doi.org/10.3389/fpsyg.2017.00490.

Goodwill, J. R. and Yasui, M. (2022). Mental health service utilization, school experiences, and religious involvement among a national sample of black adolescents who attempted suicide: Examining within and cross-race group differences. *Child & Adolescent Social Work Journal*. Advance online publication. https://doi.org/10.1007/s10560-022-00888-8.

Hadley, S. and Yancy, G. (2012). Therapeutic uses of rap and hip-hop. Abingdon: Routledge.

Halfon N. and Forrest, C. B. (2018). *The emerging theoretical framework of life course health development*. In N. Halfon, C. Forrest, R. Lerner and E. Faustman (eds.), *Handbook of Life Course Health Development*. Springer, Cham.

Hambrick, E. P., Brawner, T. W., Perry, B. D., Brandt, K., Hofmeister, C. and Collins, J. O. (2019). Beyond the ACE score: Examining relationships between timing of developmental adversity, relational health and developmental outcomes in children. *Archives of Psychiatric Nursing*, 33(3): 238–247. https://doi-org.libproxy.txstate.edu/10.1016/ j.apnu.2018.11.001.

Harper, P. T. H. and Emdin, C. (2022). *Cultivating science genius through hip-hop development and reality pedagogy.* In A. G. Robins, L. Knibbs, T. N. Ingram, M. N. Weaver Jr., and A. A. Hilton (eds.), *Young, Gifted and Missing: The Underrepresentation of African American Males in Science, Technology, Engineering and Mathematics Disciplines*, vol. 25. Bingley: Emerald Publishing, pp. 99–113. https://doi.org/10.1108/S1479-3644202 20000025008.

Jasiri X. (2023). *Hood.* In H. S. Alim, J. Chang, and C. P. Wong (eds.), *Freedom Moves: Hip Hop Knowledges, Pedagogies, and Futures*, pp. 159–179. Oakland, CA: University of California Press.

Kahsay, E., and Mezuk, B. (2022). The association between John Henryism and depression and suicidal ideation among African-American and Caribbean Black adolescents in the United States. *Journal of Adolescent Health*, 71: 721–728.

Kessler, R. C., Berglund, P., Demler, O., Jin, R., Merikangas, K. R., and Walters, E. E. (2005). Lifetime prevalence and age-of-onset distributions of DSM-IV disorders in the national comorbidity survey replication. *Archives of General Psychiatry*, 62(6): 593– 602. doi: 10.1001/archpsyc.62.6.593.

Koelsch, S. (2015). Music-evoked emotions: principles, brain correlates, and implications for therapy. *Annals of the New York Academy of Sciences*, 1337(1): 193–201. https://doi. org/10.1111/nyas.12684.

Levstek, M. and Banerjee, R. (2021). A model of psychological mechanisms of inclusive music-making: Empowerment of marginalized young people. *Music & Science*, 4: 1– 18. https://doaj.org/article/1ae4bb8795cb4e918ac101609aa619a8.

Levy, I. P. (2019). Hip-Hop and spoken word therapy in urban school counseling. *Professional School Counseling*, 22(1b): 1–11.

Levy, I. P., Emdin, C. and Adjapong, E. (2022). Lyric writing as an emotion processing intervention for school counselors: Hip-Hop spoken word therapy and motivational interviewing. *Journal of Poetry Therapy*, 35(2): 114–130. https://doi.org/10.1080/08893 675.2021.2004372.

Levy, I. and Travis, R. (2020). The critical cycle of mixtape creation: Reducing stress via three different group counseling styles. *Journal for Specialists in Group Work*, 45(4): 307–330. https://doi-org.libproxy.txstate.edu/10.1080/01933922.2020.1826614.

Levy, I. P. and Wong, C. P. (2022). Processing a white supremacist insurrection through Hip-Hop mixtape making: A school counseling intervention. *Equity & Excellence in Education*, 55(4): 395–407. https://doi-org.libproxy.txstate.edu/10.1080/10665 684.2022.2158398.

MacKinnon, L. (2012). The neurosequential model of therapeutics: An interview with Bruce Perry. *Australian and New Zealand Journal of Family Therapy*, 33(3), 210–218. https://doi.org/10.1017/aft.2012.25.

Malchiodi, C. A. (2023). *Handbook of expressive arts therapy.* C. A. Malchiodi (Ed.). New York, NY: Guilford Press.

Mau, W.-C., Li, J. and Hoetmer, K. (2016). Transforming high school counseling: Counselors roles, practices, and expectations for student success. *Administrative Issues Journal: Connecting Education, Practice, and Research*, 6(2): 83–95. https://doi. org/10.5929/2016.6.2.5.

McFerran, K. S. and Saarikallio, S. (2014). Depending on music to feel better: Being conscious of responsibility when appropriating the power of music. *The Arts in Psychotherapy*, 41(1): 89–97. https://doi.org/10.1016/j.aip.2013.11.007.

McFerran, K. S., Garrido, S., O, G. L., Grocke, D. and Sawyer, S. M. (2015). Examining the relationship between self-reported mood management and music preferences of Australian teenagers. *Nordic Journal of Music Therapy*, 24(3): 187–203. https://doi.org/10.1080/08098131.2014.908942.

McFerran, K. S., Hense, C., Koike, A. and Rickwood, D. (2018). Intentional music use to reduce psychological distress in adolescents accessing primary mental health care. *Clinical Child Psychology and Psychiatry*, 23(4): 567–581. https://doi.org/10.1177/1359104518767231.

McFerran, K. S., Lai, H. I., Chang, W., Acquaro, D., Chin, T. C., Stokes, H. and Alexander Hew Dale Crooke. (2020). Music, rhythm and trauma: A critical interpretive synthesis of research literature. *Frontiers in Psychology*, 11. https://doi.org/10.3389/fpsyg.2020.00324.

McGrath, J. J., Saha, S., Al-Hamzawi, A., Andrade, L., Benjet, C., Bromet, E. J., ... and Kessler, R. C. (2016). The bidirectional associations between psychotic experiences and DSM-IV mental disorders. *American Journal of Psychiatry*, 173(10): 997–1006.

Munson, M. R., Jaccard, J., Moore, K. L., Rodwin, A. H., Shimizu, R., Cole, A. R., Scott, J. L. D., Narendorf, S. C., Davis, M., Gilmer, T. and Stanhope, V. (2022). Impact of a brief intervention to improve engagement in a recovery program for young adults with serious mental illness. *Schizophrenia Research*, 250: 104–111. https://doi.org/10.1016/j.schres.2022.11.008.

Munson, M. R., Jaccard, J., Scott, J. L. D., Moore, K. L., Narendorf, S. C., Cole, A. R., Shimizu, R., Rodwin, A. H., Jenefsky, N., Davis, M. and Gilmer, T. (2021). Outcomes of a metaintervention to improve treatment engagement among young adults with serious mental illnesses: Application of a pilot randomized explanatory design. *Journal of Adolescent Health*, 69(5): 790–796. https://doi.org/10.1016/j.jadohealth.2021.04.023.

Mushonga, S. and Van Breda, A. (2021). Nonhuman systems as a source of interactional resilience among university students raised by alcohol-abusing caregivers in Lesotho. *Social Work/Maatskaplike Werk*, 57(4): 425–442. https://doi.org/10.15270/57-4-967.

Nafar, T., Nafar, S., Jreri, M., Offendum, O. and Salti, R. (2023). 3. 'Al-shaab yurid isqat al-nitham!': Sustaining revolution in Palestine and Syria through Hip Hop, vol. 3. University of California Press. https://doi-org.libproxy.txstate.edu/10.1525/9780520382817-006.

National Academies Press [NAS/NAP] (2016). *Ending discrimination against people with mental and substance use disorders: The evidence for stigma change*. Washington, DC: National Academies Press.

National Academies Press [NAS/NAP] (2022). Tools for supporting emotional wellbeing in children and youth. https://nap.nationalacademies.org/resource/other/dbasse/wellbeing-tools/interactive/.

Newall, M., and Machi, S. (2020). Mental health experiences differ across race, gender and age. *IPSOS*. https://www.ipsos.com/en-us/news-polls/mental-health-covid-19.

Ortega-Williams, A. (2021). Organizing as 'collective-self' care among African American youth in precarious times. *Journal of African American Studies*, 25(1): 3–21. https://doi.org/10.1007/s12111-020-09506-2.

Paris, D. and Alim, H. S. (2017). *Culturally sustaining pedagogies: Teaching and learning for justice in a changing world*. New York, NY: Teachers College Press.

Racine, N., McArthur, B. A., Cooke, J. E., Eirich, R., Zhu, J., and Madigan, S. (2021). Global prevalence of depressive and anxiety symptoms in children and adolescents during COVID-19: a meta-analysis. *JAMA Pediatrics*, 175(11): 1142–1150.

Radez, J., Reardon, T., Creswell, C., Lawrence, P. J., Evdoka-Burton, G. and Waite, P. (2021). Why do children and adolescents (not) seek and access professional help for their mental health problems? A systematic review of quantitative and qualitative studies. *European Child & Adolescent Psychiatry*, 30(2), 183–211. https://doi.org/10.1007/s00787-019-01469-4.

Reinert, M., Fritze, D., and Nguyen, T. (2021). *The state of mental health in America 2022*. Alexandria, VA: Mental Health America.

Reis, A., Saheb, R., Parish, P., Earl, A., Klupp, N. and Sperandei, S. (2021). How I cope at university: Self-directed stress management strategies of Australian students. *Stress & Health: Journal of the International Society for the Investigation of Stress*, 37(5): 1010–1025.

Rodwin, A. H., Shimizu, R., Travis Jr, R., James, K. J., Banya, M., and Munson, M. R. (2022). A systematic review of music-based interventions to improve treatment engagement and mental health outcomes for adolescents and young adults. *Child and Adolescent Social Work Journal*, 1–30.

Russ, S. A., Hotez, E., Berghaus, M., Verbiest, S., Hoover, C., Schor, E. L. and Halfon, N. (2022). What makes an intervention a life course intervention? *Pediatrics*, 149: S1–S11. https://doi.org/10.1542/peds.2021-053509D.

Schwan, K. J., Fallon, B., and Milne, B. (2018). "The one thing that actually helps": Art creation as a self-care and health-promoting practice amongst youth experiencing homelessness. *Children and Youth Services Review*, 93: 355–364.

Simons, L. G. and Steele, M. E. (2020). The negative impact of economic hardship on adolescent academic engagement: An examination parental investment and family stress processes. *Journal of Youth & Adolescence*, 49(5): 973–990. https://doi.org/10.1007/s10964-020-01210-4.

Spector, P. E. (2019). Do not cross me: Optimizing the use of cross-sectional designs. *Journal of Business & Psychology*, 34(2): 125–137. https://doi-org.libproxy.txstate.edu/10.1007/s10869-018-09613-8.

Spors, A. V. (2022). *Caring systems: Making relational, gameful self-care technologies for mental health [Dissertation/Thesis]*. University of Nottingham.

Stewart Rose, L. and Countryman, J. (2021). When youth musicking is play. *Research Studies in Music Education*, 43(3): 465–480.

Substance Abuse and Mental Health Services Administration [SAMHSA]. (2020). *Key substance use and mental health indicators in the United States: Results from the 2019 national survey on drug use and health*. https://www.samhsa.gov/data/release/2019-national-survey-drug-use-and-health-nsduh-releases.

Taylor, R. D., Oberle, E., Durlak, J. A. and Weissberg, R. P. (2017). Promoting positive youth development through school-based social and emotional learning interventions: A meta-analysis of follow-up effects. *Child Development*, 88(4): 1156–1171.

Town, R., Hayes, D., Fonagy, P. and Stapley, E. (2022). A qualitative investigation of LGBTQ+ young people's experiences and perceptions of self-managing their mental health. *European Child & Adolescent Psychiatry*, 31(9): 1441–1454. https://doi.org/10.1007/s00787-021-01783-w.

Travis, R. (2013). Rap music and the empowerment of today's youth: Evidence in everyday music listening, music therapy, and commercial rap music. *Child & Adolescent Social Work Journal*, 30(2): 139–167. https://doi.org/10.1007/s10560-012-0285-x.

Travis, R. (2016). *The healing power of Hip Hop*. Westport, CT: Praeger.

Travis, R. and Bowman, S. W. (2012). Ethnic identity, self-esteem and variability in perceptions of rap music's empowering and risky influences. *Journal of Youth Studies*, 15(4): 455–478.

Travis, R. and Bowman, S. W. (2015). Validation of the individual and community empowerment inventory: A measure of rap music engagement among first-year college students. *Journal of Human Behavior in the Social Environment*, 25(2): 90–108. https://doi.org/10.1080/10911359.2014.974433.

Travis, R., Bowman, S. W., Levy, I. and Crooke, A. (2020, January 16). *Factors contributing to the intentional use of music for therapeutic benefits and community improvement [oral paper]*. Society for Social Work and Research (SSWR) Annual Meeting. Washington DC.

Travis Jr, R., and Deepak, A. (2011). Empowerment in context: Lessons from hip-hop culture for social work practice. *Journal of ethnic and cultural diversity in social work*, 20(3): 203–222.

Travis, R., Gann, E., Crooke, A. H. and Jenkins, S. M. (2021). Using therapeutic beat making and lyrics for empowerment. *Journal of Social Work*, 21(3): 551–574. https://doi-org.libproxy.txstate.edu/10.1177/1468017320911346.

Travis, R., Gann, E., Crooke, A. H. D. and Jenkins, S. M. (2019). Hip Hop, empowerment, and therapeutic beat-making: Potential solutions for summer learning loss, depression, and anxiety in youth. *Journal of Human Behavior in the Social Environment*, 29(6), 744–765. https://doi-org.libproxy.txstate.edu/10.1080/10911359.2019.1607646.

Travis, R. and Leech, T. G. J. (2014). Empowerment-based positive youth development: A new understanding of healthy development for African American youth. *Journal of Research on Adolescence*, 24(1): 93.

Travis, R., Rodwin, A. H. and Allcorn, A. (2019). Hip Hop, empowerment, and clinical practice for homeless adults with severe mental illness. *Social Work with Groups*, 42(2): 83–100. https://doi.org/10.1080/01609513.2018.1486776.

Tyson, E. H. (2004). Rap music in social work practice with African-American and Latino youth. *Journal of Human Behavior in the Social Environment*, 8(4): 1–21. https://doi.org/10.1300/J137v08n04_01.

Viega, M. (2016). Exploring the discourse in Hip Hop and implications for music therapy practice. *Music Therapy Perspectives*, 34: 138–146. https://doi.org/10.1093/mtp/miv035.

Viega, M. (2018). A humanistic understanding of the use of digital technology in therapeutic songwriting. *Music Therapy Perspectives*, 36(2): 152–160. https://doi.org/10.1093/mtp/miy014.

Washington, A. R. (2018). Integrating hip-hop culture and rap music into social justice counseling with Black males. *Journal of Counseling & Development*, 96(1): 97–105. https://doi.org/10.1002/jcad.12181.

World Health Organization [WHO]. (2023). Depressive disorder (depression). https://www.who.int/news-room/fact-sheets/detail/depression.

Zogby, J. (2022, January 17). *As teens return to school after holidays, stress levels are highest ever; 58% report knowing someone who has 'considered self-harm'*. Forbes. https://www.forbes.com/sites/johnzogby/2022/01/17/as-teens-return-to-school-after-holidays-stress-levels-are-highest-ever-58-report-knowing-someone-who-has-considered-self-harm/?sh=71b05b21d806.

9

Becoming a Therapeutic Hip Hop Mentor

Kiran Manley

I am a balancing act
I come with past hurts
I came to spin dreams
I believe
Sunshine gleams in
Glowing hearts with
Fresh hopes

'Hip hop is neither beholden to the past nor running blindly into the future—it is a culture of possibility. It is a culture of now'.

(Haupt and Rollefson, 2021: 4)

Introduction

This chapter explores therapeutic Hip Hop as a culturally competent mental health intervention for marginalised communities. It presents a picture of inequality within the United Kingdom through a bricolage of empirical research and autoethnographic writing based on the author's MSc training in 'Creative Writing for Therapeutic Purposes' (CWTP). It elevates and celebrates the cultural identity and lived experience of a researcher, participant, and service-user in order to promote culturally competent helping practice, given the inequalities faced by Global Majority[1] people in White Majority countries.

Autoethnography can be defined as 'an approach to research and writing that seeks to describe and systematically analyze (*graphy*) personal experience (*auto*) in order to understand cultural experience (*ethno*)' (Ellis *et al.*, 2010: 1). According to Ellis *et al.* (2010), 'This approach challenges canonical

Kiran Manley, *Becoming a Therapeutic Hip Hop Mentor* In: *Music for Inclusion and Healing in Schools and Beyond.*
Edited by: Pete Dale, Pamela Burnard, and Raphael Travis Jr., Oxford University Press. © Oxford University Press 2023.
DOI: 10.1093/oso/9780197692677.003.0010

ways of doing research and representing others' and 'treats research as a political, socially-just and socially-conscious act' (p. 1).

CWTP refers to expressive writing, narrative therapy, poetry therapy, bibliotherapy, and journal therapy. It is a growing field of research and practice based on humanistic and person-centred approaches, emphasising people's potential for growth, change, and movement in a positive direction in their lives (Metanoia Institute, 2023). Practitioners abide by the same standards for practice and codes of ethics as counsellors and therapists.

Therapeutic Hip Hop refers here to CWTP combined with Hip Hop. The terms 'Hip Hop' and 'rap' and 'counselling' and 'therapy' are applied interchangeably throughout the chapter. As a forty-three-year-old British Indian woman born in England, I tell the story of how my evidence-based therapeutic Hip Hop practice began. The model combines CWTP approaches with Hip Hop and UK bass culture. It is rooted in the notion of self-empowerment through creativity and self-care.

The Hero's Journey refers to a twelve-stage narrative structure identified across world myths by Joseph Campbell (Campbell, 1968). His work was developed further by Chris Vogler in relation to screenwriting (Vogler, 1998). Both align story archetypes with those discussed by Carl Jung in terms of human psychological development. Hence, the Hero's Journey presents a helpful conceptual framework for reflective, therapeutic writing around Hip Hop, including songwriting and journalling. Rap lyrics and music videos may act as stimuli for peer-discussion and creative exploration, within a supported group. Due to limitations of space, the Hero's Journey will not be explored further here.

The model presented in this chapter was devised to bring Hip Hop Therapy to the United Kingdom in a way that represents and includes the United Kingdom's music scene. Our Hip Hop culture is very different from that of the United States. UK nightclubs are brimming with house, UK garage, and, now more than ever, drum and bass and jungle—but not Hip Hop. Here, ravers' ears are more tuned towards the Jamaican sound systems that birthed Hip Hop. It makes straight sense that Hip Hop Therapy in the United Kingdom includes local and culturally specific music forms, enabling it to reach a greater audience. Hip Hop is, after all, a democratic, postmodern, and universal folk art in itself.

Knowledge of Hip Hop's therapeutic potential is socially constructed by the author-researcher, MCs, rappers, marginalised communities, and the professionals who serve them. Though there is still much to learn, it is hoped that this chapter will spark questions, ideas, and debate to further develop the field of therapeutic Hip Hop. Let us bathe in its healing waters and dance in its thick, sticky beats.

Hip Hop HEALS CIC

Hip Hop HEALS (HHH), a Community Interest Company (CIC), is the United Kingdom's first therapeutic Hip Hop (or Hip Hop Therapy) organisation. We are a social enterprise, based in Birmingham, United Kingdom (UK). Our aim is to reduce suicide rates for men, young people, and those from Global Majority ethnic backgrounds in the United Kingdom. Sadly, suicide is their biggest killer above any disease or injury, which we will explore more later. Each group is well represented within Hip Hop culture. Therefore, bringing therapeutic Hip Hop into mental health interventions for them could help reduce dropout rates by making expressive arts and counselling more relevant. The following autoethnographic account, presented in an author-researcher mode, shares my journey in activating a brand-new approach to therapeutic Hip Hop, starting in the United Kingdom.

Philosophical and Theoretical Foundations

Hip Hop includes everyone from around the globe, from 'Pete and Bas' (the grime grandads spitting in Estuary[2] London accents with 2 million YouTube hits on their first single 'Dents in a Peugeot') to the gully boys and hijabi girls of South Asia.

Poststructuralism and social constructivism underpin Hip Hop HEALS' research and development of programmes. Accordingly, truth is viewed as local and yet universally accessible through myth (Vogler 1998). Meaning, meanwhile, is viewed as socially constructed with participants and colleagues positioned as co-researchers and lived experience experts. This maintains the person-centred nature of our action-research and ongoing inquiry into the therapeutic aspects of Hip Hop, in line with narrative therapy (Combs and Freedman, 1996; Payne, 2006).

Creative Writing for Therapeutic Purposes

In 2011, I began the Metanoia Institute's MSc in Creative Writing for Therapeutic Purposes. It was the first time the course had run and was the first of its kind anywhere in the world. CWTP follows the same practice guidelines as counsellors, psychologists, and expressive arts therapists, with strict codes for ethics and safety. As such, CWTP practitioners are expected to seek regular supervision and engage in professional development with an ongoing reflective practice. Trainees learn to deliver group therapeutic creative writing workshops for five to twelve people in short- and long-term programmes. Each week during my time on the course, a new visiting lecturer would bring tales of their practice from settings ranging from eating-disorder hospitals to prisons to end-of-life hospice care. Our faithful programme director Claire Williamson steered the course, with a leadership panel of experts in counselling, expressive writing, and literature.

In the next section, I offer a summary of my research background and the key ideas behind Hip Hop HEALS and our therapeutic Hip Hop model.

Research Background

Professor Carolyn Ellis' work on autoethnography helped me understand how to harness the power of story to bridge the gap between CWTP and Hip Hop. She posits social science as human science, arguing for the inclusion of people's stories in research. When we consider them as a legitimate form of data and insight into social and cultural phenomena, people from *inside* a culture such as Hip Hop may help those *outside* to better understand its norms, mores, and codes.

In 2012, I was considering a thesis topic for my MSc. I was compelled to include lyrics from the underground music I loved within my CWTP practice. As I prepared the Literature Review, I discovered two things that completely changed the course of my life. Firstly, through reading about trauma, I realised I myself was traumatised by an earlier bereavement (more on this later in the chapter). Secondly, I discovered Hip Hop Therapy. I began to think about how I might adapt it to include UK music genres such as jungle and drum and bass, in the hope of making it more relevant to the communities around me.

In the next section, I share a brief account of how therapeutic Hip Hop supported my own trauma healing and then go on to explain how Hip Hop HEALS came into being.

CWTP and Hip Hop

Rap originated as a youth culture born of struggle (Rose, 1993). Levy and TaeHyuk Keum (2014) state that, in 'post-industrialized Bronx, NY . . . the birth of Hip-hop was inherently therapeutic' as a 'platform for individuals, who needed a voice, to speak back against inequalities they faced' (pp. 217–218). However, Viega (2012) argues that Hip Hop is rarely connected with healing or therapeutic activity. Perhaps as a consequence, there does not appear to be an existing field of research linking the therapeutic nature of Hip Hop song lyrics in CWTP.

By combining Hip Hop with CWTP, I was able to process my own difficult emotional memories and symptoms of trauma. It was liberating. Flashbacks paused. My mood improved. My mind stopped circling around the same distressing memories like vultures. I found ways to disarm them by channelling my thoughts onto a blank page. I could put difficult times to bed and appreciate how I had grown through them, rather than berating myself as weak for not doing so, as a failure, as a fraud of a person. I now know that I was working through things, shifting and changing so I could grow. I discharged traumatic images through symbol and metaphor, containing them through tight structural forms in poetry. Hip Hop lyrics are a form of poetry, hence I propose that therapeutic Hip Hop has huge healing potential for trauma, PTSD, and grief. This forms the basis of Hip Hop HEALS' work, which is summarised next.

Our Work

Hip Hop HEALS' model of therapeutic Hip Hop is evidence-based. Knowledge of how Hip Hop offers therapeutic potential for marginalised people is socially constructed between the author-researcher, MCs, Hip Hop Therapists, community professionals, and Hip Hop HEALS' board and youth panel. As a result, lived experience informs practice. Human stories pertaining to Hip Hop's impact on well-being are gleaned through an active and ongoing consultation process, for example, through our podcast: Glowitheflow. MCs and Hip Hop Therapists tell us how they got started. They share lyric tips to encourage the audience to get writing. Importantly, they explain how it helped them and, thus, act as role models for engagement in self-care through creativity.

We also use therapeutic Hip Hop to spread public-health messaging and social-media-based psychoeducation, with a focus on trauma. We spread self-care and self-intervention tools to empower the public. Our arts-based intervention is an alternative to the Western medical model. 'Meds' have their place, no doubt, but when someone dies or departs, a tablet may not be what people crave: rather, they might crave connection and understanding from others. This is why our model is rooted in group-therapy facilitation. Our programmes present a safe space for healing, with peer support. Ultimately, we want people to generate an ongoing practice of sustainable self-care, leading to increased self-efficacy and personal flourishing.

Figure 9.1 Photo of a Youth Panel Young Man Learning to DJ, Using a DJ Mixer and DJ Controllers; Kiz Smiling in the Background. © Kiz Manley and Sam Frankwood.

Aims and Activities

We want all people to have access to culturally competent, therapeutic Hip Hop because its principles can be applied to any cultural form—its central tenet is 'Knowledge of Self'. Living your authentic story is the key to a full and happy life, according to Hip Hop.

Our aim is to make the therapeutic process more accessible for people experiencing mental health inequalities and marginalisation, particularly Global Majority people, young people, men, and Black people. All of these suffer from huge disparities in mental health outcomes. All feature heavily in Hip Hop and 'UK bass' music deriving from Jamaica's sound-system culture, including reggae, dub, UK garage, jungle, and drum and bass. Accordingly, Hip Hop HEALS tailors its Hip Hop Therapy techniques to meet the needs of local UK audiences.

We do this through a range of ways and means, which I have highlighted using italics:

Therapeutic Hip Hop Programmes for marginalised people (for example, those in recovery from mental illness, homelessness, and offending): Our workshops provide self-care tools for self-intervention, to complement existing mental health service-provision and medication. The latter are important and useful, but they do not always meet everyone's needs.

Hip Hop HEALS Trauma-Informed Academy, kindly funded by the Baring Foundation: We conducted community consultation and action-research to help us create culturally competent training in therapeutic Hip Hop. Two pilot programmes for community leaders and helping professionals were externally evaluated, with a report due for release in 2023. A series of trauma-informed Hip Hop webinars also provided free training online, with experts in trauma and Hip Hop. These are marketed and edited by our Youth Panel, and remain on our YouTube channel as a permanent resource.

Visiting Lectureships: Lectures are conducted at University College London for the MASc Creative Health course and University of the West of England in Bristol for the MA Music Therapy course.

Glowitheflow Podcast: The podcast amplifies the lived experience stories of rappers, MCs, and Hip Hop Therapists. Guests have all used Hip

Hop therapeutically. They share techniques that helped them access Hip Hop's healing powers in order to encourage others to do the same.

Targeted Health Promotion and Health Marketing: Public Health initiatives occur via social media and our youth-panel-designed Creativity Booster Packs.

Public Speaking: Live and real-time public engagement at conferences, universities, and festivals; also, guest interviews on podcasts and panels.

Inclusive Board

We are led by an inclusive Board of Directors. Three are Global Majority people from Indian, Caribbean, and Chinese backgrounds. Two are disabled, one with mental ill-health and one who is registered blind. One member has a PTSD diagnosis. Rather than assuming diversity is a problem to be solved, practitioners of inclusion assume that it is a rich resource to be tapped into and enjoyed (Ferdman and Deane, 2013: xxii). Representing diverse people with equity to challenge inequality is key to our work.

Diverse Youth Panel

Our youth panel volunteers are graduates in their twenties. All have experienced marginalisation through ethnicity, health, or Adverse Childhood Events (ACEs). Together, we coproduce Hip Hop HEALS' branding, social media, and marketing to help keep our podcast and Trauma-Informed Hip Hop Academy relevant to our target audiences. Members offer their growing expertise in exchange for work-experience opportunities. We provide them with a safe space to apply their education and training with us in a live workplace to boost employability. We support them with mentoring and references for jobs. On a more fun tip, we train them in therapeutic DJing methods as a form of self-care education. I would like to give a 'shout out' here to Pirate Studios, who gifted us with hundreds of pounds worth of free studio credit to do this.

In the next section I explore therapeutic Hip Hop in response to mental health inequalities in the United Kingdom.

Hip Hop Therapy: A Fluid Definition

Hip Hop Therapy was originally a social work intervention. Dr. Edgar Tyson, who coined the term, was a social worker. His concept of Hip Hop Therapy (HHT) refers to a social work intervention for young people. According to the *hiphoptherapy.com* website, the 'original model has evolved into a theoretical framework with significant global resonance, much like the culture itself'. HHT, the website suggests, entails 'the purposeful use of Hip Hop culture in a therapeutic relationship, and it operates in the context of a co-constructed treatment plan with specific goals and measurable outcomes' (Hall and Tyson, 2018). HHT is thus 'a revolutionary approach to mental health treatment that espouses the profound impact of Hip Hop culture and its capacity to promote individual and communal transformation' (ibid.). The *hiphoptherapy.com* website is emphatic that HHT 'embodies a wide array of interventions that mix the inherently cathartic components of Hip Hop culture with various well-established treatment modalities, from music, poetry and other expressive therapies to psychodynamic, cognitive behavioral, dialectical behavioral, solution-focused and narrative therapy' (ibid.).

Today, HHT constitutes a burgeoning mental health intervention with many offshoots and manifestations forming around the world. There is ongoing debate regarding which elements of this work may be referred to as 'therapy' and 'therapeutic', due to the inequalities regarding who has access to qualify and gain accreditation as therapists. Let us consider the United Kingdom's mental health inequalities first, before we explore the therapy/ therapeutic debate. Both can only be considered briefly here, which is regrettable since these topics are deeply complex.

Mental Health Inequalities in the United Kingdom

According to an online report by Williams *et al.* (2020) 'Health inequalities are avoidable, unfair and systematic differences in health between different groups of people'. The Mental Health Foundation, meanwhile, states that '[t]he risks of mental ill-health are not equally distributed'. Whilst '[t]he likelihood of our developing a mental health problem is influenced by our biology', it is also influenced by 'the circumstances in which we are born, grow, live and age' (ibid.). Consequently, '[t]hose who face the most significant disadvantages in life also face the greatest risks to their mental health' (Mental Health Foundation, 2023).

The Centre for Mental Health makes a similar point: there are 'many determinants in our lives which influence our mental health', ranging 'from positive parenting and a safe place to live, to experiencing abuse, oppression, discrimination, or growing up in poverty' (Centre for Mental Health, 2020). These '[d]eterminants of mental health interact with inequalities in society, putting some people at a far higher risk of poor mental health than others' (ibid.).

Clearly, then, people in the United Kingdom experience different mental health challenges (and, consequently, different care) depending on determinants including ethnicity, class, and gender, among others. The Centre for Mental Health reports that those who dwell 'in the 10% most de-prived communities are more than three times as likely to be detained under the Mental Health Act and twice as likely to die by suicide as the least de-prived 10%' (Centre for Mental Health, 2020). Meanwhile, '[f]our times as many Black people and twice as many Asian people are detained under the Mental Health Act as white people', whilst '[h]alf of LGBT+ people (52%) said they had experienced depression in the last year' (ibid.). Simultaneously, '[a]lmost half of trans people (46%) and 31% of lesbian, gay and bisexual people had thought about taking their own life in the last year' (ibid.). Individuals suffering chronic physical illnesses 'are at least twice as likely to have a mental health difficulty as those without', and 'people with SMI [Severe Mental Illness] on average have 15 to 20 years shorter life expectancy than the ge-neral population' (Powis, 2019).

Are we, as a society, doing all we can to combat these issues? Sadly, the Mind mental health charity's website reports that mental health services 'aren't practical or respectful', whilst 'the people running those services often talk down to people and don't take mental health problems seriously' (Schryver et al., 2021: 57). Additionally, those in poverty 'do not feel that their experiences are represented, and they feel left out of the conversation which compounds 'a sense that openly talking about mental health is a White middle-class privilege and that the "less palatable" aspects of mental health are not represented' (Schryver et al., 2021: 19).

The above demonstrates how people's mental health needs are not being met equitably, at least in the United Kingdom. I propose therapeutic Hip Hop could offer a solution, which I will explain in more depth shortly. Before we get to that, we need to understand some of the barriers that currently prevent it from being spread more widely.

The Hip Hop Therapy/Therapeutic Hip Hop Debate

There is a lively debate around whether the term 'therapy' is appropriate to describe what Hip Hop Therapists do. Space constrains us from delving deeply into this matter, but we need to at least touch upon it. (Please don't shoot the messenger.)

To become a counsellor in the United Kingdom, no formal qualifications are required. However, for accreditation with the British Association for Counselling and Psychotherapy (BACP), you need a degree; an online short course will not cut it. This means people on the register are deemed safe to conduct therapy because they possess the correct skills and training to conduct safe, ethical practice. For example, they can build with patients 'a co-constructed treatment plan with specific goals and measurable outcomes', to re-quote Dr. Edgar Tyson (Hall and Tyson, 2018).

However, when BACP surveyed their membership, they found the average counsellor is female, aged fifty-three, and 'falls into the "affluent achiever" bracket ("detached house, luxury car, buys wine and books on the internet, has an iPhone")' (Brown, 2017). Clearly, then, counselling is generally a female profession primarily populated by individuals who are middle-aged and middle-class. However, the profile of people needing help is significantly different from that, as we have seen.

A key area of the debate that is signalled in the title of the present section of this chapter posits that anyone using the term 'therapy' to describe what they do should be a qualified therapist who is registered with a professional body. This maintains good standards for safe, ethical practice.[3] Such organisations provide training, guidance, and a register of trusted, accredited practitioners for the public to safely rely on. Professional therapists are expected to take certain steps to look after themselves such as undertake supervision[4] and engage in Continuous Professional Development (CPD) training to stay up-to-date with new research. All of these are essential components for good counselling practice. Furthermore, all are likely to seem fair when we consider that therapy without proper protocol and safeguards creates huge risks for all involved.

In keeping with this line of reasoning, Hip Hop Therapists cannot offer 'therapy' in the United Kingdom per se because HHT is not recognised as a therapy by the United Kingdom's Allied Health Professional register. The latter recognises only four arts therapies: music, drama, art, and dance therapy. To qualify for each, you need a master's degree, a prerequisite for which is of course a bachelor degree: a therapist recognised as such by the United Kingdom's Allied Health Professional register, then, will be a highly qualified individual.

Tyson's definition of HHT could only be offered by a qualified therapist or arts-based therapist. Anything else could be considered 'therapeutic Hip Hop' but not HHT proper. I have delivered numerous therapeutic Hip Hop projects, including:

1. *Cotton: On*, a project led by Fleet Arts in conjunction with Derbyshire Council's Belper Youth Council. The project explored rap as protest art, exploring the town of Belper's links to slavery and the eventual abolition of slavery with reference to the current Black Lives Matter Movement. www.fleet-arts.org/cotton-on. www.fleet-arts.org/cotton-on.
2. *Survivor Arts Project*, led by the University of Birmingham. This is an ongoing social-worker-training project, where Hip Hop HEALS shares psychoeducation on self-care and therapeutic Hip Hop methods to use within the community. https://www.youtube.com/watch?v=n22D mcMuPSc.
3. *Hear My Voice Project*, a Birmingham 2022 Commonwealth Games–linked project based around lived-experience stories about Birmingham, UK, and Perth, Australia. The stories were rapped over music produced with local people. Listen here: https://tinyurl.com/ brummagemrap.

Positive outcomes for well-being *can* be achieved without qualifications and accreditation. Meanwhile, the people who (at present, at least) might be *able* to register as therapists offering Hip Hop Therapy do not typically mirror the communities who would benefit from it. However, communities often help each other cope effectively with life's challenges without degree qualifications in therapy. They may not follow the same protocols as a licensed professional, but therapeutic activities in the community can and typically do offer safe interventions, often with little or no training. Furthermore, poorer

CASE STUDY: COTTON:ON PROJECT

A year-long youth project exploring slavery, with Belper youth council and Fleet Arts.
Outcomes: protest zines, banners, youth-led podcasts, community art exhibitions.

- WELLBEING FOCUS: built safe space/trust, youth-driven to amplify voice
- SELF-CARE TOOLS: psychoeducation for ongoing independent self-regulation
- AFFECT TALK: offered to label emotional responses - topics were tough
- OFFERED MYSELF AS EMOTIONALLY AVAILABLE ADULT: gave safety cues
- 3rd PERSON: narrative therapy device applied to create an alien character. Town's uncomfortable history told with curiosity/reflection/distance NEUROSCIENCE: offered bottom up/top down explanations of brain during creative process, explaining calming effects of expressive arts activities

Figure 9.2 Belper Case Study Activities and Outcomes

communities do not access education equitably. Consequently, they are un-likely to be able to offer traditional therapy in their communities by training to the levels required to conduct it under the accredited label. Nonetheless, it can be assumed that there *are* people within communities who *do* match the profile of the people who need it most. They may be able to offer the Hip Hop Therapy model suggested by Tyson's definition above or create their own alternatives within a supported process of coproduction.

Ultimately, local people see what goes on in their streets. They roll their sleeves up and dig in. People who share similar areas or life experiences are easy to relate to because they speak the same language and breathe the same air. This is welcomed by many who are in desperate need of therapeutic support.

Mind, a company that focuses on the benefits of mental health treat-ment, reported that individuals experiencing poverty 'often feel like they are not listened to or taken seriously in many aspects of their life—they see themselves as caught in a system that at best fails to empathise, and at worst ignores or insults them' (Schryver *et al.*, 2021: 57). 'As a result, many in this audience express a strong desire to receive support from someone with similar lived experiences to them who is also appropriately quali-fied', the Mind report adds (ibid.). This shared experience of mental health problems, poverty, and/or financial worries can create a valuable 'shortcut' to 'understanding their situation and establishing trust' (Schryver *et al.*,

2021: 57). Promisingly, the report explains that certain organisations, and particularly ones in the youth-work field, 'are addressing the perceived gap between therapists and clients by recruiting younger case workers who come from similar backgrounds, effectively "rebranding" them as coaches or similar' (ibid.).

'Lived experience groups have become increasingly involved in systems change work in their local areas', the Centre for Enterprise (CFE) Research group have reported (CFE Research, 2020: 3). Despite this, the professional therapeutic community is still a long way from demographically representing those in UK society who, arguably, need therapeutic support more badly than any other demographic groups, as seen in the BACP membership survey (Brown, 2017). Representation, and more specifically race representation, is central to this. We will now look at that matter in relation to other helping professions.

Music Therapy

The British Association of Music Therapists (BAMT) surveyed music therapists and issued a Diversity Report in response to member concerns following George Floyd's death and the Black Lives Matter campaign. 73.08 percent of respondents identified themselves as white British whilst none identified as Bangledeshi, 'Any other Black background', nor 'White and Black African', nor 'Gypsy/Traveller and Arab' (Langford *et al.*, 2020: 22). The remaining ethnic groups were: Irish (3.14%); Multiple ethnicity/Other (3.14%); Any other Asian background (2.16%); Chinese (1.96%); White and Asian (1.77%); Any other mixed/multiple ethnic background (1.57%); Indian (0.79%); Caribbean (0.79%); Any other ethnic group (0.79%); African (0.59%); Prefer not to say (0.59%); Pakistani (0.2%); White and Black Caribbean (0.2%) (ibid.). Meanwhile, the BAMT report is clear that the '[h]igh cost of training makes courses accessible only to applicants from a privileged, middle class background' (Langford *et al.*, 2020: 6).

These findings demonstrate that diversity of race, ethnicity and social class are sorely lacking within the field of Music Therapy. Furthermore, it appears that people with white privilege in the profession have been guilty of 'gaslighting' colleagues and trainees who speak up: 'Non-white Qualified and Trainee Music Therapists shared experiences of being rejected, mocked or made to feel that their contributions on topics such as cultural practice and racial representation were inadequate by lecturers, placement supervisors and their fellow trainees' (Langford *et al.*, 2020: 7).

Awareness is the first step towards change. It is encouraging, therefore, to see that BAMT is making a huge push to improve diversity and inclusion within music therapy, since issuing the report.

Teaching

When I was growing up, my teachers were mainly white, despite the fact that I grew up in Birmingham—one of the most diverse cities in the United Kingdom. I was mainly taught about white culture, white history, and white society. You probably will not notice this if you are white, but if your parents are immigrants, from ex-colonies, believe me, you will notice.

Today, the British government's website reports that, as of November 2021, only 14.9 percent of teachers signalled as 'belonging to an ethnic minority group' (Department of Education, 2021). Furthermore, 'Teachers identifying in an ethnic minority group are not equally represented at leadership positions'. In 2021, 15.3 percent of white British teachers are reported to have been in 'leadership positions', sharply contrasting with 8.1 percent of Asian or Asian British teachers and 9.3 percent of Black or Black British teachers (ibid.). This is highly significant when we consider the important role that teachers play in early life.

Children's Literature

There were no Black or Brown characters leading my story books at school. My older sister Raj exposed me to literature of the world so I would feel included. I saw children like me as powerful leaders of their own narratives. Unfortunately, my experiences are not matched in wider children's literature.

WordsRated, a publishing industry research body, reports there are 3.5 times as many children's bestsellers by a white author as there are bestsellers by a Black author (McLoughlin, 2021). Meanwhile, just 12.12 percent of children's books are about Black or African characters, and just 7.64 percent of children's books are written by Black or African authors (ibid.).

The world of music is different in this regard. The rappers interviewed during my research and in my podcast have reported feelings of empowerment upon seeing MCs who look like them within mainstream culture. I felt the same way growing up. My older siblings played music I have since come to love: from reggae to rap and bhangra to the blues—all originating from ex-colonies.

Seeing people of colour in the art I consume makes me feel connected to others like me, and more open to the messages presented. I *feel* relevant and more than accepted: *wanted*.

In the mid-1990s, I discovered Hip Hop. It told stories I could relate to: stories about being 'Other'.[5] So how does this translate to music for inclusion and healing in schools and beyond?

Multiculturalism in Counselling

In 2010, Counselling Pyschology Quarterly published a model for multicultural competence in 'culture-infused counselling'. It posited cultural identity as fluid and dynamic, stating its importance in relation to the therapeutic relationship between counsellor and client:

> Cultural, personal, contextual, and universal factors integrate to form the personal cultural identities of both the counsellor and the client. These personal cultural identities may have a dramatic impact on the success of the counselling process and must be taken into account in both theory and practice.
>
> (Collins and Arthur, 2010: 217)

Furthermore, it states: 'The experiences, norms, values, and practices of particular cultural groups may dramatically impact the nature of service required to meet their needs' (Collins and Arthur, 2010: 219). The following section explores how therapeutic Hip Hop could present a culture-infused counselling or creative health intervention.

Creative Health

Creative health refers to arts, culture, and nature activities that have benefits for health and well-being. In 2021, the Baring Foundation human-rights charity published a report entitled *Creatively Minded and Ethnically Diverse*. It raised key issues regarding inequality, mental illness, and the whitewashed nature of participatory arts in the United Kingdom: 'Though people from all parts of the population can be affected by mental health problems, the differential impact on the diagnosis and access to treatment for racialised communities is stark' (Baring Foundation, 2021: 2). A core problem would appear to be that 'diverse-led organisations' are rarely 'specifically devoted to arts and health work', whilst 'ethnically diverse people were not well represented, either as service users or within the workforce of the arts and health organisations' in the report's findings (ibid.).

In 2017, the UK government's All-Party Parliamentary Group (APPG) on Arts, Health and Wellbeing published the report *Creative health: The arts for health and wellbeing* (2017). The report's three central messages were the arts can help 'keep us well', 'help meet major challenges [in] health and social care', and 'save money' (All-Party Parliamentary Group on Arts, Health and Wellbeing, 2017: 4).

The question is which artforms will be allowed in the helping space and who will be excluded and ignored?

Hip Hop is a Black art form.
Reggae is a Black art form.
Jungle is a Black art form.

Does it not stand to reason, therefore, that these forms are well placed to enable equity of services? These musical forms present abundant and bounteous opportunities to bring culture into the healing space but are under-researched and excluded, pushed to the margins by White Majority helping professionals, researchers, and policy decision-makers. People like me, who are drawn to such music, with its message of protest and resistance, are left in the gutters of the United Kingdom's mental health system. One of the worse manifestations of this can be seen in disparities regarding race and those who complete suicide: 'suicide rates are higher among young men of Black African and Black Caribbean origin, and among middle-aged Black

African, Black Caribbean and South Asian women, than among their White British counterparts' (McDald and Kousoulis, 2020: 25). As a British Indian woman, I fall into this high-risk category.

In October 2021, the National Centre for Creative Health (NCCH) led a five-year review, following on from the APPG's 2017 report. Commissioners gathered up-to-date information and evidence to influence future government policy on creative health. A series of roundtables were held with experts and people with relevant lived experience. A recording entitled 'Creative Health Review—Mental Health and Wellbeing across the Life Course Roundtable' is accessible at the time of writing via YouTube.

I was invited to join in. It was inspiring to hear the young beneficiaries of creative health share their experiences and the powerful lived experience stories of the panel. However, given the panel theme was: 'What are the current challenges in mental health and wellbeing, and how can creative health help to tackle these challenges?', I expected the panel itself to be more representative. I called out inequality, exclusion, and underrepresentation of diverse people in the creative health world. I spoke about the marginalisation of certain groups and questioned their exclusion from the panel itself.

I raised the fact that suicide is the number one killer of men and young people in the United Kingdom. I said we were failing as a society because our children and men were killing themselves more than any disease: roughly three-quarters of registered suicides in 2020 were for men (3,925 deaths, 75.1% of the total), which is in line with the trends of the last quarter century at least (Office For National Statistics, 2021).

When I cited this, everyone's faces dropped. The facts are hard to swallow, but we all have a role to play in making sustainable change. Again, how does this translate to music for inclusion and healing in schools and beyond?

Hip Hop for Inclusion

Hip Hop is a Black art form that emerged from impoverished communities in the South Bronx, New York, USA. It spread across the globe to become one of the most popular music genres of our times. It tells tales of poverty. Poverty breeds mental illness. Rappers share life experiences and stories of racism, oppression, voicelessness, and exclusion.

In the post-pandemic United Kingdom, this is more pertinent than ever: 'child poverty rates are set to soar, with a predicted 35% of children living in relative poverty by 2023–2024', constituting 'the highest percentage since modern records began in 1961' (Hagell and Shah, 2023). As stated previously, Hip Hop has represented and continues to represent poverty and youth. Poverty creates ideal conditions for mental illness to thrive.

So who am I and why do I care? I have two master's degrees and am a fully qualified secondary-school teacher. If I wanted, I could just use those to live comfortably.

Figure 9.3 Kiz in Front of a Graffiti Piece

But life took a funny turn for me very early on.

Let me tell you my story . . .

Hello. My Name Is . . .

. . . Kiz, a forty-three-year-old Brummie. I was born in 1979 to Harjit and Madan (RIP). Mom and Dad migrated from India in the 1960s.

I've loved and lost many people. Music helped. Writing healed.

My experience of self-healing catalysed my transition from a secondary-school English and drama teacher to therapeutic Hip Hop writing mentor.

Trigger Warning

The following contains graphic references to mental illness and potentially emotionally distressing topics including: car accidents; death; grief, trauma, and Post Traumatic Stress Disorder (referred to hereafter as PTSD).

My Story

In June 2000, I stopped walking. There was nothing physically wrong: my left leg would just buckle and collapse underneath me. I later learnt it was trauma.

My life had just been turned upside down, inside out. On May 27, 2000, my beloved older sister Promila (R.I.P.) had a fatal car accident. The police inquest could find no cause for the crash. My family went into deep shock.

Three months after Pam's death, still unable to walk, my physiotherapist told me there was no physical cause for my immobility and that I would be referred back to my doctor.

I burst into tears. My osteopath had said the same. No one could find anything wrong with me.

I repeated to my doctor a major fact that she had dismissed on my first visit: that my sister had just died. She didn't even say sorry to hear that. She wasn't *listening* to me. Imagine being in my shoes and how this made me *feel*.

I explained I was looking after my mom and dad during a time of crisis, and was labouring in their newsagents shop daily to keep the bills paid. How was I to continue if I could not walk?

My doctor sent me to a psychiatrist. After one session, I began walking again. I learnt that my subconscious mind could have transformed the pain of losing my sister to my knee, being too much to bear, and even more surprisingly, that it could have been guilt manifesting as physical pain.

We discussed how, at the time of the car accident, I was blissfully unaware that my dad was in hospital and that Pam was taking the three-hour trip from her home in Plymouth to visit him. My university friends and I had all bought tickets for one last rave together at Homelands Festival. The night before, we had glitzed ourselves up in cocktail dresses and tuxedos to attend our Summer Graduation Ball at Cardiff Castle.

I went from dancing the night away to drum and bass and techno to visiting my sister in Intensive Care. Though I was able to walk again, I became deeply dissociated and started experiencing vicarious or 'secondary' trauma.

During twenty years of trauma symptoms, no one explained what I was going through or how I could get well; not one doctor, not a single counsellor, and certainly no friends or family—none of us knew what was 'wrong' with me.

I later learnt that Black and Brown people like me are more likely to be jailed or sectioned when experiencing mental illness whilst our white counterparts receive 'softer' interventions such as counselling or medication.

When my Pops eventually passed in 2010, I experimented with expressive writing methods. I became free of trauma symptoms and a writer's block that began when Promila died.

Poems erupted from my pen in one blast, emerging fully formed and complete. Afterwards, I felt lighter and stopped being invaded by certain flashbacks and intrusive memory loops.

I trained in therapeutic writing. My research and practice now includes UK bass music culture to appeal to others like myself.

Though I recognise the benefits, I chose not to take medication for grief and trauma. I feel they are natural human responses to life-changing events. However, the alternative that I was offered was talking therapy with white-coated professionals who were largely out of touch with my cultural experience.

I'm a junglist, a raver, and a Hip Hop Head. I turned to music when my life got tough. I thought expressive arts therapies and creative health modalities would help but felt excluded. Most practitioners were white. They had a completely different upbringing to me, being mainly middle class. I noticed lots were trained in Western classical arts rather than the alternative arts and music cultures that appealed to me: Jamaican bass music, US Hip Hop culture, and other expressions of contemporary music culture that are missing from the creative health landscape in the United Kingdom.

I want to change this.

Music makes me happy. Writing helps me flourish. My purpose now is to share what I have learnt about Hip Hop's healing powers so others may benefit.

So, I founded Hip Hop HEALS project in 2012 to promote Hip Hop as a therapeutic tool. Today, I facilitate writing workshops and training in therapeutic Hip Hop to help marginalised people access culturally competent mental health interventions. In 2021, we became a legally registered nonprofit that prizes and promotes Hip Hop's creative powers for trauma healing. Please visit our website: hiphophealsuk.org and join us on social media @ hiphophealsuk.

Narrative, Therapeutic Hip Hop Research, and Practice

As a trauma survivor, I became interested in sharing alternative modes to medication and talking therapies for trauma rehabilitation. I wanted to know why they were still primary routes to trauma care via the National Health Service (NHS), whilst others involving the arts and nature have largely been ignored until recently, with the rise of the arts and health movement. Moreover, I wanted to know why my own PTSD had remained undiagnosed for so long, despite clear symptoms.

Disturbingly, race affects mental health outcomes and access to the right help. It appears that structural racism could be a factor here. What the 'right' help for you and I looks like, in practical terms, could be worlds apart. By opening up research and policy to different and varied stories of what works, or *could* work, we have a better chance of creating authentic counselling approaches and mental health interventions for those who need it most.

Making our work more inclusive is an act of love.

I challenge you to spread love more with a healthful dose of therapeutic Hip Hop, and maybe just a spoonful of funky breaks to help you get down.

Conclusion

The 'World of Research' tends toward positivism. It is often binary. However, one size does not fit all. Where human experience is concerned, there are many ways of doing things. Mental health services could be expanded to include more varied approaches, with people driving change by sharing what works from them. Rap is a great medium for this. We just need to listen.

Hip Hop sits outside of the establishment. It questions and challenges the status quo and offers alternative viewpoints. Stories of experience from within Hip Hop culture can be used to explain how it could be healing to those from outside of the culture.

Let us close now with an extract from my thesis.

Two imagined characters: 'MC Mentor' and 'Tormenta MC' discuss rap's therapeutic potential in a poetic representation of interview data, based on the lived experience of rap as therapeutic, by two rappers and the researcher, me.

MC TORMENTA
you can hear in the tunes, 'nuff tunes
what you've gone through in your head that
fuckin' scarred you for life
that's what it's for:
tunes of heartache and tunes of hardship
when they was spittin'
anti-government
anti-everything
what everyone's *for*, they was against
the opposite, the opposite!

MC MENTOR
KRS One said: 'Gangstas and pimps and drug dealers:
they are part of Hip Hop
not *the*
core of Hip Hop'.
when people try and *present* Hip Hop as being
that **an'** *not all*
the rest of it

Figure 9.4 MC Performing at a Nightclub. © Kiz Manley and Thumbs Photography.

> *that's the problem* **basically,** *it's part of the ghetto*
> so it's *always* gonna be *intertwined*

Narrative therapists position *people* as experts in their own lives (Payne, 2006). Hence the two rappers were interviewed and respected as co-researchers with equal power to myself, as researcher. Resultantly, rappers' own voices and opinions regarding the phenomena under investigation, namely whether rap could be therapeutic, were centralised within the data-collection process. Stories were also drawn from my own journey through healing traumatised grief and PTSD using CWTP. I went on to use the findings in Hip Hop HEALS' programme design.

Like this, lived experience should be at the centre of mental health intervention research and design.

Rap tells stories. Let us listen deeply to the potent tales offered by MCs. Its lyrics represent the realities of many whose needs are not being met through existing mental health services.

Going back to the Hero's Journey, in stories, a mentor figure holds wisdom because they have walked the path of the hero (Campbell, 1968; Vogler, 1998). Our stories are valuable resources whose sharing may help others.

Here in the United Kingdom, our bass music culture could really help us shape an effective and culturally inclusive form of therapeutic Hip Hop and Hip Hop Therapy. I encourage you to explore your own local music cultures to find ways of helping people in a way that is meaningful for them. It could make a world of difference.

To hear fruitful lived experience stories of Hip Hop's therapeutic powers, direct from rappers and Hip Hop Therapists, please listen to our Glowitheflow podcast: hiphophealsuk.org/podcast.

References

All-Party Parliamentary Group on Arts, Health and Wellbeing (2017). *Creative health: The arts for health and wellbeing.* All Party Parliamentary Group on Arts, Health, and Wellbeing. https://www.culturehealthandwellbeing.org.uk/appg-inquiry/

Baring Foundation (2021). *Creatively minded and ethnically diverse: Increasing creative opportunities for people with mental health problems from ethnically diverse backgrounds.* London: Baring Foundation. https://cdn.baringfoundation.org.uk/wp-content/uploads/BF_Creatively-minded-ethnically-diverse_WEB_LR.pdf.

Brown, S. (2017). Is counselling women's work? *Therapy Today,* 28(2). https://www.bacp.co.uk/bacp-journals/therapy-today/2017/march-2017/is-counselling-womens-work/.

Campbell, J. (1968). *The hero with a thousand faces.* Princeton, NJ: Princeton University Press.

Centre for Mental Health (2020). *Mental Health inequalities: Factsheet.* London: Centre for Mental Health. https://www.centreformentalhealth.org.uk/publications/mental-health-inequalities-factsheet.

CFE Research (2020). *The role of lived experience in creating systems change: Evaluation of fulfilling lives: Supporting people with multiple needs.* Leicester: CFE Research. https://www.bht.org.uk/wp-content/uploads/2021/03/The-role-of-lived-experience-in-creating-systems-change-2020-1.pdf.

Collins, S. and Arthur, N. (2010). Culture-infused counselling: A model for developing multicultural competence. *Counselling Psychology Quarterly,* 23(2): 217–233. https://doi.org/10.1080/09515071003798212.

Combs, G. and Freedman, J. (1996) *Narrative therapy: The social construction of preferred realities.* Norton.

Ellis, C., Adams, T. E. and Bochner, A.P. (2010). Autoethnography: An overview. *Forum Qualitative Sozialforschung / Forum: Qualitative Social Research*, 12(1). https://doi.org/10.17169/fqs-12.1.1589.

Ferdman, B. M. and Deane, B. R. (eds.) (2013). *Diversity at work: The practice of inclusion* (pp. i–54). Jossey-Bass.

Hagell, A. and Shah, R. (2023). *Highlighting the health inequalities faced by young people in the UK*. The Health Foundation. https://www.health.org.uk/news-and-comment/blogs/highlighting-the-health-inequalities-faced-by-young-people-in-the-uk.

Hall, J. C. and Tyson, E. (2018). *Turning the tables on therapy*. https://www.hiphoptherapy.com/.

Haupt, A. and Rollefson, J. G. (2021). Hip hop's third space: Imagined community and the global hip hop nation. *Global Hip Hop Studies*, 2(1): 3–6. https://doi.org/10.1386/ghhs_00029_2.

Department of Education. (2021). *School Workforce in England, reporting year 2021*. UK Department of Education. https://explore-education-statistics.service.gov.uk/find-statistics/school-workforce-in-england.

Langford, A., Rizkallah, M. and Maddocks, C. (2020). *Diversity report*. British Association for Music Therapy. https://www.bamt.org/resources/diversity-report.

Levy, I. and TaeHyuk Keum, B. (2014). Hip-Hop emotional exploration in men. *Journal of Poetry Therapy*, 27(4): 217–223. https://doi.org/10.1080/08893675.2014.949528.

McLoughlin, D. (2022). *23% decrease in Black characters in children's bestsellers as BLM bounce fades*. WordsRated. https://wordsrated.com/representation-childrens-literature/.

Mental Health Foundation (2023). *Black, Asian and minority ethnic (BAME) communities*. Mental Health Foundation. https://www.mentalhealth.org.uk/explore-mental-health/a-z-topics/black-asian-and-minority-ethnic-bame-communities.

McDald, S. and Kousoulis, A. (2020). *Tackling social inequalities to reduce mental health problems: How everyone can flourish equally A Mental Health Foundation report*. Mental Health Foundation. https://www.mentalhealth.org.uk/sites/default/files/2022-04/MHF-tackling-inequalities-report.pdf.

Metanoia Institute. (2023). *Practitioner certificate creative writing for therapeutic purposes (CWTP) for therapists*. Metanoia Institute. https://www.metanoia.ac.uk/programmes/career-development-pathways/practitioner-certificate-creative-writing-for-therapeutic-purposes-cwtp-for-therapists/.

Office For National Statistics. (2021). *Suicides in England and Wales: 2021 registrations*. Office for National Statistics. https://www.ons.gov.uk/peoplepopulationandcommunity/birthsdeathsandmarriages/deaths/bulletins/suicidesintheunitedkingdom/2020registrations.

Payne, M. (2006). *Narrative therapy*. Sage.

Powis, S. H. (2019). *Achieving more for people with severe mental illness*. National Health Service. https://www.engl.and.nhs.uk/blog/achieving-more-for-people-with-severe-mental-illness/

Rose, T. (1993). *Black noise: Rap music and black culture in contemporary America*. 1st ed. Wesleyan University Press.

Schryver, C. D., Hartley, R., Ellingham, J., Watson, C. and Jansen, C. (2021). *Mind: Fighting for the MH of people living in poverty: Research findings report prepared by 2CV for Mind*. 2CV. https://www.mind.org.uk/media/12428/final_poverty-scoping-research-report.pdf.

Viega, M. (2012). The Hero's Journey in Hip-Hop and its applications in music therapy. In S. Hadley and G. Yancy (eds.), *Therapeutic Uses of Rap and Hip-Hop*. Routledge, pp. 57–78.

Vogler, C. (1998). *The writer's journey: Mythic structure for storytellers and screenwriters*. Pan Books.

Williams, E., Buck, D., Babalola, G. and Maguire, E. (2020). *What are health inequalities?* The King's Fund. https://www.kingsfund.org.uk/publications/what-are-health-inequalities.

10

Global Inclusion and Healing Through Therapeutic Beat Making

Elliot Gann and Alex H. D. Crooke

Introduction

This chapter offers a narrative journey through the mission of one Hip Hop non-profit (Today's Future Sound) to offer opportunities for individual and community healing through arts and culture. Unique to this journey is how different levels of community have been integrated into a cohesive vision to foster a healthy, connected, global society. This has included a wide range of events, open to public workshops, programs in institutional settings, and artwork releases. To illustrate the rich tapestry that these different elements create, a number of graphics taken from actual events and musical releases are presented below. Each of these illustrations is accompanied by a brief description of who and what they represent. These illustrations have been paired with a brief introduction and some background information about Today's Future Sound, as well as several firsthand reflections from its founder, and first author, Dr. Elliot Gann. We hope this format offers a some-what more sensory approach to engaging in the content; an example of what is possible in the arts and community well-being space through organic and integrated connection with members of the community itself. We regret that the images are not in color in this chapter, but you can view them in their full vibrant splendor at https://todaysfuturesound.org/.

Beat Making

A room full of people out of their chairs, standing together, 'stomp, clap, stomp, clap' together in synchrony keeping the beat to the oh-so-familiar melody of Michael Jackson's 'Billie Jean'. After doing this, when participants

Elliot Gann and Alex H. D. Crooke, *Global Inclusion and Healing Through Therapeutic Beat Making* In: *Music for Inclusion and Healing in Schools and Beyond*. Edited by: Pete Dale, Pamela Burnard, and Raphael Travis Jr., Oxford University Press. © Oxford University Press 2023. DOI: 10.1093/oso/9780197692677.003.0011 are asked how they feel, verbal responses are usually some type of positive reaction . . . 'energized' or 'happy' or 'excited!' But, for functional purposes this lesson is physically/kinesthetically engaging (via stomped and clapped-out kicks and snares for the song) as well as a visual representation in order to engage multiple intelligences and different learning styles to understand concepts. The nonprofit organization Today's Future Sound (TFS) has a comprehensively developed curriculum and lesson plans to not only promote functional music and beat-making skills but also facilitate well-being through a process called Therapeutic Beat Making (TBM) (Travis *et al.*, 2021).

The Billie Jean exercise is an introduction to the basics of time signature, counting beats, and bars, and it directly relates to programming drums and drum breaks. The exercise also features an introduction to different sampling techniques like looping, sample chopping, adding effects, arrangement, song structure, live performance, and composition of harmony and melody. This culminates in a final 'beat tape' or instrumental album with original artwork conceived by the students and illustrated by 'Ron the Graphics Guy', the in-house TFS artist and graffiti expert.

Additionally, a live performance of the beats often happens within the local community. Part of Hip Hop–based education and pedagogy is the sharing out of beats that students have made at the end of each session in a 'beat cypher'. This parallels the process of beat cyphers that TFS does in adult contexts (including an informal beat cypher for the beginning of TFS staff meetings). In this way, TFS integrates the structure and tradition of Hip Hop and cyphers, staying true to Hip Hop–based education and pedagogy (Adjapong and Levy, 2021). Hip Hop is a culture that is 'lived' experientially. It is not just a tool to teach content; rather, the process, creativity, and originality are valued.

Today's Future Sound

Today's Future Sound (TFS) is a non-profit community arts organisation based in Oakland, CA, USA. Set up in 2010 with minimal staff, TFS was initially designed to deliver Hip Hop education and beat-making programs for under-resourced youth in the Bay Area. Nearly fifteen years later, it is now an organisation with a core team of eight staff in Oakland running six weekly programs in schools and juvenile halls, as well as a wider team of nearly one hundred casual employees, volunteers, and sister-programs spread across five continents (Today's Future Sound, 2022). The current vision of TFS is to connect beat makers and individuals/groups from the Hip Hop community from different geographical, linguistic, cultural, and socioeconomic backgrounds, across multiple generations, and educate them about the value of beat making and community events *from an educational, mental health (psychoeducation included), and social perspective.*

Therapeutic Beat Making

Therapeutic Beat Making (TBM) is a model, framework, and strategy used by TFS, developed by Dr. Elliot Gann through years of research and therapeutic practice. It is grounded in Hip Hop and beat-making culture, and informed by a range of theories, principles, practices, and experiences. These include Psychoanalytic/Psychodynamic principles such as that our unconscious thoughts, fantasies, wishes, and anxieties drive our behaviour (Freud and Strachey, 1900; Freud, 1958). Interpersonal neurobiology principles view integration of different aspects of the self as key to well-being (Siegel, 2012). Polyvagal theory relates to the role of the central vagal nerve in regulating emotions and relationships with our social and physical worlds (Porges, 2009). Trauma research such as that by Van der Kolk (2005), prioritizes how to be responsive to complex trauma, underscores the relationship between the mind and body, and emphasizes the importance of maintaining a safe environment for youth. Hip Hop–based education and pedagogy (Adjapong and Levy, 2021) grounds practice in the empowering values of and the artistic elements of Hip Hop culture for the purposes of learning and therapeutic growth. Finally, the TBM is also informed by Dr. Elliot Gann's personal experiences and journey with Hip Hop beat making.

TBM is geared toward work with youth, and primarily operationalized with school-aged youth in traditional and non-traditional educational settings. TFS and TBM strategies consider how youth learn before, during, and after school, and across a range of developmental settings. TFS operates in classrooms, in after-school and gap time (i.e., summer, winter, and spring break) programs, and within juvenile-justice and alternative-education settings.

Three Dimensions of TBM

The three operating dimensions of TBM are: (1) Relationship/Relational, (2) Expressive, and (3) Self-Concept (Self-Esteem and Self-Efficacy) (Travis, Gann, Crooke, and Jenkins, 2021). When answering the very practical question of how beat making and Hip Hop can be used as a therapeutic intervention, first and foremost we must recognize the culturally and developmentally responsive nature of the modality of Hip Hop beat making. It is highly effective in terms of engagement (i.e., a precursor to relationship building), building rapport/relationship building, creating connections in nonverbal ways, and being non-stigmatizing.

Culturally, Hip Hop has historically been the most popular form of music (Hillyard, 2015), and impactful within popular culture and youth culture helping to shape styles and trends (Ahmed, 2022; Nielsen, 2018). Beat making is well respected as a part of Hip Hop culture, with Hip Hop as an empowering force within Black and Brown communities, and with beat making represented historically across the Black diaspora with roots in drumming and rhythm (Travis, 2016).

Relational and Expressive

Since the therapeutic relationship is one of the highest predictors of positive therapeutic outcome in any form of therapy and therapeutic intervention (Browne *et al.*, 2021; Hauber and Boon, 2022), TFS and TBM prioritizes this as a fundamental part of creating optimal outcomes for therapeutic interventions and also for learning and knowledge sharing. The therapeutic relationship is also critical for exploring and expressing difficult emotions that may be hard to access or verbalize. It may be easier to express and release (catharsis) these emotions musically (Evans, 2019; Travis and Bowman, 2015). Simultaneously, the repetitive rhythms, whether tapped out in real time or simply listened to, whether head nodded and danced to or rapped to, and so on, can help to regulate anxiety and an activated stress response and nervous system (McFerran *et al.*, 2020; Rodwin *et al.*, 2022). The rhythmic joining and connectedness in the 'oneness' of the synchronized rhythmic activity can also help to foster the relationship and decrease perceived isolation that may be a correlate of trauma, anxiety, or other mental health struggles.

The Self and Skills

As for the impact of self-concept, self-esteem and self-efficacy can be fostered through the mastery of skill sets. This competency building is extremely important because of the extensive expertise and skills that are necessary in beat making, producing, and related Hip Hop–driven activities. For example, skills include learning about melody, rhythm, chords, programming, sampling, and infinitely more. Significant functional music skills are involved in beat making in general, and then more specifically in the use of digital technology associated with beat making and production, including digital music equipment such as the Ableton Push Series, the SP-404, digital turntables, and simply a computer/laptop. Additionally, participants learn software applications such as Ableton Live, Logic Pro, Serato Studio, and Fruity Loops. Participants use equipment and software together to skillfully express themselves and their identity, and to create art (i.e., Hip Hop artifacts, of rhythmic beats and instrumental songs) (Crooke and McFerran, 2019). There are also the skills associated with becoming an emerging independent creative professional, including digital presentation of self within social-media spaces, entrepreneurial skills, branding, promotion, critical media literacy, creative knowledge exchange, and enhancing social affiliations within a broader social media ecology (Evans, 2022: 408). All of this is in addition to the inherent content knowledge and literacies and corresponding multiple intelligences (Gardner, 2008; Shearer and Karanian, 2017) involved in beat making (i.e., including, but not limited to, technological, musical, and mathematical and scientific concepts).

The History of Today's Future Sound

The First TBM Groups

The TBM groups were first developed and piloted by Dr. Elliot Gann Director of TFS, an Oakland, California-based licensed clinical psychologist and beat maker known as 'Phillipdrummond', in his own creative practice. Dr. Gann's doctoral clinical placement was at a public charter school in Oakland. During his placement, he observed Beats, Rhymes and Life (now BRL Inc.) and their Therapeutic Activity Groups (TAGs) for his dissertation research. He did previous clinical work with adults with severe and persistent mental health issues in psychosocial group homes in Santa Barbara following his under-graduate work. Dr. Gann also worked with pre- and early adolescent males in individual practice during his graduate studies. He did this one-on-one prac-tice in addition to teaching middle-school students DJ-ing, and organizing Hip Hop artists at UC Santa Barbara with the student organization 'Hip Hop Club at UCSB' that he founded and directed as an undergraduate student. In graduate school in the San Francisco Bay Area, he was active with a variety of Hip Hop nonprofit organizations.

During his clinical practicum training, Dr. Gann would sometimes bring his turntables to the elementary school practicum placement, or when he was training at a county public clinic (e.g., into individual sessions or groups for youth on the Autistic Spectrum). He found that this was highly effective in engaging students and sometimes led to clinical breakthroughs and ways for students to express themselves differently than traditional play therapy methods.

The Post-doc Years

Following these early TBM groups Dr. Gann did his postdoctoral placement, running workshops around the Bay Area in various settings. He joined forces with renowned beat maker and finger drummer, Durazzo, who had founded the first iteration of Today's Future Sound. Durazzo left TFS to pursue his artistic career, and Dr. Gann continued recruiting from his network of Hip Hop artists in the Bay Area, where he ran monthly beat battles and MC competitions with local artists. In 2012, Dr. Gann started 'Beats4Lunch', a lunchtime beat-making program in Khalil Jacobs-Fantauzzi's classroom at West Oakland Middle School (of the renowned Fantauzzi brothers, noted filmmakers and activists).

The TFS Global Expansion

In 2017, TFS began its ongoing work in Alameda County Juvenile Hall, within the probation system. Also in 2017, Dr. Gann began volunteering in El Salvador with local artists to help launch an autonomous TBM-based program there. He put on the first beat battle in El Salvador. Dr. Gann and TFS have done similar work not only across the United States, but also in

Canada, Peru, Colombia, Chile, Australia, New Zealand, Mexico, Denmark, the United Kingdom, South Africa, France, Hong Kong, and Spain. Much of this work involved co-creative collaborations with local individuals. For example, he organized 'TEAMBeats Cape Town' in South Africa with Emile YX? and his program *Heal the Hood*. He also virtually trained and helped launch an autonomous program in Barcelona, Spain.

Programs for Adults and the Global Beat Cypher

Through the delivery of this work, it became apparent that, not only is such an intervention valuable for youth in primary and secondary schools, and in community and juvenile-justice settings, but it can also be used effectively with young and older adults in a variety of settings. This includes virtual settings, like the Today's Future Sound #GlobalBeatCypher, a weekly virtual cypher that is live streamed via multiple social-media platforms with adult beat makers from all over the world participating. This was designed as a response to the COVID-19 pandemic, to combat anti-Asian racism and xenophobia, as well as to provide a group community-based version of TBM during the pandemic 'lockdown'. It supported both virtual community building and a joining-in opportunity within a virtual space. #GlobalBeatCypher subsequently initiated in-person events that brought together participants, many of whom had previously only known each other through the livestream or virtually.

Global Diplomacy and Multinational Volunteerism.

These #GlobalBeatCypher in-person events have now happened across the United States, drawing virtual participants to visit the United States from Canada and as far as Chile. In turn, this has led to multinational collaborative volunteer projects like *TEAMBeats Chile* and *TEAMBeats Mexico* supported by nongovernmental organizations like *Partners of the Americas*, *Universidad de Concepcion*, and governmental organizations like the US State Department and its Next Level program. These projects brought members of TFS together with members of the #GlobalBeatCypher. Not only did this enable meeting in person for Hip Hop beat making events and showcases, but it also enabled the training of local Chilean and Mexican artists, respectively, in the TBM model. TFS also donated equipment to local Mexican/Chilean artists and community-based organizations. Finally, the TBM model and pedagogy were shared in bilingual trainings and formats. This brought a range of local Mexican and Chilean artists into other communities to volunteer, learn, and teach/share their skills and time.

Live Events, Community, and Relationships

TFS has facilitated live beat cyphers and beat battles for many years, and these spaces— which cater to beat makers/producers— have created a special dedicated environment that is normally unavailable (particularly for 'bedroom' and independent producers). The cyphers and battles also perpetuate beat making as a subculture and bring beat makers to the fore/spotlight. In a way, this represents a return to the origins of Hip Hop culture and music where the focus on the DJ was paramount. Often, beat makers tend to be more introverted than rappers, often remaining more isolated in their passionate pursuit of the nonverbal aspect of Hip Hop and electronic music. Performing and presenting their music in front of peers and being given physical and metaphorical venues where they can perform their beats decreases the level of anxiety for beat makers, who 'speak with beats' and share similar passions and sensibilities. Indeed, interacting through and around beat making (the 'Relationship and Relational' aspect of the process) is a vital component of TBM for individual or small-group youth interventions. The live events and virtual cyphers, battles, and showcases have been a place to gather and commune, leading to friendship, comradery, collaboration (artistic, social, and professional), networking, knowledge exchange, and a place to recruit volunteers and staff for TFS programs.

The TFS 'Beat Tapes'

#GlobalBeatCypher

One of the hallmarks of the TFS model and outcomes are the beat tapes, which are integral to the TBM model and groups for youth, but also serve to archive the #GlobalBeatCypher events, battles, and showcases beyond the archives and livestreams on YouTube and Instagram (Figure 10.1). Beat tapes also help promote these artists and share their talents with the local

Figure 10.1 Global Beat Cypher Flyer and Social Media Post

community, and TFS's global community by uploading these free beat tapes (or instrumental compilations) for free download and streaming to Today's Future Sound's Soundcloud and Bandcamp pages.

Hemlock Beats

Pictured here is an album cover illustrated by in-house artist, Ron the Graphics Guy, a former graffiti artist based in Atlanta, Georgia (Figure 10.2). Ron takes verbal instructions that are written down by TFS instructors based on group brainstorming of students to create a collaborative design for their beat tape that is posted on the TFS SoundCloud and Bandcamp pages for free downloading

Figure 10.2 Hemlock Beats, Beat Tape Cover by Ron The Graphics Guy and Glendy

and streaming. In this case, students elected to have their picture taken and then be drawn as cartoon characters. A student who preferred to focus on visual aspects helped to draw the title 'Hemlock beats', which is why the cover is on lined notebook paper, since a smartphone photo was taken of her text and sent to Ron, who illustrated the faces of students and TFS staff based on photos.

Wookie Raptor Beats

Wookie Raptor Beats, taken from a class in the San Francisco Bay Area, was the result of a collaborative brainstorm of middle and high school students, demonstrating the group process in mixing (and in the true Hip Hop sense, 'remixing' ideas) different characters, concepts, and movies/movie characters (Figure 10.3). When asked what they wanted on their album cover for the compilation album of their beats, one student suggested Wookies (fictional species of animal from the film franchise 'Star Wars'), with another suggesting raptors (a shortened version of the 'velociraptor' dinosaur from the film franchise 'Jurassic Park.'). A third student suggested that the Wookies be riding the raptors and marauding the local community. Often, the instructor or Dr. Gann will prompt students to think about something on the cover that represents their community and where they are from—in this case the Golden Gate Bridge and Transamerica Building serve as identifiers and landmarks.

Figure 10.3 Wookie Raptor Beats, Beat Tape Cover by Ron The Graphics Guy

Auburn Beats

Below are two versions of the 'Auburn Beats' beat-tape student-compilation album cover. One cover is illustrated by the TFS in-house illustrator, Ron the Graphics Guy (Figure 10.4), and one cover is by a student (Figure 10.5). The student offered to draw an alternate version of the album cover and went home and illustrated the history of Hip Hop after learning about it for the first time. Similar to the 'Hemlocks Beats' text being drawn by a student, this student contribution is core to the ethos of TFS and TBM. All effort is given to allow space for integrating other elements of Hip Hop culture like graffiti/the visual arts. In this cover art, the girls can be seen weaning hijabs, which some of the students at the school do as a cultural practice. Many students come

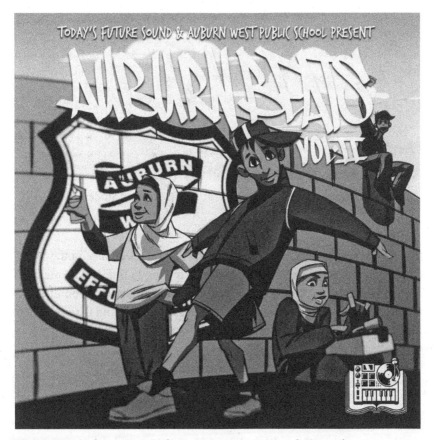

Figure 10.4 Auburn Beats Volume II, Beat Tape Cover by Ron The Graphics Guy

Figure 10.5 Auburn Beats Volume II, Beat Tape Cover by a Student

from Lebanese families, and students wanted to represent this on the album cover. You also see different students participating in different elements of Hip Hop, such as Breaking (i.e., the largest character in the foreground), graffiti (i.e., the girl with spray can on left side of the picture), and DJing and beat making, with the student on the right-hand side of the illustration.

Tassie Tiger Tacos (Australia)

Tassie Tiger Tacos came out of a short-run (two-day) intensive workshop provided in conjunction with a Hobart, Tasmania-based arts organization,

KickStart Arts. A grant-based project, the research outcomes on this project showed that girls and young women valued having a safe place to learn about beat making and enter into the production sphere of Hip Hop. For their beat-tape cover the workshop members decided to geographically mark and represent their area by including Mount Wellington (at the foot of which Hobart sits) and 'Bridgewater Jerry', a weather phenomenon considered unique to the area, in which fog is seen to 'spill down' from the mountain, covering the town (Figure 10.6). They also requested a Tasmanian Tiger holding and giving out tacos, in order to represent equity and taking care of the community. They also asked for an Aboriginal flag tattoo (see left arm) to acknowledge the traditional custodians of the land.

Figure 10.6 Tassie Tiger Tacos, Beat Tape Cover by Ron The Graphics Guy

Next, the accompanying flyer was for the beat battle and showcase done in the community the same weekend as the two-day workshops (Figure 10.7). The simultaneity of the showcase and workshop is typical of the way that TFS attempts to engage not only youth but also adults in the communities. This two-generation approach helps to get adults involved, educate them about the work, and ultimately give back to the community beyond just the youth. In this case, it also presented an opportunity for the older workshop participants to attend a beat-making community event, and meet other beat makers in their own community, thus activating connections to the wider Hip Hop community.

Figure 10.7 Tassy Fire Beat Battle and Showcase Flyer by Ron The Graphics Guy

StreetBeats: Healing Through Hip Hop

The StreetBeats series of events started out as an answer to white supremacist and racist rallies happening across the United States in 2017. Instead TFS conducted these interactive events to celebrate diversity, inclusion, and self-expression through the universal language of music. 'StreetBeats: Healing Through Hip Hop' included free beat-making workshops conducted throughout the San Francisco Bay Area in public parks, community/youth centers, and other community settings. These workshops were also intended to have therapeutic impacts for a diverse array of youth, as well as create further cross-cultural contact and understanding. Events brought beats back to the streets, from where beats and Hip Hop were born.

Dr. Gann aka Phillipdrummond was also invited to be an artist-in-residence at the Village Artists' Corner in partnership with the Asian Art Museum, and he was asked to engage local communities to help speak to the experience of the Asian diaspora. StreetBeats brought in several different Hip Hop and funk-style dancers, many of whom were Asian American, as well as Asian American beat makers and producers who performed live in front of the Asian Art Museum. StreetBeats also helped facilitate free beat making lessons from TFS staff, which included sampling music from across the Asian diaspora to create the 'StreetBeats' beat tape. Artist and youth participants were illustrated by TFS in-house illustrator, Ron the Graphics Guy, based on photographs and video stills (Figure 10.8). Four iterations of this event happened in the spring of 2018 with the resulting music and beats compiled onto this beat tape.

New York City

TFS has worked intensively throughout New York City since 2013, from Chinatown in lower Manhattan, to The Point CDC, and to Mott Haven Community High School with JC Hall's H.E.A.T. and Hip Hop Therapy Studio program. Dr. Gann and TFS not only have brought over and led California-based instructors to teach there, but also have done beat battles and beat cyphers in the NYC community. Alongside the beat battles and beat cyphers, local tri-state area beat makers from New York and New Jersey are also recruited to teach workshops in their communities.

Figure 10.8 Streetbeats, Beat Tape Cover by Ron The Graphics Guy

The collaborative workshops with TFS and regional New York–area beat makers came to the attention of the VH1 Save the Music Foundation. As a result, Dr. Gann received support for annual beat-making workshops in a variety of public-school settings across the different boroughs of New York City. At one workshop, Dr. Gann recruited over thirty-five beat makers from New York and New Jersey to teach more than eighty students at one time at PS 130, Parkside Elementary School in Brooklyn. Beat scene/Hip Hop and electronic music luminaries such as Suzi Analog, Brainorchestra, Brock Berrigan, and many more worked directly with students. The following year TFS and Save the Music Foundation did a collaborative workshop at the Thurgood Marshall School in Harlem, and MTA Beats was born. The MTA

Figure 10.9 MTA Beats, Beat Tape Cover by Ron The Graphics Guy

Beats beat tape (Figure 10.9) depicts a NYC MTA subway car robot/transformer making beats on a beat machine.

JacksonBeats

TFS's and Dr. Gann's ongoing documenting and sharing of workshops via social media has led to invitations for TFS from across the country and globe, to provide workshops and training in TBM. Teachers/educators, mental health clinicians, artists, administrators, and more reach out in anticipation of the value of TBM in their local communities. An example is former Jackson, Mississippi, councilman and lawyer Melvin Priester, Jr., who knew Dr. Gann personally while living in San Francisco, and reached out to Dr. Gann to bring the program and workshops to his own community.

The collaboration led to local practitioner trainings, annual teaching trips at local community centers and schools for youth identified as underserved, as well as beat battles/showcases in the community. These showcases brought together producers from across the Southern United States, including one invited producer who started a similar initiative to TFS in Birmingham, Alabama. In fact, it was through this Birmingham-based artist and activist, RyneSoul, aka Lashondra Hemphill, that TFS connected with Ron the Graphics Guy. The 'JacksonBeats' cover (Figure 10.10) was illustrated by local Jackson-based volunteer and artist Ian Hanson. The JacksonBeats beat tape is a compilation of beats made by youth at the Vergy P. Middleton Center in a public park setting.

Figure 10.10 Jacksonbeats, Beat Tape Cover by Ian Hanson

Conclusion

By presenting the work of Today's Future Sound (TFS), as well as the Therapuetic Beat Making (TBM) model, this chapter has aimed to provide a powerful example of how engaging with Hip Hop culture can lead to personal and community well-being. More specifically, it has aimed to illustrate those initiatives such as TFS, which are explicitly trauma informed, culturally sustaining, and authentically embedded within community, and can lead to increased connection, social support, and resilience in every corner of the globe. As discussed above, such outcomes are made possible through the unique yet organic combination of live events, community and school programs, and therapeutic sessions, and the interdependent relationship among all of these elements. Each is also anchored by a deep respect and appreciation of individuals, their cultures, their unique strengths, and their social realities. The examples provided also demonstrate the potential for culturally centred community-arts initiatives to foster connection across generational, cultural, and geographical divides. Above all, the programs, events, and models in this chapter demonstrate the value of meeting communities where they are at—by connecting through a globally recognised artform—and actively providing opportunities to celebrate both individual and collective identities.

References

Adjapong, E. and Levy, I. (2021). Hip-hop can heal: Addressing mental health through hip-hop in the urban classroom. *The New Educator*, 17(3): 242–263. https://doi.org/10.1080/1547688X.2020.1849884.

Ahmed, I. (2022). *Is hip-hop's dominance slipping? 'My concern is the magic is gone'*. Billboard Pro. https://www.billboard.com/pro/hip-hop-music-most-popular-genre-dominance-slipping/.

Browne, J., Wright, A. C., Berry, K., Mueser, K. T., Cather, C., Penn, D. L. and Kurtz, M. M. (2021). The alliance-outcome relationship in individual psychosocial treatment for schizophrenia and early psychosis: A meta-analysis. *Schizophrenia Research*, 231: 154–163. https://doi-org.libproxy.txstate.edu/10.1016/j.schres.2021.04.002.

Evans, J. (2019). 'Deeper than rap': Cultivating Racial identity and critical voices through Hip-Hop recording practices in the music classroom. *Journal of Media Literacy Education*, 11(3): 20–36.

Evans, J. M. (2022). Exploring social media contexts for cultivating connected learning with Black youth in urban communities: The case of Dreamer Studio. *Qualitative Sociology*, 45(3): 393–411.

Freud, S. (1958). A note on the unconscious in psychoanalysis. In *The Standard Edition of the Complete Psychological Works of Sigmund Freud, Volume XII (1911–1913): The Case of Schreber, Papers on Technique and Other Works*, pp. 255–266. Psychoanalytic Electronic Publishing.

Freud, S. and Strachey, J. (1900). *The interpretation of dreams*, vol. 4. Crows Nest, Australia: Allen & Unwin.

Gardner, Howard E. (2008). *Multiple intelligences: New horizons in theory and practice*. New York, NY: Basic Books. ProQuest Ebook Central.

Hauber, K. and Boon, A. (2022). First-session therapeutic relationship and outcome in high-risk adolescents intensive group psychotherapeutic programme. *Frontiers in Psychology*, 13. https://doi-org.libproxy.txstate.edu/10.3389/fpsyg.2022.916888.

Hillyard, K. (2015). Hip-hop is the most listened to genre in the world. NME. http://www.nme.com/news/music/various-artists-1151-1214849.

McFerran, K. S., Lai, H. I. C., Chang, W.-H., Acquaro, D., Chin, T. C., Stokes, H. and Crooke, A. H. D. (2020). Music, rhythm and trauma: A critical interpretive synthesis of research literature. *Frontiers in Psychology*, 11(324): 1–12. https://doi.org/10.3389/fpsyg.2020.00324.

Nielsen (2018). *2017 U.S. music year-end report*. The Nielsen Company. https://www.nielsen.com/insights/2018/2017-music-us-year-end-report/

Porges, S. W. (2009). The polyvagal theory: new insights into adaptive reactions of the autonomic nervous system. *Cleveland Clinic Journal of Medicine*, 76 (Suppl. 2): S86–90. https://doi.org/10.3949/ccjm.76.s2.17.

Rodwin, A., Shimizu, R., Travis, R., James, K., Banya, M. and Munson, M. (2022). A systematic review of music-based interventions to improve treatment engagement and mental health outcomes for adolescents and young adults. *Child and Adolescent Social Work Journal*. Advance online publication. https://doi.org/10.1007/s10560-022-00893-x.

Shearer, C. B. and Karanian, J. M. (2017). The neuroscience of intelligence: Empirical support for the theory of multiple intelligences? *Trends in Neuroscience and Education*, 6, 211–223. https://doi.org/10.1016/j.tine.2017.02.002.

Siegel, D. J. (2012). *The developing mind: How relationships and the brain interact to shape who we are* (2nd ed.). New York, NY: Guilford Press.

Today's Future Sound (2022). Today's Future Sound. https://todaysfuturesound.org/ [accessed November 22, 2022].

Travis, R. (2016). *The healing power of hip hop*. Praeger.

Travis, R. and Bowman, S. (2015). Validation of the individual & community empowerment inventory: A measure of rap music engagement among first-year college students. *Journal of Human Behavior in the Social Environment*, 25(2): 90–108.

Travis, R., Gann, E., Crooke, A. and Jenkins, S. (2021). Using therapeutic beat making and lyrics for empowerment. *Journal of Social Work*, 21(3): 551–574. https://doi.org/10.1177/1468017320911346.

Van der Kolk, B. A. (2005). Developmental trauma disorder: Toward a rational diagnosis for children with complex trauma histories. *Psychiatric Annals*, 35: 401–408.

11

The Sound Pad Project

Co-Creation of Breakin', Dance Education, and an Inclusive Educational Technology

Nathan Geering and Simon Hayhoe

Introduction

The art form of Breakin' is the most physical of the Hip Hop elements and requires the practitioner to connect with their entire body on a deep level. Geering (2018) identified that Breakin' is an ideal mindful activity because in order to execute the complex dance movements you have to be in the present moment. In addition, because it requires people to connect with the music, the practitioner has to be in that present moment to execute a dance movement or freeze perfectly in time with a musical accent and/ or beat.

As trauma is not stored only in the mind but also in the body through somatic memory (van der Kolk, 1994) it means that Breakin' is an ideal artform to help process and regulate people's emotions. The artform of Breakin' has therapeutic benefits that have been used to help treat symptoms of depression, anxiety and PTSD through enabling people to process their emotions through dance movement (Geering, 2019). In addition, Breakin' has proven to be a valuable life skill to people in the sight-loss community and has been successfully taught as a means of injury prevention and to improve spatial awareness (Geering, 2019). Due to many people with visual impairment sustaining injuries from falling, it makes sense to learn Breakin' as the 'go down element' teaches people to safely get from standing upright to rolling, jumping, and spinning on the floor. The artform gives the practitioner a heightened awareness of their bodies both internally and in relation to their surroundings, which in turn equips them with the confidence to navigate unfamiliar environments.

Nathan Geering and Simon Hayhoe, *The Sound Pad Project* In: *Music for Inclusion and Healing in Schools and Beyond.* Edited by: Pete Dale, Pamela Burnard, and Raphael Travis Jr., Oxford University Press. © Oxford University Press 2023. DOI: 10.1093/oso/9780197692677.003.0012

This chapter discusses the experiences of Breakers, choreographers, and those with visual impairments who worked collaboratively to develop a participatory dance-education, educational-technology, and choreography project called Sound Pad. The project was named after a digital instrument comprised of a set of buttons or slides for manipulating sounds that allows the user to create music, record sounds as samples, and play samples of music. The project was constructed and evaluated using a combination of participatory and grounded methodology (Hayhoe, 2020), the *rationale method* practice framework (Geering, 2019), and the development of inclusive capital (Hayhoe, 2019b). This chapter aims to explore the development of this co-created sensorially and intellectually inclusive education and performance through the experiences of dancers-as-teachers, and how this experience informs these dancers' practice. In addition, it is designed to examine the commissioning of public dance performance as a means of inclusive public education, and to make performance art more culturally diverse.

The Sound Pad project had four objectives, these were to: (1) develop a participatory dance technology, collaborative choreography, and a method of teaching dance, movement, and embodiment primarily through residual vision, sound, and touch using rationale methodology; (2) encourage people with visual impairment to move more, to feel more included in mainstream dance culture, and develop a greater sense of inclusion; (3) have a greater understanding of dance as a performative art form and a public art form; and (4) to examine the encouragement of artists in their use of a multi-modal pedagogy as a tool of teaching people with disabilities through different senses (i.e., vision or residual vision, hearing and touch used in combination with music and language as a mediator). At the end of the project, the results of this endeavour were shown at a public event in Sheffield City Centre, where participant dancers performed the work of participant visually impaired choreographers.

The following chapter discusses the design, process, and evaluation of the study and is broken into the following sections: (1) the context of the Sound Pad project, and the background of the models of practice and analysis; (2) the research and practice methodology, which was based on grounded methodology and participatory practice; (3) the analysis of observations and feedback of the three phases of the project; and (4) conclusions and recommendations drawn from the study.

The Context of the Sound Pad Project

As stated above, the method of practice used to develop the Sound Pad was the rationale method, that is, a theory of expressing dance movements through onomatopoeic sounds in order to develop a sense on embodied expression, a sense of self in the surrounding space, and safer, more stable mobility. This method consequently aimed to develop inclusive capital in both the participant dancers and visually impaired participants during the project. This method and model of human capital and inclusion are now discussed in this chapter in separate sections.

The Origins and Development of Rationale Method

The rationale method was initially developed after Nathan Geering contacted SNS Bradford (a part of Bradford City Council's service provision for community groups for people with visual impairments) and began working with a visually impaired theatre director, Andrew Loretto, to explore accessibility in Breakin' (Geering, 2017). Loretto and Geering previously worked at Sheffield Theatres and CAST in Doncaster. Loretto then suggested inviting playwright Kate O'Reilly to work on a project, and both Loretto and O'Reilly worked on a residency with Rationale. During this residency and through consultancy with Sheffield Royal Society for the Blind and those responsible for visual impairment at Rotherham Council, four significant issues were established: (1) the researchers were not just investigating visual impairment but different ways of conceptualising the world; (2) there are very few visually impaired Breakers, thus there was a potential issue of exclusion that needed addressing; (3) many people with visual impairments find audio description uninteresting, thus there was a need for audio description to be made more accessible and enjoyable; and (4) few people with visual impairment in this part of South Yorkshire went to the theatre, as they found performances inaccessible.

Further research by Rationale appeared to reveal that there was a need for an initiative to engage with people with visual impairments to raise an awareness of and an interest in dance. During this research, it was also observed that dance movements by people with visual impairments needed to be very dynamic as intricate movements are difficult to detect, and that many people with residual vision tend to see things better when they look down towards the floor. Following this research, Geering hypothesised that Breakin' would be a particularly relevant method of dance for people with visual impairments, as it is extremely dynamic and much of its movement happens down at ground level. Rationale then expanded its research in this area, in particular focusing on the accessibility of three different dance forms: ballet, contemporary dance, and Breakin'. During this work, people with visual impairments watched these different dance styles—without musical accompaniment, which it was felt could have influenced their experience—and then answered specific questions about the accessibility of each form of dance. The participants' answers seemed to confirm that Breakin' was the most accessible of these three forms.

Following this research, Rationale developed a form of audio description through beatboxing to provide a richer soundscape and stimulate the imaginations of visually impaired audiences. Rationale named this the Rationale Method of Audio Description ("rationale method"). To complement the rationale method, Rationale also worked on a new form of notation, similar to Labanotation (Hutchinson, 2013). This notation had specific sound effects matched to certain movements to ensure the highest level of accuracy during audio description of dance performances. This method of audio description is now made available to professional theatre companies and television and film productions.

Breakin' is also a valuable life skill for people with visual impairments, as it greatly improves spatial awareness and acts as a form of injury prevention—it is a method of 'falling with style'. Rationale argues it is extremely important to find ways of bridging the gap between sighted and visually impaired artists and audiences, to develop cultural inclusion. Rationale also argues that understanding visual impairment has enhanced the lives of Breakers, as it flips their way of thinking to explore creativity. In addition, it unlocks new possibilities by altering dancers' vision and their perceptions of themselves. More recently, rationale method has been explored by professional dancers, actors, painters, and writers throughout the United Kingdom, Finland, and South Africa. It has also been used to enhance productivity within businesses, as it offers a technique for directors, managers, and team members to utilise different viewpoints and perspectives in highly productive ways.

Bourdieu and Yardi's Model of Capital as Knowledge and Habits

Traditional models of technical capital, which themselves evolved out of a model of cultural capital, demonstrate it is important to gain information and use it within a network to feel included (Yardi, 2009, 2010). Information is part of human history to develop and use technologies and the arts, just as it can also be said to be part of our history to seek out our heritage and the heritage of others. Thus, cultural capital, such as that described by Bourdieu (2010), can also be knowing when to use certain types of language, such as internet jargon, and with whom certain language is socially and culturally acceptable. More controversially, human capital is our moral knowledge, such as our rules about how to exclude others who do not fit our own rules of social acceptability. It could also be said that it is part of our human character to seek out inclusion as a value to feel our sense of inclusion, and this inclusion fosters our sense of value (Hayhoe, 2019a). Consequently, to develop inclusive technical capital/inclusive capital—that is, the way people with disabilities acquire habits that develop and maintain inclusion—can also then be central to our human history, as it provides us with a sense of value.

During this project, it was felt that acquiring inclusive technical capital/inclusive capital was especially important for people with visual impairments. This was largely because people with visual impairments are more likely to find barriers to accessing inclusive capitals, as their opportunities for learning, gathering information, and gaining access to spaces and places in the community are often restricted by their impairments or social attitudes (WHO, 2001). This can potentially lead to a lessening of a sense of inclusion in mainstream society, and to a growing sense of social exclusion and isolation. For instance, previous research observed that people with visual impairments often found it harder to access technologies in cultural settings, or to access the environments of cultural institutions and public artworks (Hayhoe, 2014; Hayhoe, Roger, Eldritch-Boersen, and Kelland, 2015). The physical nature of visual impairment can also lessen our access to acquiring inclusive capital (2019a)/inclusive technical capital (2019b). For instance, acquiring visual impairment later in life can make it harder to join group discussions that are an essential part of networking for gaining information or using technology.

Furthermore, some people who have visual impairments often do not learn Braille or identify themselves as being disabled. Visual impairment may also make it harder to find transport or physical networks of friends and family. Late acquired visual impairments can similarly be thought to restrict access to mainstream learning, and the spaces and places of cultural institutions that people once enjoyed, such as the theatre.

Sound Pad set out to customise an existing music technology, converting it to a multisensory accessible educational and performative instrument of pedagogy (Campbell, 2016). This would allow people of all ages and sight levels to choreograph through rationale method. The technology was thus programmed with an audio language of onomatopoeic sound effects that most accurately helped people to imagine a variety of dance movements. The technology was to have clear tactile buttons that would allow people with visual impairments the opportunity to easily differentiate between buttons that corresponded to specific sound effects through touch, sound, and residual vision. The Sound Pad project also set out to bridge the gap between sighted and visually impaired artists and audiences, as it was designed to enable: (1) people with visual impairments to communicate their choreographic ideas and movements through sound effects and choreographic methodology; (2) dancers with visual impairments to be choreographed more efficiently and to make it possible to design ensemble choreography for groups of visually impaired dancers; (3) people with visual impairments and no experience of choreography to be taught to become choreographers through rationale method and the use of this technology to develop inclusive capital; (4) people with visual impairments to be taught to choreograph remotely from their home, develop inclusive capital, and send the sound file to the dance studio for the dancers to interpret, and to make dance choreography more accessible to people with visual impairments who find it harder to travel to new places; (5) sighted and visually impaired people to use the Sound Pad to either choreograph or to be choreographed, thus promoting the inclusion of sighted and visually impaired dancers and inclusive technical capital/inclusive capital.

Research and Practice Methodology

The methodology used to develop and evaluate the project was a combination of grounded methodology (Hayhoe, 2020) and participatory practice (Hayhoe and Garcia Carrisoza, 2019; Hayhoe, 2020), that is, a research and educational methodology for co-creating teaching and learning outcomes with all forms of learners. The methodology occurred in three stages, incorporating evaluation and practice. This methodology focused specifically on the co-creation of technology, choreography, dance, and learning and was originally developed during arts-based studies of inclusion and technological development some three years ago. Grounded methodology in particular is an evolution of a more traditional methodology called grounded theory (Glaser and Strauss, 1967). In keeping with the structure of grounded methodology, the participatory practice and research were conducted using three phases of data coding and practice, formally referred to as open (first), axial (second), and selective (third) phases.

The plan for these phases is summarised in Figure 11.1 and can be outlined as follows:

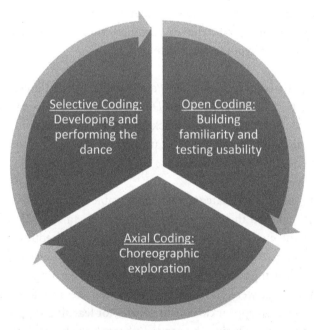

Figure 11.1 Outline of the Three Phases of Data Coding, Practice, and Analysis Used During the Project: [verbal image: an image of a circle split into three parts is displayed, with arrows showing the direction of the project in each part as it progresses. The last arrow points to the beginning of phase one, making the process ongoing].

Phase One: *Familiarising and Testing the Technology and Rationale Method.* Participants begin by familiarising themselves with the rationale method language, the Launchpad and the LPD8. After these sessions, feedback is sought on both the method and technologies. The feedback and observations of sessions are then evaluated, modifications are made to the teaching, and additions or modifications are designed to improve the usability of the technology as necessary.

Phase Two: *Choreographic Exploration.* Participants who express an interest in choreography are invited to start to choreograph movement sequences using the Launchpad and LPD8. Each participant has a set amount of time to choreograph a section of movement during each half-day session (four sessions in total), at the end of each session. This process is constantly evaluated and observed to see if movement is effectively communicated to the dancers. If needed, communication is further refined during this process to ensure movement and instructions are clearly understood. At the end of this process, the technology, learning, and choreography are more thoroughly evaluated and an initial hypothesis is created.

Phase Three: *Developing and Performing a Dance Co-created by the Participant Choreographer and Dancers.* A performance takes place to test the hypothesis, and feedback is sought. For those who struggle to leave their home, the choice of using the Launchpad to record audio sequences at home is provided.

During the first phase, categories of observable processes and practices were identified, and theories of analysis began to emerge. This provided a focus for the evaluation of the dance education and educational technology. This structure was based on a previous model developed in previous research using this methodology, which used learning environments and practices that were classified according to access preferences to examine and develop appropriate technologies for learning support (Barton and Hayhoe, 2022). During the second phase, links between variables in individual categories of practice are connected and developed into a unified epistemological model or paradigm that can be tested. In addition, if grounded methodology is used for a study of a course or workshop, as it was in this project, this linkage is done for practical purposes and provides a direction for evaluation. Between the second and third phases, an initial, testable hypothesis is then developed. During the third phase, testable evidence is used to interrogate the initial hypothesis—this data can include a workshop, course evaluations, a structured exercise, or further phases of data collection and the re-development of participatory practice. During the three phases of analysis, data is also analysed in a progressively more focused way, and all forms of data are treated as being equally important. This system of data analysis suits the reflexive, problem-solving approach to novel cultural contexts and topics, such as those found in this project, and triangulates different forms of data, data analysis, and collection methods.

In keeping with grounded methodology, data was also constantly compared during the project to refine the methodology, and the researchers regarded all forms of data collected during the project as equally important, valuable, and useable. This flexible approach to data collection suited the Sound Pad project's reflexive, problem-solving approach to new contexts, topics, and settings, which were previously unrecognized, under-scrutinized, and under-investigated. In addition, like grounded theory, grounded methodology data and theoretical approaches can also be stored for later analysis during different projects where they have more relevance.

There are differences between grounded theory and grounded methodology, and these differences were relevant in this project. For example, unlike grounded theory, grounded methodology encourages the evolution of culturally constructed theories in the style of cultural anthropologies that collect and analyse the data largely asynchronously (Geertz, 1989)— the data is thus pre-defined, as was the nature of the study in the original proposal for the Sound Pad. In addition, in grounded methodology, analysis is conducted using combinations of deductive and inductive logic (Popper, 1959, 1979). That is to say, the reflections are worked through logically for an answer, and then followed by social and cultural hypothesis testing. There are also practical differences between grounded theory and grounded methodology. Most notably, grounded methodology relies less on formal coding, and relies more on narratives developed by the researcher in order to state an original problem. Subsequently, these narratives are presented as either a thematic analysis, case studies, or a combination of both. Grounded methodology is also applicable to non-traditional research studies, such as the design and evaluation of learning or structured literature searches.

Data Collection, Preparation of the Research, and Practice and Ethics

Prior to the development of the project the Royal National Institute for the Blind, Sheffield Royal Society for the Blind and SNS Bradford were contacted in person, and members of these societies were recruited as volunteer participants either for the learning phase of the project or to provide feedback via these organisations. It was planned to recruit twenty participants of mixed ages to take part in the education, feedback, and technology elements of the project. For ethical reasons, it was also decided not to recruit young children who would not understand the nature of the project or breakin'. Twenty-one participants eventually took part in the project. The project focused on recruiting younger people for the educational elements of the project in particular, as it was hoped the educational outcomes would have particular resonance and impact in schools. However, people of all ages were asked for feedback about the technology and choreography, as it was envisaged that these elements should be as inclusive and wide-ranging as possible. As well as recruiting participants, before starting the project a suitably inclusive technology was sourced. This technology had to include sound, vision, and touch—vision was included for people with residual vision and sighted people. Eventually, an Ableton Novation Launchpad (the Launchpad) was bought.

This Sound Pad technology was chosen as it was relatively easy to teach, it could be connected to a laptop via a cable, voice samples could be loaded, and the actual instrument was a simple square device with sixty-four buttons arranged in a useable eight-by-eight array of square, good-sized buttons. Although the instrument also had other buttons and knobs arranged around the outside to program the device, the participants would not need these to develop dance choreography. More usefully, when the Launchpad was turned on it lit up, and each button could be programmed as a simple white light or a different colour, making it perceptible to people with residual vision. In addition, a similar but simpler sound pad, an AKAI Professional LPD8 (the LPD8) was sourced. This was similar to the Launchpad, but had only eight buttons in an array of four-by-two, for participants who preferred a simpler device. This again had buttons and knobs around its sides for programming and volume adjustment, but these did not need to be used during the development of choreography. During the project, there were two types of data collection: (1) participant observations (Hayhoe, 2012), some of which were voice recorded, photographed, or videoed with mobile phones (iPhone and Samsung J4); and (2) interviews with participants—these interviews were recorded using an iPhone, as the sound files could be easily fed back to the interviewees; the questions are found in Appendix A.

The methodology was informed by the British Educational Research Association's guidelines on ethical research (BERA, 2018). In accordance with these guidelines, it was a requirement that any participant in the project, whether they were a learner, a dancer, a choreographer, or a participant who provided feedback, had to provide informed consent—that is, they were either read or could read for themselves an A4 sheet describing the project and telling them their role in the project, how the data was to be used, that their participation and all data were anonymous, what the project hoped to achieve, and their right to withdraw their participation or their data from the project at any time. During the project, no participants withdrew. In addition, during the project no coercion was applied through incentives or payment, that is, participation was pro-bonum, and no financial or material reward was offered to the participants. In accordance with ethical guidelines and its promise of participant anonymity, only images of the objects made during classes and Nathan Geering were reproduced in reports, presentations, or publications resulting from this project. The images, videos, and sound files of the participants recorded during observations were subsequently only used to analyse and log the development of the project, and were downloaded and kept on a securely locked computer with password protection. Additionally, any personal data about the participants were to be destroyed six months after the end of the project.

Analysis of the Three Phases of the Project Using Inclusive Technical Capital/Inclusive Capital

Initial Tasks in the Development of the Project

As stated above, inclusive technical capital/inclusive capital is developed through the enhancement of five elements or stages of inclusion. These are illustrated in Figure 11.2. During the following evaluation of the practice, this model is used as a framework of analysis, as its aim was to develop this form of human capital through co-creation of learning, choreography, and technology. In this analysis, individual elements of inclusive technical capital/

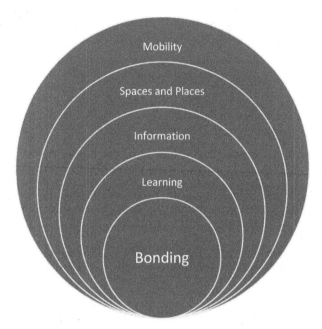

Figure 11.2 The Development of Inclusive Capital and a Sense of Inclusion: [verbal image] An image of five increasingly sized circles one within the other, with the five stages of inclusive capital in each circle.
The Development of Inclusive Capital and a Sense of Inclusion

inclusive capital will be emboldened to emphasise how and where it was developed during this project.

All three phases of practice took place during sessions at the Sheffield Royal Society for the Blind, SNS Bradford and 108 The Moor (Sheffield City Centre); and these three phases were subsequently split into children's and adult's participatory sessions. The sessions were all led by Nathan Geering and altogether included five children and sixteen adult participants. Sessions were based on groups that allowed bonding in familiar Sheffield and Bradford spaces and places between the participants and between Rationale and the participants. The dates and times of these sessions were as follows, and sessions were booked at the convenience of the venues and participants. Therefore, they did not follow a strict time pattern—the dates for these sessions can be found in Appendix B.

The children's sessions were used to develop learning about mobility and the space through dance, to generate information through familiarization with the Launchpad and LPD8, to learn choreography and breakin, to make representations of mobility that could subsequently be used to develop the technology, and to provide general feedback about the technology and the learning—thus, all the participants had importance as co-creators of learning through this knowledge-gathering and information-generation process. The same was to occur between participants in the adult sessions, where participants used the Launchpad and LPD8 then discussed what they would like to see from the technology and learning sessions, fed back on their own experiences of dance—as participants and as an audience—and provided feedback on the use of the Launchpad and LDP8.

Implementing Phase One

In the first phase of practice, samples of onomatopoeic sounds representing individual dance moves were recorded and uploaded to the Launchpad and LPD8. Participants then attended sessions to familiarize themselves with the technology, the samples used, and the notion of developing choreography with a visual impairment—this phase took place asynchronously (i.e., the adults started this phase a month after the children were introduced to the technologies). Feedback on the usability of the Launchpad and LPD8 was then gathered from participants. During this phase, Geering also started teaching participants how to use the technology, the nature of choreography, and the design of dance movement through rhythm. It was observed that rationale method could help develop many elements of inclusive technical capital/inclusive capital. For instance, the children demonstrated they could imagine mobility and their own bodies in space and place, learnt to link this embodiment to the samples of dance moves, and were happy to synthesize information about the Launchpad on their own to suggest improvements to the technology. For example, in order to develop the technology and to teach the children dance moves through embodiment, the children were asked to create representations of body movement in playdough. These playdough representations were then used to design shapes on clear buttons for the Launchpad to provide information and facilitate learning through a combination of touch, vision, sound, and language as a mediator (Hayhoe, 2018; Hayhoe, Cohen, and Garcia Carrisoza, 2019). An example of these playdough figures is shown in Figure 11.3.

From these playdough pieces, symbols were developed with the participants through co-creation that could be used as tactile information

Figure 11.3 Youth Developed Representations of Dance Movements in Playdough (General): [verbal image: An image of ten different-sized playdough figures of dance moves. They range from twirl shapes and small pieces of playdough in a circle to representations of a person with their legs split.]

and the basis for new learning. These tactile elements thus became the basis of raised buttons that could be fixed to the Launchpad and LPD8. Examples of these figures are shown in Figures 11.4 and 11.5.

Implementing Phase Two

In phase two, an initial evaluation of the feedback and observations during these early sessions showed a positive response to the Launchpad and LPD8 and the possibility of generating choreographic exploration exercises during the following sessions. The only issue that arose was that some participants found the Launchpad had too many buttons, and found it hard to use such a large array to learn choreography. Thus, for some novice users, it was felt that using LPD8 to teach choreography would be less intimidating. During analysis of interviews and observations it was also observed that participants liked music as a medium of art, some performed music beyond their school or the group, and subsequently many participants bonded through a discussion of music during the groups. In addition, many participants had previous experience of technology, they all had mobile phones, and all felt generally comfortable using technology. However, the participants had little or no experience of performative dance, especially dancing in public. Subsequently, it appeared that the participants were more comfortable using the Launchpad as a learning mediator and as a means of co-creating dance information through the language of music as it was a familiar art form; the users appeared particularly comfortable using the rationale method as music, as it proved generally easy to memorize after the initial sessions.

At the beginning of phase two, three participants also volunteered to work as choreographers with five participant dancers, and they attended further sessions to start designing movement sequences using the Launchpad and LPD8. At this point, tactile representations of the dance moves designed in phase one were molded into clear buttons and represented through raised shapes. These buttons were then stuck to the built-in buttons on the Launchpad and LPD8 with glue dots to trial this new system during

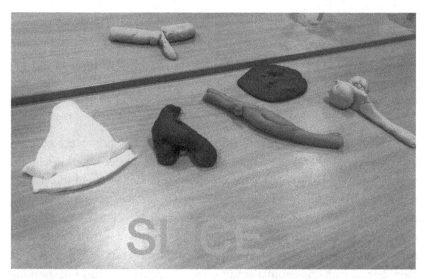

Figures 11.4 and 11.5 Youth Developed Representations of Dance Movements in Playdough (Slice and Bounce): [verbal image: Two images, one after the other and representing different sized playdough figures of named dance moves. The first image represents playdough figures of a slice—a dance move. There are six playdough figures on a table. The figures are long and thin, some split. The second image represents the figures of a bounce—another dance move. There are three figures, each of which is round, and some are like chubby human figures, set out on a tabletop.]

Figures 11.4 and 11.5 Continued

choreography sessions. Despite initial worries about possible confusion in learning choreography at the beginning of the project, as the sessions progressed and participants got to know one another, the sighted and visually impaired participants bonded as a group and appeared to develop a clear rapport. During the logs of later sessions in particular, it was noticeable that any misunderstandings and tensions caused by new forms of learning were overcome through frank conversations. Participants in particular appeared to be more honest with one another at this stage, accepting criticism and speaking freely, and subsequently the learning became more refined. Small changes in these latter stages of learning also appeared to make big differences to the development of choreography, and this new honest approach helped accelerate the process of communication and the co-creation of dance information. For example, as one dancer explained:

What was really interesting was that I didn't know his idea of a step was my idea of a step. We had to ask each other is this the kind of step you mean? So, we had to get involved more than choreographers would usually. The [technology] helped a lot.

Consequently, the testable hypothesis formed at the end of phase two of the project was that:

Once clear communication processes have been confirmed, the dancers can more easily choreograph the performance piece.

Implementing Phase Three

In the final phase of the process, the development of a choreographed sequence that could be used as a form of communication about mobility and space and place appeared to have been developed. During observations in the latter February session at 108 The Moor, for example, clear dance sequences that could be performed had been devised using rationale method, the Launchpad and the LPD8 and the dancers worked together to produce a synchronized breakdance. An example of one of these dance steps in illustrated in Figure 11.6 and performed by Geering.

Unfortunately, in mid- to late February 2020, the initial public performance of these dances had to be postponed, as widespread storms and flooding restricted travel and public attendance, and there were increasing tensions over the rising number of COVID-19 cases. However, on the 21st of February the choreography was performed at Derby Theatre to an audience of around sixty-five people. Feedback from the evening was universally positive about the performance, choreography, and the work between and within the group. For example, one audience member stated, 'The sound effects gave me a better understanding of dance moves and made the performance really enjoyable'. Whilst another audience member stated, 'I have never seen a show use accessibility in this way and thoroughly enjoyed it'. In addition, the participant dancers also provided universally positive feedback about their experiences of working with the participant choreographers and emphasised how the technology helped them alter their own understanding of mobility and space in an innovative way. For example, one dancer explained:

Figure 11.6 Example of a Breakin' (or Breakdance) Move Choreographed by a Participant and Performed by Nathan Geering: [verbal image: Nathan is moving in time to music. He is a tall man wearing blue jeans, dark-coloured trainers with red laces, and a baggy purple sweatshirt with a teddybear design on the front. He is about to spin, and one arm is outstretched to the front of his body whilst another is outstretched behind him.]

The [technology's] really good. It's easy enough to understand what [the choreographer] meant. You already had a vision of what he already wanted. And, with feeling and touching the [technology], he was able to understand what our movements were to give him a clearer idea.

Another dancer explained that the participant choreographer had challenged her expectations of what to expect from the process of designing breakin movements and sequences. However, she also felt that the participant had an image of what he wanted to achieve and communicate:

> The process has been really interesting. I found that working with [the cho-reographer] he really seems to know what he wants. You can tell he's got a vision of what he's trying to portray. And, he's not taking long to throw down what he actually wants.

Furthermore, the dancers universally felt that they had gained a personal understanding of the capability of visually impaired people beyond the cre-ation of their breakin routines as a result of working with the participant choreographers. They also described wanting to expand their experiences of working on the project to create a sustainable model of learning and co-creation:

> It's been really nice as a dancer to be creative with [the choreographers] and to create a routine . . . I didn't know what to expect, but I feel very privileged to be a part of it. Let's keep going with this, because I'm very excited to see what the future holds.

Conclusions and Recommendations

The Sound Pad project has created a unique form of co-creating, choreographing, and learning about dance sequences through imagining mobility and space, and through the co-creation of mobility. Furthermore, all the participants developed new negotiated forms of information that helped them bond, share ideas, and subsequently evolve a form of mutual inclusive technical capital/inclusive capital. In addition, visually impaired participant choreographers showed that it was possible to imagine dance sequences cre-atively through touch, sound, and residual vision and then communicate this vision to sighted dancers in an effective way. There were challenges to this process, and some dancers felt it was initially difficult to understand if what they imagined was the same as the participant choreographer. However, this confusion quickly dissipated as the sessions progressed, and both the par-ticipant dancers and choreographers appeared to evolve mutual respect and comprehension of each other's abilities. The technology and the rationale method of describing onomatopoeic sound and movement therefore seem to have particularly helped this process of communication.

Recommendations

Given these findings, the authors of this chapter recommend three points for future action: (1) The participatory practice and co-creation element of the project needs further validation with different audiences, dance companies, environments, and cultural settings. Although the process was largely successful in Sheffield and Bradford, further triangulation of these results will help to develop a more objective, culturally transferable method of working. (2) Likewise, the technology developed through co-creation and practice needs further testing in different settings and with different members of the visually impaired community. In particular, the technology at present has not been tested with participants with multiple disabilities. For example, can the rationale method help communicate the imagination of those on the autistic spectrum or those with learning difficulties? (3) The lessons learnt from this project, and particularly the development of the rationale method and model of inclusive technical capital/inclusive capital, needs to be developed as a formal method of dance and music education.

There is significant scope for dance educators to use the technology to inform their own practice and use Breakin' to increase the awareness of disability arts and the capabilities of all learners to participate in performance art on an equal basis. At first sight, Breakin' might appear as a continuous series of rapid movements, but we suggest that it offers an important opportunity for people to slow down and to connect with their inner selves, their feelings, their bodies, and their peers (Carmichael-Murphy and Geering, 2022).

References

Barton, J. and Hayhoe, S. (2022). *Emancipatory and participatory research for emerging educational researchers: Theory and case studies of research in disabled communities.* Abingdon: Routledge.

BERA (2018). *Ethical guidelines for ethical research* (4th ed.). London: British Educational Research Association.

Bourdieu, P. (2010). *Distinction.* Abingdon: Routledge Classics.

Campbell, L. (2016). Technoparticipation: Intermeshing performative pedagogy and interruption. *Body, Space & Technology,* 15: 1–14. doi: http://doi.org/10.16995/bst.16

Carmichael-Murphy, P. and Geering, N. (2022). *ACTs of creativity report: Hip Hop, breakin' and mindfulness in schools.* Sheffield: Rationale Arts.

Geering, N. (2017). Breakdance and visual impairment. *Animated Magazine,* Summer: 19–21.

Geering, N. (2019). Interview. *Hiphop Dance Almanac,* vol. 1. https://www.google.com/amp/s/www.hiphopdancealmanac.com/amp/nathan-geering-1.

Geering, N. (2019). *The Rationale method.* TEDxBradford. https://youtu.be/UmvuT1EKpcQ.

Geertz, C. (1989). Works and lives: The anthropologist as author. Palo Alto, CA: Stanford University Press.

Glaser, B. G. and Strauss, A. L. (1967). *The discovery of grounded theory: Strategies for qualitative research.* Chicago: Aldine.

Hayhoe, S. (2012). *Grounded theory and disability studies.* Amherst, NY: Cambria Press.

Hayhoe, S. (2014). An enquiry into passive and active exclusion from sensory aesthetics in museums and on the Web: Two case studies of final year students at California School for the Blind studying art works through galleries and on the web. *British Journal of Visual Impairment,* 32(1): 44–58.

Hayhoe, S. (2018). Classical philosophies on blindness and cross-modal transfer, 1688–2003. In J. Ravenscroft (ed.), *The Routledge Handbook of Visual Impairment: Social and Cultural Research.* Abingdon: Routledge, pp. 227–237.

Hayhoe, S. (2019a). Inclusive technical capital in the twenty-first century. In S. Halder and V. Argyropoulos (eds.), *Inclusion, Equity and Access for Individuals with Disabilities.* Singapore: Palgrave Macmillan. pp. 223–241. https://doi.org/10.1007/978-981-13-5962-0_11.

Hayhoe, S. (2019a). *Cultural heritage, ageing, disability, and identity: Practice, and the development of inclusive capital.* Abingdon: Routledge.

Hayhoe, S. (2019b). Inclusive technical capital in the twenty-first century. In S. Halder and V. Argyropoulos (eds.), *Inclusion, Equity and Access for Individuals with Disabilities.* Singapore: Palgrave Macmillan. pp. 223–241. https://doi.org/10.1007/978-981-13-5962-0_11.

Hayhoe, S. (2020). *An introduction to grounded methodology for emerging educational researchers.* Abingdon, UK: Routledge.

Hayhoe, S. and Garcia Carrisoza, H. G. (2019). *Accessible resources for cultural heritage EcoSystems (ARCHES) deliverables 2.4: Recommendations, guidelines and policy briefing.* Vienna, Austria: ARCHES.

Hayhoe, S., Cohen, R. and Garcia Carrisoza, H. (2019). Locke and Hume's philosophical theory of color is investigated through a case study of Esref Armagan, an artist born blind. *Journal of Blindness Innovation and Research,* 9(1): 1–9.

Hayhoe, S., Roger, K., Eldritch-Boersen, S. and Kelland, L. (2015). Developing inclusive technical capital beyond the Disabled Students' Allowance in England. *Social Inclusion,* 3(6): 29–41.

Hutchinson, A. (2013). *Labanotation.* Encyclopædia Britannica. https://www.britannica.com/art/labanotation (accessed 14th February 2020).

Popper, K. (1959). The logic of scientific discovery. London: Hutchinson & Co.

Popper, K. (1979). *Objective knowledge: An evolutionary approach* (rev. ed.). Oxford: Clarendon Press.

Van der Kolk, B. A. (1994). The body keeps the score: Memory and the evolving psychobiology of posttraumatic stress. *Harvard Review of Psychiatry* 1(5): 253–265. https://pubmed.ncbi.nlm.nih.gov/9384857/.

WHO. (2001). *International classification of functioning, disability and health: ICF.* Geneva, Switzerland: World Health Organization.

Yardi, S. (2009). Social learning and technical capital on the social web. *ACM Crossroads,* 162 (0): 9.

Yardi, S. (2010, February). A theory of technical capital. Paper presented at The TMSP Workshop, Georgia Institute of Technology, Georgia, US. http://tmsp.umd.edu/position%20papers/Yardi-SocialMediatingTech.pdf.

Appendix A

Background questions

1. Could you please tell me your age?
2. Could you please tell me your experience of dancing?
3. Could you please tell me if you have always been visually impaired or had a visual impairment from birth or when you were born?
4. Could you please tell me if you have some vision, or if you have no vision?
5. Could you please tell me if you have any other access need, such as help with walking or hearing?

Context of technology usage

1. Can you please tell me about your use of technology?
2. Do you use a PC—with a keyboard/mouse/touchpad—a tablet computer and a mobile telephone?
a. Do you use specialist tactile keyboards or sound interfaces, such as JAWS or tactile keyboards?
3. Do you use computers to make music?
4. Do you use computers to communicate with other people?
5. Do you program or code computer programs?

Context of dancing—current experience of music and dance:

1. Could you please describe your experience of music?
    a. Do you attend concerts or clubs?
    b. Do you only listen to music at home?
    c. Do you perform music?
2. Do you dance?
    a. If you dance, do you dance at home or in clubs or public dances?
    b. Do you perform dance, or have you ever performed a dance in public?

Initial impression of the Soundpad

1. If you have tried the Soundpad today, did you find it easy to use?
    i. Did you find it easy to use, and if so, why?
    ii. Did you find it interesting to use?
2. Would it be something you would like to use?
3. Can you see a benefit to using the Soundpad to plan a dance?
4. Do you identify anything we could add to the Soundpad?
5. Is there anything we could add to the Soundpad to make it easier to use?
6. Do you prefer a tactile interface?
7. What else could we do to change or program the Soundpad to make it more user friendly?

Closing questions

1. Is there anything else you think would be helpful for me to know?
2. Would it be alright to call you if I have any more questions or need clarification?

Appendix B

Children's Sessions:

- December 13th & 17th, 2019, 16.30–18.30

- January 17th, 24th, & 31st, 2020, 16.30–18.30
- February 7th, 2020, 16.30–18.30
- February 15th, 2020, 11.30–14.30
- February 17th & 18th, 2020, 10.00–16.00

Adults' Sessions:

- January 17th & 24th, 2020, 13.30–14.30
- January 20th, 2020, 10.00–12.00
- February 7th, 2020, 13.30–14.30

12

Using Social Media to Cultivate Connected Learning and Social and Emotional Support Through a Hip Hop–Based Education Programme

Jabari M. Evans

Introduction and Background

Access to spaces and places that provide pathways to creative careers in the United States has historically been stubbornly tied to race and socioeconomic background (Florida, 2019; Watkins and Cho, 2018). However, research indicates that through Connected Learning (Ito *et al.*, 2013), modern technological tools are increasingly allowing adolescents the ability to individually navigate skill development for their personal interests, develop connections with peers, and improve their networking skills (Callahan *et al.*, 2019; Watkins, 2019). Additionally, Black cyberculture on social media has been argued to galvanize Black youth to fight to overcome racism, cope with many psychological traumas, and express joy (e.g., Brock, 2020). Professional development also has been shown to manifest through online affinity spaces, social-media platforms, and their affiliated creator communities, where these youth can build kinship bonds with others who hold similar aspirations and social identities unbounded from their physical location (Gee, 2017).

These kinship- (and often neighbourhood-) driven communities are what Duffy and colleagues (2021) calls creator pods, or social-media relationships that focus on audience quality and knowledge generation. Through these pods, Black youth also receive social and emotional support in regard to racism and sexism. Social and business relationships are reflected in Hip Hop's digital communities of practice (Evans, 2020, 2021). Levy (2020) has

Jabari M. Evans, *Using Social Media to Cultivate Connected Learning and Social and Emotional Support Through a Hip Hop–Based Education Programme* In: *Music for Inclusion and Healing in Schools and Beyond.* Edited by: Pete Dale, Pamela Burnard, and Raphael Travis Jr., Oxford University Press. © Oxford University Press 2023. DOI: 10.1093/oso/9780197692677.003.0013 also noted that Hip Hop's artistic practices encourage youth of today to use digital media to express their emotions about that which it is impossible to keep silent about, increase self-esteem, protest injustices, and galvanize social movements. Although when inclusive digital affinity spaces can provide social support for Black creative youth, they are typically exclusionary to Black youth from disadvantaged socioeconomic backgrounds (Jenkins, 2007). In particular, Black youth in low-income communities often lack access to digital tools required for participation or do not know about opportunities to connect with relevant resources and thus are not given proper pathways to use social media in ways that are prosocial or facilitate their everyday emotional survival.

However, Hip Hop–based education (HHBE) programs (both in-school and after school) have been shown to disrupt those exclusionary processes by providing mentorship to youth via adults who both share their background and are part of a high-value field or career path (Ben-Eliyahu *et al.*, 2014; Raposa *et al.*, 2019). Furthermore, in the realm of social media, one can now access the world through one's own perspective and interests and actively participate with media that is consumed (Jenkins, 2007). Modern young people regularly utilize social-media platforms (e.g., Tik Tok, Twitch, and ClubHouse[1]) to digitally communicate, share information, gain knowledge with one another, and forge relationships.

This chapter explores how *Dreamer Studio* has produced significant and lasting impacts on its youth participants' transitions into creative labour beyond the physical studio setting. Dreamer Studio is located on Chicago's Southside, is partnered with a national arts nonprofit, and serves as a youth-led community-based recording studio. Housed in the basement of a local Baptist church, this unique program offers students access to a fully equipped professional music studio as a safe haven. This paper utilizes methods of digital urban ethnography (Lane, 2018) to ask how active participants, mentors, and alumni of the program organized as their artistic community of practice during COVID-19 through utilization of social-media platforms. During in-depth interviews with participants, they suggested that the self-empowerment taught in the Dreamer Studio program was an initial step towards gaining self-confidence in an occupational identity. The studio's staff, participants, and alumni self-reported three key practices to this process: (1) corralling as a pod, (2) collaborative problem solving, and (3) DIY circulation. Ultimately, I argue that participants of

Dreamer Studio are a case study of how social media provides a new opportunity for Hip Hop–based education programs to engage participants with their passions in expert ways and provide an additional sense of social and emotional support.

Twenty-first-Century Skills, DIY Careers, and Youth Participation on Social-Media Platforms

Social-media, video-sharing, and music-streaming platforms have drastically changed the digital participation strategies of aspiring musicians, as they now can move between and within platforms to self-promote themselves while seeking to professionalize their careers (Haynes and Marshall, 2018; Hesmondhalgh, 2020; Powers, 2015). Social-media platforms have been shown to greatly support the work of musicians, by providing launching pads for these burgeoning artists to speak directly to their peer communities, build personal relationships with them, and collaborate in their creative process (Baym, 2012). These relationships often now go beyond simple 'friending' to direct messaging, portal shows, and live streams of mundane activities that lead to other kinds of intimate interpersonal contact (Rendell, 2021). A rapidly professionalizing and monetizing wave of diverse, multicultural, previously amateur creatives from around the world have harnessed these platforms to incubate their own, often massive, transnational and cross-cultural creative communities (Baym, 2018).

For youth, this communication with others is largely important to occupational identity development (Watkins and Cho, 2018) and navigating today's creative workforce (Duffy, 2017). All these factors have provided a unique and precarious opportunity to Black youth in urban America, who have been shown to have a strong affinity for digital media often while nestled in communities of digital disadvantage due to their race, class, and geography (Stuart, 2020; Watkins, 2019). This has led to philanthropic efforts to seriously invest in supporting curricula to empower marginalized students to gain civic media literacy, which broadly means thinking critically about reimagining the social function of media, leveling digital inequities and the implications of technological advancements on their everyday lives (Mihailidis, 2008; Mihailidis *et al.*, 2021). In considering the digital participation of urban youth of color, interest-driven practices on social-media platforms are online activities these young people find appealing but also central as they build their creative networks and peer relations and seek cultural capital (Watkins and Cho, 2018).

Recent scholarship has argued that formal efforts engineered to provide culturally sustaining interventions for Black youth should be more focused on leveraging their creative and cultural capital in the realm of Hip Hop music (Emdin, 2021; Evans, 2021; Kramer *et al.*, 2021). For example, African American youth involvement in Hip Hop artistic practices have previously been shown to play a significant role in teaching them the importance of collaboration and innovation with technology as well as in their identity development (Love, 2015). Hip Hop communities of practice also provide both a sense of belonging and acceptance (e.g., the development and/or strengthening of relationships) to youth within peer cultures (Dimitriadis, 2009; Helmer, 2015; Seidel, 2011). Despite a proliferation of social and behavioral research pointing to the positive impact of Hip Hop music production within programmatic interventions (Levy and Travis, 2020; Petchauer, 2015), very few studies have attempted to track the impact of Hip Hop–based education (HHBE) programs towards their well-being beyond the school buildings or community centers and in the everyday lives of its participants beyond the program.

Thus, there is a need for research that examines how social-media platforms are redefining HHBE programs. Since youth are continually re-negotiating their identities and actively reinventing themselves on the platforms they participate in, there is a need to understand how programs can better accommodate (and evaluate) communities of practice as they traverse digital and physical spaces. Additionally, there is a need to understand what the hybridity of these communities means for their social and emotional development. Many scholars have claimed that Hip Hop (as a pedagogy of practice) offers an education where learners can work towards their desired aspirations via mediums or learning experiences that are familiar to them and build upon their already acquired knowledge (Emdin, 2020; Hill and Petchauer, 2013). It is also apparent that Hip Hop cultural practices provide new literacies that are linked to the positive development of African American youth (Evans, 2021). These findings suggest that measuring the successes of a HHBE program is tied to not only how participants create and listen to music, but also how they communicate with one another for social and emotional support, and the overall impacts of their well-being.

Theoretical Framework

The value of cultural production is generally organized to ensure that certain individuals are automatically advantaged or disadvantaged based on their cultural capital (knowledge, behaviours, and skills that a person can tap into to demonstrate one's cultural competence and social status), or lack thereof (Bourdieu, 1986). As an art form deeply rooted in disadvantaged urban communities, Hip Hop culture has been depicted as a social identity that has historically been viewed from a deficit standpoint (Rose, 1994). However, through the accumulation of digital clout (Hip Hop–inflected cultural capital), modern youth in Hip Hop communities of practice regularly gain social status and economic mobility through social-media platforms and participatory culture (Evans and Baym, 2022). This type of cultural capital within Black music scenes is often context-specific and can be wielded powerfully depending on the situation (Hall, 1992). To that point, previous work has been written about how Hip Hop music has served as a site of identity development and positive life outcomes for creative marginalized Black youth in urban America (Forman, 2002; Harkness, 2013; Lee, 2016; Perry, 2004; Quinn, 2004), often providing them with a cultural lens to find confidence in a society that has historically left them alienated. Not surprisingly, social-media platforms extend Hip Hop's community of practice and, in many ways, have developed as a formidable source of self-empowerment for its participants. Many scholars interested in child development in urban settings have already spoken on the power of Hip Hop production processes to drive positive mental health outcomes (e.g., self-empowerment and self-efficacy) for students of color (Levy, 2017; Sealey-Ruiz and Greene, 2011; Travis et al., 2021). Thus, one could easily argue that the connection of empowerment to competence with technological tools, a community of practice, and self-confidence for Black youth should only be made more expansive through social-media ecologies.

A concept very closely tied to the idea of Hip Hop providing Black youth with pathways for self-empowerment with digital media is Connected Learning. In a Connected Learning context, young people have increased access to a wider ecology of information, technology, and interest-driven learning communities (Ito et al., 2013). Within this framework, peer cultures and online communities provide ways for young people to learn important skills, cultivate relationships, and develop their own identities (Barron et al., 2014). Theoretically, these capabilities should provide more pathways for young people to develop deeper identification with a personal interest, and develop creativity, expertise and skill, and connection to professional aspirations (Ito *et al.*, 2013).

In those instances, the framework suggests that knowledge and knowing are associated not only with the teacher, the curriculum, or outside experts but also with every peer culture that the youth participates in. That is, learners are seen by themselves and by others as knowledgeable, committed, and accountable participants whose identities are variable, multi-vocal, and inter-active (Wenger *et al.*, 2002). Learners are held accountable for contributing to authentic problem solving, knowledge co-creation, and learning. In Connected Learning, learners are also provided with opportunities to develop interpersonal relationships and to learn with and from others. Thus, these learning environments broaden traditional forms of learner agency and accountability by expanding possibilities for engagement and bringing in new audiences with whom students collaborate and create new knowledge and understanding.

Little has been written to evaluate the role of social-media platforms to bolster a HHBE program's community of practice, or to assess how those peer cultures might contribute to how participants make their transitions into adulthood. Additionally, there is a call from researchers to better understand how these Connected Learning pathways develop for Black youth and how they make these connections among their personal interests, learning opportunities, racial identity, and real-world contexts (Emdin, 2021; Garcia, 2013; Watkins and Cho, 2018). For instance, Garcia (2013) has argued that participatory media practices are a form of civic engagement that can connect disadvantaged youth of color to an understanding of their place as citizens in larger communities. Taken a step further, one could argue that young Hip Hop artists are creating their own social movements. As such, the current study suggests that sites of Hip Hop artistic practices should be recognized and encouraged by youth advocates and researchers seeking to engage in exploring this argument, and the idea that social media can play a role in strengthening Black youth development.

As an ongoing larger project, the broader aim of my work with Dreamer Studio has been to explore how the Dreamer's program/staff and youth participants came together on social-media platforms to build community, circulating information and furthering skill development of participants. However, this chapter investigates how youth from Dreamer Studio were using social-media platforms to engage in Connected Learning and to begin to understand how the platforms themselves shaped different aspects of this process. This study extends the author's previous work on Connected Learning and Hip Hop–based education in the formal classroom (Evans, 2021) to understand how Hip Hop–based education programs meet the needs of students in out-of-school time, and how they provide learning experiences in contexts beyond the formal confines of their program facilities.

Research Questions

Given that this study seeks to examine specifically how Dreamer's community of practice aids Black youths' transition into creative work and overall well-being, this analysis was guided by the following conceptual research questions: (1) What are the critical elements of Dreamer Studio's social-media ecologies, and how does participation create Connected Learning for participants? (2) Does the engagement of these youth in Dreamer Studio's social-media ecologies present them with the opportunities to gain social and emotional support in ways that they would not otherwise have access to?

Methodology, Participants, and Profile of the Sample

The participants interviewed for this study included ten (eight male- and two female-identified) Black students aged fourteen to twenty-four years old who utilized Dreamer Studio during the 2019–2020 school year and Vel, the executive director and owner of the studio. This study received approval for all study activities from the Northwestern University Institutional Review Board (IRB) as Protocol #STU00205633 in early September 2017, was renewed in 2020, and was deemed exempt from being considered human-subjects research in 2021 by the University of South Carolina. It was not until IRB approval was obtained that data collection at the field site began. Finally, IRB study procedures for this project were modified and approved in September 2018 with the input of the executive director at Dreamer Studio (Vel) and verbal consent from the youth to use their social-media accounts for research purposes. There was no incentive for interviews or participation. To protect anonymity, pseudonyms were assigned to the name of the studio, all students, and the teacher in this study.

Data for this project was collected over a sixteen-month period and in-itially relied on in-person fieldwork, including attendance at recording-studio sessions, program workshops, live podcasts, and local open mic events. However, I found my biggest resource was observing respondents on social media, particularly Twitter, YouTube, Snapchat, and Instagram, in that chronological order. I was guided to these media by students and was allowed to friend them on each platform. This was where I also received updates on meetups that were occurring on social audio/audio sites like ClubHouse and Twitch. I immersed myself in conversations that youths were having on these platforms and then had offline conversations with students to ask questions to participants like: What does this mean? Why did you say this this way? This is in line with Lane's (2016) take on digital urban ethnography, Patton and colleagues' (2020) contextual analysis of social media, and Brock's (2018) critical techno-cultural discourse analysis (CTDA). The latter draws from technology studies, communication studies, and Critical Race Theory (CRT) in requiring researchers to include perspectives of cultural producers and seek to understand how their culture or lived experiences shape the technologies they use.

Furthermore, I have focused my work on virtual participant observations in seeking to understand the creative lives of these students outside of the program but have been forced to stay in the virtual realm due to global mandated social distancing in the midst of the COVID-19 Coronavirus pan-demic. To expand on this point, I initially asked the participants to sit for interviews in auxiliary spaces where they participated in Hip Hop culture and created music. However, due to the COVID-19 pandemic, I conducted many follow-up interviews for this study via Zoom or Apple's FaceTime, re-cording and transcribing them, before distilling recurrent themes. The anal-ysis of these data was guided by the constant comparative method (Charmaz 2014), in which bits of data were continuously contrasted with one another to develop categories and distill recurrent themes.

Finally, I used evaluation methods associated with the connected learning framework (CL) to inform my coding strategies (Ito et al., 2013). In this case study, I did not focus on CL design principles. Instead, I looked at whether the digital practices in which the students were engaged enabled the CL experiences of civic engagement and self-expression, increased accessibility to knowledge and learning experiences, and/or expanded social support for interests and empowerment for the student (Ito et al., 2013: 12). Employing MHA (Measures of Human Achievement) Labs' 21st Century Skill Building

Blocks for participatory media projects (MHA Labs, 2012), the initial codes selected to analyze field notes and online student discourse were: *personal mindset, planning for success, problem solving,* and *social awareness.* After first reading data openly as an entire data set at the same time as noting initial field notes, I selected these specific themes for more focused and integrative coding because they aligned with what I assessed to be the goals of the program described to me by the executive director of the program.

Findings

Critical Elements to Dreamer Studio as an Artistic Community

Participatory culture is a term Henry Jenkins (2007) claims is 'emerging as the culture absorbs and responds to the explosion of new media technologies which make it possible for average consumers to archive, annotate, appropriate, and recirculate media content in powerful new ways' (p. 25). Outside of mobile communication, Black youth in Chicago generally have little to no ownership of a device that gives them regular access to the Internet and its related digital tools shown to be valuable in everyday life and the workplace (Barron *et al.*, 2014). This issue not only limits their future employment options and income potential, but also hinders their academic success and overall participation with digital media (Robinson *et al.*, 2015).

In this study, participation refers to educational practices and creative processes facilitated by Dreamer's social-media ecologies. Overall, I found that Dreamer Studio encouraged its youth to develop the skills, knowledge, and kinship ties needed to be full participants in contemporary culture. I found that the studio's participants were actively given pathways for social emotional support and identity development through three critical elements:

- **Corralling as a Pod**: Developing friendships and group memberships, formal and informal, in online communities centered around Hip Hop, such as Twitter, Tik Tok and Instagram.
- **Collaborative Problem-solving:** Working together in teams, formal and informal, to complete tasks, develop and exchange new knowledge (such as through Conversations on ClubHouse).

- **DIY Circulation:** Self-distribution and consumption of media among peers and mentors (such as livestreaming on Twitch or posting music to SoundCloud, YouTube, and/or social videos on Tik Tok).

Unintentionally, it was through the logic of these elements that youth themselves described how Dreamer's online ecologies reframed the concept of artistic community and achieved program success.

Corralling as a Pod

In Hip Hop, the process of career development relies heavily on developing convenient connections, and networking with peers in order to form a creative collective to release and circulate one's creative work (Condry, 2006: 88). Evans and Baym (2022) describe this using the term 'corralling', which refers to the necessity of the posse in being a rapper and the number of hours required to build/maintain a sufficient collective, and to find uses of gratification for socio-emotional support from those different individuals. In contrast to the pre-digital era, which defined music audiences solely as spectators, when they use corralling, musicians engage fans as equals, often mobilizing the most engaged to serve in more official roles within their professional support system.

Participants in the Dreamer program continually expressed that they collectively strived to make the studio space into a platform to promote their creative work online, and construct and showcase their digital selves. Besides uploading music videos to YouTube and Soundcloud, Instagram was described as the primary platform that allowed them to communicate their artistic lives. Lamar, a rapper who was also a journalism student at a local university, also reiterated this teamwork sentiment:

> I been goin' to Dreamer for like about 5 years, I think since like the first year they opened, that's when I started goin'. I'd say like, out of a five-day week, I'd try to go through the studio like, if not every day, about 3 or 4 days a week. And even if it's not to record, even if it's not you know, to lay somethin' myself, I just go online and check in with everybody. See what everybody else has been workin' on. If anybody else needs help with anything, as far as mixin' and masterin', critiquing, marketing, anything like that . . .

Recent research has shown that videoconferencing and social video platforms provide learning opportunities just as powerful as in-person experiential learning (Hassinger-Das *et al.*, 2020). As Lamar's comments indicate, talking online with one another was not always tied to casual conversation but rather exchanging of knowledge in ways that might develop their creative skill, spawn constructive dialogue, and build their continuance commitment. DJ Gemini, aged twenty-one, explained:

> A person needs to have a vision for their brand more so than having the talent to do the job. You can make all the songs you want but people have to be in your corner for you to win. We don't just build friendships, we find collaborations (through Dreamer).

One of the primary ways artists who participated in Dreamer's community of practice collectively used social media to choreograph their professionalism was by holding digital networking sessions on Instagram Live and having listening sessions on the studio's Instagram (IG) TV channel. During these events, artists would either solicit critiques for their new music, invite studio professionals to share resources about their facility, or hold conversations about different topics regarding professional advancement.

For example, Lamar elaborated on how the artists in the studio found the most visibility for their work by promoting the Dreamer name as a social movement that anyone could join and feel important within:

> We all just keep tryin' to strike oil, really. But really just a legacy thing. We want everything to have some type of longevity to it. So, we ride for each other. You know, what I'm sayin'? All of that makes a difference. And all of that helps—and that's what makes it bigger than the music.

When Lamar says, 'tryin' to strike oil', it seemed he was speaking directly about seeking to gain financially from their creative labor. However, it was apparent that he and others at Dreamer were pursuing creative work that would give them an overall sense of hope about their everyday lives. This meant that social-media posting activities were such that participants believed they had the potential to pay off in ways beyond future economic reward: consciously or not, they were seeking to improve their own well-being through their participation in Dreamer and their creative labor.

Hip Hop–affiliated youth find friendship-driven practices on social media both appealing and necessary as they build social communities and peer relations and seek cultural capital (Watkins, 2019; Watkins and Cho, 2018). What participants like Lamar illustrated is that one of the strong points of Dreamer's community of practice was that there were participants from a variety of age ranges (and knowledge bases) who came together from different parts of Chicago. Due to this level of diversity of thought and lived experiences, the participants felt a sense of belonging to a movement larger than themselves, and felt safer to be expressive, visible, and knowledge-seeking in online spaces.

Collaborative Problem Solving and DIY Circulation

Though Vel was clearly the adult supervisor and primary teaching artist of the studio, Dreamer's overall community was far more participatory than it was 'top down'. The physical studio space was able to thrive as a place where these youth rely on both finding their truth and getting honest critique. Their conversations on the social audio platform of ClubHouse, similarly, were brutally honest, and there was a dialogic process between the artists and their studio community members in choosing how to pursue production and promotion for their work. For instance, the following quote was given by Lamar during a conversation with staff, alumni, and students of Dreamer Studio on the social audio platform of Clubhouse:

> Like, music doesn't have a user's manual. There is no way to figure out everything you need to do with some type of text. You gotta study; you gotta talk; you gotta collaborate. That's the only way you're gonna figure out what's gonna work, what's not gonna work . . . We see rappers doin' shows. We see rappers on TV. We see blah, blah, blah. How do they set those up? How do they get those opportunities? Where were they at when it happened?

In this particular quote, Lamar points out that there is an extreme level of mystery to the process of transitioning from aspirational creative laborer to being a paid professional artist. He speaks about parasocial relationships as not providing enough depth for an emerging artist to study and emulate. In that regard, Dreamer's Clubhouse conversations provided him with advice from peers that collectively were going through trials and tribulations of pursuing career pathways in Hip Hop music similar to Lamar's own. MJ, an aspiring singer/songwriter, agreed with that point:

> Honestly, I look at it as a family brand, like everybody, everybody in there from different hoods, everybody in there from like come from different backgrounds. This group is like Reddit. Like, any time I need to do something, it's my Reddit or YouTube. It's like kind of a live blog or somethin' for me, so I can see what these people's experiences are, and see if I can like, do somethin' like it, or if I should try to replicate it, or just filter it out.

MJ comments here about having people from 'different hoods and backgrounds' provided a Reddit-like resource showing that this spatial unbounding allowed them to come together more readily and make productive music and beats, select for opportunities, not only for themselves, but with each other.[2] As MJ's comments indicate, Dreamer students often referenced the family atmosphere as being paramount to their learning experiences in the program. Given that today's media tools and technologies have infinite amounts of connectivity and information to draw from, students relished the fact that they could all build off one another at any point of the day, in any location that had Wi-Fi.

In the various testimonials above, participants repeatedly used ClubHouse conversation to be engaged in connected learning. They were involved in a process that asked them to consider what issues were of importance, beyond themselves, to establish a meaningful ecosystem for young Chicago creatives from low-income communities of color. As Rebecca Black (2006) and Henry Jenkins (2007) have argued, digital cultures like these provide support systems to help youth improve their core competencies as readers and writers of new literacies. For example, through video blogs or live streaming, young people receive feedback on their music and to gain experience in communicating with a larger public, experiences that might once have been restricted to those with an enormous number of resources.

As Hip Hop's origins are from America's low-income urban communities of color (Perry, 2004), work of young women like those at Dreamer Studio is often pursued as aspirational labour (Duffy, 2017) with the hopes of creative acclaim, recognition, and financial rewards. However, many respondents cited Dreamer as being a place where they could problem solve or receive a feeling of emotional catharsis. During one Clubhouse conversation held during the COVID-19 social lockdown, Antoine elaborated on why having creative conversations online were often more helpful than the conversations he was able to have in the studio:

> It's like, alright, you know, we're gonna talk about like, career-wise, what moves you can make. How to improve your music, what you maybe can help in these portions of it. Like, if I be like, 'Man, you could really put some live instrumentation here'. Or, 'I like the way you mixed this song. Maybe lay off on the lows a little bit. Maybe to help this stand out some more . . .' Just knowing someone has your back 24/7. It gives you the freedom to experiment and still have honest and safe dialogue of what another person might think, good or bad.

As Antoine and others depicted in this section, digital spaces empowered those in the Dreamer community greatly by offering a sounding board unbounded from geography. This is not to say that everyone in the community was thriving due to their involvement in the conversations that were being had because very few students actually had the tangible successes that can be easily defined by their career status. However, through their participation in the Dreamer social-media ecology, interviewees felt that they had a trusted resource for which they could express their concerns and from which they could draw inspiration. In the end, these emerging artists expressed that while the Internet has opened opportunities for their work, it has also created a social structure for which it is nearly impossible to survive by oneself. As such, interviewees pointed out Dreamer's social media ecosystem as a vital source of information, community, and social and emotional support.

Discussion and Conclusion

Similar to cafes and barbershops, the creativity within Hip Hop recording studios builds connectivity within the communities they are nestled in. The findings of this study suggest Dreamer Studio helped its participants to participate in pursuing their career aspirations through direct experience with online publishing, social networking, and collective action. Emotional support received by students in the program was self-reported as conducive to their empowerment. In this instance, empowerment meant that through Dreamer's social-media ecologies they were given the platform to safely discuss their everyday lives. The notion that music is empowering is a concept that has long been found in many different cultures and societies. These findings appear to corroborate Travis *et al.*'s (2021) research, which clarified how individual empowerment through Hip Hop experiences like music making, can manifest as feeling better (esteem), doing better (resilience), and being better as a person (growth). This empowerment through Hip Hop also helps facilitate empowerment-based positive youth outcomes like confidence, competence, connection, and sense of community. Their community of practice did this by employing three critical elements: (1) enhancing social affiliations through corralling as a pod, (2) collaborative problem solving for creative works, and (3) DIY circulating of media for external audiences.

By facilitating their students to do creative work that they truly care about, the Dreamer Studio collective also simultaneously exposes learning equity gaps and gives voice and agency to Black youth that live within those gaps. Participants did not necessarily come to the studio in hopes of a record deal; they reported that they came to discover how to shape their relationships and skill sets. The participants also expressed that the studio's community of practice showed them how to use social media platforms to deepen their passions, supportive relationships, and access to opportunities. Though it is uncertain what the professional future will hold for these emerging musicians—signing record deals and becoming famous were the aspirations for many of them—Dreamer Studios was certainly helping prepare them for their futures by cultivating a community that can carry one another through the challenges and stresses of connecting their creative works to a larger audience in the crowded and technology-driven marketplace for attention.

Evidence from this study suggests that access to social media ecologies affiliated with creativity are just as useful to youth as their in-person creative experiences at a studio. The implications of these findings suggest that young people can use social media to join active social communities, hone skills related to their personal interests, and develop their creative career aspirations—which are all hallmarks of Connected Learning. Although social-media technologies and practices of media production are moving at a rate that outpaces empirical understanding, there are major implications in this study for understanding how young people of color in low-income communities utilize participatory media. Programs like Dreamer Studio suggest that Black youth can use Connected Learning to cultivate a community around creative work that might otherwise be marginalized or ignored. Further understanding of the socio-emotional value of Hip Hop communities of practice is still of the utmost importance, but it appears that utilizing social media as a means for Connected Learning is positively impacting the well-being of Black creative youth of Hip Hop in ways that are specific and unique to aspects of their shared racial identity.

Endnote

1. Debuting in March of 2020, Clubhouse is an audio-based social-media app. The main feature of Clubhouse is real-time virtual 'rooms' in which users can communicate with each other via audio. Users can also schedule conversations by creating events.
2. Reddit is an American social news aggregation, content rating, and discussion website.

References

Barron, B., Gomez, K., Pinkard, N. and Martin, C. (2014). *The digital youth network: Cultivating digital media citizenship in urban communities.* Cambridge, MA: MIT Press.

Baym, N. (2012). Fans or friends? Seeing social media audiences as musicians do. *Participations*, 9(2): 286–316.

Baym, N. (2018). *Playing to the crowd.* New York, NY: New York University Press.

Ben-Eliyahu, A., Rhodes, J. and Scales, P. (2014). The interest-driven pursuits of 15 year olds: 'Sparks' and their association with caring relationships and developmental outcomes. *Applied Developmental Science*, 18(2): 76–89. https://doi.org/10.1080/10888 691.2014.894414.

Black, R. (2006). Language, culture, and identity in online fanfiction. *E-Learning and Digital Media*, 3(2): 170–184. https://doi.org/10.2304/elea.2006.3.2.170.

Bourdieu, P. (2011). The forms of capital. (1986). *Cultural theory: An anthology*, 1(81–93): 949.

Brock, A. (2018). Critical technocultural discourse analysis. *New Media and Society*, 20(3): 1012–1030. https://doi.org/10.1177/1461444816677532.

Brock, A. (2020). Making a Way out of No Way: Black Cyberculture and the Black Technocultural Matrix. In *Distributed Blackness*. New York, NY: New York University Press, pp. 210–242.

Callahan, J., Ito, M., Campbell, S. and Wortman, A. (2019). *Influences on occupational identity in adolescence: A review of research and programs.* Connected Learning Alliance.

Charmaz, K. (2014). *Constructing grounded theory.* Sage Publishing.

Condry, I. (2006). *Hip-hop Japan: Rap and the paths of cultural globalization.* Durham, NC: Duke University Press.

Dimitriadis, G. (2009). *Popular culture and the sociology of education*. Abingdon: Routledge.

Duffy, B. E. (2017). *(Not) getting paid to do what you love*. London: Yale University Press.

Duffy, B. E., Pinch, A., Sannon, S. and Sawey, M. (2021). The nested precarities of creative labor on social media. *Social Media + Society*, 7(2): 1–12. https://doi.org/10.1177/20563051211021368.

Duffy, B. E. and Sawey, M. (2021). Value, service, and precarity among Instagram content creators. In S. Cunningham and D. Craig (eds.), *Creator Culture: An Introduction to Global Social Media Entertainment*. New York, NY: NYU Press, pp. 135–142.

Emdin, C. (2020). A ratchetdemic reality pedagogy and/as cultural freedom in urban education. *Educational Philosophy and Theory*, 52(9): 947–960. https://doi.org/10.1080/00131857.2019.1669446.

Emdin, C. (2021). *Ratchetdemic: Reimagining academic success*. Boston, MA: Beacon Press.

Evans, J. (2020). Connecting Black youth to critical media literacy through Hip Hop making in the music classroom. *Journal of Popular Music Education*, 4(3): 277–293.

Evans, J. (2021). Exploring Hip-Hop artistic practices as an equity and empowerment based model for media literacy education with black youth: The case of Chicago's foundations of music. PhD dissertation, Northwestern University.

Evans, J. and Baym. N. (2022). The audacity of clout(chasing): Digital strategies of black youth in Chicago DIY hip-hop. *International Journal of Communication*, 16: 1–19.

Florida, R. (2019). *The rise of the creative class*. Basic Books.

Forman, M. (2002). *The hood comes first: Race, space, and place in rap and hip-hop*. Middletown, CT: Wesleyan University Press.

Garcia, A. (2013). *Critical foundations in young adult literature: Challenging genres*, vol. 4. Dordrecht, Netherlands: Sense Publishers.

Gee, J. (2017). Affinity spaces and 21st century learning. *Educational Technology*, 1: 27–31.

Hall, S. (1992). Race, culture, and communications: Looking backward and forward at cultural studies. *Rethinking Marxism*, 5(1): 10–18.

Harkness, G. (2013). Gangs and gangsta rap in Chicago: A microscenes perspective. *Poetics*, 41(2): 151–176.

Hassinger-Das, B., Dore, R., Aloisi, K., Hossain, M., Pearce, M. and Paterra, M. (2020). Children's reality status judgments of digital media: Implications for a COVID-19 world and beyond. *Frontiers in Psychology*, 11: 1–10.

Haynes, J. and Marshall, L. (2018). Beats and tweets: Social media in the careers of independent musicians. *New Media and Society*, 20(5): 1973–1993. https://doi.org/10.1177/1461444817711404.

Helmer, J. (2015). Hip Hop's impact on the development of the self and identity. PhD dissertation, Alliant International University.

Hesmondhalgh, D. (2020). Is music streaming bad for musicians? Problems of evidence and argument. *New Media and Society*, 23(12): 3593–3615. https://doi.org/10.1177/1461444820953541.

Hill, M. and Petchauer, E. (2013). *Schooling Hip-Hop: Expanding Hip-Hop based education across the curriculum*. New York, NY: Teachers College Press.

Ito, M., Gutiérrez, K., Livingstone, S., Penuel, B., Rhodes, J., Salen, K., Schor, J., Sefton-Green, J. and Watkins, S. C. (2013). *Connected learning: An agenda for research and design*. Digital Media and Learning Research Hub.

Jenkins, H. (2007). Confronting the challenges of participatory culture: Media education for the 21st century (Part One). *Nordic Journal of Digital Literacy*, 2(1): 23–33. https://doi.org/10.18261/issn1891-943x-2007-01-03.

Kramer, C., Lester, A. and Wilcox, K. (2021). College, career, and civic readiness: Building school communities that prepare youth to thrive as 21st century citizens. *Theory and Research in Social Education*, 49(4): 602–629.

Lane, J. (2016). The digital street: An ethnographic study of networked street life in Harlem. *American Behavioral Scientist*, 60(1): 43–58.

Lee, J. (2016). *Blowin' up: Rap dreams in south central.* Chicago, IL: University of Chicago Press.

Levy, I. P. (2020). "Real Recognize Real": Hip Hop Spoken Word Therapy and Humanistic Practice. *The Journal of Humanistic Counseling*, 59(1): 38–53.

Levy, I. P. (2017). The design, implementation and evaluation of a new Hip-Hop lyricism course implemented with urban high school youth: A new pedagogical and counseling approach to meeting the emotional needs of youth. PhD dissertation, Teachers College, Columbia University.

Levy, I. and Travis, R. (2020). The critical cycle of mixtape creation: Reducing stress via three different group counseling styles. *The Journal for Specialists in Group Work*, 45(4): 307–330.

Love, Bettina (2015). What is Hip-Hop-based education doing in nice fields such as early childhood and elementary education? *Urban Education*, 50(1):106–131. https://doi.org/10.1177/0042085914563182.

MHA (2012). *MHA Overview.* Measures of Human Achievement (MHA) Labs. http://mhalabs.org/mha-overview/

Mihailidis, P. (2008). *Beyond cynicism: How media literacy can make students more engaged citizens.* Lanham, MD: University of Maryland Press.

Mihailidis, P., Ramasubramanian, S., Tully, M., Foster, B., Emily Riewestahl, E., Johnson, P. and Angove, S. (2021). Do media literacies approach equity and justice? *Journal of Media Literacy Education*, 13(2): 1–14.

Patton, D., Stevens, R., Lee, J., Eya, G. and Frey, W. (2020). You set me up: Gendered perceptions of twitter communication among black Chicago youth. *Social Media + Society*, 6(2): 1–9. https://doi.org/10.1177/2056305120913877.

Perry, I. (2004). *Prophets of the hood: Politics and poetics in Hip Hop.* Durham, NC: Duke University Press.

Petchauer, E. (2015). Starting with style. *Urban Education*, 50(1): 78–105. https://doi.org/10.1177/0042085914563181.

Powers, D. (2015). Intermediaries and intermediation. In A. Bennett and S. Waksman (eds.), *The Sage Handbook of Popular Music.* Newbury Park, CA: Sage, pp. 120–134.

Quinn, E. (2004). *Nuthin' but a "G" thang: The culture and commerce of gangsta rap.* New York, NY: Columbia University Press.

Raposa, E., Rhodes, J., Stams, G., Card, N., Burton, S., Schwartz, S., Sykes, L., Kanchewa, S., Kupersmidt, J. and Hussain, S. (2019). The effects of youth mentoring programs: A meta-analysis of outcome studies. *Journal of Youth and Adolescence*, 48(3): 423–443. https://doi.org/10.1007/s10964-019-00982-8.

Rendell, J. (2021). Staying in, rocking out: Online live music portal shows during the coronavirus pandemic. *Convergence*, 27(4): 1092–1111.

Robinson, L., Cotten, S., Ono, H., Quan-Haase, A., Mesch, G., Chen, W., Schulz, J., Hale, T. M. and Stern, M. J. (2015). Digital inequalities and why they matter. *Information, Communication and Society*, 18(2): 569–582.

Rose, T. (1994). *Black noise: Rap music and black culture in contemporary America.* Middletown, CT: Wesleyan.

Sealey-Ruiz, Y. and Greene, P. (2011). Embracing urban youth culture in the context of education. *The Urban Review*, 43(3), 339–357.

Seidel, S. (2011). *Hip hop genius: Remixing high school education*. Rowman and Littlefield Education.

Stuart, F. (2020). *Ballad of the bullet*. Princeton, NJ: Princeton University Press.

Travis Jr, R., Gann, E., Crooke, A. H. and Jenkins, S. M. (2021). Using therapeutic beat making and lyrics for empowerment. *Journal of Social Work*, 21(3): 551–574.

Watkins, C. (2019). *Don't knock the hustle: Young creatives, tech ingenuity, and the making of a new innovation economy*. Boston, MA: Beacon Press.

Watkins, S. C. and Cho, A. (2018). *The digital edge*. New York, NY: New York University Press.

Wenger, E., McDermott, R. and Snyder, W. (2002). *Cultivating communities of practice: A guide to managing knowledge*. New York, NY: Harvard Business Press.

PART III
EVALUATION AND IMPACT

13

The Hip-Hopification of Education and its Evaluation

BREIS (Student of Life Ltd)

Introduction

I would like to take you on a journey of the different phases of the Hip Hop work I carry out within education.[1] I will endeavour to take you along with me from the initial contact with a school to post-delivery of a session. Along the way there will be relevant rap quotes and a look at the internal dialogue among various entities with the intention of leaving you with a clearer understanding of Hip-Hopification. We begin at Phase One, the enquiry stage, where teachers investigate how Hip Hop can be impactful and relevant to their students. There is a back and forth that happens over the phone or via email, which sometimes ends in an invitation from the school.

PHASE ONE—The Enquiry

Dear Breis,

Hi, I am in charge of Year 5 & 6 in my school. Could I please have some more information re: these workshops? They sound fantastic for our students. What kinds of things do the workshops entail? Could there be a focus on the language within rap music as well as perception?

Please feel free to contact me on this email address.

I look forward to hearing from you

Regards
Participant

BREIS (Student of Life Ltd), *The Hip-Hopification of Education and its Evaluation* In: *Music for Inclusion and Healing in Schools and Beyond.* Edited by: Pete Dale, Pamela Burnard, and Raphael Travis Jr., Oxford University Press.
© Oxford University Press 2023. DOI: 10.1093/oso/9780197692677.003.0014

Dear Participant,

Thank you for your email. The Hip Hop Literacy workshops look at what goes into creating a rap verse. The poetic devices used, a history of the art form, some written exercises and performances from the students and myself. We can work with up to four groups in a day.

Please let me know how many groups you'd like to take part during the day. Once you are happy to go ahead, I will send a booking form for you to fill in.

King regards
Breis

This continues until the school and I are both in agreement. I send a booking form, which is filled and returned along with a list of needed equipment and resources—mainly a microphone, PA system, USB port for a power point presentation, pens, and paper. This then takes us to Phase Two.

PHASE TWO—A Meeting of Worlds

As an artist, I live in my own world. It is chaotic, rhythmical, exciting, and mathematical. When I am invited into another world, I take note of how that world operates and find a way of still operating the way I do but within the restrictions of said new world. As I approach the school I will be working in, I remind myself of why I am here.

HIP HOP AND THE MC

'It's the foundation of every nation, but what is the true meaning of education?', asked the MC.

Hip Hop had been pacing up and down. On hearing the question, he paused and looked up ahead as if looking in to the future.

'Education is derived from the Latin word "educere" or "educare" which means to train or mould. It also means to draw out or to know', he replied.

'It sounds like education is there to guide us, or find what is already inside us', rapped the MC.

'In a way it is. Education draws out the internal hidden talent of a child or person. In the broader meaning it is what equips us to handle life'.

'I see how you flow and show what you know, but what has education got to do with me though?', interrogated the MC.

'In 1833, the British government made education compulsory for children working in factories. They realised the more educated a nation gets, the more powerful it can become. (National archives, n.d.). When I was formed my purpose was to educate and to empower. When you were formed it was to educate others'. Hip Hop paused and looked the MC dead in the eye. 'You are more than what you think you are'.

I was born to put knowledge of self over a beat, to educate disenfranchised youth on the street', the MC replied in agreement.

'And there's still more work for us to do', said Hip Hop placing their hand on the MC's shoulder.

In my own life, education has always been a priority of my strict Nigerian parents. It was drummed into my siblings and me that education was the most important thing and the one thing that would make our lives a lot easier in the future. I schooled in London until the age of eight and then lived in Nigeria for the next six years. I found the difference in teaching styles difficult and took a while to adjust. When I returned to London as a teenager, I had to readjust to the United Kingdom's style of teaching. It was a bit of a car wreck. How I got through my General Certificate of Secondary Education (GCSE), A Levels (Advanced Level qualifications), and a Bachelor of Science degree is still a mystery to me.

I am greeted by the receptionist and asked to sign in to their world. As I sign in, I have officially entered this new world. I am taken to a space where the workshop will occur, and I begin to set up equipment and rearrange the space to accommodate the activities I have set for them. I set up my world within theirs—Hip Hop within education. The mic is on and tested, the volume of the background beat is adjusted to match the volume of the mic. Then I wait for the students to arrive and to be introduced to them. The students arrive with looks of curiosity and intrigue. They settle down in their seats, looking at me wondering what is in store. The teacher introduces me to the two hundred seated students. I take centre stage and begin.

PHASE THREE—Storytelling

From as far back as a four years- old I can remember always having a passion for writing and performing. This steadily grew throughout college and university and years after graduating, when I decided to become a full-time artist. One night after performing at a venue in Brixton, a poet friend of mine by the name of Malika Booker pointed out that the way I interacted with the audience would translate really well in the classroom. She proceeded to explain the work she did as a poet within education and encouraged me to think about running workshops. It seemed like a million miles away from what I believed to be doable and abandoned the notion until a year later. This was when I decided to quit my regular job and make a living as an artist. I figured I could facilitate workshops whilst I was still getting my music career on the right path. I shadowed other spoken-word artists that worked in schools, developed my style of delivery, and in a few months began delivering rap and poetry workshops in primary and secondary schools across the United Kingdom.

I combined my love of Hip Hop with my passion for education and devised a program called Hip Hop Literacy through my organisation, Student of Life. The aim was to make learning more fun and give an understanding of Hip Hop whilst simultaneously improving literacy skills. Through the art of rap and movement, I was able to engage with hard-to-reach students. I got students creating raps around different topics and subjects. We published anthologies, shot music videos, and had grand performances in front of an audience as outcomes for them. It proved to be a huge success with the children, teachers, and parents alike. I would soon come to know this as Hip Hop education and realised there were other practitioners in America using this same approach. One professor in particular from Columbia University by the name of Chris Emdin was steeped deeply in the practice of using Hip Hop in the school curriculum. On twitter, I came across a group of teachers and practitioners whose method of teaching was influenced by Hip Hop under the hashtag #HipHopEd. It was a community I was happy to be a part of and contribute towards. It reinforced the importance of the work I was doing and confirmed I was on the right path. I went on to further develop creative tools to engage students and transform learning experiences.

A few things I noticed along the way including the power of evaluation:

- Students got excited seeing an actual rapper/practitioner in their class. It made what they were learning even more real and celebrated diversity in forms of literacy and repertoires that might otherwise be positioned as new forms of thinking and engaging with the world.

- The importance of dispelling negative stereotypes around rap music and the practices of implementing the decisions we take that, over time, make knowledge and knowing, being and becoming, a matter of choices that matter.
- Rapping in other languages besides English made EAL (English as an additional language) students feel included and empowered. I did this often rapping in English, Yoruba, and Pidgin English.
- There was a high level of engagement from students who normally did not produce much and this became a form of reflexive solidarity that errs on the side of generosity that can be evidenced, thus evaluated.
- The growth in the student's confidence as a result of their participation was visible.

> *Hip is to know, it's a form of intelligence*
> *To be hip is to be update and relevant*
> *Hop is a form of movement; you can't just observe a hop*
> *You gotta hop up and do it. Hip and hop is more than music*
> *Hip is the Knowledge; Hop is the Movement*
> *Hip and Hop is intelligent movement*
>
> —*KRS-One, Hip Hop Lives (2007)*

THE MC AND THE STUDENT

'What is Hip Hop?', the wide-eyed student asked the MC.

The Master of Ceremony was delighted with the question and eager to answer. 'Hip Hop is a rebellious culture born out of the need to express and create', he began. 'It was birthed by African Americans and Latin Americans in the Bronx, New York in the 70s' (Chang, 2007).

'I thought it was a type of dance', interrupted the student.

'Well, it's more than just a type of dance. Hip Hop is rap, it's art, it's an attitude. It gave the young people living in American ghettos, a voice. It's a tool for social justice, for some it's a way out of the gang violence and poverty prevalent in their lives. For others it's pure entertainment. Its existence predates its birth, with certain elements existing before being named as they currently are'.

The student was in deep thought, taking in every word of the MC. 'The elements being rapping and dancing?'

'Yes, to be precise it's a combination of DJing, emceeing, graffiti art, and b-boying. There are other elements including beatboxing, street fashion, production, knowledge of self and entrepreneurialism. Each of these elements helped create a purpose for young people and helped them escape the harsh realities they were dealing with. For some participants who were dedicated, consistent and had a flair for their specialised practice, it would become a career'.

The student mentally replayed three words the MC had just mentioned—dedication, consistency, and flair.

PHASE FOUR—Active Engagement

Crossing borderlines with broader rhymes
I generate ideas that blow your mind
You see my awesome mind does more than rhyme
I'm thinking all the time with thoughts of mine
My thoughts are 3D and HD, all combined
Sharper than the spines on a porcupine
Signed, sealed, and delivery is full of imagery
Vividly visualised through my eyes, spoken terrifically
I'm so unique my own shadow can't even mimic me
My visions make me think into infinity
Do things differently with authenticity
And aim high specifically
'cos inside of you and inside of me
There's a genius inside that no one can see
Do you know what you want and who you wanna be?
We're bigger than we think but it's hard to see
                                          —BREIS, *Think Big*

After introducing myself and explaining the four main elements of Hip Hop, I demonstrate what I do by performing one of my songs—'Think Big'. The song is about encouraging one to believe in their capacity to achieve greatness. I teach them how to sing the chorus and encourage them to assist me at the appropriate place. This is important as I am now giving them part ownership of the performance. How good the overall performance turns out to be now depends on them performing well. Hip Hop is all about performing, so it is important the students take part in the performance. They begin to loosen up and immerse themselves in the experience, simultaneously preparing themselves for other tasks ahead. After the performance I invite the students to take part in a quick writing exercise.

We look through the text of 'Think Big' together and discuss the theme and how that applies to their lives. They discuss their imagination, their ability to dream, the potential they possess, and mental health. We look at the imagery, various perspectives, and what was interesting about them. We pick out the similes, metaphors, adjectives, and emotive language and observe how and when they are used. I give the class the option of creating their own 'Think Big' verse or writing about someone who means a lot to them. After providing them with a few more triggers, the class begins to write. I urge them to focus on their thoughts and feelings as opposed to spelling and grammar. Validating their expression by encouraging them that there is no wrong answer, only what they want to express.

PHASE FIVE—Sharing

The outcome was an outstanding verse from each student that showed his or her vulnerability, writing skill, and knowledge of self.

One by one I encourage each student to share his or her work in front of the class. Some read it like a poem; some perform it as a rap. They have gone from being the student to now being the MC. I take a back seat and allow the students to give their feedback after each verse they hear.

A young boy puts his hand up to read out his rap. He is easily the tallest boy in the class and looks older than he is. His rap is about his mum. He reads it out, as the class listens intently. He finishes the last sentence, ' . . . that's the life of me and my mum', and the whole class erupts into a cacophony of claps, wows, smiles, and even a teary eye from the teacher's assistant can be seen. The students express their delight at the story he has shared about someone who clearly means so much to him and continue to tell him what in particular they enjoyed from his rap. He is seen, his voice is heard, he is acknowledged and validated.

It is the end of the session, and I ask the students what their favourite part of the session was. For some it was hearing a professional artist perform. For

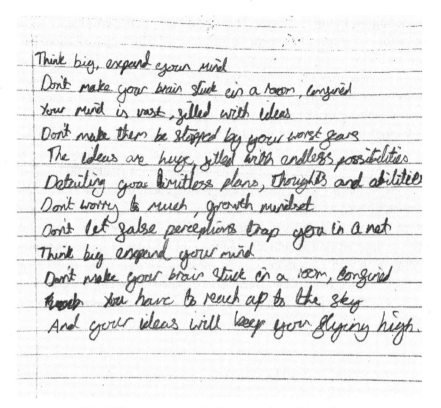

Think big, expand your mind
Don't make your brain stuck in a room, conjured
Your mind is vast, filled with ideas
Don't make them be stopped by your worst fears
The ideas are huge, filled with endless possibilities
Detailing your limitless plans, thoughts and abilities
Don't worry to much, growth mindset
Don't let false perceptions trap you in a net
Think big expand your mind
Don't make your brain stuck in a room, conjured
You have to reach up to the sky
And your ideas will keep your flying high.

Figure 13.1 Think Big verse written by Year 6 student, Salcombe
Primary School

some it was what they were able to come up with themselves. For the teachers
it was seeing how engaged the students were and how much more they now
knew about some of their students.

THE MC AND THE TEACHER

The classroom was filled with most of the teachers in the school. There were
over twenty teachers in attendance, all eager to share experiences and learn
new skills that they could implement in their respective classes. The MC was
speaking to them about the importance of creativity in the class. One of the
English teachers a few rows from the front raised her hand to ask a question.
'Could you tell us a bit more about Hip Hop Education?'

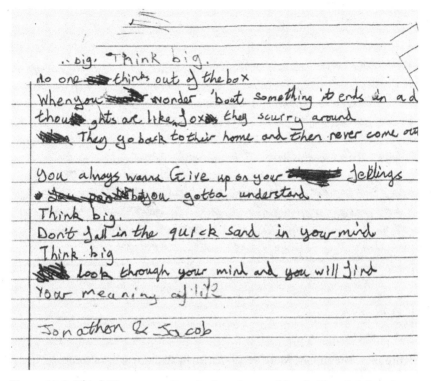

Figure 13.2 Think Big verse written by Jonathon and Jacob, Year 6, Salcombe Primary School

The MC smiled, took a quick look at his notes, and proceeded to answer. 'Hip Hop Education is looking at the creative, vibrant energy of Hip Hop and applying it in the classroom'.

The MC went on his laptop and pressed play. A Hip Hop instrumental played through the speakers. He observed the body language of some of the teachers. 'Immediately you heard this music, some of you started bobbing your head. I saw a couple of smiles creep out and some of you tensed up. This is the energy of Hip Hop. This energy can be used and utilised in many ways', said the MC.

'My approach to conducting workshops in schools is to look at the task at hand through a Hip Hop lens, specifically that of an MC (rap artist). To some degree, being a good MC is similar to being a good teacher'.

The group laughed, the MC paused and smiled again.

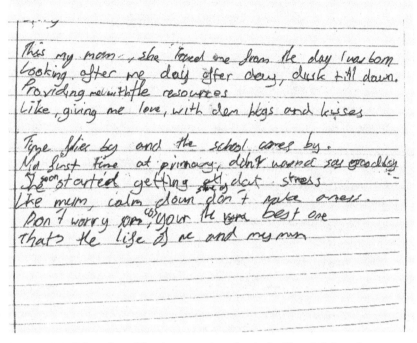

Figure 13.3 'Me and my Mum' verse written by Arda, Year 6, Salcombe Primary School

'An MC stands in front of an audience, a teacher stands in front of their class or audience. An MC must command the attention of the crowd; teachers must command the attention of their students. An MC must dazzle with their skills, engage the audience and get them to participate; a teacher must do the same. Interaction and inclusion is an integral part of my stage shows. As much as possible I get my audience to take part in the experience. Hip Hop is about participation, so a session should never be one sided. There will be times when things will go wrong on stage and you have to improvise (freestyle), similarly a teacher's lesson plan may not be effective enough in the moment and will therefore need to think on their feet to keep the lesson alive'.

'It's my job as an MC to gauge an audience and see what's working, what's not and what's missing. To know when to switch gears, when to ask the crowd to repeat after me or rap along with me. To gauge whether they've had enough, whether they need a break, when to get them energised or when to bring the energy levels down to a place of introspection. The legendary G.O.A.T. (Greatest Of All Time) MC, Rakim said,

" . . to me, MC means Move the Crowd" '.

With creative intervention, there is a possibility of hard-to-reach students getting excited by lessons, feeling like they are intelligent and capable of achieving more than they ever thought. I have so much respect for the amazing work teachers do, and what I do is in no way a critique of their work. It is more of an add-on. I produced the Hip Hop Literacy Program, to bring something different to a child's learning experience. Some schools have pushed back against what we do. To a few, the mere mention of Hip Hop throws up negative tropes of misogyny, homophobia, violence, and so on and therefore puts some head teachers off. They see Hip Hop music only through what the mainstream media machine promotes to the public; 'How can such an unruly element be used in their school?' They ask. I have had other teachers invite us in and realise that not only is the content positive, inspirational, and aspirational, but it manages to engage pupils who teachers struggle to reach. What the culture of Hip Hop does is make your voice count. It makes your words and lived experience matter. It makes you visible in a world that treats you like you are invisible.

Like I said, one of the key approaches to my delivery is connecting with the participants. Meeting them where they are at and understanding their viewpoints and experiences are just as important as what I have to deliver. Their input and perspective are what makes the work work. I had a session in a challenging PRU (Pupil Referral Unit) and had a workshop with five young men who were not exactly elated to find themselves in the session. One young man in particular was devoted to letting me know that he was not interested and was not about to make the session an easy one. I set a writing task, and all he kept talking about were his smoking and narcotic activities. Now normally these experiences would be denied, excluded, and forbidden, but I saw an opening to connect with him despite my distaste for his obsession. This was a chance to be rebellious in my approach.

Explaining to him the power of metaphors, I encouraged him to write about his 'passion' but to substitute it for something less incriminating like flowers. He began writing; the teacher and teacher's assistant were confused. He finished writing his piece and at the end could not wait to share it with everyone. He relished in the fact that everybody praised him for his work, but nobody knew what he was really talking about. This filled him with glee.

It was not so much so the task, it was more about the fact that in this instance, in this environment, his voice was not silenced or dismissed like it normally would have been. He was just redirected. When an MC is flowing, they have to flow according to what the beat is doing. Not fight it but flow with it. Similarly, I try to teach according to the energy of the group I have and not resist what they are bringing to the party. Hip Hop has always been a voice for the silenced. Alongside punk music, rap is the soundtrack to protests. In the 1970s it may have been the Sex Pistols' 'God Save the Queen', but in the student protests of December 2010 at Parliament Square it was rapper Lethal Bizzle's song 'Pow! (Forward)' that was the anthem (Hancox, 2011). In America it was Kendrick Lamar's 'Alright' that became the protest song for the Black Lives Matter movement. Rap can be a rallying cry to galvanise people and a middle finger to the establishment and all forms of injustice. In America, it is an essential tool even politicians no longer ignore. It speaks to the masses, cuts through the noise, and speaks directly to the people.

'This art form, RAP should be revered and studied in schools the same way the poetry of Shakespeare *et al.* is still studied. Rap captures the zeitgeist of modern-day trials, tribulations and triumphs of everyday people'.

BREIS (2020), *Diary Of A Creative Mind*, p. 151

PHASE SIX—A New World

My rebellious practice is to enter a world, set up my world within it, disrupt, understand, transform, and empower in no particular order and then leave a whole new world behind.

Imagine if education could solve most of our world problems today? If we could solve the problems of the world through education, wouldn't that be an amazing and exciting prospect? Yet education is not being utilised in this way. Ultimately, Hip Hop education is thinking outside the box to fix a problem, mixing different ideas together, taking something old, and making it new.

As practitioners, researchers, and educators, it is important to update our systems like we tend to do with our smartphone operating systems. Our models must exhort educationalists to be open-minded in approach, to take into account the diversity of our environments, and to be inclusive. Over the past twenty years or so, many textbooks in school have been called out for containing racially stereotypical information/propaganda. Textbooks and teaching materials need to be updated and remixed to reflect the times and to promote equity. Some approaches to teaching and learning are antiquated and no longer prepare or enrich its participants as they may once have.

So, what are my take aways for evaluating the 'Hip-Hopification of education' practices?

1. Being careful not to promise solutions to problems but rather rethinking what matters in terms what and how we value and how we care for each as a community.
2. Understanding the narrative of authentic evaluations as gestures of care and experiences that can be shared and carefully situated in the perspectives of young people.
3. Being reflexive about creating spaces and practices which include everyone.

Education is meant to prepare us for the 'real world', yet many leave educational institutions not knowing much about most things they need to— things such as how to be in a loving relationship, how to be a parent, keeping personal finances healthy, knowing and understanding who you are, and a myriad of soft skills needed to navigate life and work. If education is there to help us in the 'real world' then surely we need to understand more about ourselves. For me, this is where Hip Hop can play an important role. One of the pillars of Hip Hop is *Knowledge of self.* Understanding who we are and how to operate in this world has always been part of the program. Making this a fundamental part of learning will be crucial to our future well-being.

> *Heavenly sent to me so it was meant to be*
> *I'm already mentally who I'm meant to be eventually*
> *They couldn't see this entity's intensity immensity*
> *Didn't invest in me, but that wasn't my destiny*
> *Don't mess with me, God given energy*
> *To crush my enemy like a centipede, but I'm friendly*
> *the mic is my girl At 10 to 3, secret assignments to MC*
> *I'll do it for free but first pay my rent for me*
> *I'm ebony and every-body's telling me*
> *How to be, I won't let it be a dent in me*
> *Let me be me, the best in me is yet to be*
> *Don't need an ID card to show you my identity*

In a class of my own I tend to be essentially
A student of life, it's elementary
Not me, but a conduit I get to be
The Word in me is next to me; spell my name

This world is full of lies, everybody's in a guise
Despise and diss guys in disguise that spit lies
A bit wise behind my eyes and behind my disguise
I'm a fat guy mistaking MCs for mince pies
Throw your hands in the air, reach for the skies
I rise till I realise: I am the prize
But don't be surprised when I enter-prise
I'm blessed, I'm a blessing, I'm blessing in disguise
Disguised in a body—soul, spirit
My whole lyric no limit, so go get it
Why did he did it? 'cos flows is good for his health
Bona fide Rhymes Exist In Self

BREIS (2007), Identity

References

BREIS (2007). *Identity*. London: Student of Life Publishing.

BREIS (2020). *Diary of a creative mind*. London: Student of Life Publishing.

Chang, J. (2007). *Can't stop, won't stop: A history of the Hip Hop generation*. London: Picador.

Eric B. and Rakim (1987). Eric B. is president [song]. On *Paid in Full*. London: Zakia Records.

Hancox, D. (2011). *Pow! Anthem for kettled youth*. https://www.theguardian.com/music/2011/feb/03/pow-forward-lethal-bizzle-protests.

National Archives (No date). *1833 Factory Act: Did it solve the problems of children in factories?* https://www.nationalarchives.gov.uk/education/resources/1833-factory-act/.

14

Translating Evaluation and Research Into Practice

What Matters for Socially Engaged Arts Programmes in and Beyond Schools?

Pamela Burnard

Socially engaged *practice* describes and distinguishes between different community-based practices that are distinctively collaborative and often participatory, and involve collaboration and participation with people as the medium or material of the work. Practices are designed to forge direct intersections with the community and social issues and can involve partnerships among artist practitioners, educators, evaluators and researchers, in and across educational sectors and engaging communities (Schlemmer, 2016). These programmes are generative, communal sites for unlocking 'social energy'[1] to increase well-being, to make positive changes in communities, and to support and innovate *practice*. The role of evaluation and research in improving socially engaged arts programmes in and beyond schools cannot be underestimated in a society experiencing an accelerating pace of change.

On the one hand, *evaluation* is a reflexive process involving judgments about the quality and effectiveness of practice matters to how we draw together, understand, review, and report on socially engaged arts programmes. Furthermore, how socially engaged arts programmes empower young people leads us to think differently about educational practices that utilise the interests and resources of the community, dismantling inequalities, and creating ownership, empowerment, and responsibility among diverse individuals and groups (Hickey-Moody, 2013).

On the other hand, *research* and reporting on the impact of socially engaged arts programmes (such as the arts-mental health relationship and health effects of diverse/urban musics engagement and dance participation)

Pamela Burnard, *Translating Evaluation and Research Into Practice* In: *Music for Inclusion and Healing in Schools and Beyond.* Edited by: Pete Dale, Pamela Burnard, and Raphael Travis Jr., Oxford University Press.
© Oxford University Press 2023. DOI: 10.1093/oso/9780197692677.003.0015

is often unclear or oversimplified (Daniel and De Bruyckere, 2021). Some sources are presented as 'impact' research when they are simply opinion pieces commenting on the supposed well-being benefits of particular programmes or practices involving controlled trials that report (often unduly optimistic) evidence of the health effects of arts participation. For post-qualitative inquiries, new approaches to social inquiry often break completely with traditional qualitative methodologies. The scholar who coined and developed the concept of post-qualitative research, Elizabeth St. Pierre (2018), argues that such a break with qualitative methodologies is necessary if social researchers are to adequately respond to complex settings where thinking deeply about social music interventions and their development is an imperative (Odena, 2023). So, when teachers and arts practitioners want to evaluate their own practice and/or research their practice, they often, though not always, try to do this in partnership with researchers. Recognising the importance of translating practices into evaluation or research matters. Making visible and accessible for scrutiny what happens inside these relationships also matters within the context of socially engaged arts programmes in and beyond schools (Murphy and Espeland, 2007).

When we speak of a 'gold standard' of educational research, we view researchers as social scientists who are able to carry out randomised controlled trials to eliminate all other possible influences on the results (e.g., age, prior knowledge, socioeconomic status, parental education—the list goes on). As Shavelson and Towne (2002) wrote, in such a situation we have a 'control group that has the same experiences as the experimental group except for the "treatment" under study' (p. 69). Even if randomised controlled trials could 'prove' causation, no arts practitioner or teacher has an interest in replication; they are creative adaptors, fashioning creative practices in ways that reflect the needs of their own students, their own values, their own aims, and their own circumstances. The potential of arts activities to extend the range and types of children's and young people's opportunities to participate and to have their voices heard has been well documented (Odena, 2023; Kidman, 2018; Hickey-Moody, 2013; Hall and Jones, 2009). It is a challenge for cross-community arts practitioners, teachers, and researchers to work and think together if they hold very different views about matters of voice, partnership, and inclusiveness. This matters.

When we speak of a 'gold standard' of educational evaluation, some argue for well-conducted randomised controlled trials as the most reliable method for quality evaluations of practice reforms or evaluating a program's effectiveness. However, widespread misconceptions about what such studies involve—including their cost—have often limited their use by education officials. There are ethical obligations and multiple challenges (and indeed, impossibilities) of assigning a sample of students, teachers, or schools to a group that participates in the same program delivered in the same way or to a group that does not (the control group). In a study of the impact of creative partnerships on the well-being of children and young, McLellan *et al.* (2012) measured student well-being using surveys that were developed, piloted, and administered to 5.231 students in twenty primary and twenty secondary schools, half of which were currently engaged in Creative Partnerships programmes.

Quantifying the impacts of a large single investment in a cultural or arts project in a specific place invites the question, what has the intervention achieved that sustained investment in ongoing cultural organisations cannot? This matters for research equivalence and measuring outcomes over time that are attributed to a particular practice. This too matters. It is a challenge to reconcile assumptions on what counts as an ethical intervention, to manage expectations of many different stakeholders across highly stratified relations of power, particularly if it is branded as ideological posturing by non-government organisations to elevate the standing of a practice, or, in the case of research, an attribution of causation (see Green, 2023).

In socially engaged arts programmes, something that works for one cohort or community might not work at all for the next, even if it is the same activity or the same theme and the same practitioner/teacher. 'Evidence-informed' practice means taking a step back from 'this will work if you do it this way'. The challenges of socially engaged practices can include matters of care, and lack of time, funding, expertise, and confidence. These practices aim to create a space where, according to Laurel Richardson (1997):

(1) People feel 'safe' within it, safe to be and experiment with who they are who they are becoming; (2) people feel 'connected'—perhaps to each other, or a community, or nature, or the world they are constructing . . .; (3) people feel passionate about what they are doing, believing that their activity 'makes a difference'; and (4) people recognize, honour, and are grateful for the safe communion. (p. 185)

So, what stops teachers and arts practitioners from engaging more deeply with/in evaluation and/or translating evaluation and/or research into practice? How else could we pay attention to situations when practitioners change their ways of enacting practices because they are acting as/with evaluators or as/with researchers or simply adapting/adopting 'evidence'[2] from other evaluations or research to improve what they are doing? All of this matters.

The Arts as Sites of Care

While arts practitioners, researchers, and teaching professionals may have different goals, they are each interested not in copying anyone but learning to see and to share the issues identified by evaluation. We can see this in their collective desire for young people and the communities they are a part of, to grow, to develop, and indeed, to flourish. The issues that emerge as salient from developing appropriate evaluations are including student voices along with evidence-led based on indicators that transcend the production of desired findings. Where the study of impact cannot be separated from the conditionalities and agendas of who is interested, it is the evaluation that is not an end in itself but rather a way to transform and improve practices and programmes (Bala, 2018). This is especially so when 'paying attention' to evaluating the experience of contemporary urban arts practices, whether that be genres that constitute popular contemporary music practices such as the vocal delivery of rapping, spoken word, DJing, or Hip Hop, or any other socially engaged participatory arts programmes. As Mansfield (2022) argues, 'the arts are *sites of care* whether practised by artists, teachers or students or educational philosophers providing the forum for such discussion' (p. 422). Even the concept of 'attention' is important. 'Attention' is a concept drawn from the philosophy of French Feminist Simone Weil (2002), who was deliberately radical in terms of her concerns with waiting, pausing, suspending thought, and thereby 'paying attention'. She insisted that

> What counts in human life are not the events that dominate in the passing of years—er even the days. It is the way in which one minute is linked to the following one. And what this costs . . . in the exercise of the faculty of attention.
>
> (Weil, as cited in Goodchild, 2017: 22)

For Simone Weil (2021), we see 'attention' that translates as waiting and passing our thought, holding it close in order to make it available to the possibility of listening for and hearing the real to arrive in the moment. Evaluations are about the never-ending reflexive process involving judgments about the quality and effectiveness of practice, which matters to how we draw together, understand, review, and report on socially engaged arts programmes. This requires us to return to the essential roots of life if we are to put in place a framework for arts practices as sites of care.

Whether the evaluation is of individual participant and participatory learning and development, or of programme content and delivery, both Weil, with the potential to transform both the one who attends and the one attended to, along with Tronto's foundational work, calls our attention to the inequalities perpetuated by care (1993: 131–132). Tronto proposed, 'a flexible notion of responsibility' being a 'more attuned concept to a *politics of care* than obligation'. The politics of care is an approach to political thought and action and elucidates care as an inherently interdependent strategy in which all people can live and thrive. The politics of care invites a re-engagement with care as an ethic and a political praxis that reorients people toward new ways of relating.[3]

More recently, Yuriko Saito (2022), whose work on the aesthetics of care is primarily directed towards the interdependent relationship between the aesthetic and the ethical, pays particular attention to care as an ethical commitment and care as a condition for aesthetic experience, by cultivating an aesthetic sensibility to 'nurture the ethical attention and respect for the person being cared for' (p. 5). What she promotes that is most useful here are practices of the *care relationship in interpersonal interactions*. Saito (2022) suggests,

> Whether regarding conversations between two people or social gatherings, satisfying interactions are generated by the participants' caring attitude toward each other to create a convivial atmosphere that has distinct aesthetic features, such as a certain rhythm, collaborative creation, equality of participation and spontaneity. (p. 6)

So, what translates into practices that nurture care relationships? What translates as expressions of care at the centre of a socially engaged arts practice? What matters for evaluation and research?

Translating 'Care' at the Core of a Socially Engaged Arts Practice: What Matters?

In schools, certain contemporary arts practices (by which I refer to Hip Hop, EDM, grime, drill, house, and so on) are rarely covered in the music classroom. In contrast, in the wider society, contemporary musics are the sites into which both marginalised and non-marginalised are most likely to dive deeply. In the wider society, artists learn from one another. They go to gigs, club nights, and promo events and talk to artists and industry experts. They read reports, reflect, look at data, reflect, and often make highly detailed records or documentations of their practice. And, with their notebooks and computers full of what they do and have learned, what they reformulate, re-think, and revise affirms what is a relational practice that does not equate to any other. Beyond schools, practices (and programmes) that feature socially (and community) engaged art practices offer sites of huge potential for enhancing participation and inclusion.

For both teachers and artist practitioners, all educational sectors bear witness to the challenges of conducting evaluations or measuring impact. For any practice to be evaluated, particularly in a diverse multicultural classroom or community, quintessentially, what matters is the need to be sensitive to cultural differences.

This chapter does not have the scope to trouble the role of too-narrowly-defined arts practices in schools, nor does it critique mainstream practices that feature in systems of formal education. It also does not have scope to explore making connections between evaluation and assessment, issues of which are addressed fully in the work of Ross (1978, ch. 15), Murphy and Espeland (2007), and MacDonald *et al.* (2012). Instead, it takes into account the complexities of practice, which Puig de la Bellacasa (2017: 153) calls

> a relational ethos with a world, a process through which material constraints are co-created . . . In turn, constraints re-create relational, situated possibilities and impossibilities . . . abstract in the sense that these become more or less stabilized and can be repeated, transported, translated as the core of a practice and ask to be taken into account for a specific practice to be considered such.

But in order to produce effectively these practices in sites of care, whether affirming care as a generic activity is facilitated by teachers or arts practitioners, in or beyond school, we need to pose questions about what matters: How do we evaluate practices which develop a relational ethos with a world that is 'co-created', yet can be 're-created' with/in a socially engaged arts community? How receptive to change do practitioners/artists—more often social innovators seeking social justice—need to be for their very existence, survival, and success? What are the constraints, obligations, and requirements of a relational ethos? What matters in terms of the obligations, which Puig de la Bellacasa (2017, p. 153) argues is

> what obligates practitioners to what is 'required of a phenomenon' for it to be addressed as a focus for a particular practice. In this 'ecology of practice', constraints, requirements, and obligations hold together a 'heterogeneous collective'—competent specialists, devices, argument and material at risk—that is, phenomena whose interpretation is at stake.

What matters?

With this in mind, this chapter brings together *ways of doing* and *ways of seeing* more than merely managing the complexities of judgments about socially engaged arts practices. Rather, the aim is to identify what is translatable and relatively enduring ethically through evaluations that scrutinise what is working, what is not, for whom, and why. The impact that teaching and learning, and specifically arts engagement, have on young people, and how we benefit from engaging with 'evidence', is what matters. For those who wish to think more about and differently about their practice and want to, as Puig de la Bellacasa (2017) suggests, 'avoid both epistemological orders and relativistic accounts of scientific practices' (p. 153), what manifestos matter?

What follows are many more questions that invite practitioners (both educators and arts practitioners) to engage reflexively, which is an essential principle for social justice in educational research. As Morwenna Griffiths (1998) argues in a beautiful and useful book on the realities of practical research:

> reflexivity provides a way of acting on the knowledge that knowledge is perspectival and on the possibility that there may be a complete change of mind in the middle: that is, acting on the view that 'all knowledge and claims to knowledge are reflexive of the process, assumptions, location, history and context of knowing and the knower'. (p. 141, quoting Altheide and Johnson, 1994: 488)

The posing of questions is an important aspect of this task because our relationship with our selves is politically positioned. We need to acknowledge that. And equally we need clarity about what kinds of responsibility can be exercised as individuals and collectives.

What Matters When Practices Put Learning at the Centre?

Assumptions concerning what constitutes 'quality' matter particularly when it comes to evaluating a diverse spectrum of practices such as those that originate in Hip Hop, EDM, grime, drill, house, and so on. Is there a generic quality that pertains to diverse subgenres of musics or the braiding of intercultural music making? How does evaluation change with value creation in diverse performative musics when you need to listen carefully, not only to the words, but also to the images, rhythms, dance moves, and thoughts and feelings that complex layers of sound and meaning evoke and make visible? Are there non-normative approaches to how practices can be reconfigured in functions of material conditions in specific situations but then also evaluated, improved, and sometimes measured? What matters when focusing on the ethical as it is affecting judgments about 'quality' and as it is affecting bodies in the process of change?

My point about what matters here is that, while value-led 'evidence' might be attainable, what results from evaluations where 'quality' is not conceptualised from either a normative stance or a biosocial stance? How should evaluations work to reach new and more generative understandings about the appropriation of quality? How do we evaluate practices when practitioners are forever fighting systems with rear-guard actions against cuts in budgets and worse, the shutting down of social and educational programmes? What should and can we expect of ourselves and others? What are the latest forms of evaluation that encourage participants to examine themselves and grow in self-awareness? What are we learning for and from research that engages with intervention projects? What are the often-invisible tensions between the gatekeepers in a study and the funders? How can artist practitioners and teachers be attuned to the undercurrents between people if one is to have access to programme evaluations?

Encouraging young people to be active participants who lead on evaluations of socially engaged arts practices matters. Establishing care relationships in interpersonal interactions, or aesthetics of care as argued by Saito (2022), involves co-authoring rapport and sharing moments of the participants' experiences. The aesthetics of care benefit from the first-person account, that is, the perspective of a person engaged in practicing the care relationship. Evaluation and research need to be responsive to context and culture. Participant evaluation needs to utilise a range of different formats to ensure the full diversity of people can participate—for example, using digital journals, comment boxes, text messaging, blogs, podcasting, electronic forums, photographs, video clips, drawings, symbols, graffiti walls, or mind maps. Reflecting and learning to adapt to unplanned circumstances matters. Reviewing programmes, interventions, assessment practices, and policies, geared towards promoting social and emotional learning, healing and well-being, matter in an equitable manner for all young people. Evaluation tools come to matter differently when following and documenting the impact of care relationships, reflexivity, and equity; these are processes at the centre of socially engaged arts programmes. These are more than merely buzzwords of thinking and writing and doing. What matters is that practices are responsive to nested contexts and the relational dynamics between cultures and communities.

As Maxine Greene (1995) cogently argues:

> our very realization that the individual does not precede community means that the ground of a critical community can be opened in our teaching in and beyond schools . . . [where] to work for responsiveness to principles of equity, principles of equality, and principles of freedom, which still can be named within contexts of caring and concern . . . [requires] using their imaginations, tapping their courage—to transform. (p. 198)

Maxine Greene argued passionately for the making of active/activist citizens. Hers was a highly political vision of practitioners working with young people to consider and create a fairer future world by changing what happens in the present (Greene, 1995: 198).

What cannot be neglected is reflecting more consideration of care that engages us all as active agents empowered to contribute to better world-making. So what else is implicated in practising and promoting caring relationships?

Using Digital Technologies: What Matters?

One way to address and engage with all of these questions is through the use of digital technology. The evaluation of young people's arts engagement, as with pupil-led evaluation, documents what they do and their understanding of what this means. Engagement involves a synergistic relationship that involves participants' interaction with particular practices. Existing research tells us that engagement through digital technology ensures that affective engagement and social dimensions, which relate to the emotional connection and passion that students feel owing to their experiences of co-creating and working together, are captured as a community. It matters that the digital landscape and big data environment are responding to a novel need to explore and evaluate not only the ontological implications of the digital age but also young people's engagement as co-creators in diverse socially engaged arts practices, and their evaluation and research (Pepple, 2022).

But evaluation can be a 'perilous adventure'. As Saville Kushner argues (2017), it contains 'perils for those doing the enquiry as much as for those having it done to them' (p. xiv). The co-option of evaluation (as with evaluative research) into the bureaucracy where stakeholders are invested with political voices means we need to develop new forms of interviewing, observing, analysing, and writing through, and disseminating. The key lies in developing the use of digital creativity for rethinking its provision of innovative tools, skills, and platforms and for evaluating with a values-based or a relational ethos. Practitioners should look at examples of methodological manifestos written by evaluators, so as to see how democratic values matter.

Why Articulating a Manifesto Matters

A manifesto is a call to democratic action. One such manifesto for educational evaluation made explicit and transparent by MacDonald and Parlett (1973) invited us (a) to promote responsiveness to the needs and perspectives of differing audiences and (b) to illuminate the complex organisational, teaching, and learning processes at issue. More specifically they recommended that:

(a) *Observational data* be carefully validated and used (sometimes as a substitute for data from questioning and testing).

(b) *Progressive focusing* rather than pre-ordinate design be flexible enough to allow for responses to unanticipated events.

(c) *The central importance of evaluator positioning* (be that teacher, artist practitioner, or researcher), whether highlighted or constrained by the design, be made evident to the sponsors and audiences of the evaluation.

In an environment that is struggling with government policies that perpetuate inequity, as Lynch *et al.* (2009) argue, the loss of the capacity to develop supportive affective relations of love, care, and solidarity or of the experience of engaging in them. What matters here is the core dimension of *affective inequality* (Lynch *et al.*, 2009: 1). Care is not just a private matter. Schools should be sites of care and of intense relationality. The arts should be sites for the possibilities of:

> affective equality (developing affective relations of care and solidarity) . . . the arts engage particular kinds of content and knowledge, and are situated in major public institutions, where children can hopefully rely on 'having ample prospects for . . . caring, and solidary relationships'. (Mansfield, 2022: 422, quoting Lynch *et al.*, 2009: 2)

So, what should evaluation that manifests digital creativity, care, and affective equality look like? In two ground-breaking books, *Personalizing evaluation* (2000) and *Evaluative research methods: Managing the complexities of judgment in the field* (2017), Saville Kushner presents multiple suggestions for evaluation practices, evaluation communities, and independent evaluators. I have included them all because they are more vital than ever in a time when judgment of what is 'real' and 'effective' is deeply challenged:

1. Evaluators should provide—and be free to provide—information that government and other sponsors need as well as that which they want.
2. Evaluation and 'community' should be partners in promoting a vision of the evaluation process as one founded upon relationships that enhance and do not diminish trust.
3. Both evaluator and sponsor/funder should work closely to restore the public credibility of evaluation as an independent source of knowledge for multiple interest groups.

4. Practitioner and evaluator 'expertise' and 'activism' should be viewed pedagogically, as the capacity to create conditions that enable all stakeholders to engage in a process of mutual learning to enhance collaborative forms of action.

Juliet Hess (2019) in her seminal book *Music education for social change: Constructing an activist music education* invites more critical reflection as a starting point to set in motion how evaluation and research can translate into practice in order to push toward social change.

What Matters for Arts Practitioners in Translating Practices into Affective Evaluative Pathways?

Socially engaged arts practitioners need to evaluate embodiment beyond situated, individual subject accounts. They also need to conduct evaluation that relies on responsive feedback loops and that explores unintended outcomes that can be contextualised differently and funded from multiple sources. The concept of the *arts practitioner* traverses subjects and spaces, classes and contexts. It is an idea through which to express the creative synthesis of practice and its evaluation into embodied learning experiences. The arts practitioner understands learning as embodied, experiential, unconscious, affective. Central to the creative practitioner is *embodied expertise*, which Hickey-Moody *et al.* (2021) argue as an attuning to knowing and feeling *through* the body. Whether it is Hip Hop or rapping, young people often learn without thinking that they are learning—they sense and intuit knowledge as they pick up and author patterns, numbers, and spoken word, enabled by a safe and trusting environment that allows a diversity of approaches to open up to and author-embodied creativity. We know that all educational experiences work through creating positive or negative affects. These affects are primarily non-verbal and often pre-cognitive, which means they are feelings and confused ideas before they are intellectual endeavours. Indeed, the nature of an emotional response may prohibit an intellectual endeavour. As a concept, *affect* helps us to understand, as Deleuze explains, how affective encounters increase and/or decrease our capacity to act:

> When it [a body] encounters another mode, it can happen that this other mode is 'good' for it, that is, it enters into composition with it, or on the

contrary decomposes it and is 'bad' for it. In the first case, the existing mode passes to a greater perfection; in the second case, to a lesser perfection. Accordingly, it will be said that its power of acting or force of existing increases or diminishes, since the power of the other mode is added to it, or on the contrary is withdrawn from it, immobilized and restraining it (IV, 18 dem). The passage to a greater perfection, or the increase of the power of acting, is called an affect, or feeling, of joy; the passage to a lesser perfection or the diminution of the power of acting is called sadness. (Deleuze, 1988: 50)

Practitioners working in lower socio-economic status and culturally and linguistically diverse contexts have to work to investigate new forms of evaluating embodiment, for developing tools that focus more on the 'how' of practices, to clarify the challenges we face when doing affective evaluation and research. As Knudsen and Stage (2015) suggest, possible ways include: (1) asking questions about *affect*, (2) generating embodied data for qualitative *affect* research, and (3) identifying *affective practices* that develop affective relations of care and solidarity (p. 3).

Collecting material that includes online comments, tag clouds, viewing statistics, and accounts of bodily states, including those of the artist practitioners, is important in the creation of 'meta-strategies' (p. 3) for evaluating and researching affective practices. This is where practitioners begin by creating a positive emotional entanglement with, say, Hip Hop as embodied creativity. What matters is the role of the body in learning and teaching and specifically in cultivating affective attachments and modifying habits. Evaluation needs to recognise the importance of the bodies and the emotional landscapes of young people and to scrutinise whether these practices have a long-lasting transformative affective encounter as an outcome of these practices.

Socially engaged arts programmes are sites of hypercomplex and multisensual spaces, where affects move through bodies in ways that are sometimes difficult to see, understand, and evaluate, and yet are so vital to what evaluation and research tell us about affective practice. This matters.

Practitioners might also draw on their own learning journeys as a resource for their students, in order to show that everyone has to rework negative learning habits at some stage of their learning journey—even teachers. The classroom is only one part of the fieldwork that might be evaluated and analysed, given the robust planning and networking that occurs on a daily basis. The reflections on previous lessons and observations of students and classroom culture help to define the expectations of the entire community. Experiences can be recounted through the eyes of the key participants, open for interpretation against enforced social parameters that serve as borders. Evaluation and research comprises agreed understandings and expectations but equally enough leeway to allow for open-ended opportunities. Young people need to be given permission to explore and experience their own responses to the context of the evaluation or enquiry. Challenge is vital to practitioners' practice. Evaluation is also vital to stimulate change.

What matters is that practice with care for 'situated ethicalities is vital' (Puig de la Bellacasa, 2017: 221) because it allows young people the opportunity to participate in society, to promote their agencies and independence.

So, both evaluation and research are important to arts organisations. Both invite us to rethink our understandings of societal change. Both help and support us in exploring the relational assemblages within which young people's identities emerge and are enacted differently. It is by developing our professional creativity we drive teaching and learning enrichment. It is up to practitioners find ways to digest bite-sized research, to create a community forum to relay and exchange ideas, to translate evaluation and research into practice that privileges both youth voice and attention to inequity and injustices. Practitioners cannot and do not want to pluck evaluation or research strategies off a shelf but rather co-create a relational ethos that is integrated carefully into their reflective development as creative professionals (see Douglas Lonie's chapter in the present volume).

Increasingly, 'being in the know' as a practitioner seems to involve being 'evidence informed'—in other words, being aware of how to translate the results of evaluations or research into successful learning and to utilise these insights in your own practice. Quite right, too, you might say, and I would agree. However, becoming evidence-informed is not without its challenges and can involve walking a tightrope between two suboptimal outcomes.

On the one hand, if research is interpreted too simply, crude interventions can be condensed and disseminated as findings with 'romantic discourse about it' (Pairon, 2023: 161). Under such circumstances, the main *pay-off* of music-making is the activity itself, more than the social impact of music-making by children and young people living in an environment that severely limits them and which they can hardly change where such complex environments and difficult living conditions present harsh realities of poverty and corruption where there is no support from local or national governments (see www.simm-platform.eu, where SIMM is the abbreviation of 'Social Impact of Making Music' with research led by Lukas Pairon, who, along with others, funded an international network of researchers and music projects and programmes aimed at developing the capacity of participants to navigate to different positions in their societies).

On the other hand, entirely faithful applications of evaluations or research may not be practically possible, or desirable, in a complex socially engaged arts practice. What if studies that have been more 'ecologically valid'—as psychologists term settings or tasks that more closely resemble how the skills being studied occur in real life—use random *samples* of participants who are very different from the pupils in our everyday classrooms and communities? What if what matters to you is not prioritised, nor a shared understanding of ethical obligations of care agreed from material and affective constructs and practices as 'ethical doings'? What if what matters to you is avoided and there is no defining a code of conduct or even a normative definition of right and wrong care and of practicing the care relationship with others, which provides aspiration for better world-making and living a good and happy life?

What if practitioners are invited to partner with researchers who jump all these hurdles? Researchers can come to the party with only a singular aim, or a very limited number of aims, allowing them to isolate the specific effects of one variable. Practitioners do not have this luxury. Sites of practices are uncontrolled and noisy (in the statistical sense of being highly variable). We have to consider a huge range of interconnecting variables concurrently every time we plan any activity—as a focus of a particular practice that re-creates relational, situated possibilities and impossibilities—and this reduces our ability to quantify the effect of any single change. True fidelity to the research is, therefore, likely to be an unattainable ideal.

Where, then, is the sweet spot that matters for attempting to apply the principles of evaluation or research, which avoids both epistemological orders and relativistic accounts of scientific practices that propagate crude lethal mutations or, on the other hand, become overly entangled in the finer details?

What Are the Key Messages that Matter Most?

Rather than agonise over the minutiae of different research effects or forms of evaluation, spend your time reflecting on what went well for you in your own setting and how you could improve. This really matters. Remember, evaluations and research can be built into one's practice in a way that preserves and translates its core. Practitioners have enormous amounts of tacit expertise about the conditions under which effective practices happen, about cultivating and practising the care relationship with others, and we can sometimes, as a profession, lack the confidence to factor this into the equation. What matters is to trust yourself.

None of this is to say that we do not need to move forward on the finer details of classroom-based research. There remain many important applied questions that hold great promise for education. It is just that, according to the experts, we can all have some confidence in doing, being, and enacting the entanglements of what matters, as Maria Puig de la Bellacasa (2017) defines it, which is 'a relational ethos with a world, a process through which material constraints are co-created. In turn, constraints re-create relational, situated possibilities and impossibilities . . . And include a dimension of translatable and relatively enduring ethicality' (p. 153). Walking the path between a relational ethos and a sea of complexities may be easier than we have imagined, then. All we need to do is co-create, reflect and adjust, and trust ourselves.

Translating evaluation and research into socially engaged arts practice, in which every member is engaged and cared for, requires a concerted and coordinated effort by professionals. Equally and absolutely necessary is that encounters of caring interpersonal relationships involve perceptive, inclusive, critical, and participatory forms of interaction that involve collaboration and social purpose. Such encounters can be evaluated upon the relationships they create, represent, produce, or prompt.

References

Altheide, D. L. and Johnson, J. M. (1994). Criteria for assessing interpretive validity in qualitative research. In N. K. Denzin and Y. S. Lincoln (eds.), *Handbook of Qualitative Research*. Thousand Oaks, CA: Sage Publications, pp. 485–499.

Bala, S. (2018). *The gestures of participatory art*. Manchester: Manchester University Press.

Daniel, D. B. and De Bruyckere, P. (2021). Toward an ecological science of teaching. *Canadian Psychology/Psychologie Canadienne*, 62(4): 361–375.

Deleuze, G. (1988). *Spinoza: Practical philosophy* (R. Hurley, trans.). San Francisco: City Lights Books.

Ecorys (2017). *Arts for wellbeing: Unlocking social energy to increase wellbeing*. Ecorys. https://www.culturehive.co.uk/wp-content/uploads/2017/08/EcorysCaseStudyCPP_bait.pdf.

Goodchild, P. (2017). Weil's boat: On becoming and being. In Rozelle-Stone (ed.), *Simone Weil and Continental Philosophy*. Lanham, MD: Rowman and Littlefield, pp. 13–36.

Green, A. (2023). Conflict transformation, scalability and the non-governmental ear. In O. Odena (ed.), *Music and Social Inclusion: International Research and Practice in Complex Settings*. Abingdon: Routledge, pp. 187–201.

Greene, M. (1995). *Releasing the imagination: Essays on education, the arts and social change*. Hoboken: Jossey-Bass Publishers.

Griffiths, M. (1998). *Educational research for social justice: Getting off the fence*. Maidenhead: Open University Press.

Hall, C. and Jones, S. (2009). Creative partners: Arts practice the potential for pupil voice. *Power and Education*, 1(2): 178–188. https://doi.org/10.2304/power.2009.1.2.178.

Hess, J. (2019). *Music education for social change: Constructing an activist music education*. Routledge.

Hickey-Moody, A. (2013). *Youth, arts and education: Reassembling subjectivity through affect*. Abingdon: Routledge. https://doi.org/10.4324/9780203855829.

Hickey-Moody, A., Cook, P. J. and Portelli, N. (2021). The creative pedagogue: Enacting affective pathways for interdisciplinary embodied creativity in primary education. In P. Burnard and M. Loughrey (eds.), *Sculpting New Creativities in Primary Education*. Abingdon: Routledge, pp. 107–122.

Kidman, J. (2018). Representing youth voices in Indigenous community research: Educational experience, policy and Practice. In R. Bourke and J. Loveridge (eds.), *Radical Collegiality through Student Voice*. Berlin: Springer, pp. 55–69. https://doi.org/10.1007/978-981-13-1858-0_4.

Knudsen, B. T. and Stage, C. (2015). *Affective methodologies*. London: Palgrave Macmillan.

Kushner, S. (2017). *Evaluating research methods: Managing the complexities of judgment in the field*. Charlotte, NC: Information Age Publishing.

Kushner, S. (2000). *Personalizing evaluation*. London: Sage.

Lynch, K., Baker, J. and Lyons, M. (2009). *Affective equality: Love, care and injustice*. London: Palgrave Macmillan.

Macdonald, R., Kreutz, G. and Mitchell, L. (eds.). (2012). *Music, health and wellbeing*. Oxford: Oxford University Press.

MacDonald, B. and Parlett, M. (1973). Rethinking evaluation: Notes from the Cambridge Conference. *Cambridge Journal of Education*, 3(2): 74–82.

Mansfield, J. E. (2022). The arts as practices of care in a socially just curriculum. *Beijing International Review of Education*, 4(3): 420–444.

McLellan, R., Galton, M., Steward, S., and Page, C. (2012). The impact of Creative Partnerships on the wellbeing of children and young people. Final Report. Creative Partnerships.

Murphy, R. and Espeland, M. (2007). Prelude: Making connections in assessment and evaluation in arts education. In L. Bresler (ed.), *International Handbook of Research in Arts Education*. Berlin: Springer, pp. 337–340.

Odena, O. (2023). *Music and social inclusion: International research and practice in complex settings*. Abingdon: Routledge.

Pairon, L. (2023). The art of positive fatalism. In O. Odena (ed.), *Music and Social Inclusion: International Research and Practice in Complex Settings*. Abingdon: Routledge, pp. 161–171.

Pepple, D. G. (2022). An ecological perspective of student engagement through digital technology: Practical application and implications. *British Journal of Educational Research*, 48(6): 1216–1231.

Puig de la Bellacasa, M. (2017). *Matters of care: Speculative ethics in more than human worlds*. Minneapolis, MN: University of Minnesota Press.

Richardson, L. (1997). *Fields of play*. Rutgers University Press.

Ross, M. (1978). *The creative arts*. Portsmouth, NH: Educational Books.

Saito, Y. (2022) *Aesthetics of care*. London: Bloomsbury Academic.

Shavelson, R. J. and Towne, L. (2002). *Scientific research in education*. Washington, DC: National Academies Press.

Schlemmer, R. H. (2016). (Re)contextualising the narrative of teaching and learning. *Arts Education Policy Review*, 18(1): 1–10.

St. Pierre, E. A. (2018). Writing post qualitative inquiry. *Qualitative Inquiry*, 24(9): 603–608.

Tronto, J. C. (1993). *Moral boundaries: A political argument for an ethic of care*. Abingdon: Routledge.

Weil, S. (2002). *The need for roots: Prelude to a declaration of duties towards mankind* (A Wills, trans.). Abingdon: Routledge (Originally published 1952).

Weil, S. (2021). *Waiting for God*. Abingdon: Routledge. (Originally published 1950).

Woodly, D., Brown, R. H., Marin, M., Threadcraft, S., Harris, C. P., Syedullah, J., and Ticktin, M. (2021). The politics of care. *Contemporary Political Theory*, 20: 890–925.

15

Untangling Earphones

Power, Voice, and Agency in Participatory Music Evaluation

Douglas Lonie

Introduction

This chapter is largely based on my own voice (well, the one in my head while writing it). It is difficult to write a book chapter about impact evaluation 'objectively' because it is something I have been learning about and doing for the past fifteen years. This chapter is a reflection and discussion of that professional experience. It is not a traditional research report or summary on the basis that sharing my experience may be useful to other practitioners or researchers; particularly sharing the learning and 'unlearning'[1] I have done in the process. So, apologies upfront for privileging my voice when writing about the need to privilege other people's!

'Tangled earphones' refers to a frustration many of us have experienced. We want to listen to something privately, we know there are earphones at the bottom of our bag or drawer, functioning, semi-functioning, or not. The tangled mess we retrieve needs to be untangled and pulled apart before we can identify a functioning pair of earphones with which to listen to something clearly.[2]

In the context of this paper, I see the earphones representing different 'levels' that are regularly present in the context of participatory music impact evaluation: policy (makers and doers), practice (practitioners and organisations), and people (participants). Of course, *people* exist and are important at each level, but the way they are thought of changes at each level and can also get a bit tangled up. In fact, the process of untangling is also one of clarifying who is listening to what, or who is listening to whom. The metaphor also implies a solution that we will all be less frustrated and able

Douglas Lonie, *Untangling Earphones* In: *Music for Inclusion and Healing in Schools and Beyond*. Edited by: Pete Dale, Pamela Burnard, and Raphael Travis Jr., Oxford University Press. © Oxford University Press 2023.
DOI: 10.1093/oso/9780197692677.003.0016

to listen more clearly if we can find a way of keeping the different earphones untangled.

I begin the chapter by discussing issues of power in impact evaluation and how this should be challenged to ensure that more voices, and a broader range of experiences, can be explored and represented. The remaining discussion draws on three project case-study examples from across my work to illustrate some of the tangles that I have experienced at the different levels (the 'tangled earphones' of policy, practice, and people). *Policy* is explored with the case of a music mentoring project where I designed an evaluation tool strongly influenced by the aims of the government department that was funding the programme. *Practice* presents a case where the lead practitioner enabled us as evaluators to question and challenge some of our 'taken for granted' approaches to doing research. *People* discusses how overly rigid 'top-down' outcomes frameworks can miss the important dynamics taking place in music projects that are leading to positive change. The chapter ends with some of the strategies I have developed to 'untangle' some of these 'crossed wires', although this remains an ongoing process.

Power and Knowledge Creation in Impact Evaluation— Who Is Listening to What (and Are the Earphones Even Working)?

Issues of power and ethics are central to impact evaluation practice in all contexts, but especially when working with young people who may have complicated lives and needs. By impact evaluation, I am referring to the approaches used to determine the changes that funded interventions, in this case participatory music projects, can bring about for people, organisations, or communities.

Who holds the power to explore the changes created by education and learning interventions can vary quite widely. In social pedagogy practice,[3] for instance, relationships between participants and practitioners are often explicitly made more equal (Petrie, 2011). There is a recognition that both parties bring different skills, knowledges, and experiences to the practice situation and there is scope for mutual learning and co-creation to take place. Arguably these same principles should be applied to impact evaluation practice and attempts made to establish how knowledge and expertise is being applied, when and by whom, including the limits of such knowledge. As with social pedagogy practitioners there is an argument that those researching and exploring the impact of participatory music projects should be critically aware of their own roles in the process.

When the function of power in impact evaluation is not explicitly considered there is scope for, at best, inappropriate, and at worst, damaging methods and processes to be used. This risk is especially acute given the recent 'toolkits turn' in third-sector project design and evaluation (Belfiore and Bennett, 2010).[4] While a focus on impact is not, in itself, a bad thing (i.e., there is, arguably, a moral and ethical case for ensuring public and charitable resources achieve positive things for people and society), the need to 'prove' cases, demonstrate effectiveness, or otherwise measure and assess impact can sometimes lead to blunt and uncritical evaluation design. Participants may be asked to provide data about themselves and their experiences without fully understanding why it is being asked or what it may be used for. In attempting to demonstrate the impact of a project, as researchers we should be mindful not to use approaches that are in opposition to the practice itself. First, some context, as my own work experience is quite central to my line of argument here.

I did my PhD in the mid-2000s in a public-health research unit in a university. The PhD focused on how musical behaviour and participation were linked to young people's mental health and well-being (Lonie, 2009). In many ways the research unit represented 'best practice' in research design with new projects awarded from very qualified decision-making boards and all methods thoroughly assessed and approved by a university ethics committee. I then went to work for a charity, the National Foundation for Youth Music (mostly referred to as Youth Music), which funds around four hundred music-making projects across England at any one time, many of them using contemporary urban musics.[5] While the charity's funding comes from a range of sources, much of it comes from Arts Council England, according to priorities agreed with the UK Government Department for Digital, Culture, Media and Sport (DCMS). I then worked for a research consultancy (BOP Consulting), where my clients were often local governments, funding bodies, and large cultural organisations and institutions. This has given me direct experience of the role and function of impact evaluation in much of the policy areas that affect the funding of contemporary urban music projects and programmes.

In each phase of my work, I have tried to remain critical and reflective about the power structures at play in music programmes and how this may affect research and evaluation design and execution (Lonie, 2018). Through public discourse in seminars and conferences, I have tried to continue conversations with peers about how we can do impact evaluation in more inclusive and rigorous ways, pursuing an agenda of evaluation as exploration, rather than advocacy, or 'making a case' for funding. The conclusion of this chapter is yet another attempt to encourage practical ways that impact evaluation can be made more rigorous and inclusive.

Those funding projects seeking to achieve social change are often driven by advocacy needs (i.e., celebrating and disseminating successes), which may bias the methods used to explore change, as well as the findings that are reported and shared. Despite my own attempts to remain critical and vigilant, it is fair to say that I have also experienced, and likely been complicit in, putting the agenda of funders, and those funding them (often government departments), before the needs, expectations, or experiences of those participating in music-making projects.

Figure 15.1 illustrates a power dynamic that can often be observed in impact evaluation design and activity. It shows how, despite knowledge being generated across all levels of those involved in programme funding, the 'power' (i.e., decisions about the intended outcomes and impacts of funding, what activities are eligible, and what evaluation takes place) is often held or orchestrated by the funders, with some decision-making being devolved to the organisations receiving funds. The needs and perspectives of those taking part in project activities are rarely at the top of the pyramid. The methods that may be used to explore their experiences are rarely designed with them or adapted to the practice context in which they will be applied. The knowledge

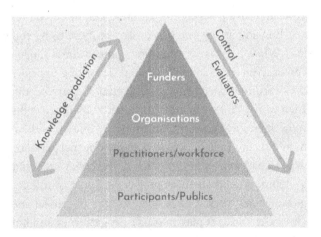

Figure 15.1 A hierarchical 'pyramid model' of impact evaluation

that is generated in the evaluation process therefore tends to be both directed by and 'held' by the funders of the work. This can often mean that negative or critical findings are less likely to be published or shared, and that evaluation practice is stalled and limited as a result.[6]

Figure 15.2 offers an alternative model for how impact evaluation could be considered, specifically the role of the evaluator as an intermediary among stakeholders (i.e., participants, practitioners, funders, and funded organisations). Evaluation, in this configuration, enables critical reflection for each of the stakeholders, as well as an opportunity for evaluation design and activities to be influenced by any of the stakeholders (i.e., the development of co-created methods, facilitating a broader range of dissemination material, and so forth). Control is removed from the diagram as the value of evaluation as a process of exploring and understanding human experience becomes the primary motivation.

Essentially the embryonic model has come from my own professional experiences, much of which I did not get quite right by foregrounding the expectations of my employers rather than designing approaches that enable people to tell their stories in ways that make sense to them.

This introductory section has considered the motivations for *impact evaluation* and the effect this can have on its design and implementation, including where issues of power and control should be considered. The

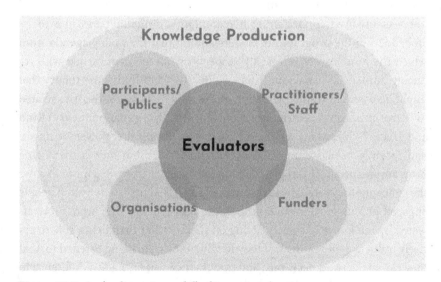

Figure 15.2 An 'embryonic model' of impact evaluation

sections below outline how a more critical approach to impact evaluation can be justified using three case studies of programmes using contemporary urban musics for young people to develop musical, personal, and social skills. The 'untangling' will hopefully be apparent in the form of key lessons learned and how each stage has informed the practice of the next, resulting in a set of ideas for how practice can develop in the future.

Earphones 1—Policy

Youth Music Mentors and the New Labour 'Respect' agenda

The Youth Music Mentors programme ran from 2006 to 2011 and was funded directly by the UK Department for Media, Culture and Sport (DCMS). The programme aimed to enable young people aged between eleven and twenty-five to develop musically and socially by being paired with a more experienced mentor. Phase 2 ran from 2008 to 2011 with funding distributed among twenty-two organisations across England. The programme stipulated that each organisation should aim to support twenty young people with at least ten sessions delivered to each, although organisations were free to decide which type of music they supported and who the mentors might be, often based on their knowledge of the needs and preferences of the young people they were working with.

I was involved in designing a *quantitative evaluation measure* to be embedded in the programme. Understanding that the policy agenda from which the funding was released ('Respect') was largely concerned with reducing anti-social behaviour, I had a dig around to find some theory that might be useful to frame the design of the tool. I landed on theories related to 'active citizenship' (Marinetto, 2003) and self-determination theory (Ryan and Deci, 2000). Many of the arguments outlining the 'power of music' had recently been summarised by Hallam (2010), but how a mentoring programme specifically might function for the participants led me to explore the concept of 'agency'. The literature had suggested that some young people engaged in anti-social behaviour because they felt that they were more affected by the forces of society acting on them, rather than being able to actively influence these forces. If they felt that they were being listened to, that they can make good decisions, and that their decisions made a difference to their lives, they may feel more inclined to take an active role in society and recognise that their 'rights' were inextricably linked to their 'responsibilities'. The measure I designed therefore asked these questions, along with the mentees' perceptions of their musical ability and their knowledge of where and how to make music locally (Leonie, 2010).

This resulted in the 'track record' tool, a bit like the outcomes star[7] but designed to look like a vinyl record (never mind that most eleven to twenty-five-25-year-olds in 2009 probably were not consuming records in quite the same way as their predecessors). The mentors were encouraged to use the tool with a mentee near the beginning and near the end of their ten sessions so that a baseline and follow-up measure of progress could be made. In total we had 280 completed baseline and follow-up questionnaires returned. The funded projects told us that the tool was not appropriate for some young people (e.g., those with certain learning difficulties), some reported that they felt the tool would compromise the model of practice being established in the mentor-mentee interaction, and others just did not want to use it. Despite these (reasonable) limitations in the universal adoption of the tool, there were positive results reported across all the dimensions we measured, particularly for musical ability and knowledge of how to continue with music making (a relief), but also for the individual dimensions and the combined score of agency (i.e., feeling you can make a difference to your life, feeling listened to, and feeling like you can make good decisions).[8]

The tool did what it set out to. We were able to say with some confidence (using terms like 'paired t-test, effect size, and validity') that the programme had increased the musical ability and agency of the young people taking part, and that this improvement could theoretically reduce potential antisocial behaviour. However, obviously there were many other factors in the participants' lives that could affect that particular outcome. The associated qualitative evaluation (conducted by Deane et al., 2011) went into much greater detail about the mechanisms of change in the mentoring process and indicated how trust and empathy were key drivers of the development of 'agency' observed in the internal quantitative evaluation. Ultimately however, both evaluations indicated that the music mentoring model was effective in line with the aims of the Respect Agenda, and that the investment from DCMS was good value for money.

Of course, by the time the programme had completed there had been a change of UK Government to a Conservative/Liberal Democrat coalition. Even before this, the out-going Labour administration had shifted their focus away from the Respect Agenda and quietly stopped funding programmes from that policy strand. These changes did not mean that anti-social behaviour, likely as a consequence or symptom of poverty, had reduced significantly, but there was a shift in policy from the new government that reconfigured the 'solution' to anti-social behaviour away from central state intervention towards charities and philanthropic actors (the so-called Big Society model).

The theory that the evaluation tool had been based on was that young people will be less likely to engage in anti-social behaviour if they feel more in control of their lives, if they are trusted and empathised with, and are developing musical and other skills in the process. This indicates an important connection between what is possible on behalf of the mentee (individual capacity) and the social conditions in which the opportunities are provided (the mentor and the organisation[s] paying for the programme). Responsibility in this case therefore extends beyond the responsibility of an individual to society. While rights are the social 'payload' of individual responsibility, there is also a responsibility for society to provide opportunities for young people to develop agency and deeper self-understanding (in relation to themselves, others, and society), something made more challenging when the economic ideology of austerity is limiting public services for young people.

Reflecting on the design of the programme and its evaluation, it seems that the concept of increasing agency to reduce anti-social behaviour, via the medium of music, in response to a central government policy, placed too much focus on the individual. The policy discourse of the Respect Agenda and latterly the 'Big Society' model is arguably based on pathologizing young people, placing the locus of control on individuals and not the broader social conditions that they find themselves in. The concept of 'finding a voice' or 'being listened to' via newfound musical ability or the idea that young people were somehow now more 'in control' seems somewhat naïve and a bit reductive given the complex socio-economic factors that are linked to poverty, alienation, and disengagement.

While I would argue that the theory driving this research was sound, the political context in which the research was done, and the findings presented were not adequately critiqued. I feel a need to open that space here, not least as part of an ethical reckoning with the young people who I was indirectly asking to fill out surveys to prove a funding case for the government.

Earphones 2—Practice

Recognising Young People as Artists—Max and the Ustudios MCs

This section focuses on a specific research project I carried out with Luke Dickens in 2011/2012 (Dickens and Lonie, 2013). Luke had been a Research Officer at Youth Music and had recently started working at a university when this work was published, developing his interests in inclusive research practice. It is fair to say that while we were both working for the charity, we felt the need to get much closer to some of the projects than perhaps the 'arm's length' design of tools described in the Youth Music Mentors example above allowed for. We had both studied cultural theory to a doctoral level and knew there were a lot of very interesting processes at play in the work being funded by Youth Music, but that a more 'hands-on' approach would be needed to properly understand it or communicate it. More specifically we felt that the focus on 'outcomes and impacts' for young people was too focused on their individual development and did not always allow for a proper consideration of the role of practice and practitioners. We needed to explore the 'how' as well as the 'what' in understanding impact.

While the mentoring model discussed above can be one successful approach, there are many different models of practice supporting young contemporary musicians. The practice and practitioners that young people are exposed to therefore also have a political dimension when considering questions of voice and agency. Some practice models are more formal and focused very clearly on qualifications or other material learning outcomes (i.e., progression to college or other education). Others are more fluid, informal, and very loosely concerned with specific developmental or musical outcomes. The spaces and places in which practice takes place can also have a huge influence on a participant's experience.

We explored these themes in research with the *Ustudios* project in Hangleton and Knoll, two housing estates near Brighton in the Southeast of England. The project received funding from Youth Music and was led by the practitioner Max Wheeler. It had run for around four years (via funding from various sources) when we conducted the research in 2011, enabling Max to build strong relationships with the participants, most of whom had been taking part on and off for the entire period.

Max had designed the project to be responsive to the musical identities of the young people taking part. While Hip Hop was the main genre being used, this was equally influenced by the tastes and interests of the young people, which also developed over the course of the four-year programme. This meant Max could bring in musical forms he was being exposed to in his broader work as a musician, as well as learn from the participants and respond to their musical influences throughout. This more 'horizontal' form of learning was a key aspect of the practice and a clear example of how Max positioned himself as a musician working with other emerging artists to make good music, rather than 'dressing up' youth work as a music intervention, or as Max put it:

> They've been to enough youth work sessions where it's like, 'Right, today we're going to get out the condom demonstration'. And it's like, 'Well that doesn't happen in a music studio, that's not professional, that's some other shit and that's not what I came down here for'. (Dickens and Lonie, 2013: 64)

The funding that was supporting the project at the time of the research was coming from a national charity with explicit public objectives for young people to 'change their lives through music'[9] and support music-making that would include and enable broader personal and social development. An emerging 'tangle' here was that in order to resource the project, its aims had to align with these national objectives, although in order to be successful, from Max's perspective at least, the project had to be focused clearly, if not exclusively, on supporting the young musicians to make the music they wanted to, to develop their music-making to the level they wanted to, and to express, through the music, their ideas, perspectives, and experiences in ways they wanted to.

The extent to which there is 'pure' agency being supported here then is obscured by the fact that the funding application and reporting would require an articulation of the practice and its impact that was aligned with the agenda of the funder (and *its* funders—ultimately trickling up to the agenda of the UK Government Department of Culture, Media and Sport).

Recognising this tension between the arguably restrictive (and unarguably political) parameters of policy and the freedom of expression that Max understood as central to the 'success' of the project was another clear motivation for us to conduct the research. A key aim of the research was to build from Max's practice, which prioritised the views, perspectives, and voices of the young artists. This meant spending time with them in the studio spaces they were working in (permanent and temporary) across and beyond the

Hangleton and Knoll housing estates, building trusting relationships with them alongside Max, asking them to share their music and to talk about the musical and lyrical ideas they were developing (often bringing in themes from their broader lives), and being open about our role as researchers, who we worked for, what the research was exploring, and what we would do with what they shared. This extended to asking how they would like to be referred to in the eventual research publications where they chose to use their MC names rather than be fully anonymised.

The three months of in-depth qualitative research that followed were essential to embed the above approaches, but also to work with Max and the young MCs to figure out how to share their stories and to present a 'development narrative' that felt authentic to their experiences and could be shared in a way that made sense to a broader research and policy community.

One way of doing this was to ensure that we were using the lyrics of the young people wherever possible as data sources in the research outputs.[10] We also played examples of the music when presenting the findings at conferences, provided links to these hosted online in published papers, and used photographs of the settings, as well as photos taken by the young people to document their experience, none of which revealed their identities, but did represent the things they identified as central to their learning experiences. The data and findings were carefully situated in the perspectives of the young people as much as possible, explicitly attempting to present the broad dynamics at play in the project. Our approach to presenting the data and findings was led by the dilemma of how to articulate the complexity of the practice, breadth, and depth of participants' experiences, while still exploring and presenting 'impact'.

Max based his practice on enabling the MCs to make music about the issues and ideas they wanted to. Often this meant exploring the broader structural aspects of poverty and deprivation, how this was linked to the MCs' relationships to the 'dominant culture' (represented by education, the police, social services, and others), and how these factors were enabling or constricting other aspects of their identities and lives, including as music artists. This process of 'conscientization' (Freire, 1998) is potentially at odds with funding agendas seeking to enable young people to 'change their lives through music'—when they realise that the change they seek is restricted by forces outside of their control. Music in this context provides a framework of understanding of conditions and circumstances, but also the limits to which these can be challenged or changed via individual or social means.

Much of the practice was based on validating young people's identities as Hip Hop artists, but within a dominant culture that stigmatized these identities (and arguably still does). The practice functioned by enabling young people's psychosocial development through 'self-actualisation' as music artists. However, those with the 'power' to fund this work further (i.e., local authorities, Youth Music, Arts Council England, DCMS) often have very different approaches to how 'valid' they consider these artistic identities. If these artistic identities are not fully recognised or appreciated, it is unlikely there will be the investment needed to develop local music markets and infrastructure for continued artistic development and/or commercial success. This potential for 'de-actualisation' as project funding ends and practice necessarily moves on is therefore also present as a component of the project's initial 'success' that could produce negative or neutral impacts in the future.

A tension also arose in the research process where we felt the need to follow academic convention in methodology design, in reporting and writing about the findings, and publishing research outputs. However, much of this convention does not encourage the sharing of multimedia data (i.e., music, photos, film) or the way that more inclusive and participatory research seeks to foreground the voices of participants, however represented. We regularly found it challenging to present descriptions of the practice or its effects, without showing actual examples of the practice, along with the artistic outputs and expressions produced. There is a need for research and policy communities to challenge some of these conventions to enable a broader understanding of what this work sounds, looks, and feels like.

Participatory principles, whether in practice, research, or dissemination, are based on equity and enabling social change through the process of participation itself. We need to challenge ourselves to consider how these principles may be compromised by convention or doing things the way they have always been done.

Earphones 3—People

Creativity and Criminality—or 'What To Do When the State Thinks You Need to Change Your Behaviour?'

The last example is from when I was working with an international research consultancy, BOP Consulting. We were commissioned by Creative

Scotland to explore how creative activities were linked to broader outcomes for children and young people. The programme that provided the context and framework for the research was called 'Cashback for Creativity' and was part of a national programme funded by the Scottish Government called 'Cashback for Communities'.[11]

Cashback for Communities has been running since 2008 and uses finance recovered under the Proceeds of Crime Act to reinvest in communities most affected by crime.[12] It has a particular focus on children and young people across services they may be more likely to miss out on due to reduced infrastructure in their communities, or relative material deprivation (e.g., sports clubs, creative activities, holidays, and trips). The funding comes from the Scottish Government Justice Department and the fund is administered by Inspiring Scotland, an independent research and evaluation organisation regularly contracted to oversee the accountability of public funding. As a result of these sources of funding the 'outcomes framework' for the Cashback for Communities programme is directly linked to the national outcomes set by the Scottish Government.[13] The outcomes framework for the fund therefore focuses on the following dimensions:

- Improving young people's confidence and 'resilience'
- Improving young people's skills
- Improving young people's well-being
- Increasing young people's 'positive destinations'
- Improving young people's behaviour
- Improving young people's educational attendance and attainment
- Reducing young people's anti-social behaviour and criminal activity[14]

On the face of it there is nothing really wrong with a government trying to improve outcomes for young people, especially those at relative disadvantage to their wealthier peers. What the Cashback for Communities outcomes framework overlooks, however, is the extent to which these outcomes are related to one another (e.g., improved confidence *through* increased skills *leading to* improved well-being), and the extent to which a temporary intervention in the form of a project grant can meaningfully affect the broader social conditions that are linked to negative outcomes across these dimensions for many young people.

In order to unpick these issues a bit, the research project funded by Creative Scotland allowed us to visit six projects funded via the Cashback for Communities programme and talk directly to the young people about what they were learning, how they were learning it, and how it may be related to their broader development. Five of the six projects we visited were using contemporary 'urban' musics, usually as part of a broader suite of creative activities (e.g., film and media, theatre). The goal of the research was to explore what specifically was happening via creative development that may be transferable to the higher-level dimensions outlined above and measured in the Cashback outcomes framework. Importantly, we did not want to ask the young people directly about their development using the outcomes 'language' outlined above, instead we just sat with them and asked them to describe what they had learned in the projects and how. Wherever possible we presented the findings using direct quotes from the young people so that the 'outcomes jargon' was being 'de-translated' back into the direct descriptions of participants' perception and experience (BOP Consulting, 2017).

The findings highlighted a sophisticated and overlapping set of processes that showed just how dynamic and interrelated the development journeys for the young people were. Rather than trying to outline the specific chronological process by which one outcome led to another, instead it was clear that there was a symbiotic relationship between development in one and development in another, and all closely tied to the activities they were taking part in. In no cases did the young people present themselves as having behaviour that needed to be changed through their participation, and in no cases did the young people discuss problems they had with anti-social behaviour or criminal activity (beyond, in some cases, being victims of bullying or at higher risk of the effects of crime).

Crucially, the role of identity was writ large through the development reported by the young people. By being seen as and treated as, and seeing themselves as, 'creative agents' and artists, the young people we spoke to were developing their confidence, competence, interpersonal skills, and making plans for their future learning and development within and outside of the supporting organisations.

Ironically the Cashback for Communities programme is a classic example of how negative identities are externally projected onto young people as they are perceived of as a 'problem' to be solved through social interventions. The implication in the outcomes framework, and its associated 'conversion targets', is that young participants must improve their (presumably bad) behaviour, increase their resilience to the effects of poverty, and reduce their antisocial behaviour and criminal activity. It is challenging to translate the overwhelmingly positive developmental impacts reported by the young people into such blunt dimensions, and there is often little appetite for complexity among those monitoring these bureaucratic processes.

This example highlights our shared responsibilities as researchers, practitioners, educators, funders, policymakers, or any other member of the 'programme milieu' to challenge the impact frameworks that we find ourselves operating within. It was only through speaking directly to around fifty young people that were taking part in this programme that the mismatch between their developmental experiences and the outcomes framework that the work was being translated into became apparent.

Our shared responsibility then is to deeply listen to the needs and experiences of the young artists we are working with and use any influence we have to create flexibility in the rigid frameworks we may find ourselves operating within. This will ultimately do greater justice to the impacts of the funded work, and to the efforts and achievements of the young people taking part in it.

Likewise, in all research and evaluation design, when people are making creative work, we can use that in the research and evaluation process, not to 'speak for itself' but to position the voice and agency on the creative process and bring that to other people, not least those who may insist that they prefer to see it represented as a number listed in an Excel spreadsheet that can be easily aggregated to the outcomes targets of a government department. The duty is on us to challenge the way developmental journeys are represented and impacts are communicated, especially when we are working with people whose voices are regularly (and often intentionally) marginalised.

Untangling Earphones—Undoing the Knots and Making it Easier to Listen to Young People and Each Other

These three earphone examples, or cases, are shared to highlight some of the ways that 'crossed wires' can lead to partial or unrepresentative accounts of the developmental processes taking place for young people in participatory music interventions. While much evaluation practice seeks to be reflexive and critically aware of the political context in which it is commissioned or conducted, often there are power dynamics built in to methodology design, data analysis, and the reporting of findings that are not wholly transparent about this 'funding milieu'. This can have the (largely unintended) effect of distorting or minimising the voices and agency of young participants, with the added irony that supporting voice and agency are often the very goals of the interventions being evaluated and a core mechanism of broader developmental outcomes.

The following final untangling tactics are presented to try and encourage more equitable evaluation practice in the future. I do not think we can ever aim for our practice to be perfect, not least because the context of our work is always changing, but we can always strive to learn from our experience and to be better.

Focus on young people as musicians first—This is a very simple but very powerful observation. When I want to talk to someone about their developmental journey or experience in the context of creative activity, I start by asking about their creative process, how what they have learned has contributed to their practice, and what they might do next. Quite often I will ask to see or hear examples of what people have learned, and where possible (and always with permissions) include this in presenting evaluation findings. Developing an artistic identity and having this validated by peers and practitioners is usually very important to participants, this should never be undermined in evaluation practice.

Be reflexive about your own voice and privilege—I have had my moments of 'imposter syndrome' or been held up as an 'expert' in something when I have felt anything but. I have been asked to make recommendations to funding decisions or strategies based on my research experience and knowledge of the field, and sometimes that 'power' has made me feel uncomfortable. Now, across all my work, I try to create space with everyone I am working with—co-researchers, participants, practitioners, and commissioners—to have an open and honest discussion about the context of the work, about my role, about the ways that the work could have an influence beyond the immediate interaction, and about the limitations of the work.

Bring 'power levels' together—Quite often evaluators are commissioned as 'objective' agents, expected to independently engage with people across the 'power levels', collecting and analysing data, interpreting findings, and feeding in knowledge from one level to the next. This misses the opportunity to bring people from these different 'levels' together and create moments to explore and critique the function of power in a programme. It also highlights the potential difference of evaluation as an opportunity for knowledge production across different agents, and evaluation as an opportunity for privileging the voice of an 'expert' evaluator over others.

Make methods accessible for everyone—Luke Dickens and I used to always say that 'people are more important than data', and it is especially important in evaluation with people who are marginalised by mainstream systems. In evaluation design it is important to remember that engaging a participant in the process (always ensuring they are happy to engage) on their own terms is more valuable than designing and administering a 'best' method. Ensuring people feel cared for and valued in evaluation processes is more important than methodological 'purity'. It is more important that people feel ok, or if possible, feel better, after taking part in your evaluation than your overall sample size or methodological design.

Explore causality and relationships between outcomes—This seems pretty basic advice, but there is danger of over-simplification that I have experienced around bureaucracies' fears of complexity. Sometimes a funder is so proud of their outcomes framework or 'theory of change' that to challenge the logic on which it is based through evaluation activity is actively discouraged. This is also related to the role and function of evaluation more generally as 'funder accountability' (i.e., 'we are achieving our targets and outcomes') or as 'learning and reflection on complex systems' (i.e., 'how can we explore what is happening in this intervention and what is being achieved or not'). Understanding how outcomes relate to each other and the mechanisms by which they are achieved is an essential aspect of the latter, but quite threatening to the former.

Challenge funders—It is important that those running and evaluating projects with young people feel able to engage critically with those funding them. Most funders are quite open and encouraging in this process, recognising the shared aims for the money being spent to have the most positive impacts possible. Nonetheless, there are often assumptions made about what needs to be done via monitoring and evaluation, and in some cases, funders themselves are encouraging bad practice in this respect. If it seems as though there is space to improve an approach to impact evaluation in a project, bring the funder to the table too, as it could likely be replicated or have a bigger influence on practice.

Ultimately, when it comes to impact evaluation, we must each take responsibility for ensuring that evaluation practice is not undermining efforts to increase participant engagement, agency, skills and competence, or voice. Being thoughtful, discussing ideas and approaches with everyone involved in a project, reading around what others are doing, and consciously challenging invisible power structures or tacit assumptions are just some of the things I aim to do when designing an evaluation. We also need to enable time and space for reflection on our practice as researchers and evaluators, this is often the best way to avoid tangles and assure regular untangling, when necessary, can take place.

References

Belfiore, E. and Bennett, O. (2010). Beyond the 'Toolkit Approach': Arts impact evaluation research and the realities of cultural policymaking. *Journal for Cultural Research*, 14(2): 121–142.

BOP Consulting (2017). *'How do you draw a rainbow the wrong way?' Understanding young people's development in creative activities*. Edinburgh: Creative Scotland.

Deane, K., Hunter, R. and Mullen, P. (2011). *Move on up: An evaluation of youth music mentors*. London: The National Foundation for Youth Music.

Dickens, L. and Lonie, D. (2013). Rap, rhythm and recognition: Lyrical practices and the politics of voice on a community music project for young people experiencing challenging circumstances. *Emotion, Space and Society*, 9: 59–71.

Freire, P. (1998). Cultural action and conscientization. *Harvard Educational Review*, 68(4): 499.

Hallam, S. (2010). The power of music: Its impact on the intellectual, social and personal development of children and young people. *International Journal of Music Education*, 28(3): 269–289.

Lonie, D. (2009). Musical identities and health over the youth-adult transition. PhD dissertation, University of Glasgow.

Lonie, D. (2010). *Attuned to engagement: The effects of a music mentoring programme on the agency and musical ability of children and young people*. London: The National Foundation for Youth Music.

Lonie, D. (2018). Measuring outcomes and demonstrating impact: Rhetoric and reality in evaluating participatory music interventions. In B. Barleet and L. Higgins (eds.), *The Oxford Handbook of Community Music*. Oxford: Oxford University Press, pp. 188–198.

MacKeith, J. (2011). The development of the outcomes star: A participatory approach to assessment and outcome measurement. *Housing Care and Support: A Journal on Policy, Research and Practice*, 14(3): 188–198. Emerald Group Publishing Ltd.

Marinetto, M. (2003). Who wants to be an active citizen? The politics and practice of community involvement. *Sociology*, 37(1): 103–120.

Petrie, P. (2011). *Communication skills for working with children and young people: Introducing social pedagogy*. Jessica Kingsley Publishers.

Ryan, R. and Deci, E. (2000). Self-determination theory and the facilitation of intrinsic motivation, social development, and well-being. *American Psychologist*, 55(1): 68–78.

16

Evaluating Young People's Voices in Spoken Word Popular Music Projects

Beate Peter

Introduction

The type of popular music that most young people engage with today differs radically from the popular music that dominated the charts before the arrival of Hip Hop, house, or techno in the 1970s and thereafter. The music sounds different. It is produced using different music-making equipment and is also consumed differently. Of the many music genres that have been created over the past fifty years, many are based on the use of the spoken voice: rap, drill, grime, trap, and more. Spoken word popular music is a clear and direct form of communication. To rap (or spit) over a beat, rather than singing a melody, provides new opportunities with regard to not only storytelling as an oral practice but also conveying meaning through 'sonic investments' (Brown, 2018) specific to spoken word popular music. These new affordances seem to be recognised by young people from a variety of backgrounds including those with challenging personal circumstances or a strained relationship with mainstream schooling (Millar et al., 2020).

Both educational and scholastic spoken word popular music projects with young people utilize these particular genres as a way to engage them through and with music. The role of music is distinctly different when considering these forms of engagement. By this I mean that engagement with music sees a focus placed on the voice young people have been given within the music as artists and narrators. Engagement through music means that young people's voice outside of the music itself might be the focus.

This chapter is concerned with young people's voices in all its iterations and the role their voices play at evaluating the success of a project. More

Beate Peter, *Evaluating Young People's Voices in Spoken Word Popular Music Projects* In: *Music for Inclusion and Healing in Schools and Beyond*. Edited by: Pete Dale, Pamela Burnard, and Raphael Travis Jr., Oxford University Press.
© Oxford University Press 2023. DOI: 10.1093/oso/9780197692677.003.0017

specifically, it addresses the relative neglect of young people's voice within the music and their role as artists in such projects.

For a discussion of *voice*, it is necessary to look at some of the factors that influence how we perceive young people's vocalisations of their viewpoints. That includes a discussion on how their collective voice is collected, interpreted, and analysed in different academic subject areas. At the same time, it includes considerations of the importance of individually recorded voices and what we hear when we listen to those voices. How is our listening shaped by ideologies, funders, project stakeholders and our own experiences as researchers? Our perceptions of *voice* influence how we understand *impact*.

According to the Cambridge Dictionary (n.d.), *impact* is 'the powerful effect that something, especially something new, has on a situation or person'. Impact, then, can become visible or expressed in a variety of ways, and such reading of impact allows for a phenomenological approach. However, in the context of higher education in the United Kingdom, the prevailing definition of *impact* is provided by the Research Excellence Framework (REF), a national assessment exercise that allocates research money according to the 'quality' of institutions' research. This definition frames impact as something measurable and quantifiable, as it is understood as: 'an effect on, change or benefit to the economy, society, culture, public policy or services, health, the environment or quality of life, beyond academia' (UKRI, online, 2022). If the former definition assumes an individual, qualitative approach to data, the latter understands impact as taking place across cohorts and as a quantitative exercise. This chapter is to advocate neither but, instead, to point at the difficulty of recording and measuring *impact* outside of a cause-effect scenario that can be planned and quantified easily.

This is particularly important for the *evaluation* of artistic projects, as creativity plays a crucial role. Creativity can be measured in many different ways, including the quality of the creative output, linking it to the level of training that is provided and received in order to be able to produce such output, or the acquisition of transferable skills. Yet, there is also an element of creativity that needs to be considered but is indefinitely harder to measure. This element is linked to notions of change and impact within a young person that might not be detectable, causal, linear, progressive. It is related to questions of creative choice. In the case of spoken word popular music projects and young people as artists, creativity might be related to the choice of words indeed, but also to not choosing specific words, to narrate a track in a particular way, to use breath, breaks, flow, or embodied articulation to convey meaning and *impact*.

The issue of capturing *impact* is then further complicated by the different ways in which various stake holders and audiences wish to see it captured. Subsequently, the framing of projects, the articulation of research questions and outcomes, the research design, the methods, and, of course, project evaluations are all shaped by not only funders' understanding of *impact* but also the importance they assign to it. This chapter does not provide answers to the questions concerning the evaluation of projects and their embedded measurement of quality and *impact*. Instead, it raises the question of what kind of change we need to capture, when we want to see it documented, and which methods help us to measure the change. It is, therefore, necessary to clearly distinguish between the *evaluation* of a project and its *assessment*. If *assessment* is 'the act of judging or deciding the amount, value, quality, or importance of something, or the judgment or decision that is made' (Cambridge Dictionary, n.d.), *evaluation* is understood to be 'the process of judging or calculating the quality, importance, amount, or value of some-thing' (Cambridge Dictionary, n.d.). The definitions differ insofar that the former focuses on a specific moment in time, whereas the latter focuses on a process. More importantly for this chapter, assessments look at how well a person performs against a threshold or standard that is set—they are diag-nostic. *Evaluations* focus on process. Here, the project itself is under scrutiny. It would be a missed opportunity to limit the evaluation of a project to one moment during the project's lifetime, most commonly at the end. Instead, *evaluation* should be considered as a permanent tool to be available to people involved in projects so that they can adjust accordingly. Although *evaluations* include qualitative judgments perhaps more than assessments, they should be included in any *assessment* of a project's success. It is, therefore, one of the aims of this chapter to promote the assessments of projects through different lenses so that *impact* can be recognised at various stages of a project and be built upon when further developing ideas and theories about young people, music, and communication.

Assuming from the relative popularity of spoken word popular music that young people wish to communicate in a clear and direct way, it is funda-mental for the evaluation of related projects to understand *voice* as appearing in multitudinous forms. Attention has to be paid to young people's *voice* both collectively and individually, and such focus has to include the *voice* as an artistic expression. In other words, for the evaluation of projects that engage young people through and with music, young people's artistic *voice* is just as important as their evaluative, reflexive voice. If we are interested in detecting and measuring change, we have to accept that it can be communicated in ways that require us to acknowledge communication as a phenomenological practice. To listen to young people in a number of different ways is particularly pertinent when they bring communication practices from their leisure time into educational projects.

Education versus Leisure

Spoken word popular music, in which the voice is used to rap, is not a prominent part of the mainstream school curriculum. Dale (2017) discusses how the OCR and AQA exam boards have implemented rapping, and he shows through a discussion of their marking criteria that this implementation fails to recognise a culturally different appreciation of music and artistic mastery. To base a good mark on the implementation of a sung hook line or the use of difficult words (pp. 120–121) means to continue to ignore the narrative that young people create through their spitting and is the result of a reliance on the traditional Western canon and a preference for the melodic development of a piece of music, the sung voice (rather than the spoken voice) or traditional notation (pp. 97–111). In fact, one might wonder whether the 'antipathy of the "classical" establishment' (Dale, 2017: 112) to include spoken word popular music is the reason why organisations outside of mainstream schooling use this kind of music successfully to engage (or re-engage) young people in education. There are a number of national charities and social enterprises that aim to provide opportunities for young people from disadvantaged backgrounds to engage with music. Youth Music, for example, enable young people to 'make, learn and earn in music' (https,//youthmusic. org.uk/about-us). Noise Solution 'strive to transform how individuals see themselves and their world, using an evidence-based approach to deliver music mentoring programmes with at risk youth' (https,//www.noisesolut ion.org/). Ruff Sqwad Arts Foundation 'aim to create meaningful cultural engagement opportunities for young people, and give them access to mainstream resources, opportunities, and progression pathways, by integrating high quality arts, youth work, industry connections, and enterprise' (https,// www.ruffsqwadarts.org/about). Similar aims are articulated by national charity Music Masters (https://musicmasters.org.uk/). These organisations work with the knowledge that young people will participate in intervention projects that engage meaningfully with the sonic character of contemporary popular music: that offer beatmaking, DJing, rapping, and suchlike. These interventions, I argue, are to be understood as genuinely educational projects, be it related to the acquisition of transferable skills, to gain access to the labour market, or to learn about its mechanisms. Moreover, the learning that is taking place is anticipated, measured, and contextualised by the youth workers and project leaders who work with the young people.

The provision of tools, skills, and knowledge is concomitant with the expectation that the young people do the learning—about the world, themselves, and their position within it. In this context, learning itself is change. The acquisition of skills and professional knowledge can be assessed easily and evidenced through their application. But there is also the learning about oneself: a reflective practice that allows young people to see themselves as persons who have changed.

A Theory of Change (ToC) can be a useful planning tool, as it focuses on process (Randles, 2013). ToC defines a problem as its starting point. With the aim to resolve the problem, it establishes connections between activities and outcomes—often in a causal relationship. These connections are based on assumptions that are made about the participation and behaviour of people. For example, the Demonstrating Impact in Music Education (DIME) group define Theory of Change as 'a means of articulating what an organisation wants to achieve in terms of outcomes for the individuals it works with, and considering whether the activities it undertakes are likely to achieve those outcomes' (DIME 2019: 2). Similarly, Belcher *et al.* (2019: 1) state that a 'Theory of Change is a model of a change process. It describes the causal relationships between a research project or program and its intended results (outputs, outcomes, and impacts), framed as a set of testable hypotheses about how and why change happens'. There is an assumption here that change occurs in a particular manner, that it is linear and progressive and also predictable. Moreover, it is assumed to be detectable and measurable, as is most likely set out when linking activities to outcomes. What a Theory of Change does not address is the *why* and *how* of young people's engagement with contemporary urban music. To answer those questions would require a more holistic, phenomenological approach that potentially makes visible unintended forms of engagement or motivations that were not anticipated. Projects that utilise the Theory of Change model might be at risk of treating the music itself, its production and consumption processes, as well as the role of young people as artists as less relevant. Popular music might only be seen as a way to reach and engage young people without asking *why* that is.

For example, in their review of the COOL Music project, Millar *et al.* (2020) state that such programmes 'are particularly suitable in engaging those at the margins of society, reaching them on their own terms through music that resonates with their own lived experience' (p. 1). The project's aims were to increase the confidence and self-esteem of its participants, and there are hints at the possibility that 'opening up' includes the consideration of young people's musical contribution. In the article's section 'breaking the rules' (that is perhaps telling in itself), the authors refer to an emerging participant-led approach and an atmosphere that encourages self-disclosure. Such consideration of the lyrical contributions of young people is a good starting point and should be built into projects as outcomes that can be evaluated. However, this opportunity was missed in this project. In their assessment of the impact of this project, Caló *et al.* (2019) admit that 'music was just a by-product of the intervention, and it was the hook to engage disadvantaged young people' (p. 994). The issue I take with this approach is that if we want to make a case for the inclusion of spoken word popular music in the school curriculum because we feel that it will be beneficial to young people not only in interventions but also in mainstream schooling, we need to find out why and how they engage: What kind of learning do young people perceive to take place? How do they measure that they have learned? What changes do they detect? What do young people want us as educators to know about themselves? And what do they want us to do with that knowledge?

In order to be able to do this, it is necessary to put music and the role it plays for young people back at centre stage. Contemporary popular music, like all the popular music that preceded it, is a tool of communication, and one that is firmly situated in the realm of leisure. Sociologists, meanwhile, continue to explore the role of leisure in the lives of young people. Blackshaw (2018), for example, argues that 'perhaps in their leisure pursuits it is not consuming that people are really after at all, but the pursuit of life itself— its highs and lows, frustrations and disappointments, the inevitable mixture of particular successes and unfulfilled dreams—and that is this what really counts' (p. 77). Blackshaw also understands leisure to be the place where young people 'attempt to reconcile the demands of individuality and community (aka freedom and security)' (Blackshaw, 2018: 75), and it appears to me that this relation is at the heart of intervention projects. I would like to take Blackshaw's thoughts on leisure as a starting point to discuss the *impact* of the kinds of contemporary popular music projects mentioned above.

By doing so, I want to discuss the communicative aspect in general and the voice(s) of participants in particular. For this reason, this chapter focuses on spoken word–based popular music that is based on rapping. As this chapter is not about genre classifications, however, it should suffice to state that I intend to invoke genres that use 'beat' (rhythmic content), rather than melody and harmony, as the foundational component. By *spoken word popular music*, then, I would gesture at beat-heavy contemporary popular music in which people rhythmically speak/spit/rap their words.

Sociologists who consider spoken word music genres as tools of communication have come up with models of explanation in order to be able to answer the questions what, how, and who young people communicate to in their tracks (Bacon, 2018; Bennett, 1999a, 1999b; Munderloh, 2017; Persaud, 2011; Rantakallio, 2019). In considering these concepts, a dimension can be added to previously described educational projects by relating individual experiences to the wider community or even society. For example, subcultural theory, as developed by the Chicago School or the Centre for Contemporary Cultural Studies in Birmingham, was to distinguish cultures according to hegemonic power positions (see Muggleton and Weinzierl, 2003 for an update on post-subcultural theory). Concepts such as that of *scenes* explained the formation of communities through production and consumption processes (Straw, 1991; Bennett and Peterson, 2004). Although scenes were originally understood as geographically fixed local communities, their character has changed in response to a world that started to be interconnected at a global level. In the of context spoken word popular music, Bennett states that: 'the commercial packaging of hip hop as a global commodity has facilitated its easy access by young people in many different parts in the world. Moreover, such appropriations have in each case involved a reworking of hip hop in ways which engage local circumstances. In every aspect then, hip hop is both a global and a local form' (Bennett, 1999b: 5).

Bennett argues with Robertson (1995) to show how popular music communities simultaneously include and exclude others through the definition of their boundaries, something that Robertson identifies as the process of glocalisation. In sociolinguistics, a field that is concerned with the way in which aspects of society impact on the use of language, similar debates take place. Alim (2009) discusses Hip Hop as a global culture, and his concept of mobile matrices that are defined as 'sets of styles, aesthetics, knowledges, and ideologies that move in and out of localities and cross-cut modalities' (p. 123) confirms the interaction between the local and the global. In addition to literature discussing the interrelationship of micro levels and macro levels in society (through music), there is a body of work by scholars from a number of different disciplines, all of whom exploring spoken word popular music for their contribution to young people's identities (Bennett, 1999a; Huq, 2003; Munderloh, 2017; Rappe, 2008; Rauch, 2010; Wilke and Rappe, 2022). What becomes apparent in the discussion on young people's involvement with spoken word popular music is their framing as not only communities of learning, but also communities of leisure.

A third body of literature is concerned with artists from spoken word popular music genres and the generation of meaning for both themselves and their consumers. Scholarly debate focuses on different aspects such as rappers' own negotiations of identity (Fleshner, 2018; Rauch, 2010; Snyder, 2018) or their narrative identity (Bruckmayr, 2020; Eberhardt and Freeman, 2015). Equally important for the discussion on communication is work on the mediating, policing, and silencing of rappers' voices (de Lacey, 2022; Dickens and Lonie, 2013; Fatsis, 2019; Nie, 2021). For example, de Lacey (2022) shows how creative practice in grime and drill music is censored, which leads to a 'denial of lived experience' (p. 14) and exemplifies the fact that 'in contemporary public and policy debates, it remains the case that sparse attention is paid to young people's accounts of their own experiences' (Dickens and Lonie, 2013: 69). Nie's (2021) analysis of Chinese Hip Hop songs before and after censorship evidences how the creative practice itself has changed, and that includes not only musical elements but also the topics that are not covered in the tracks. Rather than asking why spoken word popular music is so popular despite its oftentimes explicit reference to violence, it is marginalised. It is not appreciated in the context of leisure but situated as part of public morality and the education of value. This policing of spoken word popular music has become an urgent topic, and *Popular Music*'s special issue on 'Prosecuting and policing rap' (Quinn *et al.*, 2022) is testament on this necessary debate.

What can be learned from sociological discussions on spoken word popular music is an importance of the meaning and message that the artists convey through their music and their voices. A sociology of music entails taking stock of attitudes, beliefs, practices, and rituals at a particular moment in time with the aim to explain changes that have taken place in the past, for example modes of the production, reception, or production of music; forms of bonding; or aspects of agency and structure—all of which in response to wider technological, political, or cultural change. Intervention projects are designed with a view to initiate personal change that has yet to take place. Music, then, is an opportunity for young people to relate societal change to personal change. Accepting music as the result of negotiating tensions between individuality and community, then, the musical voices of young people in spoken word popular music projects have to be considered.

All that given, I would suggest that projects can and should function as both interventions and enquiries into the sociology of music. Projects like that already exist. For example, the *Rockmobil* that Bennet (1999a) describes is both an intervention based on the assumption that young people are drawn to projects that include popular music and an enquiry into why such intervention is needed. *Rockmobil* works by looking at *how* young people engage: this, I would assert, is a core question if we wish to measure the *impact* of projects that utilise spoken word popular music with young people. Researching rappers' voices is not new, but perhaps their inclusion into the evaluation of projects could help to better shape an understanding of *impact*.

Knowledges, Expertise, Agency, Impact: The Role of the Researcher

In the United Kingdom, universities' impact of research is assessed through the Research Excellence Framework (REF), and their definition of impact to have taken place outside of academia makes obvious the need to collaborate with external partners if academic projects are to show an impact in the real world. As with any collaboration or partnership, stakeholders bring with them a different set of experiences, knowledges, and kinds of expertise, and it is the challenge of any project design to consider these different epistemologies. Obstfeld (2017) identifies the creation of intersubjective meaning as one of the challenges of working with external partners (pp. 19–20). Creating intersubjective meaning is a question of negotiation, and such negotiations include positions of hierarchy, not only with regard to the people involved but also in relation to knowledges and experiences.

There is a number of research methodologies that have started to question the position and related power structures of the researcher and the research subjects. Moreover, they challenge these positions as fixed and work, instead, with models that suggest an equal exchange of information, skills, knowledge—equally important kinds of expertise. Koshy *et al.* (2011) summarise these methodologies as 'action research—which is also known as Participatory Action Research (PAR), community-based study, co-operative enquiry, action science and action learning', 'an approach commonly used for improving conditions and practices in a range of healthcare environments' (p. 1). Schaefer and Narimani (2021: 172) argue that there exists a dichotomy between an 'ideal' model of participatory research as imagined through total equality and a reality of very unequal partners. In their case study, it is visible through the non-academic researchers (the authors refer to them as researchers from the living environment as opposed to researchers from the sciences) starting to adopt the language of the sciences. To acknowledge different kinds of expertise without assigning values or creating hierarchies and, thus, promoting the coexistence of different kinds of expert knowledges as equally contributing has to be one of the main principles when designing projects. Moreover, different kinds of expertise have to be not only acknowledged but also communicated in a way that does not inform or create structural inequalities. The voices of all participating parties should equally inform the creation of intersubjective meaning.

Yet, reality differs. In his work with music projects that engage children who are excluded from schools, Philip Mullen (2022) understands the musicians to be facilitators. The notion of a community musician very much exemplifies this approach of professionals using their skills (expertise) to create an environment in which young people can be creative and engage with music. The research takes place when the community musicians reflect on their practice, and interventions are, if necessary, adjusted. Yet, Mullen hints at other notions of expertise. For example, he quotes one of his interviewees to comment on 'how children's knowledge of music gives them a power that is unlikely to be found in other PRU subjects' (2022: 80). He comments on popular music belonging to the younger generation and how that knowledge of and about such music makes them an expert in a field and increases their level of agency. It is exactly the question of expertise and related notions of agency that is put to question when positioning the researcher.

Unfortunately, this expertise regarding popular music is all too often dismissed as a youth cultural form of consumption. However, the young person as the expert (and musician) is a trope worth considering for its potential to answer wider questions about society and a young person's negotiation of their place within it. The knowledge that young people have about their own consumption of contemporary urban music should therefore be captured. Additionally, reflective processes should include the creation of communities or the articulation of belonging to real or imagined musical communities. Unfortunately, the time it takes to build a rapport with participants is often not factored into research projects, but this relationship-building time is crucial for researchers to capture authentic data (Peter, 2020b). This rapport is also necessary to establish if, how, and why young people decide to narrate certain life experiences and not others, both in conversations and in their tracks. The language young people use and the culture that they are part of forms an act of being and becoming that is important to acknowledge in order to help understand how young people shape parts of their identities. Alim (2009: 103) states that 'Hip Hop youth are both participants and theorists of their participation of the many translocal style communities that constitute the Global Hip Hop Nation'. Such understanding of young people as agents is not always given and reflects the different definitions and positions of researchers and layers of expertise that are called upon in projects. To be able to capture young people's own understanding and contextualisation of their lived experiences, it is crucial to consider their positions at a project planning stage: their input should be part of the decision on the shape and direction of a project.

At the core of collaborative projects are competing epistemologies that need to be negotiated and agreed upon through the creation of intersubjective meaning. As part of this process, the input of all stakeholders should be considered, and that includes various modes of communication. In spoken word popular music projects, written and performed tracks have to be accepted as other forms of participation and communication. Dickens and Lonie (2013) show successfully that lyrics serve 'as a significant means for the young participants to represent their own emotional worlds and experiences' (p. 67). At a personal level, this opportunity for young people to see themselves in the role of an artist might allow them to do it their way and move 'towards accessible and supportive modes of participation, inclusion and cultural citizenship' (Dickens and Lonie, 2013: 60).

Subsequently, *impact* has to be understood as both including a reflective element and being expressed in ways that are novel, yet tell of young people's psychological and emotional landscapes. Young people's ownership of *impact* is desired, and their voicing of it might teach other stakeholders about their experiences, learning, knowledges, and expertise as theorists of their own participation. A Theory of Change that might be used by organisations to plan their projects will have to include the consideration of a variety of communication channels. The onus is on us as researchers to develop frameworks that are able to detect and interpret all aspects of change that young people experience as a result of their involvement. That some of those changes might be articulated artistically as fear, rage, resistance, or fictional narration is a challenge that interdisciplinary scholars and teams are well equipped to address if given the space and time to 'find' impact.

Evaluation

Returning to the notion of evaluation as focusing on process, I am now turning towards the issue of recognising impact. The previous section highlighted the issue of creating intersubjective meaning as a result of stakeholders' competing epistemologies. An understanding of impact is, of course, part of these differing contexts and experiences. Therefore, it has to be accepted that impact can and will be communicated in a number of ways and at different moments in time (within or outside of a project lifecycle). A focus on process would assume the existence of a particular flexibility and space for adjustment, the questioning of evaluation points and methods— the treatment of impact as phenomenological. Yet, evaluation is oftentimes written into the project design from the very beginning and allows for limited flexibility. Thinking more radically, there is an opportunity here to include the perspectives of the young people by integrating them into the very project design. One such example is Smithson and Jones' (2021) model of Participatory Youth Practice, involving young people contributing to the design and delivery of intervention programmes. This rethinking of involvement and contribution by young people as co-producers requires a consideration of the underlying ethical principles and criteria for reflecting on such process (Schaefer and Narimani, 2021: 176). Advocating an understanding of young people as equal researchers with a form of expert knowledge that is equal to scholarly knowledge within a project necessitates the inclusion of their reflective practices, which, in turn, creates the intersubjective meaning Obstfeld (2017) identifies as challenges to collaborative and innovative projects. Overcoming these challenges can bring great rewards because, by being able to actively shape projects, young people can help to evaluate the impact that their participation has in a much more meaningful way. For example, they can evidence and reflect on impact that was perhaps not anticipated. This means that if we are interested in all the areas in which we might 'find' impact, we also need to look at 'people's behaviours, practices, imaginations, in physical and visual environments, in norms or discourses and so on'. It is only through such qualitative methods that we can 'find culture, or identity, or experience, or agency' (Mason, 2006: 22).

To be able to find impact means to be open to unintended outcomes that might emerge during a project and recognise them as being just as important as the intended outcomes against which projects are measured. Schaefer and Narimani (2021) give a great example of a research design that allows for the recognition and exploration of unintended outcomes and intended outcomes side by side. They argue for such flexibility to be written into a project design so that unintended outcomes can be responded to during a project. That includes the further exploration of outcomes with a view to advance knowledge as well as the minimising of possible adverse effects. If researchers continue to be expected to frame their project through a Theory of Change, it must be possible to articulate research questions and foci accordingly. Organisations such as Youth Music and Noise Solution continue to successfully attract funding for interventions, and their outcomes-based frameworks help to provide accountability for taxpayers' money. Nonetheless, an inclusion of qualitative methods and their qualitative, phenomenological interpretation (see Mason's dialogical explanations) should enrich intervention programmes and perhaps help to change young people's notion of their own agency.

The question that needs asking then is not so much how we can include qualitative methods and explanations but how we can frame them within a Theory of Change. For example, how do we evaluate changing notions of personal creativity or identity? How can we measure what is not consciously available to participants, or perhaps beyond the level of articulation? How can measure embodiment, culture, and affordance beyond individual subjective accounts?

We know that outcomes can be and usually are, messy and that even with the most rigorous framework in mind, they produce a variety of data and knowledges, all of which can be contextualised differently (see Mason, 2006). Acknowledging that there is not just a linear relationship between the input and output of a project is a starting point. Establishing causal relationships is only one way of making sense of data, and it would be a mistake to expect all outcomes to be relational. Considering the richness of definitions such as culture and identity, impact, when understood as 'a powerful effect that something, especially something new, has on a situation or person'

(Cambridge Dictionary, n.d.), can happen because young people respond with all their cultural-historical knowledge (Pederson and Bang, 2016). Simon Glenister, CEO and founder of Noise Solution, is right when he says 'that arts projects often revolve around grant funding from multiple sources, wherein it is dictated what data you have to collect as you are serving their agenda' (Roberts, 2022, online).

To overcome this pressure, I would argue that we need to change the way in which we design projects if we are seeking to 'find' impact. Projects need to be flexible enough to respond to a permanent feedback loop. In order to achieve this, data needs to be collected and analysed throughout the project so that unintended outcomes can be further explored for their potential. Also, there needs to be enough freedom and capacity to interpret outcomes in different contexts and from all stakeholders' perspectives. This means that the evalua-tion of a project has to be participatory in that stakeholders set the criteria for evaluation jointly, analyse the data collaboratively, and adjust their partner-ship efforts accordingly. Such call for participatory evaluation chimes with Mason's (2006) assertion that it is not only the data collection and analysis but also the contextualisation that is influenced by the research design of a pro-ject. She promotes to adapt 'multi-nodal' dialogic explanations, which means that 'the explaining that is done involves different axes and dimensions of the social experience' and that 'the ways in which these axes and dimensions are conceptualised and seen to relate or intersect can be explained in more than one way, depending on the questions that are being asked and the theoretical orientations underlying those questions' (p. 20).

To include the analysis of tracks that are produced as part of spoken word popular music projects would add a dimension that helps to bring back the focus on young people's lived experiences. As a communicative tool, these tracks are rich of data—data that might not always be in form of verbal articulations but reveals how people's concepts of self are formed and impacted on nonetheless. For example, for young people to create their concepts of *self* away from a problematic person towards the notion of a cre-ative person or even artist who is in control of their narrative, creates agency. In this context, the creation of a persona or fictional narration is as important for the expression of one's personal and group identity as is the recalling of real-life experiences (Eberhardt and Freeman, 2015; Peter, 2020a). This is be-cause the analysis of 'counter-factual characters and situations' (Dickens and Lonie 2013: 65) provides further insight into young people's understanding of their selves within a community.

In addition to the consideration of lyrics, the way voice is used also needs to be investigated. Brown (2018) discusses the use of voice as being able to convey 'more ambient scenes of belonging, enduring, or expiring [...] with artists vocalizing temporalities and affects less easily categorised or canonized in list form, less smoothly extrapolated into regional, economic, or political histories' (p. 2). She argues that by developing new strategies for listening, researchers can 'resist approaching the genre as an index of a limited range of the traumatic real' and find 'more ordinary and gradual scenes of living, enduring, and dying' (p. 3). Her advocating of Hip Hop to be listened to as an aesthetic phenomenon links with sociological theories of taste cultures (Bourdieu, 1984). In that sense, young people's choice to use 'words as weapons' (Rollefson, 2018) can be understood as an aesthetic decision that is as audible in the track as the articulation of a life decision. To police the production of spoken word popular music because of its reference to violence, in both projects and society at large, would simply be counterproductive and prevent young people from articulating that which we as researchers seek to understand.

Conclusion

Despite spoken word popular music genres being consumed by masses of young people worldwide (see Clark, 2021; FM, 2019; Taylor, 2022), they do not significantly feature in the United Kingdom's school curriculum: neither its production, nor its consumption or interpretation, is highlighted within the United Kingdom's National Curriculum for pre-GCSE children whilst the GCSE also barely touches on these important opportunities for understanding music. Intervention projects that utilize aspects of spoken word popular music production and consumption in order to engage young people plug this gap. Disengaged people seem to re-engage by tapping into an affordance that not every musical genre offers: the embodiment of sound and meaning, the ownership of one's narrative, the uncensored use of language in a creative context. This chapter set out to advocate for the inclusion of young people's voices as artists. Rappers are storytellers, so if we want to use rap as a way to engage young people, we have to listen to those stories. Moreover, the conventions, rituals, and behaviours through which these stories are told have to be considered in order to fully understand the affordance rapping provides. That includes not only the analysis of lyrical content but also aesthetic decisions related to the production of a track. However, in order to understand what it is that young people communicate through their music and to learn to detect impact, we need to go back to the drawing board. Truly believing in young people's capacity to perform cultural citizenship and thus contributing to society at large, projects need to be designed, evaluated, and assessed with space for young people's voices, and that means to take risks.

At the beginning of this chapter, I argued that it is crucial for young people to articulate what kind of learning they want to take place, how they intend to measure it, what other changes they detect, what they want to communicate to us researchers/budget holders/facilitators, and what they want us to do with that knowledge. All these questions can be answered if we include young people from the very beginning and let them help us design a project, formulate its outcomes, and develop its evaluation. Additionally, we need to take risks by creating the space and capacity to adjust projects based on an evaluation loop.

As for the question how we can measure impact, we need young people to help us 'find it', to develop a different mode of listening to their voices (Brown, 2018). As a creative methodology, such phenomenological practice can go hand in hand with more quantitatively driven methods. Mason argues that 'mixed-methods approaches raise challenges in reconciling different epistemologies and ontologies, and in integrating different forms of data and knowledge' (2006: 9). By learning from young people as stakeholders of a project what they want to communicate through their voices and also what they want to happen as a result of the communication, it can be elicited what kind of impact is desired. Smithson and Jones (2021) show how methods such as Participatory Youth Practice can lead to the meaningful participation of young people and positively impact on their participation in service design and delivery. By doing so, young people not only gain greater agency but also learn about its limits. More importantly, however, young people become the researchers and theorists of their position within communities and society at large.

In that spirit, unintended outcomes should be explored as part of ongoing evaluation. Data collection for project evaluations is usually built into its design and confirms a particular understanding and interpretation of success but also a certain directed awareness towards proposed and desired outcomes. Detecting unintended outcomes and having the space to interpret them requires time, reflection, and a certain level of openness and flexibility. Approaching spoken word popular music projects with Participatory

Action Research (see Koshy *et al*., 2011) in mind, and using both participatory methods and participatory evaluation allows for the voices of young
people to be heard and help us better understand their cultural citizenship.

References

Alim, S. H. (2009). Translocal style communities: Hip hop youth as cultural theorists of
style, language, and globalization. *Pragmatics*, 19(1): 103–127. https://doi.org/10.1075/
prag.19.1.06ali.

Bacon, E. T. (2018). Between live performance and mediated narrative: Contemporary
rap battle culture in context. In J. D. Burton and J. L. Oakes (eds.), *The Oxford Handbook
of Hip Hop Music* (online). Oxford: Oxford Academic, pp. 168–188. https://doi.org/
10.1093/oxfordhb/9780190281090.013.36.

Belcher, B., Claus, R., Davel, R., Jones, S. and Ramirez, L. (2019). *Research Theory of
Change: A practical tool for planning and evaluating change-oriented research*. https://
researcheffectiveness.ca/wp-content/uploads/sites/7/2019/08/Theory-of-Change-
Toolkit.pdf.

Bennett, A. (1999a). Hip Hop am Main: The localization of rap music and hip hop culture.
Media, Culture & Society, 21: 77–91.

Bennett, A. (1999b). Rappin on the Tyne: White Hip Hop culture in Northeast
England: An ethnographic study. *The Sociological Review*, 47(1): 1–24. https://doi.org/
10.1111/1467-954X.00160.

Bennett, A. and Peterson, R. A. (eds.) (2004). *Music scenes: Local, translocal and virtual*.
Nashville, TN: Vanderbilt University Press.

Blackshaw, T. (2018). The two rival concepts of devotional leisure: Towards an understanding of twenty-first century human creativity and the possibility of freedom.
International Journal of the Sociology of Leisure, 1(1): 75–97.

Bourdieu, P. (1984). *Distinction: A social critique of the judgement of taste*.
Harvard: Harvard University Press.

Brown, A. (2018). The strain of the voice: Hip hop's ambient vocalities. In J. D. Burton and
J. L. Oakes (eds.), *The Oxford Handbook of Hip Hop Music* (online). Oxford: Oxford
Academic. https://doi.org/10.1093/oxfordhb/9780190281090.013.3.

Bruckmayr, P. (2020). 'When I'm on the mic everything is Ḥarām': Narrative identity and
modern subjectivities among American rap artists. In D. Jung and K. Sinclair (eds.),
*Muslim Subjectivities in Global Modernity: Islamic Traditions and the Construction of
Modern Muslim Identities*. Netherlands: Brill-i-Sense, pp. 238–268.

Caló, F., Steiner, A., Millar, S. and Teasdale, S. (2019). The impact of a community-based
music intervention on the health and well-being of young people: A realist evaluation.
Health Soc Care Community, 28: 988–997. https://doi.org/10.1111/hsc.12931.

Cambridge Dictionary. (n.d.). Change. https://dictionary.cambridge.org/dictionary/engl
ish/change

Cambridge Dictionary. (n.d.). Impact. https://dictionary.cambridge.org/dictionary/engl
ish/impact

Cambridge Dictionary (n.d.). Evaluation. https://dictionary.cambridge.org/dictionary/
english/evaluation.

Clark, B. (2021, February 26). The top 10 genres in the music industry. *Musician Wave*. https://www.musicianwave.com/top-music-genres/.

Dale, P. (2017). *Engaging students with music education: DJ decks, urban music and child-centred learning*. Milton Park, Oxfordshire: Taylor & Francis. https://doi.org/10.4324/9781315718057.

De Lacey, A. (2022). Live and direct? Censorship and racialised public morality in grime and drill music. *Popular Music*, 41(4): 495–510. https://doi.org/10.1017/S026114302 2000551.

Demonstrating Impact in Music Education (DIME) (2019). *A briefing paper for the music education sector*. https://musicmasters.org.uk/wp-content/uploads/2020/09/Demonstrating-Impact-a-briefing-paper-for-the-music-education-sector.pdf.

Dickens, L., and Lonie, D. (2013). Rap, rhythm and recognition: Lyrical practices and the politics of voice on a community music project for young people experiencing challenging circumstances. *Emotion, Space and Society*, 9: 59–71. https://doi.org/10.1016/j.emospa.2012.11.003.

Eberhardt, M. and Freeman, K. (2015). 'First things first, I'm the realest': Linguistic appropriation, white privilege, and the hip-hop persona of Iggy Azalea. *Journal of Sociolinguistics*, 19(3): 303–327. https://doi.org/10.1111/josl.12128.

Fatsis, L. (2019). Policing the beats: The criminalisation of UK drill and grime music by the London Metropolitan Police. *The Sociological Review*, 67(6), 1300–1316. https://doi.org/10.1177/0038026119842480.

Fleshner, N. (2018). Prince Paul's psychoanalysis: What is it? The rap album as psychoanalytic self-exploration. In J. D. Burton and J. L. Oakes (eds.), *The Oxford Handbook of Hip Hop Music* (online). Oxford: Oxford Academic. https://doi.org/10.1093/oxfordhb/9780190281090.013.10.

FM (2019). Top 5 most popular music genres amongst modern teens. *Fame Magazine*. https://www.famemagazine.co.uk/top-5-most-popular-music-genres-among-modern-teens/.

Huq, R. (2003). Global youth cultures in localized spaces: The case of the UK new Asian dance music and French rap. In D. Muggleton and R. Weinzierl (eds.), *The post-subcultures Reader*. Oxford, Oxfordshire: Berg, pp. 195–208.

Koshy, E., Koshy, V. and Waterman, H. (2011). *Action research in healthcare*. London: Sage.

Mason, J. (2006). Mixing methods in a qualitatively driven way. *Qualitative Research*, 6(1): 9–25. https://doi.org/10.1177/1468794106058866.

Millar, S. R., Steiner, A., Caló, F. and Teasdale, S. (2020). COOL Music, a 'bottom-up' music intervention for hard-to reach young people in Scotland. *British Journal of Music Education*, 37(1): 87–98. https,//doi.org/10.1017/S0265051719000226.

Muggleton, D. and Weinzierl, R. (eds.) (2003). *The post-subcultures reader*. Oxford: Berg.

Mullen, P. (2022). *Changing voices, music making with children excluded from school*. Lausanne, Switzerland: Peter Lang.

Munderloh, M. K. (2017). Rap in Germany—Multicultural narratives of the Berlin republic. In U. Schütte (ed.), *German Popular Music: A Companion*. Berlin: de Gruyter, pp. 189–210.

Nie, K. (2021). Disperse and preserve the perverse: Computing how Hip-Hop censorship changed popular music genres in China. *Poetics*, 88: 101–590. online. https://doi.org/10.1016/j.poetic.2021.101590.

Obstfeld, D. (2017). *Getting new things done: Networks, brokerage and the assembly of innovative action*. Redwood City, CA: Stanford University Press.

Pederson, S. and Bang, J. (2016). Historicizing affordance theory: A rendezvous between ecological psychology and cultural-historical activity theory. *Theory & Psychology*, 26(6): 731–750. https://doi.org/10.1177/0959354316669021.

Persaud, E. J. (2011). The signature of Hip Hop: A sociological perspective. *International Journal of Criminology and Sociological Theory*, 4(1): 626–647.

Peter, B. (2020a). Experiential knowledge: Dance as source for popular music historiography. *Popular Music History*, 12(3): 275–294. https://doi.org/10.1558/pomh.39678

Peter, B. (2020b). Negotiating the co-curation of an online community popular music archive'. *Popular Music History*, 13(1): 58–76. https://doi.org/10.1558/pomh.39666.

Quinn, E., White, J. and Street, J. (2022). Special Issue: Prosecuting and policing rap. *Popular Music*, 41(4): 419–426.

Randles, C. (2013). A theory of change in music education. *Music Education Research*, 15(4): 471–485. https://doi.org/10.1080/14613808.2013.813926.

Rantakallio, I. M. (2019). New spirituality, atheism, and authenticity in Finnish underground rap. University of Turku. https://core.ac.uk/download/pdf/275894155.pdf.

Rappe, M. (2008). Lesen—aneignen—bedeuten: Poptheorie als pragmatische Ästhetik populärer Musik. Der Videoclip *Esperanto* von Freundeskreis. In C. Bielefeldt, U. Dahmen, and R. Grossmann (eds.), *PopMusicology. Perspektiven der Popmusikwissenschaft*. transcript Berlin: Verlag, pp. 172–183.

Rauch, M. (2010). Diasporic or playing back? Identitätsentwürfe von Mainstream Rap-Künstlern mit Migrationshintergrund in Deutschland. In H. Adam, Y.r Aydın, Z. Cetin, M. Doymus, J. Engelmann, A. Henning, and S. Witte (eds.), *Pop Kultur Diskurs. Zum Verhältnis von Gesellschaft, Kulturindustrie und Wissenschaft*. Berlin: Ventil Verlag, pp. 110–125.

Roberts, C. (2022, February 1). Capturing the noise at Noise Solution. https://www.music teachermagazine.co.uk/features/article/simon-glenister-interview-capturing-the-noise-at-noise-solution.

Robertson, R. (1995). Glocalization: Time-space and homogeneity-heterogeneity. In M. Featherstone, S. Lash, and R. Robertson (eds.), *Global Modernities*. London: Sage, pp. 26–44.

Rollefson, J. G. (2018). Hip Hop as martial art: A political economy of violence in rap music. In J. D. Burton and J. L. Oakes (eds.), *The Oxford Handbook of Hip Hop Music* (online). Oxford: Oxford Academic. https://doi.org/10.1093/oxfordhb/9780190281090.013.11.

Schaefer, I. and Narimani, P. (2021). Ethische Aspekte in der partizipativen Forschung—Reflexion von Herausforderungen und möglichen Beeinträchtigungen für Teilnehmende. *Bundesgesundheitsblatt—Gesundheitsforschung—Gesundheitsschutz*, 64: 171–178. https://doi.org/10.1007/s00103-020-03270-0.

Smithson, H. and Jones, A. (2021). Co-creating youth justice practice with young people, tackling power dynamics and enabling transformative Action. *Children & Society*, 35(3), 348–362. https,//doi.org/10.1111/chso.12441.

Snyder, T. (2018). Rappalachia: The performance of Appalachian identity in Hip Hop music. In J. D. Burton and J. L. Oakes (eds.), *The Oxford Handbook of Hip Hop Music* (online). Oxford: Oxford Academic, pp. 443–465. https://doi.org/10.1093/oxfordhb/9780190281090.013.32.

Straw, W. (1991). Systems of articulation, logics of change: Communities and scenes in popular music. *Cultural Studies*, 5(3): 368–388.

Taylor, T. E. (2022). Have no fear, hip hop is here! Creating place and space for hip hop in higher education. In J. R. Kladder (ed.), *Commercial and Popular Music in Higher Education: Expanding Notions of Musicianship and Pedagogy in Contemporary Education*. London: Routledge, pp. 174–189.

UKRI (2022, November 1). How Research England supports research excellence. https,//www.ukri.org/about-us/research-england/research-excellence/ref-impact/#,~,text=The%20Research%20Excellence%20Framework%20(REF,of%20life%2C%20bey ond%20academia%27..

Wilke, T. and Rappe, M. (eds.) (2022). *HipHop im 21. Jahrhundert: Medialität, Tradierung, Gesellschaftskritik und Bildungsaspekte einer (Jugend-)Kultur*. Berlin: Springer Verlag.

17

Evaluating Well-Being Outcomes of the Social Enterprise Noise Solution

Digital Approaches to Outcome Capture

Simon Glenister

Noise Solution is both an organisation and generically the term used to describe the intervention it delivers. That intervention is designed to improve well-being. It involves one-to-one mentoring by music producers of youth referred to the organisation by schools, mental health teams, and social-work teams. Sessions occur over twenty hours and often focus on beat making. Highlights and reflections from each session are digitally captured by young people and posted weekly, within a secure feed set up for each participant. The feed is shared with a community of family and keyworkers identified by the participant as important to them.

Attempting to communicate the 'impact' of Noise Solution has been a central part of my role as CEO for the last thirteen years. By 'impact' what I actually mean is 'outcomes' or how participants (or those around them) perceive their lives to have changed post–Noise Solution. Initially, at the heart of my efforts in this area was a desire to provide answers that effectively pre-empted questions about the efficacy of the intervention from education/social-work and mental health professionals referring to us. Questions that invariably revolve around questions of how does Noise Solution help the young people they work with, and how does it help them in their roles or the organisations they work within.

To answer those sorts of questions, the collection of outcomes data has evolved considerably over the last thirteen years. What I hope to demonstrate is that capturing data around what has or has not changed for the participant, does not have to just be a passive, linear process that only occurs after an intervention has finished. I strongly believe that collecting outcomes data, in

Simon Glenister, *Evaluating Well-Being Outcomes of the Social Enterprise Noise Solution* In: *Music for Inclusion and Healing in Schools and Beyond*. Edited by: Pete Dale, Pamela Burnard, and Raphael Travis Jr., Oxford University Press.
© Oxford University Press 2023. DOI: 10.1093/oso/9780197692677.003.0018

the active way we do now, does not just demonstrate to external people that Noise Solution has an effect on well-being but also contributes to that effect.

Capturing what happens within an intervention as a way to improve outcomes might be a counterintuitive idea to some. Before we get to why I might believe this is so, it is worth noting there seems to be a consensus that Noise Solution is doing something right. Noise Solutions ability to have and demonstrate outcomes has resulted in considerable plaudits. Organisations who have awarded or shortlisted us for national awards in 2022 alone include: Royal Society For Public Health, Price Waterhouse Cooper, Social Enterprise UK, Music Teacher Magazine and the UK Arts Council. We have also been ranked by the NatWest Social Enterprise index as a top UK 100 performing social enterprise on three occasions between 2019 and 2023, and won their 2023 impact management award.

What has helped in communicating Noise Solutions 'impact' has often been the ability to collect and demonstrate what we hope is 'believable' data (supported by research) across a breadth of domains (principally data relating to stories, finance, and numbers)—a mixed methodology if you like. Guiding principles in collecting and presenting that data have included designing data collection that does not problematise or medicalise the participant or 'get in the way' of sessions achieving their aims; data needing to be transparent; recognising limitations in data, and trying to be benchmarkable against other data sets. Any data we present needs to be presented 'in the round' amidst contextual story and number data contributing to a broad picture of the probable impact, rather than ever claiming one element to be definitive as a case for impact. Inevitably, we did not arrive at this point fully formed. It has been a journey that has informed how we think about collecting our data.

Context: Where Has Noise Solution Come From?

My musical experience comes from a career as a professional internationally touring musician with multiple recording deals. Additionally, over the last twenty-two years, I have also held various front-line roles supporting young people. I have worked within both UK local government and youth-justice settings. In 2009 I decided I wanted to fuse music production and 'beat making' with youth work. I saw it as a route to move away from traditional youth intervention, where approaches have predominantly focused on a deficit model, for example with questioning such as what are the problems and issues the individual is experiencing? What are they unable to do and how can we solve this? (Department of Health and Social Care, 2019: 24)

Instead, my intention has been to develop an approach using the medium of music production where

A strengths-based approach explores, in a collaborative way, the entire individual's abilities and their circumstances rather than making the deficit the focus of the intervention. (ibid.)

My youth work experience taught me that what could often change negative trajectories was allowing young people to discover they were good at something, anything. I just happened to have a background and interest in music technology, so I resolved to use that. I have spent many years working with young people who have often felt were unfairly labelled 'hard to reach'. This chapter is written from my perspective as a practitioner, working with what I will instead describe as Youth In Challenging Circumstances (YICC). YICC is an all-encompassing descriptor, indicative and mindful of economic difficulties, life conditions, life circumstances, and behavioural challenges young people face (Youth Music, 2016: 24). As a term, it feels pretty 'clunky', but its use here is intended to avoid the implied blame placed on young people so often inherent in other descriptions such as 'hard to reach' or 'non-attender'.

How Do We Use Music to Work with YICC?

Noise Solution presents to young people as a music organisation. Young people are referred to Noise Solution because schools or mental health teams have identified them as facing challenges. These often, though not exclusively, centre around school refusal, attendance issues, lack of motivation, low self-esteem, low engagement, neurodiversity, anxiety, depression, children in care settings struggling to thrive, or students at risk of exclusion. Or, more likely, a combination of the above.

The challenges facing youth in the United Kingdom are vast. NHS Digital compared the findings of two studies looking at how many young people present to Child Adolescent Mental Health Services (CAMHS) with diagnosable mental health challenges. In 2017 the ratio was one in nine. Post the first COVID lockdown, that had changed to one in six (Lifestyles team NHS Digital, 2021: 4). Additionally, UK newspaper *The Guardian* (2021) recently stated that it is possible that one hundred thousand young people are 'missing' or have not returned to mainstream education following the COVID pandemic (*Guardian*, 2021).

Referrals to Noise Solution predominantly come from statutory organisations in mental health, education, or UK local government authorities. These agencies seek a solution to engage where other approaches may have failed. Presenting as a musician, rather than a social worker, mental health worker, or teacher, has proven to be a highly effective way to engage YICC where other approaches may have struggled.

Working 'one to one' over twenty hours, Noise Solution pairs participants with what researchers, such as the eminent musicologist Lucy Green, would call an informal musician. A musician and or music technologist who has often learned by:

> Encountering unsought learning experiences through enculturation in the musical environment; learning through interaction with others such as peers, family, or other musicians who are not acting as teachers in formal capacities.
>
> (Green, 2002: 16)

Noise Solution musicians employ similar methods of enculturation between musician and participant within their sessions to those identified by Green. Information and technique are shared through one-to-one project-based tutoring, participant-led and often centred around music technology. Autonomy-supportive behaviour is encouraged by the musician from the participant. Musicians do not enter sessions with learning goals or curricula, but questions such as 'What do you listen to? Would you like to create that?' The focus is on their quick practical creation of music, often using Digital Audio Workstations (DAWs), to create genres of music that the participant identifies as important to them. We mostly see musicians' and participants making electronically driven genres of music, including but not exclusive to Hip Hop, grime, drill, drum and bass, and so on.

For the most part, the first five, two-hour sessions occur at participants' homes, with the remaining five occurring at commercial recording studios (local to them). Here the focus is on musicians encouraging competence supportive behaviours, where the participant gains a quick mastery in whatever music-making process they have decided to follow.

The highlights of each weekly session are digitally captured in photo, audio, and video format and shared (posted) within a bespoke cloud-based social-media-like platform developed by Noise Solution. Each individual participant has a secure feed, titled a 'MyStream'. Alongside the music created, photos, and links, there is also a video reflection at the end of each session, posted in their 'MyStream' where the participant converses with the musician. This videoed reflection is about what they felt was good or bad about the session and how this made them feel. It is intended to underline achievements by encouraging their reflection.

Predominantly, we see YICC inviting family, carers, teachers, and key workers into their 'MyStream' community. After every session with a young person, the Noise Solution platform sends automated notifications to those significant within their private community. A link brings those people the participant has invited back to the 'MyStream', where new posts are available to view and comment on. See Figure 17.1 below for an example post, where a video reflection enables the young person to showcase that week's track.

This platform intends to mirror familiar social-media experiences where identified stakeholders, predominantly family and professional keyworkers, can easily 'like' and comment on participants' posts as easily as they would within their other social-media feeds. Why go to these lengths? What is the 'MyStream' adding? Is not the creation of music within the session enough? Or might the use of the 'MyStream' within the intervention be contributing to well-being outcomes?

Well-being as a Desired Outcome

Although using music technology is Noise Solutions 'vehicle' to engage young people, it is not about creating musicians. The organisational focus is on using musical activity to create the conditions where the participant is more likely to see increases in their subjective well-being. We primarily see ourselves as a well-being organisation, not a musical one.

I fully acknowledge that 'well-being' is a complicated area of subjective reflection. It also has additional complexities of attribution around what it is that impacts explicitly on the well-being of individuals. However, the

Figure 17.1 Example post from within a Noise Solution 'MyStream' feed, where a participant post is showcasing and reflecting via video on the music created within that session, and a Noise Solution staff member, who has reacted to (and co-created) the emerging narrative through their commentary.

balance of evidence within the literature suggests that the encouragement of improved well-being through arts engagement is well worth pursuing.

Meta-analysis has found that increased well-being improves short- and long-term subjective health outcomes (Howell *et al.*, 2007: 83). While studies such as the Department for Digital Culture and Media's meta-study on well-being cite art/culture as a vehicle for improving social cohesion and well-being (Fancourt, Warran, Aughterson, 2020: 3), links have also been drawn between well-being and educational attainment. 'Children with higher levels of emotional, behavioural, social, and school well-being, on average, have higher levels of academic achievement and are more engaged in school, both concurrently and in later years' (Gutman and Vorhaus, 2012: 3). Well-being change delivered via the arts would then seem desirable to attempt with the cohort we work with, but some form of change would need to be measured to demonstrate impact on well-being.

Qualitatively, each participant's 'MyStream' feed could be said to be a built-in rolling evaluation, led by the participant, that is shared with everyone within that YICC's invited community. There are several reasons why we are collecting reflections in this way, but on a purely practical level, it allows the

YICC to let those viewing know what is and is not working for them. It helps them set the feedback agenda rather than having someone else dictate what is collected. Before we get back to why a 'MyStream' might impact well-being, this would be a timely point to briefly explore who normally, within a participatory arts context, sets agendas around what data is and is not collected.

External Influence on Impact Capture Agendas

I have often heard vocalised by arts organisations a significant disconnect around what and why impact data is collected. This is often accompanied by eye rolls whenever impact capture is mentioned. It has sometimes felt like there is a systemic distrust of **impact data collection** within the arts sector. I have heard organisations complain of collecting data not for themselves but sometimes for multiple grant funders, with different data requirements driven by competing agendas. There is an argument to be made (outside the scope of this chapter) that the collection of impact data by an arts organisation, when collected purely for the sake of evaluating an organisation's performance, is (a) a rarity and (b) in practice a different approach from that often taken by many arts organisations.

Lucky enough to be aware of potential pitfalls with grant cycles, multiple funders, and differing data agendas, Noise Solution's evolution for its first seven years saw the organisation consciously avoid grant funding. The focus was on contracts with the organisation delivering in its role as a social enterprise. For those unclear, social enterprise is a legal business structure that generally values contracts delivering income above grants. It emphasises social outcomes equally alongside commercial and financial business outcomes (Social Enterprise Mark, 2020).

Impact data is crucial to social enterprises, charities, and academics alike. I am not saying any one approach is the right one, but what and why impact data is collected can depend on your drivers for that collection. Our initial decision to collect 'MyStream' data as part of a wider breadth of impact data was due in part to Noise Solutions status as a social enterprise. One great way to demonstrate impact is by hearing from the mouths of those we work with. As a by-product, it also enabled us to make a better case for using the service, as every participant created their case study of their experience. In this way, qualitative story data and its automated collection within the culture of each session become, for Noise Solution, one pillar in its outcomes data picture. However, some audiences might prefer/trust numbers over stories.

Breadth of Data

If well-being is linked to improved outcomes that are important to health and education professionals, it follows that demonstrating any changes in well-being would be a useful metric to demonstrate. As mentioned, there is potential for Noise Solution to use 'MyStream' qualitative data to do this, but most organisations simply do not have access to the data that Noise Solution does—let alone the resource to wade through video and report on it. Additionally, historically arts organisations have been criticised for their over-reliance on qualitative data and the poor methodological rigour in analysing it (Deane, Holford, Hunter, and Mullen, 2015: 133). Within that context, changes in well-being, based on quantitative approaches, have been a key performance indicator for Noise Solution since 2016, when *The Social Investment Consultancy* (TSCI) first published an external impact report for the organisation (The Social Investment Consultancy, 2016). We initially went for an external evaluation because we wanted to be transparent with our impact reporting.

Well-being data for that report was available because Noise Solution already recognised the need to measure well-being and had adopted the use of the Shortened Warwick and Edinburgh Mental Well-being Scale (SWEMWBS) in 2015 (Warwick Medical, 2021). We will discuss in more detail the pros and cons of that particular well-being tool in a later section. Although data was initially of small sample size (n34) in the 2016 report, the initial report stated Noise Solutions impacts on well-being had achieved something called statistical significance (The Social Investment Consultancy, 2016: 18). Statistical significance is a term we will also touch on the meaning of later, but in layman's terms, the data from the well-being scale, when analysed, established that positive changes in well-being (for those who complete a set of sessions) was a statistical probability, removing any element of chance in the results.

On the face of it, this all sounds positive. There is evidence to suggest that improved well-being has positive outcomes around improved engagement, education, health, and social outcome. There is literature to suggest, for education and mental health commissioners, that demonstrating a change in well-being would likely impact positively on the populations they work with. Additionally, the TSCI report provides an external evaluation demonstrating improved well-being as a statistical probability (albeit from a small sample). Additionally, because of the capture of highlights collected within each and every session, we are also able to pair that numbers data with the stories of each participant, created by themselves, in the form of their 'MyStream'—making it possible that we could illustrate what those changes in well-being might look like. We were starting to have a breadth of data.

Let us now return to our question, 'How might the MyStream' contribute to positively impacting on well-being?' To answer this, our focus then became what is out there in terms of theory/evidence for how we might be improving well-being outcomes. What we needed was a well-evidenced theory of change.

Theory of Change

My interest in better understanding the improved well-being outcomes initially highlighted in the TSIC report led to me completing a research MEd at the Education Faculty at Cambridge University between 2016 and 2018. There, I was grateful to be introduced to various theories and methodologies around understanding and measuring well-being. That exposure to knowledge has profoundly affected the organisation's development and how it implements, operates, and thinks about its work. One macro theory of change of motivation and well-being has been particularly influential for Noise Solution. This theory now informs all aspects of the organisation's operations, design, and thinking. That theory is *Self Determination Theory* (SDT; Ryan and Deci, 2000).

What follows is a brief look at the theoretical lens of SDT, how SDT informs the development of our intervention, and, unusually (within the third sector, I believe), how SDT informs the design of the digital platform both supporting, contributing to, and evaluating the outcomes of the programme. We will also look at how we have incorporated the automation of the collection and analysis of different forms of both qualitative and quantitative data into that same digital infrastructure.

Self Determination Theory

Deci and Ryan's Self Determination Theory (SDT) is an overarching macro theorisation of the factors needed to facilitate intrinsic and extrinsic motivation and to foster that which is needed to enable well-being to flourish. In the same way that humans require food, water, or shelter, SDT postulates that for human beings to flourish and to achieve well-being, three *Basic Psychological Needs* (BPN) are required to be present. Those three BPN are autonomy, competence, and relatedness. If any of those BPN are missing, then ill-being can occur (Ryan and Deci, 2000: 61).

> by failing to provide supports for competency, autonomy and relatedness, not only of children but also of students, employees, patients, and athletes, socialising agents and organisations contribute to alienation and ill-being. (Ryan and Deci, 2000: 74)

SDT, with its understanding of how support, or frustration, of BPN impacts well-being, is a useful lens with which to examine Noise Solution's work with YICC. Why place any value or belief in SDT? As one of the two originators of SDT, Dr. Ryan has received something in the region of 450,000 citations and is considered, in academic rankings, one of the world's leading psychologists (Research.com, 2022).

That said, little has been written about the application of SDT or the impact of deficits in BPN on the well-being of YICC. There has been even less written about SDT and music when employed to work with these populations. However, Nagpaul and Chen's (2019) literature review highlights a number of studies where this area has seen some attention, including school engagement of youth in foster care, self-direction, peer mentoring and coaching, a randomised control trial looking at SDT mentoring and its impact on BPNs, and a meta-analysis of autonomy-supportive interventions (Nagpaul and Chen, 2019: 4). Promisingly, all of them cite improved outcomes using BPN supportive approaches when working with YICC.

SDT appears to provide an empirically evidenced framework to improve motivation and well-being. These basic psychological needs of autonomy, competence, and relatedness are a potential 'road map' helping inform interventions. The encouragement of these BPN has influenced how Noise Solution has utilised music as a delivery method around which to create spaces where these BPN can be encouraged. The next section examines how

Noise Solution maps these BPN to its delivery of sessions, via both the relationship within the music mentoring sessions and the supporting digital infrastructure of the 'MyStream' communities.

Viewing the Noise Solution intervention through the lens of SDT

Taken as a whole, both the practical music-making and digital supporting elements of each session are intended to combine to support the fulfilment of the three basic psychological needs.

Autonomy is intended to be encouraged by facilitating participants to co-negotiate project goals. Musicians are autonomy supportive in helping the participant choose which genre of music is created and their role within that, and additionally to feel in control of both what is captured within their 'MyStream' feed and of who it is digitally shared with at all points of the programme This is intended to contrast with deficit-based youth work approaches, that it could be argued are often autonomy frustrating.

Competency is intended to be encouraged through the quick mastery of music technology. Quick wins using technology sidestep what could be seen as traditional barriers to music making. The musician is competence supportive in guiding the achievement of co-negotiated musical goals. Participants are encouraged to use the computer as an instrument to create their compositions, succeeding quickly at something that is societally perceived to be complex (making music).

Relatedness resides within the 'MyStream' element. It is important to underline those stakeholders' communication within the 'MyStream' feed as a two-way affair. The digital feeds are each qualitative and time-bounded entities that enable the capture of weekly 'moments of flourishing' and of reflection within a musical context. Each participant's growing competence is intended to be externalised and mirrored back at them through their 'MyStream' accompanied by the comments of others they have trusted to invite. Within the 'MyStream', participants both see themselves succeeding and see themselves recognised as succeeding by others. The intention is to encourage broader reflection on the part of all stakeholders so that participants may absorb messages of positive affirmation.

In Figure 17.2 Taken from Noise Solution Impact report 2022.

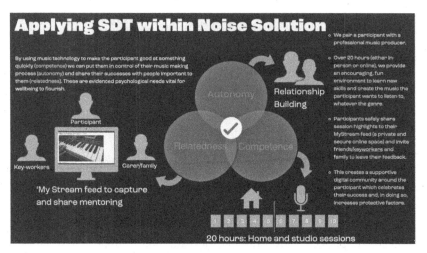

Figure 17.2 Description and visual aid to the application of SDT within a Noise Solution intervention, Noise Solution impact report, 2022.

This positive affirmation within comments left by those viewing a 'MyStream' can often starkly contrast to other areas in participants' lives where 'deficit-based' and 'problem-orientated' approaches may dominate. In their 2014 paper 'What can't music do?', DeNora and Andsell (2014) noted that narratives like this have the potential, with their inclusion of stakeholders' commentary, to contribute to a broader cultural ecology where it is

> not the music per se that accomplishes this enhancement but rather what is done with, done to and done alongside musical engagement. It is music plus people, plus practice plus other resources that can make a change for the better. (DeNora and Andsell, 2014: 8)

Indeed, the process of others seeing and engaging with the narrative may be instrumental in cementing any reflective self-realisations the process may have engendered. Talking about the similar process of digital storytelling, Davis and Weinshenker state that

> Without the ongoing support of the community, the self-realisations they report and the personal transformations they testify to are likely to

fade from consciousness without translation into action. (Davis and Weinshenker, 2012: 50)

Interaction from others both within the 'MyStream' and in conversations engendered because of them may help people internalise more readily the narrative they have created. This point is explored more fully by Robert Kegan, a constructive-developmental psychologist, discussing the mental health development of adolescents. Kegan (1994) states that, for self-reflection and change to occur, adults need to help scaffold experiences for young people where:

Self-reflection is a developmental accomplishment . . . they must step outside of their immediate categorical reality. Their experience must be transformed into an object of contemplation. (Kegan, 1994: 32)

In this way, the 'MyStream' may become a transitional object of contemplation, scaffolding reflection, and, within that process, fostering the BPN of relatedness. Potentially, this relatedness element captures and shares a developing dyadic relationship between the musician and participant—a relationship where the musician's focus is on encouraging, via music mentoring, not just relatedness but all three BPN. In theory, from an SDT perspective, this should result in an increase in participants' well-being. Does it? And if a change occurs, how does Noise Solution capture that?

Measuring 'Well-being' Change: Using SWEMWBS via the 'MyStream' Tool

To measure well-being, we need a tool. The well-being measurement scale we have embedded within a tab in each participant's 'MyStream' is the Shortened Warwick and Edinburgh Well-being Scale (SWEMWBS, Warwick Medical School, 2021). This well-being scale was chosen for a variety of reasons, not least because of the positive way in which questions were phrased (rather than from a deficit perspective). The scale is validated with years of research behind it, as it was developed through a partnership between academics and the UK National Health Service (NHS). Importantly it aligns with those guiding principles I mentioned in the opening. In choosing it, I felt it would not further problematise or medicalise YICC, and it was a scale already widely used. This meant that there was a large UK-wide existing data set of results to compare results against.

The SWEMWBS user guide describes the well-being measurement tool as a seven-item questionnaire covering subjective well-being and psychological functioning, in which all items are worded positively and address aspects of positive mental health. Questions draw subjective responses from participants on both hedonic and eudaemonic elements of well-being. SWEMWBS is scored by summing the responses to each item, answered on a one-to-five Likert scale. The minimum score is seven, and the maximum is thirty-five. It is suggested that SWEMWBS is validated as effective down to the age of eleven, though earlier documentation states thirteen (ibid.). Ease of access to completing the scale within each participant's 'MyStream' enables the musician to support, if needed, the participant in filling out the scale questions. This data is collected at two time-points, the start and end of their time with us (typically, week one and week ten). This allows for comparative analysis of bivariate data to occur against start and end changes, while also allowing for comparison of end scores against national averages, by age and gender.

In regard to how it compares with other scales used by the NHS, a 2021 investigation into benchmarking the reliability and assessing SWEMWBS sensitivity to measuring well-being change saw a research team from Warwick and Edinburgh Universities subject the measurement tool to a battery of testing. These included direct comparisons against standard mental health measures such as PHQ-9 and GAD-7, tools that are used widely within NHS mental health teams in the United Kingdom. The study concluded that SWEMWBS is highly correlated to these scales (Shah *et al.*, 2021). However, it should be noted that any correlation and psychometric testing were often carried out by the same team involved in developing SWEMWBS.

What works wellbeing, a UK independent body for well-being evidence, conducted a rapid review of the usage of WEMWBS and identified 228 studies using the scale (What works wellbeing, 2022. P.5). This paper also included results for a longer version, developed initially, called WEMWBS. This version contains fourteen items rather than seven. In comparing the validity of SWEMWBS against the longer WEMWBS,

SWEMWBS . . . has better scaling properties which means that the measurement of differences in scores may be more precise. It has been shown to be 'responsive to change' in clinical populations undergoing psychotherapy at both group and individual level. (Warwick Medical School, 2021)

Evaluative work, looking specifically at youth using the scale, saw the Warwick and Edinburgh team collate 30,000 responses to the scale from various organisations from across the United Kingdom (larger data sets of 60,000 plus are available for adults). This enabled that team to establish population score bandings and averages. From a practical perspective, drawing on this work Noise Solution can compare its own SWEMWBS scores against national population averages split into bandings of low, medium, and high levels of well-being.

SWEMWBS has a mean of 23.5, and with a standard deviation of 3.9 in UK general population samples. This means 15% of the population can be expected to have a score >27.4, so we have set the cut point at 27.5 for high well-being. Equally, 15% of the population can be expected to have a score <19.6, so we have set the cut point at 19.5. (Ng Fat L; Mindell J, Boniface, Stewart-Brown, 2016)

In respect of any well-being scale's accuracy in measuring subjective reflections, it is established that the scale is validated, compares well against other established scales, has been tested for reliability and used at scale, and provides benchmarkable UK average rankings of low, moderate, and high levels of well-being. Within these parameters what then are the results in changes to well-being that we are seeing when using this tool to measure the subjective well-being of Noise Solution participants pre and post-intervention? Additionally, how do those results compare against those UK averages?

Youth Well-being Results: Pre–post Change versus the National Average

Figure 17.3 below sets out a sample of 224 sets of start and end SWEMWBS data contributed by Noise Solution participants from the age of thirteen and upward. Breaking down by age, we see 138 participants between the ages of thirteen and fifteen—74 participants between sixteen and twenty-four and

Age Band	Gender	Average SWEMWBS Start Score	Average SWEMWBS End Score	Average SWEMWBS Score Difference	Record Count
13-15	Female	18.21	20.27	2.07	33
	Male	21.72	24.20	2.48	105
	Subtotal	20.88	23.26	2.38	138
16-24	Female	18.06	22.16	4.10	25
	Male	19.91	22.66	2.75	49
	Subtotal	19.28	22.49	3.21	74
25-39	Female	15.84	18.69	2.85	2
	Male	19.66	22.83	3.17	10
	Subtotal	19.02	22.14	3.12	12
Total		20.25	22.95	2.69	224

Figure 17.3 Age and gender split of average start and end SWEMWBS scores

12 participants between the ages of twenty-five and thirty-nine. Regarding gender, 27 percent of participants identified as female.[1]

In Figure 17.3 above in column five, we see the average score differences between start and end scores, banded by age and gender. The meaningful change threshold identified in Shah et al.'s 2021 paper on the sensitivity to change of the SWEMWBS scale is any difference between one and three (Shah et al., 2021: 1).

In Figure 17.4 below, we see a broader overview of Noise Solutions 217 SWEMWB scores compared against a UK national average score. The pie charts below show three shades of bandings. These represent delineations of below the UK national average (darkest), within two points (mid) of the UK national average, and above UK national average SWEMWBS scores (lightest).

We can see that 61 percent of participants scored their subjective well-being as sitting within the low-level banding pre-intervention. Post-intervention, low levels of well-being dropped to 38 percent. Seventeen percent (of the 217 participants represented) start with SWEMWBS scores above the UK average. Post-intervention, scores above the UK average more than doubled to 38 per cent, with a further 23 percent ending within two points of the UK average. It would be interesting to further investigate if shifts in the lower levels of well-being are more desirable and may have more impact on individual outcomes than those who, for example, shift from moderate to high levels of well-being.

Of note is that the greatest change between start and end scores was amongst sixteen- to twenty-four-year-old women, where we see an average change of 4.10 (n24). As a practitioner and CEO looking to demonstrate outcomes, our ability to granularly see these sorts of well-being change and evaluate changes demographically has led to better conversations with commissioners and funders, as we can clearly demonstrate where and with whom we see better outcomes. What else can the data tell us?

Youth Well-being Results: Statistical Significance

As well as analysing demographic bandings and giving us national comparisons to established averages, Noise Solutions cloud-based platform automatically analyses well-being data in other ways. SWEMWBS data is automatically analysed for statistical significance and range of change in

Figure 17.4 Start and end SWEMWBS scores compared against the UK national average derived from a sample of n30,000

well-being. Calculations include a T test looking for statistical significance and also range of change of well-being, calculated using Cohen's calculation. Further reading on Noise Solution's use of these statistical analysis methodologies can be found in 'Changes in well-being of youth in challenging circumstances: Evaluation after a 10-week intervention combining music mentoring and digital storytelling' (Glenister, 2018). But what does statistical significance actually mean?

As mentioned earlier, statistical significance is a term used to describe the result of a calculation that establishes the probability of a result occurring. In this case, we are looking for the probability that improvement in well-being will occur, calculated by comparing sets of start and end SWEMWBS scores. The calculation result is written in the format of a 'p' number, with 'p' standing for probability. Once calculated, the resulting p number needs to equate to a better than 95 percent probability to be considered to have removed the element of chance in results occurring. Any resulting 'p' number under .05 percent (or within the remaining 5% of the 95% benchmark) means that the result can be called statistically significant. The lower the number, the higher the probability and the better the result.

When running this analysis of statistical significance performed on the same data set as Figure 17.3 within Noise Solutions cloud-based platform (comparing start and end SWEMWBS scores), Noise Solution has maintained statistical significance at p. 0001, while seeing a greater than 0.50 shift (ranked as a large effect within shifts between start and end scores). Noise Solution results have maintained this level of statistical significance, consistently for the last six years.

You may well ask, especially if you are not an academic, why do we take the trouble to dig this deep into the data? I stated earlier that to demonstrate efficacy, we need to cover a number of domains (number, story, and financial). We also need to be able to justify and explain those results. My experience over the years has been that whatever conversation you might be having around outcomes, the other party may better relate to story, number, or financial data, so we had best have all bases covered.

No one way is definitive in demonstrating efficacy, but taken together, these different strands indicate a stronger possibility to a wider audience that the work is having positive outcomes. This quantitative data is part of that picture, and we want to present it in a way that is transparent, believable, and based in science. We are intentionally taking academic methodologies (that come with external peer-reviewed oversight) and building them into analysis to be able to demonstrate that the intervention not only improves well-being, but is statistically likely to do so.

Furthermore, the data can demonstrate where YICC start and finish compared to a national average. There is value in being able to say these scores can be compared against 30,000 other responses rather than '. . . here's a scale I've made up'. There is also value in automating that process, to be able to take Noise Solution or an external agency out of the equation and say we are not telling you this, the participants or YICC are telling you this by inputting their subjective well-being directly into the platform, alongside their 'MyStream' reflections.

This is also about flexibility of data. By that I mean, if we were to examine a set of well-being results of young women, we could ask, is it statistically significant? How do start and end scores measure against national averages? We could also pull out via their 'MyStream' the actual voice of every one of those data points within a set of data (otherwise known as a person!). Because all of our data, both qualitative and quantitative, resides in one cloud-based platform, we can link it and interrogate it in many different ways, allowing commissioners to not only see the numbers but also to directly hear the voice of each participant—allowing numbers to be illuminated by actual stories.

The Financial Significance of Positive Well-being: For Families, for Services

In the previous section, I briefly mentioned the financial impact of improved well-being. In 2019 an eight-month pro-bono study was conducted by five independent health economists and data analysts from a private data health consultancy Costello Medical. The purpose of the report was to establish what the social return on investment was of Noise Solution. In other words, for every pound spent, how many pounds were being saved by services, families, or systems? The report placed the value of Noise Solutions engagement and outcomes on well-being at a social return on investment figure (SROI) of 334 percent, or £3.34 return for every £1 spent (Costello Medical, 2019: 32).

According to Costello's report, these savings are based on a variety of estimated savings to families and services for things such as time saved due to re-engagement with education (i.e., where families are not taking time off work) or where services are not needing to engage with participants.

Estimated savings were arrived at by comparing results against pre-existing national data sets. These were contained within peer-reviewed studies of existing costs to systems within these areas. If we take Noise Solutions annual turnover and multiply it by what Costello state is a very conservative 334 percent figure, we can estimate a saving of circa one million pounds a year for families and statutory services. Again, this is another element to add to the breadth of evidence. We know well-being improves outcomes; here is our well-being scale data demonstrating change, here is what it looks like when compared against national well-being scores, here is YICC telling you their experience and what it means to them, and here is an independent estimate of what those changes in well-being are likely to equate to in cost savings.

SROI calculation is currently a simple manual process, but it would not be difficult to build in predictive cost-saving analysis and automate the reporting of it within the platform. That is one possible future route to explore, but there are others.

Where Next: Automated Audio-to-Text Linguistic and Sentiment Analysis of Video?

In a chapter that discusses digital approaches to outcome capture and evaluation, it would be remiss not to highlight what future possibilities utilising digital developments might hold. This is our 'what we might do next' section. Everything discussed here is in beta form and not currently implemented, but we have demonstrated, internally at least, that what I discuss here is possible.

Most **evaluations** you have ever seen look at the past, looking at what has already happened. Evaluative processes by necessity take place after a project has finished as organisations pull together data collected. Noise Solution is developing the automated ability to extract audio from the participant's weekly video reflections (given at the end of each weekly session) and to transcribe them to text as they are uploaded. Once in text format, the ability to sentiment analyse that data is fairly simple. By that, I mean we can extrapolate fairly easily and automatically whether someone is talking about any element of text within their reflections positively, neutrally, or negatively.

What if we could then pair that data with the linguistic analysis of that text, for example, automatically identifying concepts related to BPN within 'MyStream' video reflections—or indeed BPN absence or frustration? We would know (as someone progressed through a programme) what people were or were not saying of interest within an SDT framework and whether they were talking about it negatively, positively, or neutrally. We also have this as a beta within the platform.

It would be another short step to apply machine learning and react to that absence with automated suggestions to musicians or those viewing a 'MyStream' highlighting where BPN is not being demonstrated. Or, better still, suggest how to better satisfy BPN frustration. We are acutely aware that there are both huge ethical considerations in this as well as huge possibilities for a platform that collects the amount of data that we do. These advances in AI/machine learning technology, automatic speech-to-text, and their ability to conduct automated analysis of said transcriptions are very interesting steps to consider.

Conclusion

'There is no perfect way to capture changes in well-being' is something I find myself saying a lot when talking about Noise Solutions approach to impact capture. This is often followed by me saying, '.anyone who says there is, is selling snake oil'. I think, as a paired set of statements, these have greatly informed my approach to impact capture and analysis. It encapsulates both how hard the task is and how we need to be careful, indeed sceptical, about what and how we view the evidence.

Everything I have talked about regarding collecting data has to happen in a way that does not get in the way of what is truly important, the experience of the young person. The purpose of Noise Solution is to be strengths based, not deficit based. SDT tells us quite clearly that lack of autonomy or 'feeling controlled' is a demotivator. Acting in any way that medicalises or problematises young people can feel controlling and could therefore be considered problematic. This has often been a stumbling block for organisations as many feedback mechanisms used to capture impact can do just this and thus get in the way and feel controlling. For example, when was the last time you felt good about someone saying—'here, you have to fill out this feedback form'? Ever felt intrinsically motivated to do that, especially if it was giving you a scale asking how bad do you feel about x? No, me neither. Intentionally, as far as any Noise Solution participant is concerned, all they are doing (apart from answering seven brief positively framed well-being questions; SWEMWBS) in week one and week ten is making music and posting about it, in a way that should feel natural as it mirrors social-media experiences. Yet the breadth of data and what we can extrapolate from qualitative and quantitative data, within a digital infrastructure where everything from referral forms/engagement of family and professionals within the platform/who said what when, all collected in one data 'bucket of truth', is pretty deep.

It is quite simple what Noise Solution does. We enable young people to take control of an element of their lives (autonomy), often against a backdrop of things not going so well. We then make them good at something they care about, their music, and we do so quickly (competence). Technology allows us to mirror their success back at the young person. That same technology enables their significant adults to also experience or 'see' and engage in that success. Vitally, for the participant, that facilitates them 'feeling seen' as successful by those significant (relatedness). As mentioned in the title, we believe capturing the outcomes contributes to the outcomes.

However fantastic that might be, if we were not able to capture the data around this, then it might as well not have happened. The reality is that if you are delivering music (or any) mentoring sessions with young people or adults, someone has to pay for that to happen. Impact data is like a menu at a restaurant from which commissioners or funders can choose to buy from you or not. Did you convince them you could solve their problem enough that they would pay for your service? Were you transparent? Was your offering believable? What was the thing or things that convinced them? For Noise Solution, in those commissioning conversations, we can demonstrate the following.

We have grounding in well-being theory and what it can do to solve problems around engagement and motivation. Here is the well-being data from everyone who has engaged with us. It tells us that improved well-being is a statistical probability, and we can compare pre- and post-well-being level results against the well-being level of the rest of the country. We have halved low levels of well-being for our cohort. We can demonstrate demographically by age or gender where changes in well-being occur—oh . . . and here are the stories of every participant as they explore what those changes in well-being meant to them, stories literally from their own mouths created with the co-production of their family and key workers. We leverage these digital 'MyStream's to engage all the stakeholders in this young person's life, around a growing positive narrative. Here is why we believe that it contributes to improved well-being. Externally, we have been told these changes to well-being are worth a million pounds a year in savings to families and services.

I am not saying as an impact capture and analysis approach it is in any way perfect; well-being is subjective, after all. But, I think it is fair to say it does give a steer and insight into what the outcomes of the work are. And access to all that data certainly solves a lot of problems for Noise Solution as an organisation.

If I want to leave any kind of takeaway, it is this. You are missing a whole bag of tricks if impact data is seen as an afterthought to please someone else's agenda. Do not bolt evaluation onto the end of projects. It needs to be folded into the DNA of how an organisation engages with people, it needs to not get in the way of any work done, it needs to have breadth, and it needs to have depth. As someone once said to me at the start of my impact capture journey, if you are not sure where to start, you just need to start collecting something.

References

Costello Medical (2019). *Social return on investment report*. https://issuu.com/noisesol utionuk/docs/sroi_report_final_july [accessed January 18, 2022].

Davis, A. and Weinshenker, D. (2012). Digital Storytelling and Authoring Identity In C. Ching and B. Foley (eds.), *Constructing the Self in a Digital World*. Cambridge University, pp. 47–74.

Deane, K., Holford, A., Hunter, R. and Mullen, P. (2015). Power of equality 2. http://netw ork.youthmusic.org.uk/learning/research/power-equality-2-final-evaluation-youth-musics-musical-inclusion-programme-2012-20 [accessed January 18, 2022].

DeNora, T. and Andsell, G. (2014). What can't music do? *Psychology of Well-Being: Theory, Research and Practice*, 23(4): 1–10.

Department of Health and Social Care (2019). Strengths-based approach: Practice Framework and Practice Handbook. https://assets.publishing.service.gov.uk/gov ernment/uploads/system/uploads/attachment_data/file/7781 [accessed September 10, 2022].

Fancourt, D. Warran, K. and Aughterson, H. (2020). Evidence summary for policy: The role of arts in improving health and well-being. Report to the Department for Digital, Culture, Media & Sport. https://www.gov.uk/government/publications/evidence-summary-for-policy-the-role-of-arts-in-improving-health-and-wellbeing [accessed October 2022].

Glenister, S. (2018). Changes in well-being of youth in challenging circumstances: Evaluation after a 10-week intervention combining music mentoring and digital story-telling. *Transform*, 1(1): 59–80.

Green, L. (2002). *How popular musicians learn*. Aldershot: Ashgate.

Gutman, L. and Vorhaus, J. (2012). *The impact of pupil behaviour and well-being on educational outcomes*. https://assets.publishing.service.gov.uk/government/uploads/system/

uploads/attachment_data/file/219638/DFE-RR253.pdf [accessed October 10, 2022]. London, UK.

Howell, R., Kern, M. L. and Lyubomirsky, S. (2007). Health benefits: Meta-analytically determining the impact of well-being on objective health outcomes. *Health Psychology Review*, 1(1): 83–136.

Kegan, R. (1994). *In over our heads: The mental demands of modern life*. Harvard University Press.

Lifestyles Team, NHS Digital. (2021). *Mental health of children and young people in England, 2020: Wave 1 follow up to the 2017 survey*. https://digital.nhs.uk/data-and-information/publications/statistical/mental-health-of-children-and-young-peo ple-in-england/2020-wave-1-follow-up# [accessed September 1, 2022]. University of Cambridge and University of Exeter.

Nagpaul, T. and Chen, J. (2019). Self-determination theory as a framework for under-standing needs of youth at-risk: Perspectives of social service professionals. *Children and Youth Services Review*, 99 (1): 328–342.

Ng Fat, L., Scholes, S., Boniface, S., *et al.* (2016). Evaluating and establishing national norms for mental well-being using the short Warwick–Edinburgh Mental Well-being Scale (SWEMWBS). *Findings from the Health Survey for England. Qualitative Life Research* 26: 1129–1144.

Noise Solution. (2022). Impact report. https://issuu.com/noisesolutionuk/docs/ noise_solution_impact_report_2022?fr=xKAE9_zU1NQ   [accessed   January 18, 2022], p. 8.

Best Psychology Scientists. (2022). *Research.com*. https://research.com/scientists-ranki ngs/psychology [accessed November 2, 2022].

Ryan, R. and Deci, E. (2000). Self determination theory and the facilitation of intrinsic motivation: Social Development, and Well-Being. *American Psychologist*, 55(1): 68–78. https://doi.org/10.1037/0003-066X.55.1.68.

Savage, M. (2021). Hunt launched to find 'ghost children'. *The Guardian*. https://www.theg uardian.com/society/2021/dec/12/hunt-launched-to-find-ghost-children-missing-from-schools-in-england [accessed December 1, 2022].

Shah, N. Cader, M. Andrews, B. McCabe, R. and Stewart-Brown, S. (2021). Short Warwick-Edinburgh Mental Well-being Scale (SWEMWBS): Performance in a clinical sample in relation to PHQ-9 and GAD. *Health and Quality Life Outcomes*, 19 (260). doi:10.1186/s12955-021-01882-x.

Social Enterprise Mark. (2020). What is Social Enterprise? *Social Enterprise Mark*. https:// www.socialenterprisemark.org.uk/what-is-social-enterprise/#toggle-id-5   [accessed July 31, 2022].

The Social Investment Consultancy. (2016). Noise Solution external evaluation report. *Youth   Music*.   https://network.youthmusic.org.uk/posts/cabinet-office-funded-imp act-audit-states-noise-solution-sta [accessed July 31, 2022].

Ryan, R. and Deci E. (2000). Self-determination theory and facilitation of intrinsic mo-tivation, social development and well-being. *American Psychologist*, 55(1): 68–78. doi: 10.1037/0003-066X.55.1.68F

Warwick Medical School. (2021). Collect, score, analyse and interpret (S)WEMWBS. https://warwick.ac.uk/fac/sci/med/research/platform/wemwbs/using/howto [accessed November 10, 2022].

What Works Wellbeing. (May 2022). Rapid Review of Wellbeing Evaluation Research Using the Warwick-Edinburgh Mental Well-Being Scales (WEMWBS). [Online]. https://whatworkswellbeing.org/. Available at: https://whatworkswellbeing.org/wp-content/uploads/2022/05/WEMWBS_Rapid_Review_final.pdf   [accessed   August 21, 2023].

Youth Music. (2016). *Challenging circumstances*. https://www.youthmusic.org.uk/what-we-do/challenging-circumstances [accessed December 12, 2022].

18

Who is Heard and Who Gets to Belong in Hip Hop?

The Counterspaces of Women and Gender Minority Rappers in Finland

Inka Rantakallio

Acknowledgment of external funding: The author has received funding from the Research Council of Finland during the writing of this chapter.

Since its beginnings in New York City in the 1970s, among mainly under-privileged working-class Black and Latinx youth, Hip Hop culture and particularly Hip Hop music have been, and remain, seminal tools for creating spaces for self-expression, joy, belonging, and societal critique. By the twenty-first century, Hip Hop has become an intrinsic part of global popular culture. Yet the idea of Hip Hop as 'voices from the margins' (Rose, 1994) has not always been true in terms of the artists' gender, sexuality, or spectrum of topics: while women and LBGT+ artists have been part of the culture since its birth, they have been systematically marginalized in Hip Hop throughout its history (Guevara, 1996 [1987]; Rose, 1994; Iandoli, 2019; Strand, 2019; Rantakallio, 2021). Despite the recent global successes of female artists such as Cardi B and Megan Thee Stallion[1] or openly gay rapper Lil Nas X,[2] in contemporary mainstream Hip Hop music (often US rap), the norm is still a Black male artist with narratives of hypermasculinity and heteronormativity (Rajah, 2022: 68–69; Kehrer, 2017: 3, 20, 109).[3]

Finnish Hip Hop is an exception in comparison to the United States and most Hip Hop scenes around the world in that while most Hip Hop practitioners are heterosexual men, they are also usually white; a simple Google search of the word 'suomiräppäri' (Finnish rapper) yields pictures of almost exclusively white male artists. While this norm seems tenacious,

Inka Rantakallio, *Who is Heard and Who Gets to Belong in Hip Hop?* In: *Music for Inclusion and Healing in Schools and Beyond.* Edited by: Pete Dale, Pamela Burnard, and Raphael Travis Jr., Oxford University Press.

current Finnish Rap music is far from homogeneous and has become significantly more diverse in terms of gender and race in recent years (Westinen,
2019; Rantakallio and Strand, 2021). Yet, particularly women and non-binary
artists have been and still are underrepresented and undervalued groups in
Finnish Hip Hop.

In this chapter, I present an overview of four initiatives from the past
couple of years that have sought to advance the participation and inclusion of
women and non-binary people in Finnish Rap music. Here, *inclusion* entails
identifying what barriers cause unequal access and what types of initiatives
help bring down these barriers that currently typically exclude women and
other marginalized groups. I discuss the outcomes of these initiatives, their
evaluation, and what we can learn from them. While these four examples did
not feature systematic processes of evaluation, this chapter uses particularly
participant perspectives to discuss their impact.

Firstly, I briefly present some historical and conceptual background for
this chapter, followed by analysis of the examples. In the discussion and conclusion, I call attention to factors that advance and hinder the participation
of women and other marginalized people in Hip Hop and popular music
scenes, or what contributes to inclusion and exclusion.

Background: The Curious Case of Finnish Rap's White Male Dominance

Finnish Rap music developed in the 1980s thanks to US cultural imports
such as Hip Hop records and films and became a mainstream, chart-topping
popular cultural phenomenon during the 2010s (Sykäri *et al.*, 2019). In
recent years, women and rappers of colour have also become more numerous in the scene. Heini Strand's pioneering book on Finnish women
rappers *Hyvä Verse—Suomiräpin naiset* (*Nice verse—The women of Finnish
rap*, 2019) introduced twenty-seven artists, most of whom have begun in
the 2010s. The increased number of women and non-binary rappers also
coincided with or indeed led to (Rantakallio, 2021; Horn, 2021) the creation of a closed Facebook peer support and networking group for non-male
rappers, NiceRap, in 2017. The success of D.R.E.A.M.G.I.R.L.S (a rap group
I focus upon in what follows), which drew thousands to Finland's festival
arenas during its one-year run (2018–2019), initiated a new and public demand for women artists and a discussion around the lack of mainstream

female artists and the role of feminism in the Finnish Hip Hop scene. While similar discussions had already occurred in the early 2000s upon the creation of the Femcees Finland female rapper network (2002–2004; see Rantakallio, 2021), artistic success did not yet follow. Two decades later, the situation seems to be slowly changing, as more and more women rappers are now featured on official Spotify playlists and at festivals[4]

Also a new generation of Black and Brown rappers such as Yeboyah and Blacflaco has come to the fore in Finland in recent years. Although the racial homogeneity of Finland as 'white' is largely a cultural-historical myth and the indigenous Sámi and the Roma minorities have lived here for centuries (Hoegarts et al., 2022b: 4–6; Keskinen, 2019: 172–173), the number of Black African immigrants has increased only in the past three decades (Kelekay, 2022: 20–21). As Hoegaerts et al. (2022b: 6) and Kelekay (2022: 20) remark, Finnishness and whiteness are not interchangeable, and yet, discursively, they have often been portrayed as such. This history and norm of whiteness also contribute to how non-white groups are treated. Afro-Finns, in particular, are subjected to racism (FRA, 2018) and Finland's state-sanctioned othering and oppression of Indigenous Sámi and the Roma have also been used to prop up white racial superiority (Hoegarts et al., 2022b: 4–6; Keskinen, 2019: 175–178; Keskinen, 2021: 80–81). The predominance of whiteness is reflected in the Finnish rap scene alongside an ignorance and silence about racism (Ramstedt and Rantakallio, 2020; Rantakallio, forthcoming 2023). Meanwhile, Hip Hop (and especially US rap) have often offered representation of and knowledge about Black and Brown people to Finnish youth of colour (Kelekay, 2022: 21–22).

While not all Finnish Rap is made by heterosexual white men, they are still the often unquestioned norm in Finland, and those who do not fit the norm have been frequently labelled as 'female rapper', 'immigrant rapper', 'queer rapper', or with another epithet accentuating otherness. In the case of women, the historical devaluation of their skills and contributions to Hip Hop (Lindsey, 2015: 53; Rantakallio, 2021; see also Iandoli, 2019) is linked to the patriarchal values and structures of Hip Hop and society more generally (Rose, 2008: 118–119). For women, their lack of visibility is often explained with stereotypical assumptions such as: women are not interested in Hip Hop; women lack necessary skills, and if they were any good, they would not be marginalized; the women who appear talented must have a male ghostwriter or producer; women use their sex appeal to get to the top; women actually have it 'easier' than men because of their hypervisibility in a male-dominated genre; if some women get media exposure, women as a group are not oppressed in the music industry; and that music made by women only speaks to other women. These are just some of the stereotypes I have heard from women working in the scene and seen repeated in the media and by male rappers. The lack of female representation allows these stereotypes to go unchallenged. As author and professor of social work Brené Brown notes (2022: 177): 'Many individuals who are members of marginalized groups find themselves caught in an ever-tightening vise of two types of dehumanization—stereotyping and invisibility'.

Conceptual Framework: Intersectional Hip Hop Feminism, Whiteness Studies, Counterspaces, and Belonging

This chapter, and its approach to evaluation, builds on Hip Hop feminist theory that analyses intersecting identities and systems of social power, such as gender and race, in Hip Hop (Morgan, 2012; Pough *et al.*, 2007). As Treva B. Lindsey states (2015: 54), 'For Hip Hop feminists, excavating and clearly articulating how women and girls shape Hip Hop situate[s] the culture within a herstory of defiance and resistance'. Hip Hop feminism also includes non-binary and trans people into its analysis and thus challenges the cis-gendered norm (Lindsey, 2015: 64). Hip Hop feminism is an intersectional analytical approach that looks at how 'institutional and cultural power structures are designed to privilege those who are what Audre Lorde calls "mythically normal" while punishing everyone else' (Cooper et al., 2018: 250).

Hip Hop feminists evaluate Hip Hop culture by looking analytically and critically at content and expression, such as lyrics, sounds, and images, as well as Hip Hop's relationship with larger societal power structures, such as patriarchy and racial capitalism. Perhaps most importantly, Hip Hop feminists rely on personal narratives and perspectives (Pough, 2004: 11–13; 2007: vii–ix; Lindsey, 2015: 56–63). Listening and centering the voices of women, non-binary people, and other marginalized groups, which have always been a part of Hip Hop, is key to learning to observe how norms hinder inclusion and to creating an environment of empowerment and social justice (see also Lindsey, 2015: 54). Hip Hop feminism entails a constant process of evaluating what is harmful and what is sustainable, and thus holding artists, listeners, as well as music industry and the media accountable (Pough, 2007: vii; Rantakallio and Strand, 2021).

Hip Hop feminism has been first and foremost created *by* Black women *for* Black and Brown women, girls, and other non-cis men (Pough, 2004; Pough *et al.*, 2007; Lindsey, 2015; Cooper *et al.*, 2018). While remaining mindful of the dangers of co-optation, I argue that these critical interventions and perspectives can be applied to other local Hip Hop scenes to theorize the roles of women and other minoritized people in Hip Hop (Rantakallio, 2021; Rantakallio and Strand, 2021), if we remain critical of the contextual shift and analyse how normative whiteness shapes society and upholds racism. Feminists who are white can benefit and learn from the perspectives of Black feminists.

In my analysis, I combine Hip Hop feminist theory and critical whiteness studies (Frankenberg, 1993; Hoegarts *et al.*, 2022a). This entails paying attention to how 'White people are "raced," just as men are "gendered"' (Frankenberg, 1993: 1), how the normative whiteness of Finnish Hip Hop creates a dynamic of cultural domination (Rantakallio and Järvenpää, forthcoming 2023), and how whiteness is a normative part of Finnish national identity (Keskinen *et al.*, 2021: 60–61). The Hip Hop feminist theoretical framework is rooted in affirming Black lives (see Lindsey, 2015: 65–68); thus, any analysis relying on Hip Hop feminism must never centre whiteness, and should remain critical of the ways in which whiteness aims to centre itself. An example of the latter: I have been asked if the Hip Hop feminist criticism concerning Finnish Rap's whiteness, which aims to highlight female, non-binary, and Black and Brown voices, means that White men can no longer rap (it does not). Looking critically and evaluatively at these ways in which whiteness and patriarchy function as hegemonic power structures is necessary if we wish to provide critical antiracist feminist analysis and facilitate change towards a more equitable Hip Hop culture locally as well as globally. In other words, we should critically analyse how men as well as people racialized as white maintain domination.

Further, I use the conceptual framework of *counterspace* to analyse how the four examples discussed below represent physical and/or ideological spaces that challenge norms and stereotypes, and help create a sense of *belonging*. Belonging is difficult to define because it is often a very personal and even elusive experience that happens not only in relation to our own identity (Yuval-Davis, 2006) and sense of place (hooks, 2009) but also in relation to other people. Belonging is a fundamental human need, and 'in the absence of love and belonging, there is always suffering' (Brown, 2022: 154).

'Counterspace' was used by Solórzano *et al.* (2000) to describe how African American college students build social and academic sites of participation that challenge racial stereotypes and inequity, 'a supportive environment wherein [. . .] experiences are validated and viewed as important knowledge' (Solórzano *et al.*, 2000: 70). Counterspaces are a response to discrimination and exclusion, and thus function as social spaces where one can 'vent their frustrations and get to know others who shared their experiences of microaggressions and/or overt discrimination' (Solórzano *et al.*, 2000: 70).

Ong *et al.* (2018) applied this idea of counterspaces to women of colour working in STEM (science, technology, engineering, mathematics) and define counterspaces as physical and/or ideological spaces for minorities to express their identities, vent their thoughts, and create alternative ideas, community, and practices countering normative thinking and culture. In short, counterspace can be a separate, safer space that offers a sense of social belonging (Ong *et al.*, 2018: 210). The purpose of such spaces is to counter the stress of isolation, being overlooked, and being the only person of certain race/ethnicity, gender, and so on, as well as various micro- and macro-aggressions (Ong *et al.*, 2018: 210). I have also chosen to use counterspace as a theoretical lens in order to underscore how such spaces can challenge the status quo of heterosexual white male dominance in Hip Hop culture and rap music (see Rantakallio, 2021). Ideally, when the goal is equity, counterspaces should at some point become unnecessary. As bell hooks (2000 [1984]: 72) notes, whereas separatist spaces can be fruitful for 'the groundwork', the final goal is 'integration with equality' (see also Collins, 2013: 328, on developing critical consciousness).

Combining these perspectives, I analyse below how women and non-binary minorities in Finnish Hip Hop have created counterspaces to fight stereotypes and norms, to express their identities, and create alternative ideas, communities, and practices. These can challenge Hip Hop culture's and society's gender and racial norms and thus have the potential to impact the music scene, pushing towards inclusivity. However, if we are not able to observe how norms, such as whiteness, hinder inclusivity and oppress marginalized people, our efforts will be in vain; we must unpack and dismantle those norms. This is what counterspaces can help do: they are a response to identified exclusion and norm(s), and their objective is to increase a sense belonging of those marginalized people who create and participate in them. The opinions and experiences of participants are key to evaluating the necessity and meaning of such spaces in the lives of marginalized people, but looking at the wider context in which such spaces are created often reveals systemic issues that require further documentation and addressing (Solórzano *et al.*, 2000: 70–72; Ong *et al.*, 2018: 207–210).

In addition to being a Hip Hop scholar, I have worked as a Hip Hop journalist and DJ for several years. Lived experiences of (white) racial and (middle-) class privilege, as well as marginalization based on gender and a range of cultural and practical insights due to working within the scene, shape my knowledge production. Specifically, through my middle-class white identity, I get to feel like I belong in Finnish Hip Hop and in academia: often, the people around me look like me and talk like me, and assume that I am just like them. Yet being a woman has meant being excluded from male networks and being stereotyped concerning my DJing skills and even my research interests. One could say that I am simultaneously an insider and an outsider, as I navigate these various intersections. This leads to what Patricia Hill Collins (2013: 183) describes as an 'outsider within' position, which implies an ambiguous sense of belonging while also not belonging—an experience that I share with many women and non-binary practitioners. Further, as a queer woman, I have noticed that I frequently share spaces with queer women rappers: we frequent some of the same clubs, have friends in common, and actively pay attention to the heteronormativity in rap. These standpoints inform my analysis and application of Hip Hop feminist perspectives and how I think about belonging in Hip Hop (for more on standpoint theory, see Harding, 2004).

Next, I discuss four examples of counterspaces in Finnish Hip Hop that have sought to highlight the contributions of and offered opportunities for women and other marginalized groups to create, perform, and discuss rap music and challenge the (white) male norm. In the evaluation of these projects, I rely first and foremost on interviews and other personal accounts by the creators and participants of those spaces. Additionally, I use media articles and websites, audiovisual releases as well as my practitioner knowledge as a female Hip Hop journalist and DJ. I focus on the following cases: (1) D.R.E.A.M.G.I.R.L.S, an all-female group of eight rap/R&B artists and two DJs that took the Finnish music scene by storm in 2018–2019; (2) Matriarkaatti (Matriarchy), a Hip Hop feminist project led by two white female rappers consisting of clubs, Spotify playlist, podcast, vodcast, and an album (2017–); (3) Finnish Hip Hop feminist anthology 'Who belongs?

Writings on Hip Hop and feminism' (*Kuka kuuluu? Kirjoituksia hiphopista ja feminismistä,* 2021), where another editor and I worked with a diverse group of practitioners to co-produce a Hip Hop feminist dialogue; and (4) Monsp bootcamps and mixtapes (2020–) which highlighted up-and-coming women and non-binary artists by creating an opportunity to practice studio work and record their songs. Following the theoretical frameworks of Hip Hop feminism and counterspaces outlined above, the evaluation of the quality of inclusion in this chapter's examples is first and foremost based on the available documentation of the lived experiences (personal reflections) of the participants. I will also evaluate the response of other stakeholders to these programs. As outlined above, counterspaces are a reaction to an identified problem, a lack of inclusion; the central point of evaluation is how have these spaces increased opportunities for the representation and participation of women and non-binary artists and offered counterstory to the hegemonic male narrative.

Female/Non-binary Supergroup: D.R.E.A.M.G.I.R.L.S

The D.R.E.A.M.G.I.R.L.S showcase drew thousands to Finland's festival arenas between August 2018 and August 2019. The group of two DJs, seven rappers, and one R&B singer first performed at the renowned *Flow Festival* in Helsinki in August 2018. D.R.E.A.M.G.I.R.L.S was created by the DJ duo D.R.E.A.M (Taika Mannila and Lina Schiffer) specifically as a showcase for this purpose in cooperation with the Helsinki-based booking agency All Day Entertainment (Mannila and Schiffer, 2021: 177–178). The group consisted of two D.R.E.A.M DJs, six solo artists (Adikia, BWA, F, Nisa, Yeboyah, and as a featuring artist, rapper Mon-Sala), and one duo SOFA. One joint single, 'Koskematon RMX' (Adikia *et al.*, 2018), has been issued to date, which speaks about themes and local Finnish activists related to the #MeToo movement; the song was originally Adikia's joint single with Mon-Sala, which was extended and rewritten for D.R.E.A.M.G.I.R.L.S. In this remixed five-minute-long version, each of the artists has their own verse.

Less than a year prior to D.R.E.A.M.G.I.R.L.S' inaugural performance, in November 2017, when I was still hosting the radio show Rap Scholar, I invited over twenty women rappers on-air. The general understanding in Finland, at that time, was that there are a maximum of two or three women who rap. Due to the success of D.R.E.A.M.G.I.R.L.S' *Flow* debut (a performance that filled up a tent that fits 15,000), a showcase initially meant to be a one-off became a tour with seven additional dates of mostly festivals (Hasala 2019). Rapper Yeboyah deems that D.R.E.A.M.G.I.R.L.S 'changed things so much' in the Finnish Rap scene. In my interview, they described how the situation had been 'desperate' for women merely one year prior to D.R.E.A.M.G.I.R.L.S, but that the change began to take place rather quickly (Yeboyah, personal communication, April 20, 2022.) What they refer to with the word 'desperate' is the rampant sexism and misogyny in the Rap and music industry: the belittling and ignoring of women artists, not to mention sexual harassment. While talented women have never been lacking, it was not until the world-wide movement known as #MeToo and other, comparable initiatives that the industry realized they needed to support more women artists.

In her essay, rapper Mon-Sala evaluates the showcase's impact by stating that when a larger group like D.R.E.A.M.G.I.R.L.S came out, the media and everyone else finally had to take notice that there are many talented female rappers out there (Horn, 2021: 230). Furthermore, Mon-Sala states that D.R.E.A.M.G.I.R.L.S helped debunk the myth of women 'catfighting' and not being able to work together (Horn, 2021: 231). In media interviews (e.g., Rauhalammi, 2018) and elsewhere (Kuukka et al., 2021: 23; Horn, 2021: 231), the members have voiced their mutual support for one another. Historically, women and minorities have often banded together in order to be able to create art and music, free from gender discrimination, as evidenced in a Hip Hop context by Femtastic collective in Sweden (see Dankić, 2019) and Femcees Finland (2002–2004) and NiceRap (2017–) online peer groups in Finland (see Rantakallio 2021). In their evaluation of D.R.E.A.M.G.I.R.L.S' impact, the D.R.E.A.M DJ duo estimates that, thanks to performing at large venues for people of all ages, the group inspired a large group of listeners to support women and signalled to underrepresented people to 'go ahead' with their ar-tistic endeavours. Regarding the process, the duo admits making mistakes and learning more about intersectional thinking in feminism as they have adjusted to the needs and expectations of the artists involved during their joint journey. Further, the duo deems that although some men 'got scared' by the D.R.E.A.M.G.I.R.L.S project and there is still a long way to go for men to be more inclusive, a few male artists have by now included more women features on their albums (Mannila and Schiffer, 2021: 187–190).

D.R.E.A.M.G.I.R.L.S created a counterspace for talented female and non-binary artists in a Hip Hop scene where the biggest stages have been almost exclusively reserved for male artists. The representation offered by

D.R.E.A.M.G.I.R.L.S is undoubtedly their strongest legacy; the general public was now forced to recognize that there are several talented women and non-binary artists in the Finnish Rap scene, including Black women and women of colour. The group initiated a wider public demand for women and non-binary artists and a discussion around the role of feminism in the Finnish Hip Hop scene. Representation of 'someone like me' can even be the reason for someone to start rapping; rapper Rehtori discussed how she got the idea to start rapping only after seeing women on stage for the first time in early 2018 at the *Mimmit räppää* open mic event in Helsinki (Rehtori, personal communication, May 4, 2022).

In 2018, *Flow Festival* became one of the signees in the Keychange project (run by the PRS Foundation), which aims at improving gender equality in the music industry (Vedenpää, 2018). The festival was thus already searching for ways to improve their program; the door was open for a group like D.R.E.A.M.G.I.R.L.S to step in. Gender equality is currently mentioned as part of *Flow*'s sustainability program, and to support their values, the festival actively pays attention to the gender balance in booking artists; while the target of the Keychange pledge was equality by 2022, the festival reported having reached the goal already in 2019 when 65 percent of the artists and groups who performed at *Flow* had women or non-binary members (Flow Festival, n.d.).

Also the booking agency, *All Day*, that was involved in assembling D.R.E.A.M.G.I.R.L.S has made further efforts to evaluate and advance equality in the music industry. The agency created an equality plan in 2021 and added ethical guidelines to all their artist contracts and customer order confirmations according to which both the agency, the customer, and the artist commit to equal treatment and non-discrimination. The agency *re-evaluates* their equality plan, the diversity of their roster, and employee satisfaction yearly with the help of development discussions, anonymous feedback, personnel surveys, and artist surveys. Additionally, the agency offers equality training to their employees among other actions, and has a trainee program for underrepresented groups to further inclusion in the music industry (All Day Agency, n.d.).

Live and Digital: Matriarkaatti

Matriarkaatti, or Matriarchy, is a project led by two white female rappers, Adikia and Mon-Sala, and is comprised of clubs, open mic events, a Spotify playlist (*Matriarkaatti Monthly*, n.d.), a podcast (Matriarkaatti, 2021e), and *Matriarkaatti BTW* vodcast (2021a, 2021b, 2021c, 2021d), as well as their eponymous album (Matriarkaatti, 2022). The Finnish Hip Hop feminist platform was established in 2017. After two years of making podcast episodes on their own and organizing some club events, the two artists assembled a working group. During the selection process for working group members, they had conversations with candidates to ensure that they share feminist values (Matriarkaatti, personal communication, March 1, 2022). They received substantial funding from Kone foundation at the end of 2019, mere weeks prior to the breakout of the COVID-19 pandemic, to produce a ten-part Hip Hop feminist podcast, album (building on the themes of the podcast), and an extensive club tour around Finland. Despite long planning, the ebb-and-flow of the COVID pandemic caused the club tour to be substituted with a four-part YouTube video series *Matriarkaatti BTW* (2021a, 2021b, 2021c, 2021d), which features guest artists and was published in late 2021. Only one club event took place in Helsinki in November 2021 (organized under COVID pass rules). In my interview, they explained that the schedule of the project was also adjusted from twelve months to two years (Matriarkaatti, personal communication, March 1, 2022).

Adikia and producer at the time, Emma Kurki, describe the project as a feminist and anti-racist platform focused on Hip Hop and rap music that wants to create space for those marginalized in the Hip Hop and the wider music scene, most notably women and non-binary people. Further, they aimed to reach also those who are not yet familiar with feminist thinking and questions pertaining to equality (Matriarkaatti, personal communication, March 1, 2022). Their *Matriarkaatti Monthly* Spotify playlist (n.d.) is the only media-curated list of non-male artists' rap/R&B music releases in Finland. In their four-part *Matriarkaatti BTW* series on YouTube, they included non-binary and queer people, and one Black woman. Similarly, in their eight-part podcast, they interviewed women, queer people, and one Black non-binary person. The guests work as rap and R&B artists, researchers, and activists. The songs on the album were each made for a specific podcast episode, reflecting the themes and focus of that episode. The topics in the podcast and YouTube episodes range from cultural appropriation and racism to gender diversity, sexuality, mental health, the historical dismissal of women musicians, 'fangirling' (female fandom), and fashion. All episodes feature professional sound design. On their Instagram page, Matriarkaatti have featured short explanations about terminology and themes related to feminist and anti-racist topics (Matriarkaatti, personal communication, March 1, 2022).

Matriarkaatti's work remains grassroots and largely outside of the music industry machinery; according to my evaluation, their independence is arguably their strength, yet their impact will perhaps remain relatively small without stronger networks that would help them reach more artists, listeners, and people working in the music industry. By being independent, they can stay true to their vision of being a feminist, antiracist multimedia platform without having to conform to the often 'less political' culture of commercial entities, and can express and execute that vision by openly favouring non-male artists. However, they evaluate that they could have used more money on marketing and that their ability to impact people based on their social media reach is significantly smaller compared to commercial companies (despite having used some of their grant funding on sponsored posts) (Matriarkaatti, personal communication, March 1, 2022). Their Spotify playlist *Matriarkaatti Monthly* had roughly 600 followers ('likes') in late 2022, whereas the largest Finnish Rap playlists curated by Spotify have tens of thousands.[5] Having performed as a DJ in several of their open mics, live shows, and club events from 2019 onwards, I would estimate that the crowds have been small in comparison to other Hip Hop clubs. However, aiming only to reach mainstream crowds and spaces or 'lamenting [women's] absence in this particular Hip Hop arena can implicitly marginalize the spaces in which women and girls create, shape, and remix hip hop' (Lindsey, 2015: 59). On the whole, Matriarkaatti's consistent centering of non-male artists is unusual and thus noteworthy in any music context.

When I interviewed Matriarkaatti, they described a combination of limited time and financial resources to advertise their work and a lack of diversity in their (at the time all-white) team and to some extent among guests of the podcast. Due to the tight schedule of the studio where they recorded the podcast and vodcast, the grant provider's terms for using the grant within a fixed time frame, and COVID causing a handful of guests to cancel appearance due to quarantines and other restrictions, Matriarkaatti's assemblage of guests was not as diverse as they had planned. When planning their clubs, which have continued after the height of the pandemic (and without external funding), they have usually had more time to evaluate and adjust this aspect of the implementation, resulting in more diverse line-ups (Matriarkaatti, personal communication, March 1, 2022). They have since recruited a woman of colour as their producer/coordinator in summer 2022, suggesting that their evaluation process led to a change.

Matriarkaatti has given a platform for many new and unsigned Rap and R&B artists to perform and gain experience. This distinguishes them from many, more established clubs and festivals and allows them to offer a form of support and inclusion that has clearly been meaningful to many women and non-binary artists with little experience and networks in the industry. Implicitly and explicitly, Matriarkaatti's live events build on female-oriented 'open mic' events in Finland, such as *Mimmit Räppää* ('Chicks rapping') in Helsinki and *She's Rap* in Jyväskylä (a city in Central Finland with its own local and strong Hip Hop scene), which have been very important for non-male beginner artists to build courage to rap (as the case of Rehtori testifies above). Based on my personal participant experience where I have repeatedly witnessed artists' grateful and excited demeanour at Matriarkaatti's events on- and off-stage over the years as well as seeing artists return to perform at their events (myself included), I argue that the platform provides an important counterspace particularly for women and non-binary beginner and independent artists.

Finnish Hip Hop Feminists: 'Who Belongs?'

The Finnish Hip Hop feminist anthology *Kuka kuuluu? Kirjoituksia hiphopista ja feminismistä* (Rantakallio and Strand, 2021) can be translated as 'Who is heard?' or 'Who belongs?' with the subtitle translating as 'Writings on Hip Hop and feminism'. The book consists of essays and interview dialogues by twenty-four individuals (including the editors, i.e., chapter author and journalist Heini Strand). The book's contributors include women, minorities of colour, and LGBT+ and disabled people who work as rappers, DJs, journalists, producers, activists, and music-industry professionals. It also featured two heterosexual, white, and able-bodied men, arguably demonstrating that feminism and feminist discussions are for everybody. In the introduction to the book (which, it should be noted, is co-authored by myself), we make explicit that *Kuka kuuluu?* draws from Black Hip Hop feminist scholars such as Joan Morgan, Gwendolyn Pough, and many others, and that we wish to honor their work by adding perspectives from feminists in Finnish Hip Hop. Morgan, Pough, and other Hip Hop feminists have provided ample documentation of how Hip Hop is Black culture, that women have been integrally part of it, and that one can love Hip Hop and still offer critique about the culture.

We applied for and received a grant from Kone foundation in late 2019 to create the anthology, but still needed a publisher for it. Based upon our understanding of Hip Hop feminism as inherently polyvocal given that it 'samples and layers many voices' (Morgan, 2012: 418), we sought out a publisher who agreed to publish an anthology instead of a non-fiction book by just us two white editors (which some publishers had demanded). We then offered our authors the chance to participate either with an essay or with a transcribed and edited interview, depending on which format best suited their form of knowledge production and current situation: the assumption that everyone has the same (or even similar) resources or opportunities to produce spoken or written text is not only ableist but frequently classist. With this approach, we also wanted to avoid misrepresenting the contributors' lived experiences and worldviews on which the book is based. Whereas the essayists decided on the topics themselves, the editors suggested a broad theme for each interview based on the expertise and lived experiences of the participants.

The book critically addresses Finnish Rap's normative whiteness as well as the ambivalent relationship between US Hip Hop culture and Finnish Hip Hop. It also identifies several forms of intersecting discrimination within Hip Hop culture and music industries and society, such as racism, sexism and misogyny, objectification of curvy female bodies and fatphobia, ableism, transphobia, and homophobia. *Kuka kuuluu?* testifies that for many Finnish practitioners of colour, Hip Hop has been the only culture offering diverse representation in a white-dominated and frequently racist Finland and its popular culture. Further, it identifies Hip Hop as rooted in (diasporic) Black culture and Black and Brown joy. In essence, a central point of evaluation for social-justice work is whether it centers the views of those who are marginalized. *Kuka kuuluu?* provides a platform for marginalized voices and viewpoints and thus creates counterstory that challenges established understandings about Finnish Hip Hop culture as mostly the playground of white men. As such, the book represents an intellectual counterspace that also signals a cultural shift; whereas combining intersectional feminism with Hip Hop was not at all evident in the 1990s (Morgan, 2012), by the 2020s, Hip Hop feminism has become global.

As the book's co-editor, I have a personal investment in it, and thus assessing the book's impact is challenging for me because I naturally hope that it has been meaningful for those involved, highlighted previously marginalized diverse voices, and provided new theoretical viewpoints. We could have systematically asked for feedback from those who participated—albeit many did express public appreciation for the result and the process, and one or two also voiced criticism of some repetitiveness in the editorial process, which I consider a sign of trusting communication. The book seemingly caught the attention of and was well received among people within art, music, and culture scenes and people interested in feminism and inclusivity more generally; several people liked and shared posts about the book on Instagram. The feedback also face-to-face was exclusively positive, and people working in the music industry, including some working at major labels and a couple of male rappers, have come forward saying they have read the book and consider its message important. When I have spoken about the book to other international researchers, many have inquired about an English translation, testifying of the book's topical nature. *Kuka kuuluu* has arguably broadened understandings about Finnish Hip Hop also based on its visibility in Finnish mainstream media (e.g., Harju, 2021; Holm, 2021; Mäntylä, 2021). But only people who have liked the book have reached out to me, which presumably is not the whole truth. The book's sales have been modest, which suggests that its reach has been limited. I would estimate that, as with feminist and antiracist discussion in general, those who need to educate themselves the most often do not, whereas those who are already interested will read books such as this one. To my knowledge, the book is the first Hip Hop feminist anthology to come out of Europe, and one of few Hip Hop feminist publications that also includes an essay on disability (by a rapper with cerebral palsy; see Leminen, 2021). As such, it is a 'conversation starter' that demands people to reflect on current harmful norms in Hip Hop culture, music industry, and society.

Creating Opportunities: *Monsp* Bootcamps and Mixtapes

Monsp Records is a label focused exclusively on Finnish rap and R&B music. Founded in 1997 as an independent label, it has been a subsidiary of Warner Music Finland since 2019. Monsp appointed a new A&R, former music journalist Ida Karimaa, in early 2020, who is behind a recent initiative: a bootcamp for women and other non-male artists who wish to practice studio work (Warner, 2020). The call for participation was distributed via social media and various music media in autumn 2020. During this first bootcamp in October 2020, where established women rappers and artists of colour as well as producers mentored the participants (Warner, 2020; Vanha-Majamaa, 2020), the idea of a mixtape release with a song by each of the attendees came about. The first mixtape, *Monsp bootcamp vol. 1.*, was released digitally in January 2021. The second bootcamp took place the following autumn 2021, and *Monsp bootcamp vol. 2.* was released in January 2022. While the artists were chosen for the camps based on demos, attention was also paid to diversity as well artistic and commercial potential (Karimaa, personal communication, August 31, 2022).

Karimaa had felt that changing the male-dominated Hip Hop music scene cannot be left solely to youth centers and NGOs or collectives but must involve the music industry (Flinkkilä, 2021). In my interview, Karimaa described her frustration when repeatedly hearing how 'there just aren't any women rappers', while simultaneously hearing from women that they did not have access to networks or studios to make music (Karimaa, personal communication, August 31, 2022). She admitted that it was a 'mystery' to her that no one had done something like the bootcamps before, as she had already identified a need for this type of project while previously working as a music journalist (Karimaa, personal communication, August 31, 2022). Karimaa's description implies lack of awareness, within the music industry, of the structural and cultural obstacles women and gender-minority members face, in addition to a general lack of feminist action. This also suggests that the industry is far removed from the open mics and other venues where women have been performing their music and practicing their craft for years, as the industry has been unable to locate them. This sense of invisibility is also suggestive that larger-scale industry initiatives are necessary alongside small-scale ones like Matriarchy. Karimaa (personal communication, August 31, 2022) also mentioned that the bootcamps functioned as an opportunity for participants to vent their experiences of stereotyping and discrimination and receive peer support, which further affirms their counterspace status (cf. Solórzano *et al.*, 2000: 70; Ong *et al.*, 2018). For Karimaa (personal communication, August 31, 2022), hearing these conversations was a confirmation of her prior evaluation that the bootcamps were 'very necessary'. These experiences, and the promotion of Monsp bootcamp as a 'safe space', were also discussed openly in the media (Vanha-Majamaa, 2020; Flinkkilä, 2021). According to Karimaa (personal communication, August 31, 2022), the people responsible for the bootcamps had also had discussions about the format and purpose of the bootcamps: how to create a safe and encouraging environment for those participating, and why that is necessary for the project to reach its goal, that is, increase the number of non-male rappers and R&B artists.

The bootcamps and particularly the mixtape releases clearly provided a 'leg up' for the participants in terms of experience, being able to release music via a major label subsidiary and getting mentoring from more established artists during the camp. While the artists who took part are yet to break into the mainstream, some have had festival appearances and released more music. Further, in my interviews with two of the artists who participated, both spoke about being able to expand their professional and peer networks (Rehtori, personal communication, May 4, 2022; SiniMini, personal communication, September 8, 2022).

When I spoke with her in 2022, Karimaa confirmed that a third bootcamp and mixtape are on the way. While she 'of course' hopes that they will eventually become obsolete, the response has been enthusiastic within Warner Music Finland along with many other industry contexts, and thus the project continues (Karimaa, personal communication, August 31, 2022). According to Karimaa (personal communication, August 31, 2022), the feedback from the participants confirms that the project has been highly rewarding and meaningful, which she feels pride and joy about. This counterspace within the industry, where women and non-binary beginner artists are prioritized, has already seemingly created a small shift on Spotify's official Finnish rap playlists, as observed by Karimaa (personal communication, August 31, 2022), some of the participants (Rehtori, personal communication, May 4, 2022), and me.

Discussion: Evaluating the Role of Counterspaces in the Music Industry

The main issues that the initiatives discussed in this chapter set out to improve were representation, access, and narratives of women and non-binary people as well as other underrepresented groups in Finnish Hip Hop and rap, and thus amending stereotyping and invisibility. Key evidence in all four, fitting a Hip Hop feminist framework, has been the personal assessment of those who created and those who took part in the initiatives. The common assumption and starting point for evaluation in these spaces has been an identified need to change the dominant white male narrative and create a more diverse environment increasing belonging and inclusivity. Summarising, these initiatives can be considered as counterspaces that have helped to make marginalized artists more visible and, perhaps with the exception of the anthology, have enabled identifiable access opportunities for women and non-binary artists. The counterspaces provided by D.R.E.A.M.G.I.R.L.S, Matriarkaatti, and Monsp have functioned as sort of incubators and safer environments for marginalized groups to develop their craft. Through the combination of the Hip Hop feminist critique and counterstory of *Kuka kuuluu?*, increased visibility and networks, and above all access and resources (such as a studio time with a professional producer, opportunity to perform), these initiatives have arguably helped create a more inclusive Hip Hop music scene, that is, have produced many of the intended effects.

Based on my research, the initiatives have had a clear *impact* on the self-esteem and professional development of the artists involved as well as on the people who created these spaces. Further, they have increased interest in feminist thinking in the music industry, in the media, and among the public. In all four cases, resources such as sufficient time and money have been of the essence to achieve this. In hindsight, Strand and I could have sought additional money for the marketing of *Kuka kuuluu?*, or Matriarkaatti could have allocated a portion of their sound design budget, for example, to social-media marketing to increase the visibility and impact. To my knowledge, none of the four have implemented a systematic participatory evaluation process during or after the project, which might be useful for improving their impact and for other future projects.

Two of the projects, Matriarkaatti and Monsp, continue their work still. Continuing the broader development, however, demands that everyone (regardless of their position in the music industry) uses their power to create change and normalize inclusive thinking, that is, thinking critically about what the current norms are and how they marginalize certain groups of people. The representation of women and minorities and the creation of opportunities for them are necessary because, currently, the music industry structures are not accommodating to women and minorities and do not sufficiently recognize the existing problems such as lack of studio access and networks. There are only a handful of people like Karimaa working within these structures in an attempt to create changes while also having to deal with restrictions posed by those structures themselves; Karimaa, for example, is one of the few women A&Rs working at a major label in Finland.

She also says she would welcome other labels setting up similar initiatives as the Monsp bootcamps (Flinkkilä, 2021).

The idea is prevalent in the music industry that, if minorities were just skilful enough, they could become mainstream. This obscures the myriad structures, mechanisms, and discourses that hold this unequal status quo in place, such as lack of access and opportunities, othering via prefixes ('female', 'queer'), passively accepting that 'this is just how things are and always have been', and further, expecting minorities to do all the work towards inclusivity as if they had the power necessary to solve this situation (or what I call the 'please educate me' response). Consequently, counterspaces such as the ones discussed in this chapter have been necessary for women and non-binary artists to be able to focus on creating art and improving their self-confidence instead of having to fight dehumanizing stereotypes and invisibility. Counterspaces have also been useful for more accurately recognizing the problems, as participants have been able to vent experiences of unequal treatment that they may have been afraid or unable to share elsewhere.

As rapper Mon-Sala states in her essay in *Kuka kuuluu*, 'Dreamgirls [*sic*], Matriarchy or any other group cannot erase the problems of the music industry alone. They can however demonstrate what is wrong with the current system and what needs to change' (Horn, 2021: 235; translation by chapter author). Mannila and Schiffer, who assembled D.R.E.A.M.G.I.R.L.S, describe a glaring lack of male support (Mannila and Schiffer, 2021; Rauhalammi, 2018). Those who fit the norm often do not notice its existence and may experience difficulties understanding or believing women or other marginalized people when they try to explain why they do not feel welcome or accepted— or how they become hypervisible as the exception to the norm and thus often face unfair expectations about being exceptionally great as soon as they hit the scene. While equality training may be one way to evaluate and increase the level of awareness of such dynamics among industry professionals, also data about the number of women and BIPOC working in various roles in the industry can be a way to assess whether further action, such as quotas, might be necessary. With such actions and the abovementioned, identifiable results and knowledge from counterspaces, the need to end the marginalization experienced by women and other groups will perhaps be taken seriously, that is, their perspectives are better believed and heard.

Despite having included BIPOC and LGBT+ creators, all of the above-discussed examples are originally the initiatives of cisgender white women. This suggests that we are still far from truly equal access and resources to

even create counterspaces, let alone penetrate the mainstream consciousness or music-industry structures more permanently. On the other hand, all
initiatives were created by women who are themselves part of the music industry as artists or other actors, and thus have close insight of the problems
and what needs to change. Social-justice movements, in particular #Me
Too and Black Lives Matter, have in recent years added pressure for culture
industries to pay more attention to equity and apply various tools to reach
it—such as the 50-50 gender-equality initiative to which some festivals such
as *Flow* have committed. Nonetheless, there is still a long way to go. There is
also the risk that initiatives like the Monsp bootcamps and mixtapes are used
to 'tick the diversity box'. Without real efforts, advances towards the full inclusion of women and other marginalized groups can only be limited.

Visibility, or representation for those who are not usually visible, as
offered by D.R.E.A.M.G.I.R.L.S for example, is a tool for equity. On its own,
it is insufficient to create the level of change that is needed. However, when
paired with the provision of sustained access for minority groups, making
under-represented groups more visible can help advance change. Through
adding more voices and stories, as in *Kuka kuuluu* book or Matriarchy's
multimedia platform, we can change the narrative; but we also need to
change the structures and the culture of white cis-heteronormativity, as
the Monsp bootcamps and mixtapes have attempted to do. The recent
examples discussed above, alongside collectives and groups like Facebook
group NiceRap and, prior to that, Femcees Finland, have functioned as
counterspaces for women, trans, and nonbinary artists. These counterspaces
are still largely outside the industry structures. If the ambition is to impact
upon those structures, counterspaces alone are not sufficient. Thus far, two
members of D.R.E.A.M.G.I.R.L.S, rapper and R&B singer F and rapper
Yeboyah, are the closest to penetrating the mainstream music industry: they
have achieved major-label record deals, significant streaming numbers, and
significant cultural visibility. Arguably, however, this seems to replicate the
age-old 'there can only be one female rapper at a time' trope in Hip Hop.
Without doubt, we are yet to see women represented equally to men.

Measuring the wider, industry-level *impact* of the initiatives discussed
here is not easy: while the anecdotal evidence suggests that they have made
a qualitative difference in the lives of the participants, other impact is not
self-evident. How much time would be sufficient to see a cultural change
where equal opportunities to participate are seen as an industry-wide priority? What are the long-term impacts of the initiatives, if any? What type of

evidence counts as impact? How do we dismantle norms that are harmful? To gather evidence in relation to these questions, I have relied on interviews with those involved in the initiatives, media articles, and podcasts and vodcasts, which I coupled with my working experience in the scene as a scholar-journalist-DJ. While I believe that the chosen informants have the experiences and perspectives to assess such impact, the big picture remains blurry.

We might *measure* the wider change in the representation of minorities quantitatively: looking weekly, monthly, or yearly at the number of women, LGBTQ+, and people of colour featured on the most popular (i.e., with the most followers) Spotify playlists, in festival lineups, and nominated for industry awards, we can observe whether the percentages shift of not. But perhaps we should not settle for increased mainstream representation of women and minorities. Wider impact could mean major labels taking more responsibility for changing the still often patriarchal and racist culture of the music industry towards a more democratic one, with participatory evaluation as one key component. In terms of action, this could entail, for example, taking more financial risks in supporting the most marginalized artists, Black women and women of colour, at early stages of their careers. We can demand that rap lyrics no longer normalize misogyny, sexism, and homophobia because such language dehumanizes women and LGBT+ people and often makes these groups feel unwelcome in the industry; paying attention to language is important in actively trying to change discourse, which plays an important role in creating change and inclusivity. In addition to these forms of accountability, we can also aspire to hear more people speak out about norms that exclude marginalized people.

Conclusion: Creating Change

In spring 2022, I was a panelist in Finnish music organisations' seminar about inclusivity in the music industry. One of the other panelists, often named as one of the three most powerful people in the Finnish music industry, said that he considers it important that these discussions are also safe and welcoming for straight white cisgender men like him who do not yet know everything. Most of the time, these spaces and discussions are not safe and welcoming to people who are *not* heterosexual white able-bodied men. His comment also inadvertently suggested that only when the discussion and change happen on the terms of the most powerful can they be allowed. This kind of 'dialogue' or demands to be nice offers no change at all, nor does it benefit those who are most marginalized. Having discussions is important, but asking them to be easy gets us nowhere; as bell hooks (2000 [1984]: 66–67) states, if we always want to feel 'safe', 'we may never experience any revolutionary change, any transformation, individually or collectively'. As many have noted, growth is often uncomfortable; when the privileged feel some level of discomfort, it might indeed be one indicator for evaluation that change is taking place. This is also why I have chosen to frame the initiatives discussed in this chapter as counterspaces and not 'safe spaces', as their emphasis is on changing the status quo. However, belonging often necessitates feeling safe, and Ong *et al.* (2018) describe counterspaces as a form of safe space. Evaluating what level of discomfort and safety produces change is difficult because individuals have different backgrounds and needs, thus meeting people 'where they are at' may often be necessary. Even in counterspaces that can offer some sense of belonging, there are bound to be both inclusion and exclusion because we hold intersectional identities and do not live single-issue lives (as put famously by Black feminist author Audre Lorde).

An environment of trust, where speaking truthfully about how norms can be harmful and exclusionary is valued, and where everyone regardless of their background feels that their learning is considered important, can foster willingness to create social change. I argue that one of the most significant factors hindering inclusivity are those men and white people in positions of power who most often support only people like them. To create change, they would need to work to provide opportunities to diverse groups of people and actively question how their maleness and whiteness make them biased and unable to notice systems of oppression and discrimination—that is, to get uncomfortable. For change to become possible, it would also be necessary for those in power to critically evaluate how they themselves uphold the systems of oppression and discrimination by becoming defensive when attention is drawn to their complicity in these systems. Research about inequality is unlikely to bring change without social-justice-oriented critical action: in many instances, this will entail a look in the mirror.

In this chapter, I have traced certain norms in Finnish Hip Hop while evaluating the role and impact of counterspaces created for those who are not male (and white). In terms of structural change and wider impact—if wider is here considered a cultural change leading to increased accountability as well as increased and consistent visibility and access for women and non-binary artists—perhaps the most encouraging examples have been D.R.E.A.M.G.I.R.L.S and the Warner sub-label Monsp's bootcamps and subsequent mixtape releases. Both were initiatives created in part by people who have leverage in the industry; they were able to create spaces for artists to advance their careers through studio and performance experience and through building stronger peer and professional networks. These projects have arguably also changed public perceptions about the quality and quantity of non-male rappers in Finland.

Nira Yuval-Davis (2006: 198) notes that people often manage the fear of exclusion by trying to conform. Counterspaces instead widen the boundaries of norms. Some might say that the ideal would be to smash the norms altogether, in order to offer inclusion and a sense of belonging to those who feel excluded. In any case, it is necessary to first understand the norms that exclude people before we can change them.

References

Audio and audiovisual sources

100 *Suomi* (n.d.). [Playlist]. Spotify. https://open.spotify.com/playlist/37i9dQZF1DW Tw1ORfckhDu?si=7789283cfc974c04 [accessed September 23, 2022].

Adikia (featuring Mon-Sala, Yas Lo, SOFA, Yeboyah, Nisa, Donatella and F) (2018). Koskematon RMX. [Song]. Rutilus Musiikkimedia.

Lil Nas X (2021, March 26). *Lil Nas X—MONTERO (Call me by your name) (Official Video)* [Video]. YouTube. https://www.youtube.com/watch?v=6swmTBVI83k&ab_channel= LilNasXVEVO.

Matriarkaatti (2022). *Matriarkaatti*. [Album]. Not on label.

Matriarkaatti Monthly (n.d.). [Playlist]. Spotify. https://open.spotify.com/playlist/57L 9NphLOlSZvD4saOYfoW?si=a747d8d21122442d [accessed September 23, 2022].

Matriarkaatti (2021a, October 8). *SUKUPUOLIANARKIAA Matriarkaatti BTW episode 1 / Vieraana Pink Taco Krew* [Video]. YouTube. https://www.youtube.com/watch?v= AF6DZyttZxc&ab_channel=Matriarkaatti.

Matriarkaatti (2021b, October 15). *KAPITALISMI TEKEE SUSTA ORJAN BUCKSILLE Matriarkaatti BTW episode 2 / Vieraana Rosa Coste* [Video]. YouTube. https://www. youtube.com/watch?v=djywAwL-NL8&ab_channel=Matriarkaatti.

Matriarkaatti (2021c, October 22). *TERAPIAA PLIIS Matriarkaatti BTW episode 3 / Vieraana Pimeä Hedelmä* [Video]. YouTube. https://www.youtube.com/watch?v= 68dZPGJdiEA&ab_channel=Matriarkaatti.

Matriarkaatti (2021d, October 29). *YEAR OF THE BIMBO Matriarkaatti BTW episode 4 / Vieraana SOFA* [Video]. YouTube. https://www.youtube.com/watch?v=DV8anNSk fbE&ab_channel=Matriarkaatti.

Matriarkaatti (Hosts) (2021e). *Matriarkaatti-podcast* [Audio podcast]. Spotify.
Rap Caviar. (n.d.). [Playlist]. Spotify. https://open.spotify.com/playlist/37i9dQZF1DX
0XUsuxWHRQd?si=071543051b90469f [accessed November 7, 2022].

Literature References

All Day Agency (n.d.). *Yhdenvertaisuussuunnitelma.* https://allday.fi/yhdenvertaisuus
suunnitelma/ [accessed November 9, 2022].
Brown, B. (2022). *Atlas of the heart: Mapping meaningful connection and the language of
human experience.* Vermilion.
Collins, P. H. (2013). *On intellectual activism.* Philadelphia, PA: Temple University Press.
Cooper, B. C., Morris, S. M. and Boylorn, R. M. (2018). Introduction. In B. C. Cooper, S.
M. Morris, and R. M. Boylorn (eds.), *The Crunk Feminist Collection.* Feminist Press,
pp. 249–251.
Dankić, A. (2019). Att göra hiphop. En studie av musikpraktiker och sociala positioner.
PhD dissertation, Stockholm University. Universus Academic Press.
Flinkkilä, J. (2021, November 5). *Kaikki mukaan—hiphop-työpaja raivaa tilaa moni-
muotoisuudelle.* TeoStory. https://www.teosto.fi/teostory/kaikki-mukaan-hiphop-tyop
aja-raivaa-tilaa-monimuotoisuudelle/.
FRA (2018). *Second European Union minorities and discrimination survey: Being Black in
the EU.* Publications Office of the European Union. https://fra.europa.eu/sites/default/
files/fra_uploads/fra-2018-being-black-in-the-eu_en.pdf.
Frankenberg, R. (1993). *White women, race matters: The social construction of whiteness.*
Routledge.
Flow Festival (n.d.). *Sustainable Flow.* https://www.flowfestival.com/en/festival/sustaina
ble-flow/ [accessed November 9, 2022].
Grammys (n.d.). *Rap.* https://www.grammy.com/music-genre/rap [accessed November
7, 2022].
Guevara, Nancy. (1996 [1987]). Women writin' rappin' breaking. In W. E. Perkins (ed.),
Droppin' Science: Critical Essays on Rap Music and Hip Hop Culture. Temple University
Press, pp. 49–62. (Orig. published in M. Davis, M. Marable, F. Pfeil, and M. Sprinker
[eds.], *The Year Left II, Toward a Rainbow Socialism: Essays on Race, Ethnicity, Class and
Gender.* Verso).
Harding, S. (ed.) (2004). *The feminist standpoint theory reader: Intellectual and political
controversies.* Routledge.
Harju, S. (2021, February 14). Suomiräpin ääni murroksessa—Musiikintutkija ja dj Inka
Rantakallio kertoo, mitä on hiphop-feminismi ja miksi sitä tarvitaan. *Turun Sanomat.*
https://www.ts.fi/kulttuuri/5223881.
Hasala, I. (2019, August 24). Taika Mannila ja Lina Schiffer loivat Dreamgirls-
spektaakkelin, joka nosti artisteja päälavoille—Katso tallenne rap-ryhmän keikalta.
Helsingin Sanomat. https://www.hs.fi/kulttuuri/art-2000006214998.html.
Hoegarts, J., Liimatainen, T., Hekanaho, L. and Peterson, E. (eds.). (2022a). *Finnishness,
Whiteness and Coloniality.* Helsinki, Finland: Helsinki University Press.
Hoegarts, J., Peterson, E., Liimatainen, T. and Hekanaho, L. (2022b). Finnishness, white-
ness and coloniality: An introduction. In J. Hoegarts, T. Liimatainen, L. Hekanaho, and

E. Peterson (eds.), *Finnishness, Whiteness and Coloniality*. Helsinki University Press, pp. 1–16.

Holm, N. (2021, April 30). *Suomirapin kasvuvara*. Suomen Kuvalehti. https://suomenku valehti.fi/kulttuuri/hiphop-on-aika-seksistinen-ja-homofobinen-kulttuuri-sanoo-feministisen-rap-kirjan-toimittaja-heini-strand/.

hooks, b. (2000 [1984]). *Feminist theory: From margin to center*. 2nd ed. Routledge.

hooks, b. (2009). *Belonging: A culture of place*. Routledge.

Horn, N. (2021). Toistemme onnen sepät—Yhteistyön ja verkostojen merkitys naispuolisille tekijöille. In I. Rantakallio and H. Strand (eds.), *Kuka kuuluu? Kirjoituksia hiphopista ja feminismistä*. Kosmos, pp. 234–235.

Iandoli, K. (2019). *God save the queens: The essential history of women in Hip-Hop*. Dey Street Books.

Kehrer, L. J. (2017). Beyond Beyoncé: Intersections of race, gender, and sexuality in contemporary American Hip-Hop ca. 2010–2016. PhD dissertation, University of Rochester.

Kelekay, J. (2022). From 'something in between' to 'everything all at once': Meditations on liminality and Blackness in Afro-Finnish Hip-Hop and R&B. *Journal of Critical Mixed Race Studies*, 1(2): 18–49.

Keskinen, S. (2019). Intra-Nordic differences, colonial/racial histories and national narratives: Rewriting Finnish history. *Scandinavian Studies*, 91(1–2): 163–181.

Keskinen, S. (2021). Kolonialismin ja rasismin historiaa Suomesta käsin. In S. Keskinen, M. Seikkula, and F. Mkwesha (eds.), *Rasismi, valta ja vastarinta. Rodullistaminen, valkoisuus ja koloniaalisuus Suomessa*. Gaudeamus, pp. 69–84.

Keskinen, S., Mkwesha, F. and Seikkula, M. (2021). Teoreettisen keskustelun avaimet—rasismi, valkoisuus ja koloniaalisuuden purkaminen. In S. Keskinen, M. Seikkula, and F. Mkwesha (eds.), *Rasismi, valta ja vastarinta. Rodullistaminen, valkoisuus ja koloniaalisuus Suomessa*. Gaudeamus, pp. 45–68.

Kuukka, R., Kuittinen, S. and Noroila, F. (2021). Rap riisuu alasti—Naisen ilmaisu hiphopissa. In I. Rantakallio and H. Strand (eds.), *Kuka kuuluu? Kirjoituksia hiphopista ja feminismistä*. Kosmos, pp. 21–44.

Leminen, M. (2021). 'Jos mä osaa kävellä, nii miks mä just kävelin sun eteen?' Battle rap ja vammaisuus. In I. Rantakallio and H. Strand (eds.), *Kuka kuuluu? Kirjoituksia hiphopista ja feminismistä*. Kosmos, pp. 157–176.

Lindsey, T. B. (2015). Let me blow your mind: Hip Hop feminist futures in theory and praxis. *Urban Education*, 50(1): 52–77.

Mannila, T. and Schiffer, L. (2021). Tyttöjen unelmia—Tältä maailma näyttää. In I. Rantakallio and H. Strand (eds.), *Kuka kuuluu? Kirjoituksia hiphopista ja feminismistä*. Kosmos, pp. 175–194.

Morgan, J. (2012). Hip-hop feminist. In M. Forman and M. A. Neal (eds.), *That's the Joint: The Hip Hop Studies Reader*. 2nd ed. Routledge, pp. 413–418.

Mäntylä, E. (2021, March 3). Räpin uusi aika. *Helsingin Sanomat*. https://www.hs.fi/nyt/art-2000007836346.html.

Ong, M., Smith, J. M. and Ko, L. T. (2018). Counterspaces for women of color in STEM higher education: Marginal and central spaces for persistence and success. *Journal of Research in Science Teaching*, 55(2): 206–245.

Pough, G. D. (2004). *Check it while I wreck it: Black womanhood, Hip Hop culture, and the public sphere*. Northeastern University Press.

Pough, G. D. (2007). An introduction of sorts for Hip-Hop feminism. In G. D. Pough, E. Richardson, A. Durham and R. Raimist (eds.), *Homegirls Make Some Noise: Hip Hop Feminism Anthology*. Parker Publishing, pp. v–ix.

Pough, G., Richardson, E., Durham, A. and Raimist, R. (eds.) (2007). *Homegirls make some noise: Hip Hop feminism anthology*. Parker Publishing.

Rajah, A. (2022). I'm a 'savage': Exploring Megan Thee Stallion's use of the politics of articulation to subvert the androcentric discourses of women in Hip Hop culture. *Educational Research for Social Change*, 11(1): 57–71.

Ramstedt, K. and Rantakallio, I. (2020, October 16). Finnish rap, the far right and racism. *Toiminta Soi—Kirjoituksia yhteiskunnallisesta, toiminnallisesta ja aktivistisesta musiikintutkimuksesta*. https://www.suoni.fi/etusivu/2020/10/16/finnish-rap-far-right-and-racism.

Rantakallio, I. (2021). Femcees Finland, NiceRap ja vastatilojen voima: Suomiräpin naisten vertaisverkostojen historiaa. *Etnomusikologian Vuosikirja*, 33: 67–93.

Rantakallio, I. (Forthcoming 2024). Researcher as minority and majority: Hip hop feminist epistemologies. In K. Ramstedt and S. Välimäki (eds.), *Manifesto for Activist Music Research*. Bristol, UK: Intellect.

Rantakallio, I. and Järvenpää, T. (Forthcoming 2023). Vulnerability and white masculinities—Evangelical Christianity and new spirituality in the performance personas of Finnish rappers Ameeba and Roni Samuel. In S. Lindholm, K. Ringsager, and J. Söderman (eds.), *Nordic Noise: Hip Hop, Culture, and Community in Northern Europe*. Ashgate Popular and Folk Music Series. London: Routledge.

Rantakallio, I. and Strand, H. (eds.) (2021). *Kuka kuuluu? Kirjoituksia hiphopista ja feminismistä*. Kosmos.

Rauhalammi, I. (2018, October 26). *Suuri yleisö ajattelee, että naisten tekemä musiikki on naisille—Dreamgirls haluaa muuttaa musiikkialan rakenteita*. Yle. https://yle.fi/aihe/artikkeli/2018/10/26/ei-voi-verrata-mihinkaan-suomirap-showhun-dreamgirls-saa-yleison-itkemaan-ja.

Rose, T. (1994). *Black noise: Rap music and Black culture in contemporary America*. Wesleyan University Press.

Rose, T. (2008). *Hip Hop wars: What we talk about when we talk about Hip Hop—and why it matters*. Basic Civitas Books.

Ruisrock. (n.d.). *Our values: Equality*. https://ruisrock.fi/en/ruisrock/our-values/equality/ [accessed November 8, 2022].

Solórzano, D., Ceja, M. and Yosso, T. (2000). Critical race theory, racial microaggressions, and campus racial climate: The experiences of African American college students. *The Journal of Negro Education*, 69(1/2, Winter–Spring): *Knocking at Freedom's Door: Race, Equity, and Affirmative Action in U.S. Higher Education*: 60–73.

Strand, H. (2019). *Hyvä verse—Suomiräpin naiset*. Into.

Sykäri, V., Rantakallio, I., Westinen, E. and Cvetanović, D. (2019). Johdanto: Hiphop Suomessa 35 vuotta. In V. Sykäri, I. Rantakallio, E. Westinen, and D. Cvetanović (eds.), *Hiphop Suomessa. Puheenvuoroja tutkijoilta ja tekijöiltä*. Nuorisotutkimusseura, pp. pp. 7–32.

Vanha-Majamaa, A. (2020, October 27). *'Jos oot hyvännäköinen mimmi, ne näkee sut mieluummin yhden yön juttuna kuin vakavasti otettavana artistina'—suomirap on usein häijy naisille ja sukupuolivähemmistöille*. YleX. https://yle.fi/aihe/artikkeli/2020/10/27/jos-oot-hyvannakoinen-mimmi-ne-nakee-sut-mieluummin-yhden-yon-juttuna-kuin.

Vedenpää, V. (2018, August 10). *Suurilla kansainvälisillä festivaaleilla pian puolet naisesiintyjiä—Suomesta mukana ainoastaan Flow Festival: 'Ei aivan ongelmatonta'.* Yle Uutiset. https://yle.fi/uutiset/3-10347552.

Warner. (2020, September 3). *Monsp ja HMC publishing järjestävät maksuttoman rapbootcampin lokakuussa.* https://warnermusic.fi/2020/09/03/monsp-ja-hmc-publishing-jarjestavat-maksuttoman-rap-bootcampin-lokakuussa/.

Westinen, E. (2019). Kuulumisen ja etnisyyden neuvottelua monimuotoisessa suomiräpissä. In V. Sykäri, I. Rantakallio, E. Westinen, and D. Cvetanović (eds.), *Hiphop Suomessa. Puheenvuoroja tutkijoilta ja tekijöiltä.* Nuorisotutkimusseura, pp. 232–267.

Yuval-Davis, N. 2006. Belonging and the politics of belonging. *Patterns of Prejudice*, 40(3): 197–214.

Notes

Foreword

1. Kuttin Kandi, videoconference interview with Mark Katz, November 21, 2018.
2. David Spellmon, email message to the author, January 14, 2023.
3. Junious Brickhouse, telephone conversation with Mark Katz, January 27, 2023.
4. Deidre Smith, Facebook post, January 7, 2023.
5. For an account of the speech and its reception, see Nicholas Graham, 'Michael Eric Dyson's 1996 Commencement Speech', *For the Record*, December 15, 2016, https://blogs.lib.unc.edu/uarms/2016/12/15/michael-eric-dysons-1996-commencement-speech/.
6. The new curriculum is profiled in Jared (2023).
7. Breakfast Jam Facebook page, https://www.facebook.com/BreakFastJam.
8. Kaweesi Mark, email message to Mark Katz, January 27, 2023.

Chapter 1

1. The neologism 'legal penal system'—not unlike the abolitionist catchphrase 'criminal legal system'—is adopted here to problematise, refute, and refuse the term 'criminal justice system', insisting that the latter is a system of laws that (literally) *creates* 'crime' (both as a concept and a reality) through turning certain activities into punishable offences. This is not to deny that violence and harm exist, or that there are people who commit violent acts that cause harm. Rather, it is to stress that 'crime' is a political category that condemns, stigmatises, marginalizes, and racialises violence as the inherent trait, individual anomaly, cultural pathology, and personal responsibility of 'deviant' individuals and groups. Notions like 'law' and 'justice', therefore, are not understood here as interchangeable or synonymous. As Ben Quigley (2007: 15) argues, '[w]e must never confuse law and justice. What is legal is often not just. And what is just is often not at all legal'. Legal practitioners, therefore, do not (necessarily) observe principles and ideas of 'justice', but enforce 'the law'—the technical and legal(istic) restrictions on the behaviour, actions, and activities of 'the public'. While 'justice' denotes and embodies notions and ethical standards of fairness, 'the law' is 'the technical embodiment of attempts to order society' (Williams, 1993: 139). What we refer to or think as 'the law', therefore, simply refers to 'written law, codes, [and] systems of obedience' (Williams, 1993: 138), *not* that higher, 'just' ethical plane that we think that the law signifies, or stands for. For that reason, the term 'legal penal system' is

used throughout this chapter to stress that the state's juridical infrastructure delivers punishments, not justice— using 'the law' as an instrument of political (mis)rule.

2. The term 'Black' is used here to refer to cultural practices that are rooted in, evolve from, and establish a dialogue with cultural traditions of the African diaspora. Although the term 'Black' has come to include 'African, African-Caribbean, Asian and other visible minority ethnic communities who are oppressed by racism' (Maylor 2009: 373), it is used here to exclusively refer to 'African Diasporic Blackness' (Andrews, 2016: 2063–2064). This is not meant to deny the term its coalitional meaning or potential in global anti-racist movements, but to apply it more narrowly to Afro-diasporic culture(s). Much of such usage draws inspiration from Stuart Hall's (1993, 1975) extremely insightful thinking about the 'Black' in Black or Afro-diasporic (popular) culture. Furthermore, while rap culture should not and cannot be understood in 'exclusively racial/ethnic terms' (Gunter and Watt, 2009: 520) (especially in the context of contemporary urban multiculture), the (kin)aesthetic, linguistic, and musical codes that define it are nevertheless informed by and borrow from Black or Afro-diasporic culture. For an excellent discussion of how rappers 'across [and beyond] lines of color' (Kelley, 2008: x) engage with the music, but do so *in* and *through* the sonic and poetic signature(s) of Afro-diasporic culture(s), see Perry (2004: 12, 13, and 25).

3. Nicknamed 'rap on trial', this body of research first emerged in the United States (Kubrin and Nielson, 2014; Nielson and Dennis, 2019) but took root soon after in the United Kingdom (Quinn, 2018; Fatsis *et al.*, 2021; Owusu-Bempah, 2022a, 2022b), and elsewhere (Basu and Lemell, 2006; Lippman, 2019; Carinos, 2020; Roks and Van Den Broek, 2020; Åberg and Tyvelä, forthcoming). For a digital compendium to scholarly research related to 'rap on trial', see Charis Kubrin's valuable website: https://endrapontrial.org/research/. For another digital repository of reports, scholarship, and legal resources on the criminalisation of rap in the United Kingdom, see: https://sites.manchester.ac.uk/prosecuting-rap/home/about/. For a special journal issue devoted to the prosecution and policing of rap, see the latest issue of *Popular Music* (Available at: https://www.cambridge.org/core/journals/popular-music/firstview).

4. The New York Senate Bill S7527, (nick)named: the 'Rap on trial' Bill (Dillon, 2021; Joshi, 2022), '[e]stablishes an assumption of the inadmissibility of evidence of a defendant's creative or artistic expression', unless prosecutors can 'affirmatively prove that the evidence is admissible by clear and convincing evidence'. The full text can be accessed at: https://www.nysenate.gov/legislation/bills/2021/s7527.

5. Following the American examples cited above, such prosecutorial arguments *can* (and *should*) be challenged on legal grounds, but, to my knowledge, this is almost never done. The rationale for objecting to the use of drill-related material in court rests on the argument that the (ab)use of such 'evidence' may have an adverse effect on the fairness of the proceedings (citing Section 78, Police and Criminal Evidence Act 1984), due to the insubstantial probative value of rap lyrics (citing Section 101, Criminal Justice Act 2003) and concerns about freedom of expression of rappers (citing Article 10 of the Human Rights Act).

6. In addition to representatives of law reform and human rights charities and youth workers, two academic colleagues and this chapter's author were invited to contribute

to two such Listening Exercises organised by the CPS on drill music, in January and April 2022. As well as offering insights and evidence from our extensive research and experience as an expert witness in cases that rely on drill lyrics and videos as 'evidence', we were additionally asked to comment on an embargoed version of the CPS's draft legal guidance on gangs, drill, and social media, before the April 2022 meeting. As such, the announcement that the CPS is or was 'unaware' of the (mis)use of drill in criminal trials naturally sounds rather alarming. In the light of the above, it is also puzzling to see the same criminalising rhetoric in full force at a CPS article, published in June 2022, which insists on erroneously define drill music as: 'a type of hip-hop often featuring lyrics referring to drug dealing and street crime. A darker side of this genre can see lyrics linked to gang violence and threats to kill, which, if relevant to a case, may form part of the evidence' (CPS, 2022). Leaving aside the obvious *faux pas* of conflating rap with hip-hop—when the former refers to rapping over an instrumental track while the latter refers to a broader music culture that can, but does not always, feature rap(ping) in it—the same criminalising logic that is criticised in this chapter, is also hard to miss.

7. Ancillary orders are imposed on offenders by the court in addition to an actual sentence. See CPS (2019) for more details.

8. Such practices have recently received considerable media attention, following the Oversight Board's overturning of Meta's decision to remove a UK drill music video from Instagram, on the grounds that policing online content in this manner can 'amplify bias' as well as undermining 'respect for due process and transparency'. To read the Oversight Board's decision in full, see: https://www.oversightboard.com/news/413988857616451-oversight-board-overturns-meta-s-decision-in-uk-drill-music-case/.

9. It is perhaps useful to remind ourselves that such 'experts' for the prosecution are laughed out in the auditorium (and the lecture theatre too!), but are taken seriously in the courtroom—urging us to think (twice!) about just how high standards of evidence actually are in court proceedings. A recent sellout play, *The UK Drill Project*, satirises this flagrant disregard for assessing the suitability of cops-as-experts, or the specialised knowledge they claim to have, by targeting two serving officers (nicknamed PC Bar and PC Railings) who are engaged in such work as appendages to the Crown in cases that involve drill material as evidence (Pritchard, 2022). For a more academic take on this very issue, see: Ward and Fouladvand (2021).

10. For a potted history of how UK grime and UK drill have been policed against, see: Fatsis, 2019a, 2019b, and 2019d.

11. In a more fictional vein, the folly of guilt by association that joint enterprise is based on is brilliantly captured in a short play by interdisciplinary artist Jay Bernard (2021). Bernard's critique of the racialisation in joint enterprise prosecutions takes the form of a monologue about a young woman whose teenage friendship ties become 'evidence' of gang association—as an 'accomplice' who is treated as 'parasitic' and 'culturally complicit' to acts of violence she never committed.

12. 'Whiteness' here does not refer to skin colour or physiological traits. Rather, it is understood as a political term that describes ways of being *structurally* 'white'—a social

identity *and* a social structure that upholds it. 'Whiteness' is therefore approached here as an ontology (a way of *being*), a racist ideology (a way of *seeing*), and a power relation (a way of *doing*) that enables the domination, authority, and perceived humanity of those who are racialised and identify themselves as 'white'. As Olsen (2004: 43) aptly puts it: whiteness has historically been 'not a biological status but a political color that distinguished the free from the unfree, the equal from inferior, the citizen from the slave'. This echoes similar perspectives on 'race' and racialisation that approach 'whiteness' and 'blackness' as 'the colour of [people's] politics and not the colour of [their] skins' (Sivanandan, 2008: xviii).

13. The track is unearthed from the author's own vinyl record collection, but can be accessed online at: http://bitingtick.blogspot.com/2016/07/banning-of-records-att ila-hun.html. The information about the *Banning of Records* being itself banned and comes from a relevant entry in the Discography of American Historical Recordings (DAHR): https://adp.library.ucsb.edu/index.php/mastertalent/detail/302219/Ati lla_the_Hun_Quevedo_Raymond.

14. For similar discussions on the policing of calypso, see: Cowley (1996) and Hill (1997: esp. 16–17, 32–33, 43, and 67).

15. 'Spitting' in the rap lexicon is a synonym of rhythmic speech; rhyming/rapping.

Chapter 2

1. Reference numbers for our AQA UAS units are: 105527, 105553, 105554, 105648, 105649, 105650, and 105651.

Chapter 4

1. It is interesting that this happened around thirty years after Elvis, 'rock 'n' roll', and all that became known in the United Kingdom: we can note that the landmark Hip Hop record 'The Message' by Grandmaster Flash and the Furious Five was issued just over thirty years before now; perhaps, then, music education in the United Kingdom takes around thirty years to catch up with landmark innovations.

Chapter 9

1. Global Majority refers to 'the group of people in the world who do not consider them- selves or are not considered to be white' (https://dictionary.cambridge.org/, 2023).

2. Estuary English is an English accent associated with the area along the River Thames and its estuary, including London.

3. 'Ethics' here means to 'do no harm' to oneself nor others through one's professional practice.

4. 'Supervision', put simply, means training and counselling for counsellors by a trained professional. It is a pivotal part of one's safe and ethical practice. Therefore, all therapeutic practitioners should undertake supervision.

5. Otherness refers to: the quality or state of being other or different. The overarching concept 'feeling of otherness' highlights that, rather than a static, binary experience, individuals moved across a continuum ranging from the excluding experience of feeling stigmatised and othered, to the inclusive experience of integration.

Chapter 12

1. Debuting in March of 2020, Clubhouse is an audio-based social-media app. The main feature of Clubhouse is real-time virtual 'rooms' in which users can communicate with each other via audio. Users can also schedule conversations by creating events.

2. Reddit is an American social news aggregation, content rating, and discussion website.

Chapter 13

1. This chapter has been reproduced with permission from publisher Brill-i-Sense, where it was originally published in a volume: P. Burnard, E. Mackinlay, D. Rousell, and T. Dragovic (eds.) (2022), *Doing rebellious research in and beyond the academy.*

Chapter 14

1. 'Social energy' is generated when residents come together to make a positive change in their community, and it is one of the key ways in which well-being runs through programmes such as 'Arts for Wellbeing' (see Ecorys, 2017) and many other programmes featured in this volume.

2. Evidence can be summarised as being 'evidence-based' where scientific evidence is used to decide what works or 'evidence-informed' where scientific evidence is used to make choices about what could work, taking your own context into consideration. 'Research-informed' is where scientific research is used to make deliberate choices in your own context and to evaluate these choices (Daniel and De Bruyckere, 2021).

3. Since the outbreak of the COVID-19 pandemic, discussions about the politics of care have proliferated within and beyond schools, the academy, and social movements. Within and beyond schools, care is an ethic; care does more than require a posture of

mutual respect, responsibility, and obligation between individuals; political care is a site of mutual aid, consciousness raising, and delivery of more just relations of power (Woodly, Brown Marin, *et al.*, 2021).

Chapter 15

1. The concept of 'unlearning' came up in the discussion of the first seminar of the series and indicates how as researchers and practitioners we should be reflexive about some of our taken-for-granted beliefs and ideas and be open to alternative ways of knowing. The visual minutes of the session can be accessed here https://cuminetwork.wordpress.com/virtual/ (accessed January 14, 2023).
2. I know lots of people use wireless earphones these days, but that ruins the metaphor so let us just pretend that the frustrating tangled-wires experience remains an issue.
3. Social pedagogy is a holistic approach to education where children and young people are treated as equal social beings to those educating them. It is largely based on clear communication and encourages reflective practice at its core (i.e., reflection on how ways of being can affect the way that children and young people respond to an education interaction). For a fuller discussion of the tenets as relevant to this chapter see *Communication skills for working with children and young people* by Pat Petrie (2011).
4. By 'toolkits turn' I am referencing the observations by Belfiore and Bennett, amongst others, that some impact evaluation is being applied 'off the shelf' using pre-designed variables and methods that may not be relevant or appropriate to the intervention or those taking part in it.
5. https://youthmusic.org.uk/ (accessed January 14, 2023).
6. These are generalisations to some degree, as there are many organisations and funders who are actively attempting to disrupt this power structure and support efforts in co-created and participatory impact evaluation design. Indeed, my observations here are historical; Youth Music's evaluation practice has progressed somewhat since I worked there ten years ago.
7. https://www.outcomesstar.org.uk/ (accessed October 10, 2022).
8. The full results can be seen in Lonie (2010).
9. https://youthmusic.org.uk/about-us (accessed October 9, 2022).
10. The outputs were two presentations at academic conferences, two academic papers, two 'youth arts' sector conferences in 2012 and 2013, and now, the presentation for the CUMIN seminar in March 2022 that led to this paper.
11. https://cashbackforcommunities.org/ (accessed on January 14, 2023).
12. People living in the most deprived areas according to the Scottish Index of Multiple Deprivation.
13. There are 'national outcomes' relating to children and young people and culture, among many others, guiding the policy-making of the Scottish Government, https://nationalperformance.gov.scot/national-outcomes (accessed October 14, 2022).

14. These outcomes are updated for each three-year 'phase' of the programme, current and historical programme outcomes can be seen here https://cashbackforcommunit ies.org/ (accessed January 14, 2023).

Chapter 17

1. 'Noise Solution' has widened gender responses to include non-binary options, but they are not available for this earlier set of data.

Chapter 18

1. For reference, see the music video for their joint single 'WAP' (Cardi B, 2020).
2. For reference, see the music video for the single 'Montero (Call me by your name)' (Lil Nas X, 2021). The song name alludes to the movie, *Call me by your name* (2017), that narrates the gay romance of two young men.
3. This racial and gender norm of mainstream rap becomes evident also when looking at, for example, Spotify's most popular curated rap music playlist *Rap Caviar* (n.d.) or Grammy winners or nominees in the rap categories (Grammys, n.d.): both feature a clear majority of Black male artists. In the context of this article, I wish to draw attention to this aspect in order to situate the Finnish context and its differing racial norms.
4. One example in the Finnish context is one of the country's oldest popular music festivals, *Ruisrock*. The festival is a Keychange signee and had several Finnish women rappers perform at the festival in 2019 and 2022 (the festival was not organized in 2020 or 2021 due to COVID). The festival claims to have achieved the 50-50 gender balance among its performers in 2019 (Ruisrock, n.d.).
5. I looked at the two at that time largest Finnish Rap Spotify playlists, *Suomiräpin Järkäleet* and *Aitoa Suomiräppiä*, in February 2021 soon after *Kuka Kuuluu* and the first Monsp mixtape were released (Rantakallio, 2021). The percentage of women on the lists in early 2021 was around 7 percent and 3 percent, whereas in late 2022, it was 21 percent and 4 percent, respectively. *Suomiräpin Järkäleet* was still updated weekly in 2021 and had over 60,000 followers. However, at the time of writing (November 2022), the playlist has not been updated since April 28, 2022, and has only ca. 16,000 followers. A new Finnish Rap playlist *100 Suomi* (n.d.) with considerably more followers (over 70,000) has been added to Spotify in early 2022. In November 2022, the number of women artists on that list was roughly 8 percent.

Glossary

affect: the many ways to conceptualise 'affect'. Here are some definitions: (1) Emotions and qualitatively experienced feelings seen as vital to shaping social values, gender ideals and collective groups: (2) a pre-personal intensity that shifts the capacity for a body (of any kind) to think, feel, and act in relation with other bodies. Whether considered as subjective emotion or impersonal intensity, affects circulate amongst bodies in ways that are collectively modulated and yet largely unconscious.

affective practices: affective relations of care and solidarity.

artist practitioners: teaching artists or creative practitioners.

attention: a concept drawn from the philosophy of French Feminist Simone Weil that means 'waiting, pausing, suspending thought' and thereby 'paying attention'.

AQA: a UK exam board which awards GCSE qualifications to schools across England, Wales, and Northern Ireland.

beatboxing: a musical style or technique, especially in Hip Hop, in which the sounds and rhythms of percussion instruments or sound effects are simulated by using the mouth and voice.

beat making: the practice of composing (i.e., creating and recontextualizing) music with the use of electronic music technology. Often it is loop-based music that emphasizes drumming and rhythmic components, with sampled or synthesized sound. It has significant developmental origins within Hip Hop culture despite current use across musical genres.

best practice: established quality standards of conduct in a sector or discipline. It may be established informally (e.g., through a network of professional peers with a shared understanding) or formally (e.g., through a written 'code of practice').

Bourdieusian: an argument or element of an argument that recalls the theories of noted French sociologist Pierre Bourdieu.

breakdancers/breakdancing: see Breakin

breakin': an energetic style of dance typically performed to Hip Hop music, characterized by stylized footwork and acrobatic or athletic movements. It originated among African American and Latino people in New York City during the early 1970s. Historically, many have referred to Breakin' (or Breaking) as 'breakdancing', but the former term is preferred, in capitalised form, by many practitioners.

calypso: a style of Caribbean music that originated in the early to mid-nineteenth century and spread across the Caribbean and the wider world by the mid-twentieth century; the music's roots are said to stem from the eighteenth century.

composting: a philosophical, political, and practical process put forward by Donna Haraway for undoing the relations of domination that subordinate nonhuman lives to human interests.

connected learning: environments that are typically grounded in production, providing learners opportunities to create, distribute, curate, and critique products. Research suggests that these environments work best when filled with peers and mentors who share interests and can work collaboratively on shared projects or with common goals in mind. Learners should have access to the resources, tools, and materials they need to pursue their interests. Ideally, learning experiences should be designed as part of networks—including schools, homes, and informal interest communities—that help to make pathways for increased participation and deeper learning transparent and accessible.

counterspace: the physical and/or ideological spaces created for and by marginalised people where they can express their identities and thoughts, and create alternative ideas, communities, and practices that challenge normative thinking and culture. Counterspaces are a response to discrimination and exclusion and thus meant to offer a sense of social belonging through shared experiences and support.

CPS: the UK's 'Crown Prosecution Service', which prosecutes criminal cases that have been investigated by the police and/or other investigative organisations.

DAO: a Decentralised Autonomous Organisation in which control is not centralised and significant power and/or influence is wielded by the users within the DAO.

DJ (or 'deejay'): originally an abbreviation for 'disc jockey', at its most fundamental level a DJ is someone who plays music for audiences; in Hip Hop and post-Hip Hop contexts, DJ decks can be categorised as a musical instrument through which recordings are mixed, spliced, reconfigured, and/or tampered in a wide range of ways. Some DJs can be described as 'turntablists', but this term is not synonymous with DJing: turntablism is likely to include 'scratching' and/or advanced technical skills, whereas some DJs eschew such technical performance and simply play the recordings with little or no alteration.

DnB: An abbreviation of 'Drum and Bass', a genre of music that originated in the United Kingdom in the late 1980s/early 1990s.

drill: a relatively new rap subgenre with origins in Chicago and with a particular character in the form of 'UK drill'. Drill broke into the UK mainstream in 2018 amid claims that it was to blame for rising levels of violence and 'criminality'. Relative to other rap music, UK drill is moodier and darker in sound and more graphic in its violent imagery.

Each One Teach One: a proverbial dictum said to have emerged from the learning practices of African slaves in America whereby educational benefits (learning to read and so forth) would be passed along through a conscious process of sharing designed to counteract the fact that slaves were denied any education. More recently, the phrase has been widely used in Hip Hop culture to encourage a comparable sharing of skills and knowledges.

EBacc (English Baccalaureate): a 'performance measure' through which schools in England are compared. The EBacc combination is English Literature *and* English Language, Maths, GCSE coverage of the three Sciences (Biology, Chemistry, and Physics), a Foreign Language (ancient and modern are both accepted), and either Geography or History. Music and the Arts are not included in the EBacc combination. Schools in England are tracked and compared according to how many learners achieve the EBacc combination.

EDM: Electronic Dance Music, which means different things to different people but can generally be taken to mean the kinds of electronically generated dance music that will be often found in clubs.

educational research: the scientific field of study that examines education and learning processes and the human attributes, interactions, organisations, and institutions that shape educational outcomes. Educational research involves systematic collection and analysis of data related to the field of education. There are four general types of educational research: (1) Descriptive (for example, survey, historical, content analysis, qualitative, and postqualitative); (2) Associational (for example, correlational, causal-comparative); (3) Intervention (for example, experimental, quasi-experimental, action research).

empowering music engagement: listening to music or other music experiences that facilitate attitudes and behaviours with the potential to help people *get better* in some way. The individual and community-related forms of better include to feel better (esteem), to do better (resilience), to be better (growth), to better belong (community), and better conditions ([social] change). At the individual level, music experiences may contribute to individual empowerment through greater esteem, stronger identity, handling adversity, demonstrated resilience, prosocial and health-enhancing attitudes and behaviours, skill-building, and preventing victimization. These are the personal dimensions aligned with feeling, doing, and being better. Community empowerment is related to embracing one's culture, appreciation of cultural resilience, sociopolitical development, and collective action for equity, justice, and collective well-being. These community-level dimensions are associated with better belonging and better conditions.

estate: areas of social housing commonly built in the 1950s, 1960s, or 1970s in the United Kingdom such as a block of flats, a collection of blocks of flats, or a large area of housing often originally built as a 'council estate'.

ethico-onto-epistemology: the notion of 'ethico-onto-epistem-ology' was first coined by physicist-philosopher Karen Barad to point at the inseparability of ethics, ontology, and epistemology when engaging in (scientific) knowledge production, with scientific practices, and with the world itself and its inhabitants—human and non-human beings.

evaluation: a reflexive process involving judgments about the quality and effectiveness of practice matters to how we draw together, understand, review, and report on socially engaged arts programmes.

evidence-based: where scientific evidence is used to decide what works.

GCSE: the General Certificate of Secondary Education, which replaced the older GCE (commonly known as the 'O-level') in 1988, is the standard qualification for children of sixteen years of age in England, Wales, and Northern Ireland. There are alternatives to the GCSE such as the BTEC qualification, but the GCSE is considered the standard academic qualification in the United Kingdom outside of Scotland.

gender minority: a person who is not cis-gender, that is, whose gender identity differs from the one assigned at birth; includes (but is not limited to) non-binary, gender fluid/diverse, intersex, and trans people.

glocalisation: the process of the local and the global sphere mutually influencing each other.

grime: a Hip Hop–informed style with roots in the 1990s 'UK garage' scene that originated in London during the first decade of this century and has grown, through the huge success of artists from Wiley and Dizzee Rascal to Stormzy and innumerable other UK artists, to an immensely influential status today. Whilst grime is Hip Hop informed, it is by no means synonymous with Hip Hop: rather, grime has become an *oeuvre* of its own.

Hip Hop culture: a culture with the values of self and community improvement, anchored in five creative elements, MCing (rapping), deejaying, Breaking (break-dancing), graffiti, and knowledge of self. The modern era of Hip Hop out of the South Bronx (NY) is credited as starting among predominantly Black and Latinx youth and communities (Afro-Caribbean, Latinx-Caribbean, and African American) in 1973. But the more distal roots of Hip Hop can be found among Jamaican and Reggae culture with sound systems, toasting and chanting, the spoken word creations of the Last Poets and Watts Prophets of the 1960s, the Jubalaires of the mid-twentieth century, the Celebratory Dancing from Kaduna Nigeria, and the thirteenth-century traditions of West African Griots. Hip Hop is now at once contemporary and youth oriented, but also multigenerational and global, speaking to a wide range of marginalised populations.

Hip-Hopification of education: defined and practised by BREIS (Brother Reaching Each Inner Soul), Hip-Hopification of education is looking at the creative vibrant energy of Hip Hop and applying it in the classroom. It is about captivating audience with lyrical wizardry and a command of a chosen topic. It is about participation, interaction, inclusion, improvisation, connective with and steering audience towards a safe space where they can learn.

Humboldtian: a holistic approach to education from the nineteenth century entailing both research and study, so named due to its historical link to Wilhelm von Humboldt.

impact evaluation: the process of establishing the short- and long-term changes taking place due to an intervention of some form. It generally includes research design (i.e., designing methods such as surveys, interviews, focus groups, or desk-based research), analysis, and reporting of results. It is a process often used by those funding interventions (public and private) to assess the outcomes of their investment.

impact studies: studies that isolate the effect of an intervention by assuring that there is 'clean' comparison between a treatment group that received the intervention and a comparison group that is just the same except that it did not get the intervention.

informal learning: learning that happens outside of the formal environment of the classroom, the practice room, and the school. In music-education literature, informal learning has been identified as the standard mode of learning in popular music, where many (most, probably) professional performers have not received any formal musical training.

intra-action: a Karen Baradian term used to replace 'interaction', which necessitates pre-established bodies that then participate in action with each other. Intra-action understands agency as not an inherent property of an individual or human to be exercised, but as a dynamism of forces.

key stage: a period of schooling in the United Kingdom, with KS3 (Key Stage 3) being eleven to thirteen years of age (or fourteen years of age in some schools today) and KS4 being thirteen (or sometimes fourteen) to sixteen years of age.

launchpads: technology for triggering samples, often with a colourful set of sixty-four touch pads. Leading manufacturers of this technology include Ableton and Novation.

Liberty: the United Kingdom's largest civil-liberties organization, campaigning for everyone in the United Kingdom to be treated fairly, with dignity and respect; 'Liberty is ordinary people standing up to power', the organisation proclaims for itself.

marginalisation: social, economic, and often historical exclusion of groups of people from power in society, typically based on for example race, ethnicity, gender, sexuality, religion, or (dis)ability.

Music Hub: in 2012, the United Kingdom reconfigured the longstanding 'music service' model (whereby government funding was distributed to individual counties or a region within a county), replacing these with 'Hubs'. The basic delivery is similar however: provision of music-related learning opportunities, invariably including conventional musical instrument tuition (violin, guitar, trumpet, drums) but fairly rarely including DJ tuition or similar.

Nordic Bildung: in addition to being the name of a particular organisation in Denmark, Nordic Bildung (or 'Folkbildning') is the general name for learning for life, for fun, learning for the sake of learning and studying as undertaken in the Nordic countries (Denmark, Finland, Iceland, Norway, and Sweden).

Norm: a practice or behaviour considered as normal, standard, preferable, and expected.

Ofsted: the UK Government's 'Office for Standards in Education', which visits schools around the United Kingdom with HMI (Her Majesty's Inspectors) working alongside non-HMI 'lay inspectors' to evaluate the quality of teaching and learning, the rigour of child protection and suchlike. Ofsted will sometimes classify a school as 'unsatisfactory' or 'requires improvement', which can trigger a process that may even result in the school being closed: it is common, therefore, for teaching practitioners and the management teams they work for to be highly fearful of an Ofsted inspection.

participatory culture: a culture with relatively low barriers to artistic expression and civic engagement, strong support for creating and sharing one's creations, and some type of informal mentorship whereby what is known by the most experienced is passed along to novices. It is a culture in which private individuals are not just consumers but producers of media and further play a role in the shaping of mass media content (Jenkins, 2006).

participatory music: elective music education and learning that often takes place in non-formal (i.e., out of school) contexts. Participatory music is usually led by one or more practitioner(s) and often includes practical demonstrations, group work, and 'learning by doing'. It often includes diverse musical genres and is responsive to the identities and interests of those taking part.

participatory music-making: a term coined by Thomas Turino (2008) that characterizes activities that take place when people actively engage in a music interaction, and his concept emphasises music-making as predominantly social in nature.

post-qualitative enquiry: a concept proposed predominantly by education scholar Elizabeth St Pierre to describe new approaches to social inquiry that break completely with traditional qualitative methodologies. St Pierre argues that such a break with qualitative methodology is necessary if social researchers are to adequately respond to post-structuralist, and posthumanist deconstructions of the liberal humanist subject.

research-informed: where scientific research is used to make deliberate choices in your own context and to evaluate these choices (Daniel and De Bruyckere, 2021).

risky music engagement: listening to music or other music experiences that facilitate attitudes and behaviours with the potential to decrease mental or physical well-being of the individual or others. The specific types of risk are both overt and subtle. More overt risky engagement includes music listening associated with greater comfort with or thinking about substance use, misogyny, risky sexual behaviors, violence, and illicit drug sales to make money. Empowerment and risk can occur alongside each other so that even as people engage music in ways that allow them to feel or do better in some areas of well-being, it can also *simultaneously* contribute to attitudes or behaviors that can decrease mental or physical well-being of oneself or others (Travis, 2016: 69). For example, youth may be empowered and learn to feel better, emotionally or about themselves, through materialism, by the victimisation of others, misogyny, or through a reliance on external validation. Attitudes and behaviours may develop or be reinforced through lyrics that align with these dynamics.

SATB: Soprano-Alto-Tenor-Bass, which is the classic 'voice' arrangement for four-part harmony.

spitting: often used as a synonym for rapping; sometimes defined as freestyle rapping.

socially engaged: arts practices and programmes referring to any artform that involves people and communities in collaborative, participatory engagement with the medium or material of the art in social interaction. They do not typically operate through traditional audience models that separate professional arts and the public or audience.

spoken word popular music: not a genre classification but a description of an aesthetic; beat-heavy contemporary popular music in which people rhythmically speak/spit/rap their words.

Therapeutic Beat Making (TBM): a comprehensive, multidimensional theory and model that proposes therapeutic value in creating and recontextualising music with electronic music technology (i.e., 'beat making'). The proposed therapeutic benefits of TBM include three dimensions: (1) Relational, (2) Expressive, and (3) Self-Concept.

Western art music: a term that is often preferred by musicologists compared to the more vague 'classical music', primarily because the later eighteenth-century and early nineteenth-century classical period is just one among several eras within the Western art-music field (with the classical period being preceded by the baroque and renaissance periods and followed by the romantic and modernist periods).

Index